W9-AFA-774

THE APPARITIONAL LESBIAN

GENDER AND CULTURE

Carolyn G. Heilbrun and Nancy K. Miller, editors

THE
APPARITIONAL
LESBIAN

FEMALE

HOMOSEXUALITY

AND

MODERN

CULTURE

COLUMBIA

UNIVERSITY

PRESS

NEW

YORK

TERRY CASTLE

COLUMBIA UNIVERSITY PRESS

NEW YORK CHICHESTER, WEST SUSSEX

Copyright © 1993 Columbia University Press
All rights reserved

Library of Congress Cataloging-in-Publication Data

Castle, Terry.
    The apparitional lesbian: female homosexuality and modern culture /
Terry Castle.
        p.   cm. — (Gender and culture)
    Includes bibliographical references and index.
    ISBN 0-231-07652-5
    1. Lesbianism in literature.   2. Women in literature.
    3. Homosexuality and literature.   4. Literature, Modern—History and
criticism.   I. Title.   II. Series.
PN56.L45C37   1993
809'.89206643—dc20   93-13830
                                                          CIP

⊗

Casebound editions of
Columbia University Press books
are printed on permanent
and durable acid-free paper.

Printed in the United States of America
C 10 9 8 7 6 5 4 3 2 1

To Beverley Talbott, with love

CONTENTS

ACKNOWLEDGMENTS

S e v e r a l chapters here began life as essays in various periodicals: I would like to thank the editors of the *Kenyon Review*, *Textual Practice*, the *Women's Review of Books*, *Representations*, and the *New Republic* for allowing me to reprint them (with some alterations) here. To the friends and colleagues who supported this project from its inception I owe many and deep thanks—above all, to Nancy Miller, who along with Carolyn Heilbrun and Jennifer Crewe at Columbia University Press, made this book possible in the first place. Nancy has been that rare combination, a steadfast friend and an honest critic; I would not have done without either her warm encouragement or well-judged criticisms. In turn, I am grateful to Carolyn and Jennifer for their enthusiasm and useful advice, as I am to Martha Vicinus, who read the manuscript in its late stages and helped me—in a compelling way—to see what it should be.

To others who helped me generously along the way I offer thanks: to Paul Alkon, Linda Anderson, Robin Becker, John Bender, Corinne Blackmer, Joe Bristow, Bliss Carnochan, Marjorie Garber, Linda Kerr, Seth Lerer, Herbie Lindenberger, Joss Marsh, Diane Middlebrook, Randy Nakayama, Susan Pensak, Marjorie Perloff, Lou Roberts, Patricia Juliana Smith, John Tinker, and Leon Wieseltier. My long-lost English cousin, Bridget Castle, has been an inspiration—as have Cleo Eulau, Kristin Midelfort, Stephen Orgel, and Rob Polhemus, without whose good will and friendship my life would be much impoverished. I owe most of all, however, to Beverley Talbott, to whom I dedicate this book with love.

THE APPARITIONAL LESBIAN

1

One of several ghosts haunting this book is that of Greta Garbo, who died in April 1990, just after I'd started working on the volume's signature piece, "The Apparitional Lesbian." Quite by accident a local cinema was featuring a Garbo retrospective that very week, and along with many others I went to see her—in the luminous, surreal *Queen Christina*—out of a shared sense of tribute. In the strangest of that film's many strange moments— when Garbo-as-Christina, moving as if in a somnambulistic trance, walks slowly around the room in an inn where she has just spent a night of passionate love with the Spanish ambassador, "memorizing" each object and piece of furniture with her hands and eyes, only to end, dreamily, by uttering a weird private soliloquy about the crystals of snow drifting silently down outside the window—I found myself struck by the uncanniness of it all: a lesbian actress, portraying a notoriously lesbian queen, in one of the classic heterosexual love scenes in Hollywood film. Wasn't it odd? Yet no one seemed to notice, except perhaps Garbo herself. What else (I fantasized) was the impervious speech about the snow—delivered improvisationally and sotto voce, like a kind of mysterious fugue—but a way of absenting herself, of layering with irony everything that had come before? She was signaling, I figured, showing us that she *knew*. Was it not obvious? Yet to judge by the trusting faces of my fellow audience members—as happily ensconced in illusion, it seemed, as the Spanish ambassador—apparently not.

When it comes to lesbians—or so I argue in the following chapters—many people have trouble seeing what's in front of them. The lesbian remains a kind of "ghost effect" in the cinema world of modern life: elusive, vaporous, difficult to spot—even when she is there, in plain view, mortal and magnificent, at the center of the screen. Some may even deny that she exists at all. Though hardly surprising, it was still unsettling to find after Garbo's death how many obituaries either touched only fleetingly on her love of women or neglected to mention it at all. And this with a woman whose lovers (like Mercedes de Acosta) published memoirs about her, who conventionally spoke of herself using male nouns and pronouns ("When I was a young boy in Sweden . . . " etc.) and who was once described by Gore Vidal, with ineffable camp precision, as a "perfect gentleman, who spent forty years looking for the perfect pullover."[1]

My primary goal in this book has been to bring the lesbian back into focus, as it were, in all her worldliness, comedy, and humanity. It is too easy to think of her as distant and strange and standoffish: as alienated from the real or "everyday" world the rest of us inhabit. The lesbian is never with us, it seems, but always somewhere else: in the shadows, in the margins, hidden from history, out of sight, out of mind, a wanderer in the dusk, a lost soul, a tragic mistake, a pale denizen of the night. She is far away and she is dire. (She has seldom seemed as accessible, for instance, as her ingratiating twin brother, the male homosexual.) What we never expect is precisely this: to find

Greta Garbo as Queen Christina, 1933.
*Courtesy of the Margaret Herrick Library, Academy
of Motion Picture Arts and Sciences.*

her in the midst of things, as familiar and crucial as an old friend, as solid and sexy as the proverbial right-hand man, as intelligent and human and funny and real as Garbo.

The task of refocusing, I admit, is not an easy one. It wasn't easy for me to begin this book; only a kind of spectral visitation prompted me to do it at all. As late as 1989, I was still entrenched in my "official" academic speciality—eighteenth-century English literature—and trying feverishly to get on with what I invariably referred to (without irony) as my "big book." The subject of the big book, interestingly, was to have been ghosts—and, in particular, the waning of belief in apparitions in Western culture after the Enlightenment. To this end, I had spent almost two years doing research and writing outlines, and my study overflowed with books and piles of notes—on ghosts and psychology, ghosts and religion, ghosts and art, ghosts and literature, ghosts and the self. The result of all this obsessional labor (or so I fondly imagined) would be nothing less than an "apparitional" history of modern consciousness.

Before I could get very far with this grandiose scheme, however, a ghost of my own came back to haunt me. For weeks I struggled to find a way to begin, only to discover that the more I thought about "the apparitional," the more vaporous and elusive and impossible the subject became. One evening, after a particularly dispiriting session at the computer, I found myself—in a Garbo-like fugue of my own— jotting down the first words of the autobiographical essay that appears here under the title "First Ed." Immediately I was struck with a panicky feeling of playing hookey; this wasn't what I was supposed to be doing at all. What was I doing trying to conjure up a long-lost lesbian (in male drag!) I used to see at a YWCA in 1964? What about the big book? My mind seemed to have gone walkabout. But the relief was also unmistakable. I could "see" the ineffable Ed as clearly as if she stood there. Indeed, as I worked on the piece over the next few days, with the growing realization that it was possible to write about something other than vapor, I felt scandalously energized—as if, paradoxically, a great weight had lifted. Casting my old notes aside with strange exhilaration, I proceeded to plan out the first of the essays included in this volume.

In retrospect everything makes more sense than it did at the time. Lesbianism had always been a "phantom" in my scholarly work—a theme that I often yearned to write about (and sometimes did in carefully veiled ways) yet for a variety of reasons felt unable to address directly. The big book, I realize now, was a last-ditch attempt to avoid the issue. Yet even so I was constantly torn. (Throughout the 1980s I had watched enviously as other lesbian and gay scholars, braver souls than I, had begun writing openly on homosexuality in various academic books and journals.) By arriving so suddenly and unaccountably, the eponymous "Ed" released me from my inhibitions. And, in turn, in conjuring up this spectral visitor from my own lesbian past, I had unwittingly turned toward—or let myself be captured by—my real subject.

Why is it so difficult to see the lesbian—even when she is there, quite plainly, in front of us? In part because she has been "ghosted"— or made to seem invisible—by culture itself. It would be putting it mildly to say that the lesbian represents a threat to patriarchal protocol: Western civilization has for centuries been haunted by a fear of "women without men"—of women indifferent or resistant to male desire. Precisely because she challenges the moral, sexual, and psychic authority of men so thoroughly, the "Amazon" has always provoked anxiety and hatred. As the lesbian philosopher Monique Wittig has put it, "The refusal to become (or to remain) heterosexual always meant to refuse to become a man or a woman, consciously or not. For a lesbian this goes further than the refusal of the *role* 'woman.' It is the refusal of the economic, ideological, and political power of a man."[2] Under the circumstances it's perhaps no wonder that so many men (and some women) have sought to see the lesbian "disappeared." By refusing to undergo the symbolic emasculation that Western society demands of its female members—indeed depends upon—the woman who desires another woman has always set herself apart (if only by default) as outlaw and troublemaker.

Historically this ghosting of the lesbian has taken a number of forms. One will search in vain for any unambiguously lesbian heroines in the annals of modern civilization: from Sappho to Greta Garbo, Queen Christina to Eleanor Roosevelt, virtually every distinguished woman suspected of homosexuality has had her biography sanitized at one point or another in the interest of order and public safety. Lesbian contributions to culture have been routinely suppressed or ignored, lesbian-themed works of art censored and destroyed, and would-be apologists—like Radclyffe Hall in the 1920s—silenced and dismissed.* Politically speaking, the lesbian is usually treated as a nonperson—without rights or citizenship—or else as a sinister bugaboo to be driven from the scene at once. (In a recent diatribe against a proposed equal rights amendment in Iowa, for example, the fundamentalist clergyman Pat Robertson warned of "a socialist, anti-family political movement that encourages women to leave their husbands, kill their children, practice witchcraft, destroy

*Radclyffe Hall's fictional defense of love between women, *The Well of Loneliness*, was ruled obscene under the provisions of the 1857 Obscene Publications Act and banned in England shortly after its publication in 1928. In a newspaper editorial published before the trial, James Douglas, editor of the *Sunday Express*, declared, "I would rather give a healthy boy or a healthy girl a phial of prussic acid than this novel. Poison kills the body, but moral poison kills the soul." The ban was not successfully challenged until 1949. See Baker, *Our Three Selves*, pp. 223–44 and 353.

capitalism and become lesbians."³) As soon as the lesbian is named, in other words, she is dehumanized.

The law has traditionally ignored female homosexuality—not out of indifference, I would argue, but out of morbid paranoia. It is true that in contrast with male homosexuality—an offense punishable by death in some European countries until the nineteenth century— lesbianism has seldom been prohibited or proscribed in so many words.⁴ Yet this seeming obliviousness should not deceive us. Behind such silence, one can often detect an anxiety too severe to allow for direct articulation. When members of the House of Lords decided in 1921, for example, not to amend the antihomosexual Criminal Law Amendment Act of 1885 to include acts of "gross indecency" be- tween women, it was not because they deemed the threat of lesbian- ism an inconsequential one—quite the contrary—but because they were afraid that by the very act of mentioning it, they might spread such unspeakable "filthiness" even further. The result of such denial: the transformation of the lesbian into a sort of juridical phantasm.⁵

Nowhere has the work of ghosting been carried on more intensely than in the realm of literature and popular fantasy. Western writing over the centuries is from one angle a kind of derealization machine: insert the lesbian and watch her disappear. Actual spectral metaphors are crucial to the business of derealization: in Denis Diderot's *La Reli- gieuse* (1760), for example, an evil mother superior who lusts after her nuns is a weird and vaunting "specter," while in Baudelaire's *Les Fleurs du mal* (1857) a pair of tormented female lovers are sickly "phan- toms" wandering eternally in a ghastly living hell. In Henry James's *The Bostonians* (1886), the woman-loving Olive Chancellor, with her cold white hands and oddly glittering eyes, chills all around her with her eerie and "unreal" passion for the nubile Verena Tarrant. Similar sapphic apparitions continue to haunt twentieth-century literature as well, especially in pulp fiction and drama.⁶

Once the lesbian has been defined as ghostly—the better to drain her of any sensual or moral authority—she can then be exorcized. In *The Bostonians*, as in similar works by Balzac, Gautier, Flaubert, Zola, Charlotte Brontë, Hawthorne, Wilkie Collins, Sheridan LeFanu, Maupassant, Colette, Proust, Arnold Bennett, D. H. Lawrence, Compton Mackenzie, Wyndham Lewis, Dorothy Strachey, Dorothy Baker, Ernest Hemingway, Sinclair Lewis, Mary Renault, Rosamund Lehmann, Jean-Paul Sartre, Lillian Hellman, and countless other Anglo-European writers who have dilated on the lesbian theme, the spectral lesbian is ultimately expelled from the "real" world of the fiction—as if vaporized by the forces of heterosexual propriety. Thus Olive Chancellor, humiliated and excoriated by her rival Basil Ransom, who literally drags her adored Verena away from her in the last scene in James's novel, undergoes there a strange bodily and psychic etiolation, becoming paler and paler, weaker and weaker, until on the last page she seems to disappear altogether.[7]

Given such murderous allegorizing, it is perhaps not surprising how many lesbians in real life have engaged in a sort of self-ghosting, hiding or camouflaging their sexual desires or withdrawing voluntarily from society in order to escape such hostility.[8] The Garboesque retreat into secrecy and silence can be a lifesaver. (So too the decorous *mariage de convenance*, like that between Vita Sackville-West and Harold Nicolson, or H.D. and Richard Aldington.) Yet this is not the whole story. As the litany of distinguished names in the foregoing paragraph suggests, the very frequency with which the lesbian has been "apparitionalized" in the Western imagination also testifies to her peculiar cultural power. Only something very palpable—at a deeper level—has the capacity to "haunt" us so thoroughly. This is a point that Radclyffe Hall seems to have grasped when she used the ghost metaphor at the end of *The Well of Loneliness* (1928) to conjure up a paradoxical affirmation of lesbian existence. In the final pages of that much-maligned yet still fiercely compelling fiction, when the melancholy heroine Stephen Gordon imagines herself surrounded by a hallucinatory "legion" of spirits—the ghosts of all the women, past and present, who have suffered over their homosexuality—the true uncanniness of the metaphor abruptly reveals itself. Communing with her "unbidden guests" in a weird, visionary convulsion, a sort of fantastic orgasm of the spirit, Stephen's own homosexual being is mysteriously affirmed. She undergoes a quickening—her "barren womb" becomes "fruitful." And in the novel's famous last line, the ghosts begin to speak through her, as in one ecstatic and thunderous voice: "Give us also the right to our existence!"[9]

What Radclyffe Hall's allegory of inspiration suggests is this: that within the very imagery of negativity lies the possibility of recovery—a way of conjuring up, or bringing back into view, that which has been denied. Take the metaphor far enough, and the invisible will rematerialize; the spirit will become flesh. It is an insight I have tried to apply in various ways in this book. Although the eight essays in this volume differ in mode and style—two being explicitly autobiographical ("First Ed" and "In Praise of Brigitte Fassbaender"), three historical and biographical ("The Diaries of Anne Lister," "Marie Antoinette Obsession," and "The Gaiety of Janet Flanner"), and three literary critical ("The Apparitional Lesbian," "Sylvia Townsend Warner and the Counterplot of Lesbian Fiction" and "Haunted by Olive Chancellor")—each is at bottom a kind of invocation: an attempt to call up, precisely by confronting the different kinds of denial and disembodiment with which she is usually associated, the much-ghosted yet nonetheless vital lesbian subject.

At this point it is fair to ask—exactly who *is* this spectral lesbian subject I claim to be invoking? Let me first list a few things I think she is not:

1. *She is not a recent invention.* I fly in the face here, I realize, of that theory—popularized by historians of sexuality influenced by the late Michel Foucault—which holds that lesbianism, at least in the flagrantly sexualized sense that we usually understand the term today, is by and large a fabrication of late nineteenth- and early twentieth-century male sexologists. Before Krafft-Ebing, Havelock Ellis, Sigmund Freud, and others "invented" the notion of female sexual deviance around 1900, or so the argument usually runs, there was no such thing as lesbian identity, nor any self-avowedly "homosexual" behavior on the part of individual women. The lesbian only became possible, supposedly, after she was "produced" by turn-of-the-century clinicians. The argument is bolstered by the fact that *lesbian* and *homosexual* are indeed relatively recent terms, first given currency by medical writers in the later nineteenth century. What did women do who happened to desire one another before the crucial nomenclature appeared? According to the most extreme proponents of the sexological model, they mainly sat about doing needlework, pressing flowers into albums, and writing romantic letters to one another. If they ever got into bed together, it was strictly platonic: a matter of a few cuddles and "darlings" and a lot of epistemic confusion.[10]

None of this seems very persuasive to me—and not only because it

relies so heavily on a condescending belief in the intellectual and erotic naiveté of women of past epochs. What the advocates of the "no
lesbians before 1900" theory forget is that there are myriad ways of
discovering one's desire. Take again the matter of literature and literary representation. As the late Jeannette Foster demonstrated in 1956
in her brilliant (and unjustly ignored) bibliographic study, *Sex Variant
Women in Literature*, love between women has been a motif in European art and culture since classical times and a prominent literary
topos at least since the Renaissance. It is true that a great deal of writing dealing with lesbianism has been produced by men and is often
satirical or pornographic or "underground" in nature. But do we then
assume that women never had access to this flourishing popular tradition, or that they somehow managed (until Freud) to remain indifferent to its often luxuriant sexual imagery? Common sense alone
suggests otherwise. It is difficult, I maintain, to contemplate passages
in Juvenal's *Satires*, Martial's *Epigrams*, Ovid's *Metamorphoses*, Arios-
to's *Orlando Furioso*, Aretino's *Dialogues*, Sir Philip Sidney's *Arcadia*,
Shakespeare's *As You Like It* or *Twelfth Night*, Ben Jonson's *Volpone*,
John Donne's *Satires, Epigrams, and Verse Letters*, John Cleland's *Memoirs of a Woman of Pleasure*, Samuel Richardson's *Pamela*, Diderot's
La Religieuse, Laclos's *Les Liaisons dangereuses*, Coleridge's *Christabel*,
Christina Rossetti's *Goblin Market*, Balzac's *La Fille aux yeux d'or*,
Swinburne's *Poems and Ballads* or *Lesbia Brandon*, or Zola's *Nana*—
fairly well-known works all—without certain ticklish ideas popping
instantly into one's head. For all of its mystifications, literature is
(still) the mirror of what is known: and Western civilization, it seems,
has always known on some level about lesbians.

A similar point might be made about terminology. *Lesbian* and *homosexual* may indeed be neologisms, but there have always been *other*
words—a whole slangy mob of them—for pointing to (or taking aim
at) the lover of women: *tribade, fricatrice, sapphist, roaring girl, amazon,
freak, romp, dyke, bull dagger, tommy*.[11] Even the seemingly innocent
odd woman or *odd girl* occur with such enticing regularity in early
lesbian-themed writing as to suggest the possibility of a host of lost or
suppressed code terms.* And where there are words—even comic or

---

*A subterranean "lesbian" meaning may be present in *odd* and its derivatives—I would
argue—as early as 1755. In the scandalous autobiography she published in that year, the

10

A POLEMICAL
INTRODUCTION

taboo or salacious ones—there is identity. As I argue in two of the
essays in this volume, "The Diaries of Anne Lister" and "Marie Antoinette Obsession," one can find striking evidence of a certain incipient lesbian self-awareness well before the so-called invention of the
lesbian around 1900. In the first essay I reflect on the interesting case
of Anne Lister (1791–1840), a little-known English woman who managed to carry on a brisk and highly satisfactory homosexual love life in
rural Yorkshire in the 1820s. (Although circumspect in her public
dealings, Lister wrote freely in her diary about her "oddity," as she
called it, finding philosophical justification for it in the writings of
Rousseau and Byron.) And in the second, dealing with the homoerotic cult that grew up around Marie Antoinette in nineteenth-century
England and France, I suggest that such libidinal self-awareness may
not in fact have been so uncommon. Because rumors of Marie Antoinette's own homosexuality were widespread throughout the nineteenth century, those who venerated her memory, I argue, were often
affirming—at times quite explicitly—their own lesbian impulses. As
more archival research is carried out on the lives of women of the past,
I predict that more of these instances of "premature" lesbian self-
awareness will materialize, casting further doubt on the recent-
invention hypothesis. The work of lesbian and gay historiography
has only just begun.[12]

2. *She is not asexual.* This is really only a corollary of 1. One of the

---

transvestite English actress Charlotte Charke referred to herself as an "odd mortal" and
repeatedly called attention to the "oddity" of her history, which included episodes of traveling about for long periods in male costume with a woman who posed as her wife. Anne
Lister, writing in her diary in the 1820s, spoke of her sexual desire for other women as her
"oddity" or "odd freak": encountering a similarly inclined lady named Miss Pickford in
1823, she described feeling "oddish." Later in the nineteenth century, and on into the twentieth, the word inevitably crops up whenever female-female desire is hinted at—especially
in fiction. Thus Basil Ransom, meeting Olive Chancellor for the first time in *The Bostonians*,
finds himself thinking that "she *was* a very odd cousin of his, was this Boston cousin of his"
(64). After the youthful Stephen Gordon refuses a male suitor in Radclyffe Hall's *The Well of
Loneliness*, it is whispered of her (by her neighbors) "that she had always been odd, and now
for some reason she seemed odder than ever" (107). Nor can it be altogether a coincidence, I
think, that the word appears so often in the titles of lesbian-themed books. One need only
think of Ann Bannon's *Odd Girl Out* (1957), one of a series of pulp novels about Beebo
Brinker, a lesbian in Greenwich Village in the 1950s; Elizabeth Jane Howard's *Odd Girl Out*
(1972), about a young woman who nearly wrecks a marriage by sleeping first with the husband then with the wife; or, indeed, Lillian Faderman's *Odd Girls and Twilight Lovers* (1991),
on the history of American lesbian life in the twentieth century.

reasons that historians of sexuality have been so eager to treat lesbianism as a recently "invented" (and therefore limited) phenomenon, it
seems to me, is because it is so difficult—still—for many people to
acknowledge that women can and do have sexual relations with one
another. The less of it there is, it seems, the better. We may laugh at
Queen Victoria's fabled disbelief when informed by her ministers—
during parliamentary deliberations over the aforesaid Criminal Law
Amendment Act—that, yes, sex between women was technically
possible. Yet it is remarkable how often similar imaginative "block-
ages" afflict the more sophisticated. It is telling, I think, that when
the first volume of Anne Lister's diary was published in 1988 it was
immediately rumored to be a hoax, precisely on account of its often
jaunty sexual explicitness. (In one entry the indefatigable Lister describes "going to" her lover M. three times in one night; elsewhere she
fantasizes about having a penis, taking a female friend into a toolshed
and fucking her.) It was impossible, the rumor went, that a woman of
the 1820s could have had such a rambunctious and enjoyable sex life:
women just didn't do that then. Yet lurking behind this assumption, I
think, was another: that they don't do it now either. Even among
some feminist historians, paradoxically, one could detect this morbid
refusal to visualize—as if lesbianism and "not doing it" were somehow perversely synonymous.[13]

I have tried to maneuver around this rather more insidious and ascetical kind of denial by focusing whenever possible on the embodied
and erotic aspects of lesbian experience. I am skeptical, for example,
when scholars or critics argue—as one did not so long ago—that lesbianism is simply another form of female "homosocial" bonding,
blandly analogous to "the bond of mother and daughter [. . .] the
bond of sister and sister, women's friendship, 'networking,' and the
active struggles of feminism."[14] In the essay "Sylvia Townsend
Warner and the Counterplot of Lesbian Fiction," I suggest that the
weakness of this theory lies in the way that it obscures the specificity,
one might almost say melodrama, of lesbian desire—its incorrigibly
lascivious surge toward the body of another woman. Yet I try to "recar-
nalize" matters elsewhere too—as when I cogitate, in "The Gaiety of
Janet Flanner," on Janet Flanner's delightedly sensual appreciation of
Ingres's female nudes or, in "In Praise of Brigitte Fassbaender," on the
exquisite libidinal pleasure to be derived from the voice and body of
the opera singer.

3. *She is not a gay man.* This might seem obvious, yet often (strangely) is not. When a conservative religious leader recently denounced "gays, lesbians, and prostitutes" as "the source of AIDS" and urged a return to "normal life," one sensed (along with the hysterical moral scapegoating and near gothic sex panic) a certain conceptual blurring at work: of no account, seemingly, was the fact that lesbians actually had a relatively low rate of HIV infection in the 1980s—far lower than that of gay men or prostitutes, or indeed virtually any other category of person, gay or straight, recognized by the Centers for Disease Control. Since lesbians, like gay men, engaged in "homosexual practices," they were as "guilty"—in the Torquemadan eyes of the demonizer—as their depraved brothers-in-sin.[15]

We might call this kind of nonseeing a sort of ghosting through assimilation. As soon as the lesbian is lumped in—for better or for worse—with her male homosexual counterpart, the singularity of her experience (sexual and otherwise) tends to become obscured. We "forget" about the lesbian by focusing instead on gay men. Such forgetting can even occur, ironically enough, at the very instant the lesbian is asserting herself most vehemently. Presenting "The Apparitional Lesbian" to various scholarly audiences over the past year, I could not help but notice how often the first question I would receive after delivering my talk was "But what about gay men?" or some version thereof—as though I had implicitly committed an offense against good manners by daring to speak of lesbianism without mentioning male homosexuality. Even among sophisticated and open-minded listeners, it was extremely difficult, I found, to keep the lesbian focus—so strong the collective reflex to shift back toward the topic of love between men, as if that, paradoxically, were somehow less peculiar or less threatening than love between women.

Thus it is that I have mostly avoided—when speaking of lesbianism in this book—the use of pseudo-umbrella terms such as *gay* or *queer*, and have resisted placing my version of lesbian phenomenology under the currently fashionable rubric of queer theory. The term *queer* has lately become popular in activist and progressive academic circles in part, it seems to me, precisely because it makes it easy to enfold female homosexuality back "into" male homosexuality and disembody the lesbian once again. I sympathize with the views expressed by lesbian playwright Holly Hughes during a recent roundtable discussion of queer theory published in the *Village Voice:*

I'm ambivalent about the term *queer*. I think it's useful in certain ways—it has the cringe factor, it's confrontational. And there is something about the experience of being an outsider that's embedded in the word. When you throw it back in people's faces, it can produce a certain sense of empowerment. It also has limitations. In some ways, it reminds me of the word *gay*. I worked really hard to get *lesbian* into usage, and so did a lot of people who came before me. Lumping us together [with gay men] erases the differences, the inequalities between us.[16]

The work of Eve Sedgwick, currently the most eloquent proponent of "queer theory" in the academic world, has been in this respect both an inspiration and a goad. While no one can discount the immensely valuable work that Sedgwick has done in bringing the subject of homosexuality into the intellectual mainstream (and the canny reader will find the volatile traces of her influence throughout this book) there is an important sense in which the subject of lesbianism simply does not concern her. In her 1985 book, *Between Men: English Literature and Male Homosocial Desire*, the nervous avoidance of the topic of lesbianism is striking—is even, as I point out in the aforementioned Townsend Warner piece, an enabling condition of that book's argument. And even in her most recent book, *Epistemology of the Closet* (1990)—though she here defends her masculinist bent far more gracefully and compellingly than she did in *Between Men*—the focus on men and male homosexuality remains fairly unremitting. (Her great theme, as she notes in her introduction, is that "chronic, now endemic crisis of homo/heterosexual definition, indicatively male, dating from the end of the nineteenth century" and the writers she chooses to illuminate the theme are Melville, Wilde, Nietzsche, James, and Proust.) To the extent that "queer theory" still seems, at least in its Sedgwickian incarnation, to denote primarily the study of male homosexuality, I find myself at odds with both its language and its universalizing aspirations.[17]

4. *She is not a nonsense.* Here too, finally, I am flagrantly out of step with current thinking. Especially among younger lesbian and gay scholars trained in Continental philosophy (including a number of the so-called queer theorists) it has recently become popular to contest, along deconstructionist lines, the very meaningfulness of terms such as *lesbian* or *gay* or *homosexual* or *coming out*. No one knows what these words really signify, the argument goes; they lack linguistic

transparency. The claims put forward in support of this position are sometimes dizzying. Here is one such critic (herself lesbian) going after *lesbian*, for example, with all pistons firing:

> What or who is it that is "out," made manifest and fully disclosed, when and if I reveal myself as a lesbian? What is it that is now known, anything? What remains permanently concealed by the very linguistic act that offers up the promise of a transparent revelation of sexuality? Can sexuality even remain sexuality once it submits to a criterion of transparency and disclosure, or does it perhaps cease to be sexuality precisely when the semblance of full explicitness is achieved?

"To claim that is what I *am*," she continues, "is to suggest a provisional totalization of this 'I' "—

> But if the I can so determine itself, then that which it excludes in order to make that determination remains constitutive of the determination itself. In other words, such a statement presupposes that the "I" exceeds its determination, and even produces that very excess in and by the act which seeks to exhaust the semantic field of that "I." In the act which would disclose the true and full content of that "I," a certain radical *concealment* is thereby produced. For it is always finally unclear what is meant by invoking the lesbian-signifier, since its signification is always to some degree out of one's control, but also because its *specificity* can only be demarcated by exclusions that return to disrupt its claim to coherence.[18]

Frankly, I disagree: I don't find it "always finally unclear what is meant by invoking the lesbian-signifier." In this I am, I suppose, a kind of closet Wittgensteinian. I believe that we live in a world in which the word *lesbian* still makes sense, and that it is possible to use the word frequently, even lyrically, and still be understood. I am reminded of a student in a course I was giving on lesbianism and literature who persisted in quizzing me, often fiercely, about what I meant by the term. Was a lesbian simply any woman who had sex with women? What then of the woman who had sex with women but denied that she was a lesbian? What about women who had sex with women but also had sex with men? What about women who wanted to have sex with women but didn't? Or wanted to but couldn't? And so on and so on, to the bizarre hypothetical case of a physically handicapped married woman, unable to have sex with her husband (or anyone else), who considered herself heterosexual, yet unconsciously desired to have sex with women. Inevitably I responded to such questions by saying that I used the term in the "ordinary" or "dictionary" or "vernacular" sense. (A lesbian, according to *Webster's Ninth*, is a woman "characterized by a tendency to direct sexual desire toward another of the same sex.") And indeed, I still maintain, if in ordinary speech I say, "I am a lesbian," the meaning is instantly (even dangerously) clear: I am a woman whose primary emotional and erotic allegiance is to my own sex. Usage both confers and delimits meaning: the word is part of a "language game," as Wittgenstein might say, in which we all know the rules.[19]

That the meaning of *lesbian* is in practice more stable and accessible than some of its would-be deconstructors would allow can be demonstrated, I think, by the following somewhat comic example. In my opening paragraph I refer to Greta Garbo as a lesbian, despite the fact, as some readers will know, she occasionally had affairs with men as well as women. Why not refer to her, more properly, as a bisexual? Because I think it more *meaningful* to refer to her as a lesbian. And I am not the only person to think so. When asked by an orchestra manager in 1938 about his purported affair with the Swedish actress, the conductor Leopold Stokowski responded, "Jerry, have you ever made love to a lesbian? It's wunnnderful . . . !"[20] Yes, it *is* wunnnderful. But we know that it's wunnnderful because the word "means" here in a way we immediately grasp: that while Garbo sometimes makes love to men, she would rather make love to women. Indeed the very point of the joke lies in this immanence of meaning: it is precisely Garbo's preference, paradoxically, that makes her—in the maestro's eyes—so delectably enticing.[21]

Who then *is* the much-ghosted being I am seeking to call back to life in this book? I can characterize her best, I think, by borrowing a term from the literary critic Edward Said. In a recent essay on minority literature and the politics of identity, Said spoke eloquently of "the useful notion of worldliness." Worldliness, according to Said, is that humane and expansive faculty of mind which allows one to see things "in a global setting"—as part and parcel of a larger world of "formal articulations." Worldliness is the very opposite of "separatism"; it has nothing to do with fetishizing one element of experience over another. Rather than haunting "some tiny, defensively constituted corner of the world," the truly worldly individual seeks to inhabit "the large, many-windowed house of culture as a whole."[22]

The lesbian I have tried to invoke in this book is above all a *worldly* being in the Saidian sense. Which isn't to say that she isn't often "worldly" in a more conventional sense too. Once again, we seldom envision her as such: as civilized, witty, full of style and point and savoir faire. As far as cultural stereotypes go, gay men have always seemed to monopolize the wit-and-sophistication department, with the lesbian hopelessly bringing up the rear—a grim and uncouth figure in lumpy tweeds or ill-fitting motorcycle jacket. And yet when we look at the lives and accomplishments of actual women, what stereotype could in fact be more false? Who more "civilized" than Janet Flanner, for fifty years the Paris correspondent of the *New Yorker?* Or Gertrude Stein, with her salon? Or Wanda Landowska, the great musician and sublime interpreter of Bach? Or Berenice Abbott, the celebrated photographer? Or Marguerite Yourcenar, the first woman writer admitted into the Académie Française?

Who more sophisticated than Elizabeth Bishop? Or wittier than the peculiarly devastating Violet Trefusis? (Trefusis on the cave paintings at Lascaux: "Trops mignons, ces Cromagnons.")[23] Or more apropos than the young British novelist Jeanette Winterson? In Winterson's recent lesbian coming-of-age novel, *Oranges Are Not the Only Fruit* (1985), there is a marvelous passage in which the precocious narrator describes making a little Wagnerian "tableau" out of Easter eggshells for a school competition:

> We cut a cardboard box to set the scene, Elsie doing the back-drop, me doing the rocks out of half-egg shells. We stayed up all night on the dramatis personae, because of the detail. We had chosen the most exciting bit, "Brunhilda Confronts Her Father." I did Brunhilda, and Elsie did Wodin. Brunhilda had a helmet made out of a thimble with little feather wings from Elsie's pillow. "She needs a spear," said Elsie. "I'll give you a cocktail stick only don't tell anyone what I use it for." As a final touch I cut off some of my own hair and made it into Brunhilda's hair. Wodin was a masterpiece, a double-yoker brown egg, with a Ritz cracker shield and a drawn-on eye-patch. We made him a match-box chariot that was just too small. "Dramatic empha-

sis," said Elsie. The next day I took it to school and placed it beside the others; there was no comparison. Imagine my horror when it didn't win. I was not a selfish child and, understanding the nature of genius, would have happily bowed to another's talent, but not to three eggs covered in cotton wool, entitled "Easter Bunnies."[24]

It is precisely in the subtle juxtaposition here between great and small, the grandiloquent and the miniaturized, infantine pomposity and grownup irony, that Winterson reveals herself as the reigning mistress of postmodern lesbian drollery.

And yet it is the more profound sort of worldliness—that expansive, outward-looking, and multifaceted humanity described by Said—that I wish in the end to associate with my lesbian subject. We need to recognize how fully, if invisibly, the lesbian has always been integrated into the very fabric of cultural life. This is a paradox of course: just how thoroughly, despite all the hostility ranged against her, she has managed to insert herself into the larger world of human affairs. None of the women invoked in this book—from the adventuresome Anne Lister to the cosmopolitan Flanner—ever let a sense of sexual alienation or "marginality" stand in the way of her curiosity, self-education, or ambition: each sought to participate to the utmost in the rich communal life of her time (and usually did). Such openness to experience may in fact be typical of the homosexual woman; and not only because she has so often had to work in the so-called "real world" to support herself. The very feeling of being obliterated by one's society may prompt a wish to assert oneself all the more aggressively—to enter more fully, as it were, into the larger scheme of things. Certainly, as is often the case with minority groups, lesbians have made contributions to culture out of all proportion to their actual numbers.

I was struck anew by this paradox not long ago while reading a somewhat gossipy (but very good) biography of Marlene Dietrich. In a chapter on Dietrich's long-standing affair with the flamboyant screenwriter and poet Mercedes de Acosta—the same de Acosta who also managed to captivate Garbo—the author (the film and theater historian Donald Spoto) describes de Acosta as "a charter member of America's creative lesbian community" of the 1930s and 1940s. In a brief yet amazing footnote he goes on to explain that "among a legion, this group included Edna St. Vincent Millay, Willa Cather and Anita Loos (writers); Cheryl Crawford, Elizabeth Marbury, Eva Le Gallienne, Alla Nazimova, Katharine Cornell, Blanche Yurka, Natasha Rambova and Mary Martin (in the theater); Janet Gaynor, Jean Arthur, Kay Francis and Dorothy Arzner (in Hollywood)."[25]

What staggers here is the almost comic sense of surplus: we aren't used to thinking of lesbians as "legion" or as playing any crucially significant part in anything so mainstream as "the theater" or "Hollywood." Spoto's impressive catalogue of names is, among other things, a startling affirmation of lesbian accomplishment. Yet it's only the tip of the iceberg. Lesbian creativity has been responsible, it could be argued, for much that we take for granted in modern culture, especially (though not solely) in the world of the arts. How to appreciate modernism itself, for example, without recognizing the brilliant contributions made by Gertrude Stein, Djuna Barnes, Virginia Woolf, Sylvia Beach, Natalie Barney, Romaine Brooks, Margaret Anderson, Jane Heap, Jane Bowles, Marie Laurencin, Tamara de Lempicka, Gluck, Florence Henri, or Eileen Gray? How to understand twentieth-century Anglo-American poetry without acknowledging the rich and variegated talents of Millay, Amy Lowell, H.D., Charlotte Mew, Marianne Moore, Elizabeth Bishop, Muriel Rukeyser, Adrienne Rich, May Swenson, Audre Lorde, Olga Broumas, or Marilyn Hacker? Nor is the lesbian influence only to be found in the realm of so-called high culture. It is impossible to appreciate the blues, I would maintain, or the history of American jazz and popular song, without taking into account the unforgettable contributions of Bessie Smith, Ma Rainey, Gladys Bentley, Ethel Waters, Mabel Mercer, Alberta Hunter, or Janis Joplin.

In the essays that follow I have sought to affirm this kind of worldliness: the connection between lesbian experience and human experience as a whole. Whether writing about actual women, works of literature, or cultural institutions such as the opera, I have tried to break down the imaginative and ideological barriers that keep us from seeing (in Spoto's term) that "legion" of lesbians in our midst. Indeed, if a single grand theme shapes this collection, it is that there are always "more" lesbians to be found in the world than one expects—that lesbians are indeed "everywhere," and always have been. For too long our thinking has been dominated by a kind of scarcity model: either

Out into the world: Garbo in the final scene of *Queen Christina. Courtesy of the
Lester Glassner Collection.*

there aren't any lesbians at all, or too few of them to matter. It is time,
I maintain, to focus on presence instead of absence, plenitude instead
of scarcity.

For only by looking at what's in front us do we undo the repressive
magic of the naysayers—of all those who would wish the lesbian
away. Only thus do we call the lesbian back from that "world of vapors" to which she has been consigned. And once we begin to look,
we may find her looking back at us: making eye contact, delighted to
be seen at last. I don't claim to be immune to this flirtatious answering
gaze, and some readers will undoubtedly find my approach here too
rapturous and utopian, others too facetious. (I manage, in different
ways, to find the spectacle of lesbian desire both sublime and comic.)
Yet there is a certain value in casting aside inhibition. In seeking out
the lesbian who is everywhere, one often finds a part of oneself. Like a
ghost come back to life, or Garbo in her greatest role, the lesbian offers us new and vital information about what it is to be human.

A Postscript on the Arrangement of Chapters

With one exception, the chapters in this book appear in the order in which they were composed. Along with the importunate "Ed," the earliest essays here, "The Apparitional Lesbian" and "Sylvia Townsend Warner and the Counterplot of Lesbian Fiction," written in 1989 and 1990, were important ground-clearing pieces for me; through the writing of them, I was able to lay out in a synoptic and schematic way the larger themes of the book as a whole. In the chapters that follow—on Anne Lister, Marie Antoinette, *The Bostonians*, Janet Flanner, and lesbianism and opera—I develop the idea of "the apparitional lesbian" in a more detailed and self-consciously diachronic way: each might be considered a kind of case history, or specimen moment, in the evolution of lesbian sensibility from 1800 to the present.

2

FIRST ED

F i r s t, E d—who, for all the sense of dra-
ma her memory evokes, is surrounded with a certain haze, a nimbus
of uncertainty. Did our encounter, the one I remember, take place in
1963 or 1964? It must, I think, have been 1964, if only because the
Dixie Cups' "Chapel of Love" (a crucial clue) was on the radio that
summer, lilting out of dashboards all over San Diego, along with
"Don't Worry Baby," "Pretty Woman," and "I Want to Hold Your
Hand." It was the summer that my father's large brown and white
Oldsmobile got a cracked block from the heat, and his hair, which had
gone gray after my mother divorced him, went completely white, like
Marie Antoinette's. A few months later the Dodgers, resplendent
with Koufax, won the Series, and I and my fellow sixth-graders, tran-

22

sistors in hand, celebrated with loud huzzahs on the rough gravel playgrounds of Whittier Elementary School.

All during the long hot months of vacation, I went once a week for a swimming lesson at the old YWCA downtown at 10th and C Street. We had recently returned (my mother, my younger sister, and I) from two years on the English coast, where we had lived in a gloomy village near Dover. My British-born mother had taken us there—in a flurry of misguided nostalgia and emotional confusion—immediately after her divorce in 1961, and we had stayed on, in a strange state of immobility and shared melancholia, until mid-1963. In the summer of 1964, however, things seemed better. While my sister and I reaccustomed ourselves to the unfamiliar sunshine, my mother exulted in being back in California, in living as a "bachelorette" (with two children) in the pink Buena Vista apartments, and in the hope—not yet dashed by various Jamesian revelations—of her imminent marriage to the handsome Chuck, the mustachioed ensign in the Navy with whom she had committed the sweetest of adulteries before her divorce.

My mother had been a swimming instructor for the Y during the ten years she had been married to my father, and the organization kept her loyalty, being associated with water, freedom, light, pools, and "living in San Diego"—with everything, indeed, that she had dreamed of as a teenager working for the gasworks in St. Albans. She herself had taken a number of classes at the downtown Y: the intermediate and advanced swim course, synchronized swimming, and beginning and advanced lifeguard training, during which she learned to divest herself of numerous layers of clothing, including laced snow boots, while submerged in eight feet of water. Despite my mother's demonstrated aquatic skills, however, I adamantly refused to let her teach me any of them, and remained, at the relatively advanced age of ten, a coy nonswimmer. After several abortive sessions at the bathroom sink, during which she tried to make me open my eyes under water, it became clear that I was not going to learn anything under her tutelage, but would require instruction from some more neutral party. Hence my introduction to the Y, the children's evening swim program, and the delicious orchestrated flutterings of breast, elbow, and ankle.

The YWCA was an antiquated building by southern California

standards—Julia Morganish, from the teens or twenties, though not a work of her hand. It preserved the dowdy grandeur of turn-of-the-century California women's buildings, manifest in its square white facade, Mission-style touches, and cool, cavernous interior. Of the actual decor of the building, I remember little: only, vaguely, some seedy fifties leatherette furniture parked at odd angles in the reception area, peeling bulletin boards, the ancient candy machine expelling Paydays and Snickers with a frightful death rattle, and the small front office staffed—inevitably—by a middle aged, short-haired woman in slacks. The place had an interesting air of desolation: various lost or ill-fitting souls lingered in the front area especially—off-duty sailors, people speaking Spanish, Negroes and Filipinas, mysterious solitary women. I never saw any of the guest rooms, and did not know that they existed: it would not have occurred to me that anyone might actually live there.

The indoor pool was deep in the netherworld of the building, seemingly underground—a greenish, Bayreuthian extravagance, reeking of chlorine and steam. Entering from the women's locker room, one found oneself immediately at one of the pool's deep-end corners. A wobbly diving board jutted out here in dangerous invitation, while at the opposite end a set of pale scalloped steps beckoned to the less adventurous. Running around the pool on all sides was an ornate white tile gutter, cheerfully decorated—by the same wayward deco hand, presumably, that had done the steps—with tiny mosaic flowers and swastikas. The water itself was cloudy, awash with dead moths and floating Band-Aids, but nonetheless, in its foggy Byzantine way, also warm-seeming and attractive. A slippery tiled walkway, inset with more flowers and swastikas and the imprinted words DO NOT RUN, completed the scene. Along this elevated platform our blond-haired teacher, an athletic woman named Pam, would slap up and down in bathing suit and bare feet, calling out instructions in a plaintive Midwestern tongue.

We were five or six in all, a sprinkling of little girls in cotton suits with elastic waists, and one or two even smaller boys in minuscule trunks. Under Pam's guidance we soon mastered the basics: the dog paddle, a variety of elementary crawls and backstrokes, flapping side-strokes, "sculling" and "treading water"—all with much gasping and excitement. It was on one of these occasions, while struggling to float on my back without inhaling water, that I must first have seen Ed. The ceiling over the pool was high up, some thirty or forty feet, with tall windows of opaque glass near the roof line, through which a few dim green rays of evening sunlight would sometimes penetrate to the fluorescent fug below. A dusty balcony overhung the pool at this level, stacked with seldom-used folding chairs for the spectators who came to observe the water ballet displays put on by the synchronized swimming class. Ed stood up there aloft, along with a few seamen in whites, waiting for the adult free swim hour that immediately followed our class.

Even from my unusual angle I could see that Ed was spectacularly good-looking—in a hoodish fifties way that had not yet, by mid-1964, been utterly superseded by the incoming styles of the era. I might grace my bedroom bulletin board with the toothy images of John, Paul, George, and Ringo, but Ed's "look" (as I knew even then) was far more compelling. Indeed I felt oddly giddy those times when she met my gaze—as though our positions had reversed, water and air had changed places, and I was the one looking down from above. She wore men's clothes of a decade earlier, Sears and Roebuck style, the tightest of black pants (with a discreet fly), a dark leather belt and white shirt, a thin striped tie, and, as I saw later, the same pointy-toed black dress shoes worn by the Mexican "bad boys" at Clairemont High School, down the street from the Buena Vista apartments. Her hair was excessively, almost frighteningly groomed into a narrow scandalous pompadour, and had been oiled with brilliantine to a rich black-brown, against which her face stood out with stark and ravishing paleness. She appeared to be in her late twenties or early thirties—definitely "old" to me—though something about the drastic formality of her costume also gave her the look of a teenage boy, one dressed up, perhaps, for a senior prom. She spoke to no one, smoked a cigarette, and seemed, despite her great beauty, consumed by sadness. She had a thin face of the sort I would later find irresistible in women.

One evening, more sultry than usual, my mother, who normally dropped me off and picked me up after class in the front foyer, was unable to collect me, owing to some sudden disorder in the radiator of our bulbous green Studebaker. My teacher, Pam, and her mother, the gamy old Peg, a short tanned woman who wore pants and also taught swimming classes at the Y, agreed to drive me home to Clairemont in their car. As soon as they had closed up the office we were to leave.

I had already finished changing and sat by myself in the locker room, waiting for my ride, when Ed came in. The other little girls were long gone. The floor was still wet with the footprints of the departed; the thick damp air hung about like a dream. At the same time everything seemed to open up, as if I—or she and I together—had suddenly entered a clearing in a forest. Ed said nothing, yet seemed, in some distant way, to recognize me. I sat still, not knowing where to go. She scrutinized me ambiguously for a few moments. Then, as if some complex agreement had been reached between us, she began to strip away, vertiginously, the emblems of her manhood.

Ed, Ed, my first, my only undressing. She moved gracefully, like a Pierrot, her pallid face a mask in the dim light. She removed her jacket and unbuckled her belt first, laying them carefully on the bench next to me. Then she slipped off her shoes and socks. I gazed down at her bare feet. Her eyes met mine and looked away. Then she loosened her tie with one hand, and pulled it off, followed by her heavy cuff links. Glancing again in my direction, she began to unbutton her shirt, twisting her torso in an uneasy fashion as she did so. She wore, heart-stoppingly, a woman's white brassiere. This she unhooked slowly from behind, and watching me intently now, let her breasts fall forward. Her breasts were full and had dark nipples. She stopped to flick back some wet-looking strands of hair that had come down, Dion-like, over her brow. Then rather more quickly, with a practiced masculine gesture, she began to undo her fly. She removed her trousers, revealing a pair of loose Jockey shorts. She hesitated a moment before uncovering the soft hairiness beneath—that mystery against which I would thrust my head, blindly, in years to come. I stared childishly at the curly black V between her legs. She took off her watch, a man's gold Timex, last of all.

Her transfiguration was not complete, of course: now she took out a rusty-looking woman's swimsuit from a metal locker and began, uncannily, stepping into it. She became a woman. Then she folded up her clothes neatly and put them away. Still she did not speak—nor, it seemed, did she ever remove her eyes from mine.

I am aware, too late, how almost painfully sexy Ed was—and perhaps, at the level of hallucination, intended to be. Even now I seem to see the disquieting movement of her chest and shoulders as she leaned over the bench between us, the damp pressed-in look of her thighs when she began to pull the resistant nylon swimsuit up her body, her breasts poignantly hanging, then confined, with the aid of diffident fingers, in the suit's stiff built-in cups. Indeed, I seem to be assisting her, leaning into her, even (slyly) inhaling her. She bends slightly at the knees, balances herself with one hand against the locker, begins to hold me around the neck—but this is a fantasy of the present. In that moment my feelings were of a far more polite, delicate, even senti-mental nature. Astonishment gave way to, resolved into, embarrass-ment. When at last Ed drew on, over the dark crown of her head, a flowered Esther Williams-style bathing cap—the final clownish touch of femininity—I felt, obscurely, the pathos of her transforma-tion: she had become somehow less than herself. But her eyes, with their mute, impassive challenge, never faltered. They seemed to say, I own you now. And I realized too, though I had no words for it at the time, how much I adored her, and what tumult lay ahead.

The other women came and got me soon enough—Ed must have gone—for the next thing I remember is sitting deep in the well of the backseat of my teacher's Plymouth, the warm night breeze blowing in my face, and the lights of downtown glinting in the background as we drove away. Pam and her mother talked in a desultory, friendly way in the front seat. They used slang with each other and swore softly—almost as if I weren't there, or were much older, which I enjoyed. I looked at the back of their heads, at Pam's blond nape and her moth-er's cropped gray thatch, while the sounds of the radio—KCBQ—wafted sweetly through the summer air:

> We're going to the chapel
> And we're
> Gonna get ma-a-a-rried
>
> Going to the Chapel of Love

Then, as we wound our way down 101 through Balboa Park, un-der the tall bridge by the zoo, the two of them began—as if to the music—to talk about Ed. They seemed to know her; they spoke al-most tenderly, referring to her by name. Ed looked more like a guy than ever, my teacher remarked. The words hung about softly in the

air. I began listening hard, as I did at school. Her mother, Peg, reflected for a moment, then glanced back and smiled at me in the dark,
enigmatically, before murmuring in reply, "Yeah, but she don't have
the superior plumbing system." And into the night we sped away.

Many years later, when I had just turned twenty-two, and lay in
bed with a much older woman with whom I was greatly in love, I told
the story of Ed, this story, for the first time. I was already getting on
Helen's nerves by that point; she tried to find the fastest way through
my postcoital maunderings. Ed was, she concluded, "just an exter-
nalization." As she often reminded me, Helen had spent fifty thousand dollars a year for eight years of psychoanalysis in Chicago. She
wore her hair in a long braid down her back to represent, she told me,
her "missing part." She was thin and dark, and, when she wasn't
teaching, wore a man's watch and lumberman's jacket. My mother,
she said, "sounded like a hysteric." A lot of things happened later,
and I finally got to resenting Helen back, but that's a winter, not a
summer story.

3

THE

APPARITIONAL

LESBIAN

To try to write the literary history of lesbianism is to confront, from the start, something ghostly: an impalpability, a misting over, an evaporation, or "whiting out" of possibility. Take, for example, that first (and strangest) of lesbian love stories, Daniel Defoe's *The Apparition of Mrs. Veal* (1706). The heroine of this spectral yarn (which Defoe presents in typically hoaxing fashion as unvarnished "fact") is one Mrs. Bargrave, who lives in Canterbury with a cruel and unfeeling husband. While lamenting her sad state one morning, Mrs. Bargrave is amazed to see her oldest and dearest friend, Mrs. Veal, coming up the street to her door. The two friends have been estranged ever since Mrs. Veal, "a Maiden Gentlewoman of about 30 Years of Age," began keeping house for a brother in

Dover. Overcome with joy, Mrs. Bargrave greets her long-lost companion and moves to kiss her. Just as the clock strikes noon, writes
Defoe, "their Lips almost touched," but "*Mrs. Veal* drew her hand
cross her own Eyes, and said, '*I am not very well,*' and so waved it."[1]

The touch of lips deferred, the two nonetheless converse lovingly.
Mrs. Veal tells Mrs. Bargrave she is about to set off on a journey, and
wished to see her again before doing so. She begs Mrs. Bargrave's forgiveness for the lapse in their friendship and reminds her of their former happy days, when they read "Drelincourt's Book of Death" together and comforted one another in affliction. Moved, Mrs.
Bargrave fetches a devotional poem on Christian love, "Friendship in
Perfection," and they read it aloud, musing on God's will and the
happiness to come in the hereafter. "Dear Mrs. *Bargrave,*" exclaims
Mrs. Veal, "I shall love you forever." Then she draws her hand once
again over her eyes. "*Don't you think I am mightily impaired by my Fits?*"
she asks. (Mrs. Veal has suffered in the past from falling sickness.)
"No," Mrs. Bargrave replies, "I think you look as well as I ever knew
you" (4). Not long after, Mrs. Veal departs, as if in embarrassed
haste.

It is not until the next day, when Mrs. Bargrave goes to look for
Mrs. Veal at a nearby relative's, that the eerie truth is revealed: her
friend has in fact been dead for two days, having succumbed to "fits"
at exactly the stroke of noon on the day before Mrs. Bargrave saw her.
The supposed "Mrs. Veal" was nothing less than an apparition. Suddenly it all makes sense. The spirit was undoubtedly heaven-sent, an
excited Mrs. Bargrave now tells her friends, for all of its actions, including the mysterious "waving" off of her attempted kiss, displayed
its "Wonderful Love to her, and Care of her, that she should not be
affrighted." And Defoe himself, in his role of supposed reporter, con-
curs: the specter's great errand, he concludes, was "to comfort Mrs.
Bargrave in her Affliction, and to ask her Forgiveness for her Breach of
Friendship, and with a Pious Discourse to encourage her" (8). From
this we learn "that there is a Life to come after this, and a Just God
who will retribute to every one according to the Deeds done in the
Body" (preface).

Why call this bizarre little fable a lesbian love story? One could,
conceivably, read into its sparse and somewhat lugubrious detail a
richer, more secular, and sensational narrative—cunningly secreted

inside the uplifting homily on Christian doctrine. Mrs. Bargrave, the unhappy wife, and Mrs. Veal, the maiden gentlewoman—such a story might go—have in fact been clandestine lovers; they have been estranged by circumstances; Mrs. Veal dies; Mrs. Bargrave's vision is a kind of hysterical projection, in which the passion she feels for her dead friend is phantasmatically renewed. Defoe even gives a certain amount of evidence for this sort of fantasia. All the men mentioned in the story are either evil or unsympathetic: Mrs. Bargrave's husband is "barbarous"; Mrs. Veal's brother tries to stop Mrs. Bargrave from spreading the story of his sister's spectral visit. We are invited to imagine a male conspiracy against the lovers: they have been kept apart in life; they will be alienated (or so the brother hopes) in death. The fact that Defoe sometimes hints at erotic relationships between women elsewhere in his fiction—witness *Roxana*—might make such a "reading between the lines" seem even more enticing.[2]

And yet, this does not feel quite right: one is troubled by a certain crassness, anachronism, even narcissism in the reading. Is it not a peculiarly late twentieth-century moral and sexual infantilism that wishes to read into every story from the past some hidden scandal or provocation? And hasn't Defoe made it clear—more or less—that the relationship between Mrs. Bargrave and Mrs. Veal is strictly an incorporeal one? Mrs. Veal, after all, is an apparition—a mere collection of vapors—so much so that Mrs. Bargrave, as we are explicitly reminded, cannot even kiss her.

At the risk of dealing in paradoxes, I would like to argue that it is in fact the very ghostliness—the seeming ineffability—of the connection between Mrs. Bargrave and Mrs. Veal that makes *The Apparition of Mrs. Veal* an archetypally lesbian story. The kiss that doesn't happen, the kiss that *can't* happen, because one of the women involved has become a ghost (or else is direly haunted by ghosts) seems to me a crucial metaphor for the history of lesbian literary representation since the early eighteenth century. Given the threat that sexual love between women inevitably poses to the workings of patriarchal arrangement, it has often been felt necessary to deny the carnal *bravada* of lesbian existence. The hoary misogynist challenge, "But what do lesbians do?" insinuates as much: *This cannot be. There is no place for this.* It is perhaps not so surprising that at least until around 1900 lesbianism manifests itself in the Western literary imagination primarily as an absence, as chimera or *amor impossibilia*—a kind of love that, by definition, cannot exist. Even when "there" (like Stein's Oakland) it is "not there": inhabiting only a recessive, indeterminate, misted-over space in the collective literary psyche. Like the kiss between Mrs. Bargrave and Mrs. Veal, it is reduced to a ghost effect: to ambiguity and taboo. It cannot be perceived, except apparitionally.

But how, one might object, to recognize (enough to remark) something as elusive as a ghost effect? By way of answer let us turn to another work, also from the eighteenth century, in which a similar apparitionality envelops—and ultimately obscures—the representational field. The work is Diderot's *La Religieuse* (1760), long recognized as a masterpiece of the erotic, though of what sort of eros its admirers (and detractors) have often been at a loss to specify.[3] We recall the story: Diderot's pathetic heroine, Suzanne Simonin, forced to become a nun by her selfish and obdurate family, is imprisoned within a series of corrupt convents, each worse than the last, where she is singled out for cruel and incessant persecution by her superiors. In letters smuggled out to various lawyers and secular officials, Suzanne recounts her sufferings and begs for release, though her cries for help go unheard. Diderot's first-person narrative itself masquerades as one of these letters, supposedly addressed to the Marquis de Croismare. Yet it also doubles as Diderot's own sensationalist assault on cloistered religious communities and the inhuman "wickedness" perpetrated within them.

As most of its modern commentators have remarked, a fear of sexual relations between women seems to suffuse—if not to rule—Diderot's story.[4] And yet how is this fear insinuated? Ineluctably, by shadow play—through a kind of linguistic necromancy, or calling up, of ghosts. Take Diderot's sleight-of-hand, for example, in the scene early in the novel in which the vicious mother superior at Longchamp, the first convent in which Suzanne is incarcerated, forces her to undergo a sadistic mock death as a punishment for disobedience. After being made to lie in a coffin, being drenched with freezing holy water, and trodden upon (as "a corpse") by her fellow nuns, the pitiful Suzanne is confined to her cell, without blankets, crucifix, or food. That night, at the behest of the superior, other nuns break into her room, shrieking and overturning objects, so that

> those who were not in the conspiracy alleged that strange things were
> going on in my cell, that they had heard mournful voices, shoutings

and the rattlings of chains, and that I held communion with ghosts and evil spirits, that I must have made a pact with the devil and that my corridor should be vacated at once.[5]

A young nun, infected by the atmosphere of collective paranoia, sees Suzanne wandering in the corridor, becomes hysterical with terror, and flings herself into the bewildered Suzanne's arms. At this point, Suzanne tells the marquis, "the most criminal-sounding story was made out of it." Namely,

> that the demon of impurity had possessed me, and I was credited with intentions I dare not mention, and unnatural desires to which they attributed the obvious disarray of the young nun. Of course I am not a man, and I don't know what can be imagined about one woman and another, still less about one woman alone, but as my bed had no curtains and people came in and out of my room at all hours, what can I say, Sir? For all their circumspect behaviour, their modest eyes and the chastity of their talk, these women must be very corrupt at heart— anyway they know that you can commit indecent acts alone, which I don't know, and so I have never quite understood what they accused me of, and they expressed themselves in such veiled terms that I never knew how to answer them.   (85–86)

An irrational yet potent symbolic logic is at work here: to be taken for a ghost is to be "credited" with unnatural desires. No other incriminating acts need be represented, no fleeting palpitation recorded—it is enough to become phantomlike in the sight of others, to change oneself (or be changed) from mortified flesh to baffled apparition. To "be a ghost" is to long, unspeakably, after one's own sex. At the same time—Diderot slyly suggests—the demonic opposite is also true: to love another woman is to lose one's solidity in the world, to evanesce, and fade into the spectral.

The notorious final section of *La Religieuse*—in which Suzanne is moved to a new convent and falls under the erotic sway of its depraved superior, "Madame ***"—shows this last uncanny transformation most powerfully. Suzanne, we recollect, after being half-seduced by Madame *** (who visits her nightly in her cell and excites her with ambiguous caresses), becomes afraid for her soul and begins to avoid her, on the advice of her confessor. Maddened by the young nun's rebuffs, Madame *** pursues her like a specter, day and night.

"If I went downstairs," writes Suzanne, "I would find her at the bottom, and she would be waiting for me at the top when I went up again" (169). Surprised by her on one occasion in the convent chapel, Suzanne actually mistakes the superior for an apparition, owing to what she calls a "strange effect" of the imagination, complicated by an optical illusion: "her position in relation to the church lamp had been such that only her face and the tips of her fingers had been lit up, the rest was in shadow, and that had given her a weird appearance" (165).

As the superior's sexual obsession finally lapses into outright dementia—following upon a church inquiry instigated by Suzanne into abuses at the convent—her ghostly status is confirmed. As she passes "from melancholy to piety and from piety to frenzy," she becomes a nightwalker in the convent, raving, subject to terrible hallucinations, surrounded by imaginary phantasms. Sometimes, Suzanne tells the marquis, when she would come upon Madame ***—barefoot, veiled, and in white—in the convent corridors, or being bled in the convent infirmary, the madwoman would cover her eyes and turn away, as though possessed. "I dare not describe all the indecent things she did and said in her delirium," says Suzanne; "She kept on putting her hand to her forehead as though trying to drive away unwanted thoughts or visions—what visions I don't know. She buried her head in the bed and covered her face with her sheets. 'It is the tempter!' she cried, 'it is he! What a strange shape he has put on! Get some holy water and sprinkle it over me. . . . Stop, stop, he's gone now' " (182). Exiled to a world of diabolical spirits, surrounded by horrific shapes she tries feebly to "fend off" with a crucifix, the naked and emaciated Madame *** finally expires in an exhalation of curses—a ghost indeed of her former sensual and worldly self.

How are we to read such scenes? One is struck at once by the curious repetition of gesture: like the ghostly Mrs. Veal, putting hand to eyes and "waving" off the kiss of Mrs. Bargrave, Madame *** raises her hand repeatedly to her face to obliterate those visions—the ghosts of her former love—that haunt and torment her. As if in closeup in some lost avant-garde film, the isolated hand over the eyes, caught forever in Manichaean black and white, makes the gesture of blockage, as though to cede into the void the memory (or hope) of a fleshly passion. But somewhat more insistently than in *The Apparition of Mrs.*

Veal, the blocking motion is visible here as an authorial gesture as well—as the displaced representation, or symbolic show, of Diderovian motive. What better way to exorcize the threat of female homosexuality than by treating it as ghostly? By "waving" off, so to speak, the lesbian dimension of his own story, even as his heroine Suzanne exculpates herself from any complicity in the superior's erotic mania, Diderot establishes his credentials as law-abiding, slightly flirtatious, homophobic man of letters—the same man who could jealously complain to his lover Sophie Volland about the unnaturally "voluptuous and loving way" in which her own sister often embraced her.*

The literary history of lesbianism, I would like to argue, is first of all a history of derealization. Diderot's blocking gesture is symptomatic: in nearly all of the art of the eighteenth and nineteenth centuries, lesbianism, or its possibility, can only be represented to the degree that it is simultaneously "derealized," through a blanching authorial infusion of spectral metaphors. (I speak here of so-called polite or mainstream writing; the shadow discourse of pornography is of course another matter, and demands a separate analysis.⁶) One woman or the other must be a ghost, or on the way to becoming one. Passion is excited, only to be obscured, disembodied, decarnalized. The vision is inevitably waved off. Panic seems to underwrite these obsessional spectralizing gestures: a panic over love, female pleasure, and the possibility of women breaking free—together—from their male sexual overseers. Homophobia is the order of the day, entertains itself (wryly or gothically) with phantoms, then exorcizes them.

One might easily compile an anthology of spectralizing moments from the eighteenth-, nineteenth-, and even early twentieth-century literature of lesbianism. After the melodramatics of *La Religieuse*, one might turn, for example, to Théophile Gautier's *Mademoiselle de Maupin*, a novel that, despite its different tone and sensibility

---

*See, for example, Diderot's letter to Volland of September 17, 1760 (in *Diderot's Letters to Sophie Volland*), in which he animadverts on her sister's "curiously" erotic way with her (60). In a letter written August 3, 1759, Diderot coped with his imagined rival by transforming her, through simile, into airy nothingness. "It does not make me unhappy to be her successor," he wrote, "indeed it rather pleases me. It is as if I were pressing her soul between yours and mine. She is like a snowflake which will perhaps melt away between two coals of fire" (21). And later, after warning Sophie not to kiss her sister's portrait too often lest he find out, he says: "I put my lips to yours and kiss them, even if your sister's kisses are still there. But no, there's nothing there; hers are so light and airy" (24).

(comical-fantastic rather than morbid-sublime), also presents the sexual love of woman for woman as an essentially phantasmatic enterprise. Rosette, the lover of the narrator D'Albert, has fallen in love with Théodore, a mysterious young visitor to her country estate. What she does not know (nor any of the other characters) is that Théodore is in reality a woman in disguise, the handsome adventurer Madeleine de Maupin. Clad only in the most apparitional of nightgowns ("so clinging and so diaphanous that it showed her nipples, like those statues of bathing women covered with wet drapery"), Rosette comes to Théodore/Madeleine's room one moonlit evening and pleads with her to make love to her. When "Théodore" (assuming that Rosette is deluded about her sex) is reluctant, Rosette takes matters into her own hands. Although, she explains, "you find it wearisome to see me following your steps like this, like a loving ghost which can only follow you and would like to merge with your body . . . I cannot help doing it."[7] Then she pulls Théodore/Madeleine toward her and their lips meet in a ghostly, "almost imperceptible kiss" (306).

Aroused by Rosette to the point that she can no longer tell whether she is "in heaven or on earth, here or elsewhere, dead or living," "Théodore" now wonders for a fleeting instant what it would be like to give some "semblance of reality to this shadow of pleasure which my lovely mistress embraced with such ardour" (307). But how to turn shadow into substance? Her question goes unanswered, for just as Rosette slips naked into her bed, Rosette's brother, Alcibiades, bursts farcically into the room, sword in hand, to prevent the rape he imagines to be taking place. His mocking accusations underline the already free-floating spectral metaphorics of the scene: "It appears, then, my very dear and very virtuous sister, that having judged in your wisdom that my lord Théodore's bed was softer than yours, you came to sleep here? Or perhaps there are ghosts in your room, and you thought that you would be safer in this one, under his protection?" (308). After wounding Alcibiades in an impromptu duel and fleeing on horseback into the woods around Rosette's house, Théodore/Madeleine is herself pursued by seeming phantoms:

> The branches of the trees, all heavy with dew, struck against my face and made it wet; one would have said that the old trees were stretching out their arms to hold me back and keep me for the love of their

chatelaine. If I had been in another frame of mind, or a little super-
stitious, I could easily have believed that they were so many ghosts
who wanted to seize me and that they were showing me their fists.
(312)

Though carefully designed to maximize readerly titillation,
Gautier's stagey scene of lesbian coitus interruptus is also a paradoxical statement on sexual ontology. Such spectral coupling as that between Rosette and Madeleine de Maupin must needs be interrupted,
because otherwise *it might prove itself to exist*. What would happen,
Gautier seems to ask, were Rosette to realize the true sex of her lover?
The anxiety that pursues the novelist—or so his compulsive slippage
into the language of the apparitional here suggests—is not so much
that the ethereal Rosette might start back in blank dismay, but that
the discovery of absence instead of presence (a haunting vacuity
where the phallus should be) might bring with it its own perverse and
unexpected joy. Yet Gautier can no more tolerate eros without a phallus than the dripping branches of the trees can hold back Madeleine
de Maupin on behalf of their infatuated "chatelaine." Indeed, lest
Rosette or her would-be lover bring into being some giddying new
embodiment of love, the *amor impossibilia* must remain just that—a
phantom or shadow in the comic narrative of desire.*

Similar negations haunt the nineteenth-century poetry of lesbianism. In Baudelaire's "Femmes damnées," for example, one of the numerous lesbian-obsessed poems in *Les Fleurs du mal* (1857), Delphine
and Hippolyte, the tortured lovers, are presented as damned spirits,
enslaved by a sterile passion and doomed to wander ceaselessly in a
hell of their own creation. Although Delphine's spectral kiss falls on
Hippolyte's mouth—as Rosette's does on Madeleine de Maupin's—
so "lightly" as to be barely perceptible ("Mes baisers sont légers

---

*The trees brushing Madeleine de Maupin's face bring to mind, of course, that waving
gesture which I am suggesting often subverts the literary representation of lesbian desire. Yet here the gesture is displaced—with its meaning seemingly inverted—onto those
anthropomorphic trees, which, like ghosts, want to *preserve* the possibility of a sexual union
between Madeleine and Rosette. How to deal with the apparent contradiction? One way, it
seems to me, would be to read "into" the narrative a second, unmentioned gesture: that of
the rider, who finding her eyes momentarily blinded with dew, reflexively brushes back the
very branches that brush her. In this second, hypothetical waving—so automatic as to pre-
clude mention—will be found that motion of avoidance so often accompanying the literary
threat of female homosexuality.

comme ces éphémères / Qui caressent le soir les grands lacs transparents"), its psychic weight is enough to impel Hippolyte into haunting torments:

> Je sens fondre sur moi de lourdes épouvantes
> Et de noirs bataillons de fantômes épars,
> Qui veulent me conduire en des routes mouvantes
> Qu'un horizon sanglant ferme de toutes parts.

> [I bear a weight of terrors, and dark hosts
> Of phantoms haunt my steps and seem to lead.
> I walk, compelled, behind these beckoning ghosts
> Down sliding roads and under skies that bleed.][8]

Breathing "la fraîcheur des tombeaux" on her lover's breast, she longs for oblivion. But in a morbid excoriation in the concluding stanzas of the poem the poet himself addresses the ghost-ridden couple, condemning them forever to a world of shades:

> —Descendez, descendez, lamentables victimes,
> Descendez le chemin de l'enfer éternel!
> Plongez au plus profond du gouffre où tous les crimes,
> Flagellés par un vent qui ne vient pas du ciel,

> Bouillonnent pêle-mêle avec un bruit d'orage.
> Ombres folles, courez au but de vos désirs;
> Jamais vous ne pourrez assouvir votre rage,
> Et votre châtiment naîtra de vos plaisirs.   (ll.85–92)

> [Hence, lamentable victims, get you hence!
> Hells yawn beneath, your road is straight and steep.
> Where all the crimes receive their recompense
> Wind-whipped and seething in the lowest deep

> With a huge roaring as of storms and fires,
> Go down, mad phantoms, doomed to seek in vain
> The ne'er-won goal of unassuaged desires,
> And in your pleasures find eternal pain!]

In Swinburne's would-be Baudelairean "Faustine" (1862), a similar fate is reserved for the wicked Roman empress Faustine, in whom "stray breaths of Sapphic song that blew / Through Mitylene" once "shook the fierce quivering blood" by night. Worn out by that "shameless nameless love" that makes "Hell's iron gin" shut "like a trap that breaks the soul," Faustine is surrounded in death by the phantoms of women she has debauched in life:

> And when your veins were void and dead,
>   What ghosts unclean
> Swarmed round the straitened barren bed
>   That hid Faustine?
>
> What sterile growths of sexless root
>   Or epicene?
> What flower of kisses without fruit
>   Of love, Faustine?[9]

And in "The Lesbian Hell" (1898), a bizarre poem by Baudelaire and Swinburne's turn-of-the-century epigone, the poet and occultist Aleister Crowley,

> Pale women fleet around, whose infinite
>   Long sorrow and desire have torn their wombs,
> Whose empty fruitlessness assails the night
>   With hollow repercussion, like dim tombs
>   Wherein some vampire glooms.
>
> Pale women sickening for some sister breast;
>   Lone sisterhood of voiceless melancholy
> That wanders in this Hell, desiring rest
>   From that desire that dwells forever free,
>   Monstrous, a storm, a sea.[10]

Drawing "the unsubstantial shapes / Of other women" to them with kisses that burn cold "on the lips whose purple blood escapes," the inhabitants of "lesbian hell" roam the earth,

> Like mists uprisen from the frosty moon
> Like shadows fleeting in a seer's glass,
>   Beckoning, yearning, amorous of the noon
>   When earth dreams on in swoon.   (ll.27–30)

When we turn to late nineteenth- and early twentieth-century fiction, the apparitional lesbian is equally ubiquitous—even in works such as Henry James's *The Bostonians* (1886) in which the homophobic fantasy that generates (and evacuates) her is disguised within a more realistic and neutral-seeming representational context. How else, perhaps, to regard the ineffable Olive Chancellor, defeated in her love for Verena Tarrant by the all-too palpable Basil Ransom, than as a more repressed version of those pale females, "sickening for some sister breast," who wander unappeased through late Victorian decadent fantasy? The ascetical Olive, who "glides" through rooms and greets strangers with a freezing touch of her slender white hand ("at once cold and limp") is indeed the ghost-woman of James's novel, chilling all around her with her preternatural-seeming passion for the lovely and puerile Verena. (Her connection with Olive, Basil warns Verena, is "the most unreal, accidental, illusory thing in the world.")[11] And like the evil exhalations of Swinburnean afflatus, Olive too will ultimately be exiled to an asexual "land of vapors" (319). When Basil, in the tumultuous last scene of the novel, comes to drag Verena away "by muscular force" from the Music Hall in Boston where she is about to give an oration on women's rights, Olive, at her creator's behest, lapses at once into impotent, agonized insubstantiality. "Dry, desperate, rigid," writes James, "yet she wavered and seemed uncertain; her pale, glittering eyes straining forward, as if they were looking for death." To the triumphant Basil she is a "vision"—an unearthly "presentment" of "blighted hope and wounded pride" (432). Unable in the end to compete—in this most crudely embodied of Jamesian erotic struggles—Olive simply "disappears" on the last page of the novel, retreating to the unseen stage of the auditorium, where she will search for words to explain her loss (434).

In *Extraordinary Women* (1928), his farcical satire on the expatriate lesbian colony on Capri, Compton Mackenzie (hailed by James in 1915 as "the greatest talent of his generation") tells a somewhat more facetious, but similarly dysphoric tale. Rory Freemantle, a hardboiled older Englishwoman living on the island of "Sirene" (Capri), is in love with the elusive Rosalba Donsante, a boyishly beautiful heiress notorious for her numerous international lesbian love affairs. Nurturing a fantasy that Rosalba will find her stolid, cigar-smoking habits more appealing than the "fine-spun web of emotion" offered by previous lovers—these last, she reflects, "had embarked upon a friendship with her in the way they might have embarked upon a novel by Henry James"[12]—Rory remodels an ancient villa for Rosalba overlooking the Bay of Naples and populates it with two white peacocks to symbolize their love. When Rosalba, arriving to take possession, answers her friend's question about how she likes it by doing a charming striptease in her new bedroom, the awkward Rory is understandably thrilled.

Given the novel's tone of mock-jaded sophistication (and Mackenzie's seemingly *un*-Jamesian frankness regarding female-female liaisons) one might expect the situation here to resolve, however fleetingly, into a representation of lesbian passion. Yet almost at once an irruption of spectral metaphors betokens yet another scene of blockage and evaporation. The "vivid light" outside the villa, the narrator observes, had given the walls of the bedroom "a kind of semi-translucency like moonstone, a strange noontide ghostliness in which Rosalba's body glowed with such a warmth of life as almost to seem lighted from within like a paper lantern, as if indeed its shadow might faintly incarnadine the floor" (140). Enchanted by this magical effect, which seen from another angle seems "to solidify [Rosalba's] body to flesh again," Rory looks quickly out of the window to make sure no workmen are passing by, "so conscious was she now of a challenge in Rosalba's attitude which would make her nudity a scandal even here in this cloud-cuckoo palace swung between sea and sky" (141). In so doing her eye unluckily falls on the two white peacocks meant to signify herself and Rosalba:

> The quality of their plumage gave to them from whatever angle the sun caught it a lightness that humanity could not keep. Their tails trailed along like smoke—no, hardly so opaque as smoke, but like a creeping mist. . . . They seemed indeed all plumed with thistledown, those vain imponderable birds, those wraiths stepping so delicately and contemptuously beside the cypress-trees darkly clustering. (141)

"Ah, look," Rory is moved to exclaim, "look, dearest, there are the white peacocks that will walk here always like our two ghosts, when perhaps sometimes we are not together here." But the effect of this melting speech is not what she expects:

> Rosalba jumped back from the window and made the sign to protect herself from the evil eye.

"*Pavoni! Pavoni!*" she cried. "*Sei pazza?* Oh, I think you are quite mad to bring those horrible birds here."

And as if in her nakedness she were somehow more dangerously exposed to their influence she began to fling on her clothes hurriedly. (141–42)

While the peacocks scream in dismay and the pitiful Rory pleads unsuccessfully with Rosalba to stay, the narrator himself intrudes, making an oddly italicized gesture at his own creations: "*And here of your courtesy let the chronicler lay down his pen a moment and, after closing his own fist, project his own little finger and his own forefinger to ward off the omen of evil influence, because he is, to tell the truth, as much afraid of peacocks as Rosalba*" (142).

We recognize in this flourish, of course, exactly that waving off or exorcism gesture we have seen elsewhere in the literature of lesbianism: the uncanny movement of the hand that at once blocks and obscures the embodiment of female-female eros. Mackenzie, to be sure, coyly displaces the exorcizing motion away from its obvious target: not Rory and Rosalba making love, but two wraithlike peacocks on a terrace is the "evil" spectacle, ostensibly, that we are not meant to see. And yet the very self-consciousness of the narrator's gesture, the almost Fieldingesque fake prudery, makes his real object apparent. What will remain invisible here and throughout this comedy of "extraordinary women," paradoxically, is precisely that "incarnadined" lust—rosy, bumptious and taboo—that binds them one to one another.

Similar metaphors, along with similar inhibiting gestures, proliferate also, finally, in two of the best-known early twentieth-century lesbian novels written by women. Mary Renault's *The Friendly Young Ladies*, set in the 1930s and published in 1944, begins with a radical enough premise: two bohemian women, Leo and Helen, live together in a distinctly eroticized intimacy on a houseboat on the Thames. For the first half of the novel, told mainly from the point of view of Leo's younger sister, Elsie, Renault sets up what appears to be a richly ironical tale of adolescent misunderstanding. Convinced that the boyish Leo, who ran away from home, conceals some scandalous heterosexual past, Elsie is completely blind to the far more obvious fact that Leo and Helen are lovers. In contrast, Elsie's older friend Peter—a doctor and would-be Freudian—immediately discovers in the trouser-clad Leo and glamorous Helen "all kinds of possibilities" for professional speculation.[13]

In the second half of the novel, Renault retreats, however, from this plot of mistaken sexual identity, veering off into a far more conventional, even bathetic, love story. Leo, we learn, has turned to the love of women mainly on account of a traumatic heterosexual experience suffered earlier in life. In the arms of the understanding Joe, a writer friend who also lives on the river, she abruptly overcomes her antipathy to men, and in the last pages of the novel leaves Helen to go off to Arizona with him. What we might call the crucial spectralizing moment in the novel occurs as Leo wakes from her first (and revelatory) night of love with Joe. Then, writes Renault, "the ghost of their old companionship seemed to be lying here beside them, with a face of its own like the face of a dead boy struck down quickly in a smile. . . . Go ahead, said the ghost, smiling at her" (258).

Here the apparitional metaphor works, as it were, in reverse—to negate, or white out, what has come before: the unspoken yet implied sexual intimacy between Leo and Helen. For the dead boy, in Renault's rather overworked symbolism, is of course none other than Leo herself—Leo as she was in her earlier masculine aspect, when (as she puts it to herself) she could be friendly with Joe "man to man" (258). At the same time "he" is also, by insinuation, Leo the lover of Helen—now replaced by the "woman" ("naked and newly born") who lies in Joe's healing embrace. Encircled by her male lover, blocked off from her own narrative past, Leo the lesbian becomes Leo the ghost: incapable of speech (except to encourage Leo the "woman" to go ahead), incapable of protest, incapable of retrieving an otherwise sophisticated novel from its own surprisingly crushing final banality.*

---

*After this retreat into homophobic convention, one is perhaps not so surprised by the afterword Renault composed for the 1984 Pantheon edition of her novel. Here, in a scornful comparison of *The Well of Loneliness* with *Extraordinary Women*, Renault comes solidly down on the side of Mackenzie's book, which she praises for its "civilised" representation of its characters' loves. Radclyffe Hall, by contrast, is condemned as graceless and vulgar—the sort of writer, Renault complains, who, had she lived into the 1980s, would undoubtedly have used the ludicrous term "gay" to describe her "bellyaching" characters (p. 283). It is true that in both *The Charioteer* (1959) and her acclaimed series of historical novels about ancient Greece, Renault (who never married and lived most of her life with another woman) dealt—with remarkable sensitivity—with the subject of male homosexuality. Yet her gravitation here toward the evasive Mackenzie—and mandarin disdain for Radclyffe Hall—suggest that she never attained a corresponding imaginative freedom, paradoxically, regarding female same-sex love.

And in Dorothy Strachey's semiautobiographical *Olivia*, published under the pseudonym "Olivia" in 1949, we are back, as though by sorcery, in the claustrophobic emotional landscape of Diderot's *La Religieuse*. Here again the oppressive, hysteria-inducing all-female institution (a turn-of-the-century girls' boarding school near Paris); here again the manipulative/seductive woman-in-authority (the beautiful headmistress Mademoiselle Julie); and here again a naive, apparently sexually inexperienced heroine (the sixteen-year-old schoolgirl Olivia). Unlike Diderot's Suzanne, however, who remains strangely aloof from the desire she evokes, Olivia is no emotional cipher: intoxicated by Mademoiselle Julie's caressing voice and searching glances, she broods incessantly about her, dwelling above all on her mysterious relationship with the "invalidish" Mademoiselle Cara, the fellow teacher with whom Mademoiselle Julie shares her living quarters. Unable to eat or sleep, pursued by "cloudy" fancies (especially after the headmistress begins singling her out for intimate goodnight kisses), Olivia finds herself aching for "some vague blessing, some unimaginable satisfaction, which seemed to be tantalizingly near but which all the same, I knew was unattainable—a blessing, which, if I could only grasp it, would quench my thirst, still my pulses, give me an Elysian peace."[14]

That such wraith-obsessed desire will remain forever frustrated we already suspect when Olivia, dressed in Oriental veils and watchfully observed by Mademoiselle Julie, dances with another girl at the school's annual Mardi Gras fancy-dress ball.* Ghosts hover ominously in the background as Georgie, the other girl, aroused by Olivia's obvious excitement, confesses that she has once been in love. "We danced every waltz together," says Olivia, "but we knew well

---

*Scenes of plays and costume parties are a staple in novels having to do with girls' schools— and usually betoken a moment at which lesbian undercurrents in the fiction come to a crest. Comparable travesty scenes can be found in Brigid Brophy's *King of a Rainy Country* (1956) and Christine Crow's *Miss X, or the Wolf Woman* (1990). In the former, the heroine kisses another girl during a school production of *As You Like It* (the same play staged within *Mademoiselle de Maupin*); in the latter, the heroine performs the "Dance of the Maenads" from Euripides' *The Bacchae*—"a dance which, with a slight initial shock of my own, some might even say brazen, audacity, I now found myself beginning slowly and rhythmically to perform with who else but Miss X herself as sole spectator and judge" (60). All of these scenes can be traced back, it seems to me, to the "fete" scene in Charlotte Brontë's *Villette*, during which Lucy Snowe and Ginevra Fanshaw act a love scene together, with Lucy in quasi-male dress. See *Villette*, chapter 14.

enough that we were not dancing with each other, that one of us was clasping, the other being clasped by the phantom of her own dreams" (68). And they flit into view again when Mademoiselle Julie fails to come to Olivia's room that night to give her her promised bedtime kiss. When the baffled Olivia goes with "sickened heart and faltering steps" to see her the next day, the elusive headmistress coolly reprimands her for pursuing *"des chimères"*—at the expense of her studies (71).

These same soul-destroying spirits—deathly emblems of the *amor impossibilia* between woman and woman—are everywhere at the novel's melodramatic conclusion. After Mademoiselle Cara is found dead of an overdose, Mademoiselle Julie enigmatically allows Olivia to come into her room and sleep in her own bed, while she herself keeps a lonely waking vigil. Olivia spends the night in barely suppressed bliss. The next day, however, she learns that Mademoiselle Julie is to give up her post to go to Canada with another teacher and is summoned—in shock—to bid the headmistress farewell. Her hopes for some passionate acknowledgment of the previous night's apparent communion are cruelly disappointed. Warning Olivia that she wants "no scene," Mademoiselle Julie begins a strange, seemingly dissociated monologue in which she touches elliptically on their relationship—

> "It has been a struggle all my life—but I have always been victorious—I was proud of my victory." And then her voice changed, broke, deepened, softened, became a murmur: "I wonder now whether defeat wouldn't have been better for us all—as well as sweeter."

—then, after raising Olivia to an almost intolerable pitch of emotion, abruptly breaks off:

> "You, Olivia, will never be victorious, but if you are defeated—" how she looked at me! "when you are defeated—" she looked at me in a way that made my heart stand still and the blood rush to my face, to my forehead, till I seemed to be wrapped in flame—then she suddenly broke off and brushed her hands across her eyes, as if brushing away an importunate vision. When I saw them again, they were extinguished and lifeless.
> "I don't know what I'm saying," she went on dully. "I've got a headache. Good-bye." (102)

The scene is indeed a "victory" (in Mademoiselle Julie's ironic term) of psychosexual blockage. With the now-familiar gesture, that delicate, vicious pass over the eyes that is also a kind of self-blinding, Mademoiselle Julie brushes away the vision she is unable to endure— of Olivia's breathless proximity, of herself surrendering to the very longings she has "struggled" all her life to deny. At the same time, her gesture signals a moment of ultimate representational blockage in Strachey's novel itself. Though lesbianism is the great unspoken theme of *Olivia*—its treasured inward dream and motivating fantasy—the sexual love of woman for woman exists within the repressive framework of the fiction only as haunting chimera, as that which, by definition, may be sensed but never *seen*. By the end the reader is left as blind and unseeing as Mademoiselle Julie. As for Olivia, the love-struck heroine, she is left grasping after the flimsiest of apparitions: in the final pages of the novel, shortly after Mademoiselle Julie has indeed gone to Canada, Olivia receives the news of her death (108).

Dysphoric examples of the spectral metaphor could perhaps be multiplied indefinitely. Certainly it would be easy enough to find such manifestations in the works of other writers—in Balzac and Dickens, Charlotte Brontë, Wilkie Collins, Gissing, Sheridan LeFanu, Colette and Proust, Isak Dinesen, D. H. Lawrence, Clemence Dane, Wyndham Lewis, Rosamund Lehmann, Lillian Hellman. Indeed, so typically hostile and oppressive are the uses to which the spectral metaphor is put, one might almost speak of a "great tradition" of antilesbian writing—a dubious shadow canon of works in which women who desire other women repeatedly find themselves vaporized by metaphor and translated into (empty) fictional space. As one male character warns another in Edouard Bourdet's *The Captive* (1926), after learning that his friend is in love with a homosexual woman, "Fly from her . . . do you hear? Otherwise you are lost! Otherwise you'll spend your existence pursuing a phantom which you can never overtake. One can never overtake them! They are shadows. They must be left to dwell alone among themselves in the kingdom of shadows!"* And just as

---

*Bourdet, *The Captive*, p. 149. Consider also Colette's maxim in *Ces Plaisirs* (1932): "We can never bring enough twilight, silence, and gravity to surround the embrace of two women." Meditating on those "fairylands of love" inhabited by the famous Ladies of Langollen (who

lesbians get turned "into" ghosts in such literature, ghosts—to their discredit—also get turned into lesbians. To the extent for example that the mysterious Miss Jessel in Henry James's *The Turn of the Screw* manifests herself as an apparition hungering "infamously" after little Flora, it is tempting also to read her as a cryptolesbian: in the sinister metaphorical dynamic of James's story the two identities, ghost and girl-lover, seem indeed to become endlessly and horrifyingly inter-changeable.[15]

And yet without unsaying, as it were, the negative power of the apparitional metaphor, I would like to complicate the somewhat re-lentless (and pessimistic) argument laid out here. Up to this point I have focused exclusively on the insubstantiality of the apparitional lesbian—her weightlessness, her sterility, her annoyingly diffident response to the imperatives of physical desire. She epitomizes "not-thereness": now you see her, but mostly you don't. Or do you? For the supernatural metaphor itself, obviously, suggests a different and perhaps more subtle way of thinking about the matter. A ghost, ac-cording to *Webster's Ninth*, is a spirit believed to appear in a "bodily likeness." To haunt, we find, is "to visit often," "to recur constantly and spontaneously," "to stay around or persist," or "to reappear con-tinually." The ghost, in other words, is a paradox. Though nonexis-tent, it nonetheless *appears*. Indeed, so vividly does it appear—if only in the "mind's eye"—one feels unable to get away from it. It is surely in the latter, colloquial, and uncanny sense that Renée Vivien invokes the ghostly metaphor in her ecstatic sapphic reverie, *Une Femme m'ap-parut* (*A Woman Appeared to Me*; 1903). To be haunted by a woman—in the magical speech of desire—is ineluctably to see her.[16]

What of the spectral metaphor and the lesbian writer? For her, one suspects, "seeing ghosts" may be a matter—not so much of derealization—but of rhapsodical embodiment: a ritual calling up, or *apophrades*, in the old mystical sense. The dead are indeed brought back to life; the absent loved one returns. For the spectral vernacular, it turns out, contains its own powerful and perverse magic. Used

---

eloped together in 1778 and lived together in Wales in rural seclusion for over fifty years), Colette professes the conviction that their love, "nourished on very little," had to have been chaste—the "delicate solidarity" of "two sweet, foolish creatures . . . loyal to a delusion." See Colette, *The Pure and the Impure*, pp. 113 and 127.

imaginatively—repossessed, so to speak—the very trope that evaporates can also solidify. In the strangest turn of all, perhaps, the lesbian body itself returns: and the feeble, elegiac waving off—the gesture of would-be exorcism—becomes instead a new and passionate beckoning.

The intimate writings of women, not surprisingly, hint at such transvaluation. Violet Trefusis, writing to Vita Sackville-West from Cornwall at the height of their turbulent love affair in the summer of 1919, speaks of being possessed by her, as though she were present:

> Now it's Clovelly, I separated from you, but nevertheless haunted by you day and night. . . . The nights of music and ineffable longing for you—I used to stand by the open window, between the music and the garden. And in the garden were irises which cast very black shadows, and sometimes I would catch my breath: *surely* that was a figure in a leopard-skin that darted out into the dappled moonlight . . . [17]

"O mercy," she exclaims (as if incanting) "the things I want to write!"—

> You remember the caresses. . . .
> It seems I have never wanted you as I do now—
> When I think of your mouth. . . .
> When I think of . . . other things, all the blood rushes to my head, and I can almost imagine. . . .   (150)

And again: "the house is haunted by your presence, and the sound of your voice calling me" (164).

Virginia Woolf, writing to the same Sackville-West in 1927, toward the end of their own love affair, playfully invites her to come with her to Hampton Court: "We'll dine; we'll haunt the terrace."[18] Later on she asks "dear Mrs. Nicholson," "Ain't it romantic—this visionary and aetherial presence brooding diaphanous over Gordon Square, like a silver spangled cloud? What are we to call her?"[19]

And in *For Sylvia*, the autobiographical memoir she composed for her lover, Sylvia Townsend Warner, in 1949, the poet Valentine Ackland uses the imagery of the spectral to conjure up a poignant vision of their emotional and physical bond. Thinking back to the cottage in Norfolk she and Townsend Warner shared in the 1930s, Ackland writes,

I dream of it now, too often, and when I am dead for sure my ghost will haunt there, loving and grieving—there, and along the Drove at Chaldon, where my Love stood beside the thorn tree and vowed her troth to me. Because of that vow and because of our life together I do not think that she will leave me alone, even when I am a ghost; and if she will walk with me, we will be happy—as we have always been, even in despair, together.*

But we need not confine ourselves to private invocations. The ghost metaphor also reappears, strikingly metamorphosed, in twentieth-century lesbian fiction. Perhaps inevitably Radclyffe Hall's *The Well of Loneliness* (1928) provides the paradigm. True, the story of Stephen Gordon's discovery of her sexual identity is composed in a powerfully dysphoric register, and in the novel's early chapters especially, a number of spectral metaphors, deployed in the traditional negative manner, help to advance this melancholy effect. In her maladroit and unhappy youth, Stephen is both a specter in the sight of others and a victim herself of tormenting erotic ghosts. Witness the passage in which Stephen's parents, Sir Philip and Anna, first suspect the truth about their daughter's frighteningly alien sexual nature:

---

*Ackland, *For Sylvia*, p. 132. The spectral metaphor crops up interestingly in lesbian slang of the 1930s. Witness the following scene in the pseudonymous *Diana: A Strange Autobiography* (1939), when the author enters a lesbian bar for the first time and strikes up a conversation with one of the regulars:

"Do you mind telling me," she said, "if you are one of us or a spook?"
I was embarrassed to be ignorant of lesbian jargon. Elizabeth had to explain what she meant by "spook":
"A woman who for some reason or other strays into lesbianism as second best. And stays because she likes it better."
"Once a woman is a spook she almost never prefers a man again," she went on like a teacher. "She may marry if she wants a home and children, but chances are she has a lesbian lover."

See Diana Frederics, *Diana*, pp. 123–24. The term *shadow* seems to have had a similar denotation. As Robert A. Schanke points out in a recent biography of the lesbian actress Eva Le Gallienne, when the husband of Le Galliene's lover, the starlet Josie Hutchinson, filed for divorce from Hutchinson in 1930, naming Le Gallienne as co-respondent, "headlines in the *New York Daily News* read 'Le Gallienne Shadow Actress is divorced,' 'shadow' being the common euphemism at the time for women who loved other women." "Some people will regard this as a new angle in the old love triangle," wrote a columnist in the *New York Daily Mirror*, "but the affinity of one girl for another is as old as the pyramids." See Schanke, *Shattered Applause*, p. 88.

He knew already, and she knew that he knew. Yet neither of them spoke it, this most unhappy thing, and their silence spread round them like a poisonous miasma. The spectre that was Stephen would seem to be watching, and Sir Philip would gently release himself from Anna, while she, looking up, would see his tired eyes, not angry any more, only very unhappy.[20]

Later, when Stephen falls miserably in love with Angela Crossby—the married woman who first flirts with, then spurns her—it is Angela who becomes a cruel and teasing ghost: "Pacing restlessly up and down her bedroom, Stephen would be thinking of Angela Crossby—haunted, tormented by Angela's words that day in the garden: 'Could you marry me, Stephen?' and then by those other pitiless words: 'Can I help it if you're—what you obviously are?' " (152). After Angela takes a male lover, Stephen finds herself haunting the rose garden outside Angela's house, like some wretched "earth-bound spirit" (184).

In later chapters, however, ghosts of a different sort begin to haunt Stephen. It is worth recollecting, I think, that Radclyffe Hall herself was for most of her life an ardent spiritualist—a participant in seances and table rappings in the teens and twenties, a believer in apparitions, and a contributor on several occasions (with her lover Una Troubridge) to the *Journal of the Society for Psychical Research*. For almost twenty years, much in the manner of patients consulting a psychoanalyst, she and Troubridge communicated regularly with Hall's deceased lover "Ladye" (Mabel Batten) through a spirit medium, Mrs. Leonard. In Batten's words from beyond the grave Hall and Troubridge seem to have found not only day-to-day solace but a kind of mystic sanction for their own sexual relationship. The very dedication of *The Well of Loneliness*—"TO OUR THREE SELVES"—is an acknowledgment of the occult yet inspiring erotic triangle out of which Radclyffe Hall's novel itself was born.[21]

Yet Stephen, too, is a necromancer, and experiences her own ultimately liberating communion with spirits. We get a hint of what is to come in the famous "recognition" scene, midway through the novel. Here, like the heroine in some sapphic *Mysteries of Udolpho*, Stephen opens a locked bookcase in her dead father's study and discovers the works of the sexologist Krafft-Ebing, heavily annotated—with her own name—in her father's handwriting. While the room grows dusky with shadows, Stephen (who until now has felt nothing but bewilderment over her erotic longings) begins to read with increasing excitement. "Then suddenly," writes Radclyffe Hall, "she had got to her feet and was talking aloud—she was talking to her father: 'You knew! All the time you knew this thing, but because of your pity you wouldn't tell me' " (204). Confronting the phantasm of Sir Philip, whose tender understanding of her nature she now recognizes, Stephen also, as it were, confronts herself. For as his spectral presence instructs her, she is indeed one of those "thousands" marked out by God as different from the sexual norm. To be haunted thus, one might say, is to encounter one's own palpably lesbian self.

But the theme of spectral communion is realized even more starkly in *The Well*'s climactic final scenes. Tormented by self-hatred, Stephen has become convinced that her young lover Mary should live a more "normal" life—by marrying a man—and so deceives her into thinking she has been unfaithful. Falling for the ruse, Mary sorrowfully departs for Canada with Martin Hallam, who is in love with her. A despondent Stephen then returns alone to their flat on the Rue Jacob, only to find herself surrounded by "terrible" shapes—the hallucinatory images of those who have died, or suffered unspeakable anguish, over their lesbianism:

> The room seemed to be thronging with people. Who were they, these strangers with the miserable eyes? And yet, were they all strangers? Surely that was Wanda? And someone with a neat little hole in her side—Jamie clasping Barbara by the hand; Barbara with the white flowers of death on her bosom. Oh, but they were many, these unbidden guests, and they called very softly at first and then louder. They were calling her by name, saying: "Stephen Stephen!" The quick, the dead, and the yet unborn—all calling her, softly at first and then louder. (436)

Among these haunting Baudelairean shades there are some, Stephen sees, with "shaking, white-skinned, effeminate fingers"—male denizens of the homosexual underworld she has frequented with Mary—who reproach her bitterly for abandoning them: " 'You and your kind have stolen our birthright; you have taken our strength and have given us your weakness!' " The female spirits then join in, while moving ever closer: " 'We are coming, Stephen—we are still coming

on, and our name is legion—you dare not disown us!'" (436–37).
Reeling back in guilty horror, Stephen raises her arms as if "to ward
them off," but the phantoms close "in and in" like a vividly pursuing
horde. Then, writes Hall,

> They possessed her. Her barren womb became fruitful—it ached
> with its fearful and sterile burden. It ached with the fierce yet helpless
> children who would clamour in vain for their right to salvation. They
> would turn first to God, and then to the world, and then to her. . . .
> And now there was only voice, one demand; her own voice into
> which those millions had entered. A voice like the awful, deep rolling
> of thunder; a demand like the gathering together of great waters. A
> terrifying voice that made her ears throb, that made her brain throb,
> that shook her very entrails, until she must stagger and all but fall be-
> neath this appalling burden of sound that strangled her in its will to be
> uttered.   (437)

The novel ends with Stephen—shuddering like one in orgasm or
labor—gasping out a dire collective plea for acceptance: "Acknowledge us, oh God, before the whole world. Give us also the right to our
existence!" (437).

The less-than-pious reader may well have to suppress a laugh here;
the style is pure Radclyffe Hall—hieratic, overwrought, full of melodramatic, dismal pomp. But infelicities of tone and taste should not
distract us from the startling transformation the novelist also works
on the conventional spectral figure. The blocking movement is there
of course: by raising her arms as if to "ward off" the oncoming phantoms, Radclyffe Hall's self-loathing heroine somewhat oafishly pantomimes the repressive theatrics we have seen before in Defoe, Diderot, Mackenzie, and Strachey. But it's a useless move now—in fact
seems to draw in, rather than repel, the encroaching host. It's as if—
to mar Stevie Smith—Stephen were not drowning but waving. And
what ensues, despite the maundering mock religiosity of Hall's presentation, is a loopy, delirious, untrammeled consummation: a kind
of sex scene with ghosts. Overlaid and penetrated by the apparitional, Stephen is "possessed" in a fantastic convulsion indistinguishable
in the end from sexual gratification. And while she labors and pants,
struggling to give birth to a new erotic truth, all the pale and rejected
revenants of the lesbian literary tradition seem to pervade her, to find

embodiment within her—engrossing their voices within hers in a plangent affirmation of existence.

Radclyffe Hall's rewriting of tradition, it is true, might be considered incomplete: we do not get to gaze into Stephen's future or see what changes to her character will result from such wild intercourse with spirits. Whether Stephen will now evolve into an emphatically carnal being of the sort that Radclyffe Hall was herself remains to be seen. (The novelist in a letter to one of her lovers: "You must come here at once as you promised . . . I must have you—I *must*—I *must*—I *must*.")[22] Radclyffe Hall wrote, alas, no sequel to *The Well of Loneliness*. But what we do have is in its own way perhaps enough: a spectacular first breakout from the coils of homophobic repetition. By embracing the apparitional, by realizing its potential, so to speak, within her own body, Stephen Gordon also acts out a fierce and liberating movement from denial to acceptance. In place of the pristine half-truths of repression, she finds passionate congruence; in place of morbid evasion, the creative ferment of a desire encompassed and acknowledged.

And Radclyffe Hall's successors, one could argue, in fact write the sequel. Virtually every English or American lesbian novel composed since 1928 has been in one sense or another a response to, or trespass upon, *The Well of Loneliness*; one can sense its lingering emotional aftershocks even in such disaffected and ultimately retrograde works as *The Friendly Young Ladies* and *Olivia*.* (In some cases, as in Elizabeth Jolley's surreal *The Well* from 1986, the appropriation of Radclyffe Hall is at once brazen and mysterious.)[23] But the way in which Radclyffe Hall's followers have emulated her most interestingly, perhaps, has been precisely in restaging this uncanny transvaluation of the apparitional—by returning again and again to the ghostly metaphor and conjuring from it a multifarious imagery of erotic possibility.

---

*Consider the following passage from *Olivia*, with its Radclyffe Hall-like resonances and uncanny play on the crucial word "loneliness": "Greatness and loneliness. 'Puissant et solitaire.' To live above the crowd in loneliness. To be condemned to loneliness by the greatness of one's qualities. To be condemned to live apart, however much one wanted the contact of warm human companionship. To be the Lord's anointed! Strange and dreadful fate! I forgot where I was as I thought of it" (p. 60). The narrator is glossing De Vigny's *Moïse*, which she and Mademoiselle Julie have just read aloud, but her words also eerily recall another "anointed" one: Stephen Gordon, likewise "condemned to live apart" in perpetual loneliness.

In the interest of brevity (and with an eye towards my not-too-distant conclusion), I will confine myself here to several relatively recent examples, though a couple of classic lesbian novels of the twenties and thirties deserve to be mentioned in passing. Woolf's *Orlando* (1928)—published a few months after *The Well of Loneliness*, but a sequel only in the strictly chronological sense—also puts the traditional spectral metaphor to its own (comically) subversive uses. How else perhaps to understand that disarming moment when the soon-to-be-female Orlando, awakening after a strange seven-day nap in the mid-seventeenth century, seems unable to remember his impassioned affair with Sasha, the Russian princess, consummated on the frozen banks of the Thames during the previous century? Then, writes Woolf, "he would listen when people spoke of the great frost or the skating or the carnival, but he never gave any sign, except by passing his hand across his brow as if to wipe away some cloud, of having witnessed them himself."[24]

One could argue, I suppose, that the spectral figure behind the "cloud" image here works negatively—is perhaps even a token that Orlando, in preparation for his imminent sex-change, must "forget" his passion for Sasha in order that this passion not be reinterpreted, retroactively, as lesbian in nature. By waving at the "cloud" he/she exorcizes the incriminating memory of those nights on the ice with Sasha, locked in the melting "delights of love" (45). And yet Woolf's ambiguous syntax actually enforces a quite opposite reading. The very gesture which at first seems meant to drive away the ghost of Sasha is in fact the "sign" that she is remembered. The gesture of exorcism becomes indistinguishable from the gesture of recollection. And Sasha will continue to be recollected in this manner—gathered together in Orlando's memory—throughout the novel. Returning to England in the early eighteenth century from Constantinople (where he has in fact turned into a woman), Orlando feels "scampering up and down within her, like some derisive ghost who in another instant will pick up her skirts and flaunt out of sight, Sasha the lost, Sasha the memory, whose reality she had proved just now so surprisingly" (163). And later, in the twentieth century, Sasha appears again—as an "apparition in grey fur," glimpsed by Orlando on the "ground-floor department of Messrs. Marshall & Snelgrove" (300).

With each of these comic returns, Woolf celebrates the unsettling power of the imagination to retrieve the object of desire, to bring her back—fully clothed or in arousing deshabille—into the ecstatic purview of the lover. "Haunted!" cries Orlando in the novel's final pages, "haunted ever since I was a child" (313). It is not surprising that Vita Sackville-West, reading *Orlando* for the first time and realizing that it was in part Woolf's symbolic commemoration of their own love affair, declared herself "dazzled, bewitched, enchanted, under a spell."[25]

And something of the same flesh-awakening magic is present—though more darkly—in *Nightwood*, the elliptical lesbian masterpiece published by Djuna Barnes in 1936. Robin Vote and Nora Flood, the novel's central pair of lovers, are "so 'haunted' of each other," writes Barnes, "that separation was impossible."[26] In "going about the house, in passing each other, they would fall into an agonized embrace" (57). For love, like a wraith,

> becomes the deposit of the heart, analogous in all degrees to the "findings" in a tomb. As in one will be charted the taken place of the body, the raiment, the utensils necessary to its other life, so in the heart of the lover will be traced, as an indelible shadow, that which he loves. In Nora's heart lay the fossil of Robin, intaglio of her identity, and about it for its maintenance ran Nora's blood. Thus the body of Robin could never be unloved, corrupt or put away. (56)

Though Nora's internalizing embrace of Robin is presented as a mode of disquiet—part of the intimate anguish of the night—Barnes, by the very extremity of her imagery, also affirms the sensuality of the spectral. To be possessed of an apparition is to feel her within, like some primitive disorder, in the depths of one's own being.

When we turn to more recent lesbian fiction, that written since the Second World War, the apparitional lesbian is even more vividly realized. I refer here not only to those numerous "pulp" productions popular from the thirties on—works such as *Love Like a Shadow* (1935), *White Ladies* (1935), *Who Walk in Darkness* (1951), *Women in the Shadows* (1959), *The Shades of Evil* (1960), *Twilight Girl* (1961), *Twilight Lovers* (1964), *The Ghosts* (1965), *Sex in the Shadows* (1965), and so on—in which the invocation of the spectral is inextricably bound up with the seductive unveiling of a "secret" sapphic world in bohemia or the bars.[27] (Renault's *The Friendly Young Ladies*, it's worth noting, first appeared in the United States in 1945 under the crepuscular title of *The*

Middle Mist.) Pulp fiction, of course, mimics that trend toward representational candor which one can detect in mainstream lesbian writing from *The Well of Loneliness* on.[28] But only by looking at rather more ambitious and self-conscious literary works, I think, can we fully appreciate the way in which the apparitional lesbian is "brought back to life"—imbued with breadth, heft, and charisma—in the later twentieth-century lesbian imagination.

Maureen Duffy's experimental fiction *The Microcosm* (1966), perhaps the most underrated of modern English lesbian novels, is actually set in a world of ghosts: in an underground London women's bar (transparently modeled on the Gateways) called the House of Shades. Here Matt, the central character—so butch and so morose that even her creator habitually refers to her using masculine pronouns—mourns the death of Carl, another butch, who (it is implied) has committed suicide. While Carl's spirit hovers nearby, Matt plumbs the familiar, *Well*-like depths of sapphic alienation:

> Sometimes I think we're all dead down here, shadows, a house of shades, echoes of the world above where girls are blown about the streets like flowers on long stalks and young men strut by on turkeycock legs thrusting against the March winds, all a little more dead by your real dying since you've come to haunt this place, your laughter jazz-noted, harsh, the dusty floor recoiling under the thudding feet, a glimpse of remembered features in a face in profile, the shock of a turning head. We wait for you to come down the stairs every evening, lifting a hand, a grin; shedding a coat, a scarf; the possibility always there.[29]

And later, caught up in the melancholy gaiety of another drink-clouded evening, she finds herself musing: "The dead have possessed you, dead hopes like children in limbo, every vital feeling a ghost of itself; the face of a zombie looking back at you from the glass" (238).

And yet the novel itself offers an escape from Matt's relentlessly morbid imaginings. Duffy, in a 1988 afterword to *The Microcosm*, describes how the work grew out of a series of tape-recorded interviews she did with a number of lesbian women in England in the early 1960s.[30] In a succession of long ventriloquistic set pieces—strategically juxtaposed against Matt's own stream-of-consciousness reveries—Duffy recreates the voices of these women, along with others recovered from an imagined lesbian past. (In one especially breathtaking sequence, Duffy paraphrases for almost thirty pages from the autobiography of Charlotte Charke, the eighteenth-century transvestite actress who published her *Life* in 1755.)[31] Each of the women who "speak" within the novel, such as the comical Feathers, who declares herself a psychic and a believer in "spiritual things," are linked by their connection to Matt or the House of Shades—that microcosm of lesbian life to which all are drawn. The result is a brilliant, shifting group portrait, shot through with both naturalistic and supernaturalistic touches.

Duffy's characters are subject to erotic longing, but only, paradoxically, because consummation—suggested by the womblike sensuous space of the House of Shades itself—is always imminent. Even the dour Matt seems to realize this, when in the absence of her lover Rae (who has stayed home) she dances with another young woman. "She is slight as a grass stalk in the wind, nothing in my arms," she thinks to herself. Yet at the same time Matt recognizes that the sense of ghostliness is illusory. "We dance a little apart, bodies not touching, as people do who know their flesh take fire quickly and who respect each other too much to play with it" (19). As for the down-to-earth Feathers, who lives with a dog-loving girlfriend named Bill, she finds a weirdly vital satisfaction in dreaming itself: "I can listen to music and have the most beautiful love affair in my mind. The great thing is of course that it can't fade whereas the other sort, what some people would call the real thing, will always fade. I've learnt that much anyway" (253). With its own surreal, quasi-documentary style and eerie commemoration of actual lesbian voices, *The Microcosm* at once gives credence to such fantastic notions and disarms the classically homophobic distinction between the "phantasmatic" and the "real." The women of the novel may live in a house of shades, but it is one in which love, in all of its richly embodied lineaments, is nonetheless always possible.[32]

In both Margaret Erhart's *Unusual Company* (1987) and Christine Crow's *Miss X, or The Wolf Woman* (1990), making love with a ghost is the necessary prelude to lesbian sexual awakening. Franny, the young narrator of Erhart's dreamlike fiction, meets a mysterious older woman, Claire, in a New York bookshop, and is immediately struck by her resemblance to "a ghost in flight."[33] Like Stephen Gordon spying on

Angela Crossby, Franny begins to haunt Claire's apartment building, eavesdropping on what appear to be the sounds of sexual intercourse emanating from her apartment. After several weeks, during which Franny finds herself wondering whether the invisible Claire really exists, Claire discovers her and invites her in: the sounds turn out to be a tape recording of whale noises. Franny and Claire peer together through binoculars at people in neighboring apartments, then fall onto Claire's bed, where Claire undresses Franny: " 'Beautiful shoulders,' she said. 'Beautiful breasts. I thought I'd cry, Franny, I really did, if I got through all those coats and sweaters and under the last layer there was nothing but air' " (38). Claire then takes Franny's virginity, declaring (when Franny bleeds), "What a thing you are!" (43).

Midway through the fiction, Franny muses on their lovemaking, emphasizing—in one of the more curious turns of the spectral metaphor to date—its encompassing physicality:

> When I made love to her she was never not with me, I'm certain of that. In the beginning we would drag each other to bed almost every afternoon, talking, dreaming aloud, touching. I was still amazed by the softness, hers and mine both. It had something to do with skin, not flesh, because god knows I was boney. Another thing too: We weren't huge people, but together there felt like so much of us. "I know what you mean," said Claire. "Women's bodies are everywhere; not just what fills the space, but the space too. A man seems to come from one place and be one thing. Poor men. No wonder they make miserable ghosts." (86)

For the rest of the novel, which turns in its later stages toward a kind of lesbian picaresque, with Claire leaving Franny for a "spiritual community" in Micronesia, and Franny traveling west to California and Santa Fe, where she and Claire are ultimately (though unhappily) reunited, she holds onto this truth: "that she was not this lover or that, but this one, the one I would always love, the only one I would love" (216).

By contrast, in the comical *Miss X*, a kind of wayward postmodern rewrite of *Olivia*, such effusively carnal lovemaking seems at first glance impossible. Mary Wolfe, the novel's would-be wolfish narrator, recounts the sad history of her schoolgirl infatuation with her "homoseXual" headmistress, the now-dead "Miss X." (It is Mary's appropriately obsessional typographic conceit to capitalize every appearance of the letter "X" in her tale.) After "intoXicating" her with French poetry ("LuXe, calme, volupté") and stolen kisses ("XXXX") in her study, the tweedy and flirtatious Miss X, it seems, let her "Head Girl" down rather badly. During a weekend visit to "OXford" (Mary had won a scholarship to one of the women's colleges), Miss X rented a double room for them at the "Radclyffe Hall Hotel," but having drunk rather too much, fell ponderously asleep while the breathless Mary was left crouching "X-legged" by the side of her bed, a "ghostly white shape" suffering in "vivid darkness."[34]

Traumatized by this rejection (along with Miss X's numerous other amorous "double Xsings"), Mary is suitably self-pitying. "If the style of my narrative often lacks the compleXity of mature refleXion," she intones elegiacally, "it is doubtless because the ghostly self which beckons me there in the shadows has never ceased all these years to cry out for a hearing, waiting in the wings till its tale be told" (4). Yet before she can really sort out the "miXed up" details of her tale—which remain jumbled and obscure—she is interrupted by "eXciting" (though "eXasperating") outbursts from the dead Miss X: "Miss X! Miss X! It is I, Miss X, your old Headmistress, come back to haunt you without your knowing me, crying in vain to the empty air!" (24).

Gradually her spectral "X-beloved" imparts a "paradoXical" vision of erotic communion. It is not just that Mary finds "homoseXual" satisfaction with someone else—a feminist academic named Annabel, who enters the narrative midway and in the hope of "eXorcizing" its "heteroseXist hypostatization," begins advising Mary on how her "teXt" (*Miss X* itself) should end. At the climactic moment of her supposedly "eXcruciating" tale, after a sentimental visit to Miss X's old house, Mary finds her dead teacher ("dressed in a distinctly wolfish night-cap and white flannel nightdress like the phantom grandmother in *Little Red Riding Hood*") entering her dreams for the first time:

> With mutual fervour—"Come here, Mary," "Come here, Miss X"— obviously she'd mistaken my tears for kisses—we pulled each other down on the little turret bed amongst the swaying branches and *fucked and fucked the whole damned night, skin, blood, bone and breast and all*, as Annabel in good old Anglo-SaXon language would say. ("SiX letters

beginning with 'f' this time, from L. *futo*, 'to have conneXion with a woman'—Oh well.") (201)

"Father Xmas entering the Nursery at twilight?" Mary asks herself after this "eXstatic" reunion, "Little Red Riding Hood in bed with the Wolf?" No, she concludes: "Like all good Freudian Xmas presents, the best dreams always unwrap themselves" (201).

Similar transformations, one suspects, could be found elsewhere in recent lesbian-themed fiction. Diligent ghost-hunters will find much to ponder in the works of—among others—Sybille Bedford, Françoise Mallet, Elizabeth Bowen, Dorothy Baker, Rosemary Manning, Patricia Highsmith, Brigid Brophy, Eveline Mahyère, Violette Leduc, Shirley Jackson, Edna O'Brien, Elizabeth Jane Howard, Pat Arrowsmith, Elizabeth Jolley, Alice Walker, Jane Rule, Bertha Harris, May Sarton, Audre Lorde, Joanna Russ, Kay Dick, Antonia Byatt, Jeanette Winterson, Rebecca Brown, and Jane DeLynn.* I will wrap up my own brief survey, however, with a snapshot, so to speak, from another very recent lesbian novel. In Sarah Schulman's *After Delores* (1988), a lyrical tale of love lost and found on New York's gritty Lower East Side, the nameless narrator (another Miss X) is trying without success to forget her lover Delores, who has left her for another woman. One is hardly dumbfounded by the melancholy opening pass of her story: "I walked out in the snow trying to get away from Delores's ghost. It was sitting back in the apartment waiting for me."[35]

But the crucial moment in Schulman's novel (which shifts brilliantly between farce, gumshoe melodrama, and glowing, delirious romance) has more to do with remembrance than denial. The narra-

---

*Works especially inviting such scrutiny include Highsmith's *The Price of Salt* (1952), Mallet's *The Illusionist* (1952), Brophy's *King of a Rainy Country* (1956) and *The Finishing Touch* (1963), Mahyère's *I Will Not Serve* (1958), Jackson's *The Haunting of Hill House* (1959), Manning's *The Chinese Garden* (1962), Baker's *Cassandra at the Wedding* (1962), Bedford's *A Favourite of the Gods* (1963) and *A Compass Error* (1969), Bowen's *The Little Girls* (1964), Leduc's *Thérèse and Isabelle* (1967), Rule's *This Is Not For You* (1970), Arrowsmith's *Somewhere Like This* (1970), Howard's *Odd Girl Out* (1972), Russ's *The Female Man* (1975), Sarton's *Mrs. Stevens Hears the Mermaids Singing* (1975), Harris's *Lover* (1976), Lorde's *Zami: A New Spelling of My Name* (1982), Walker's *The Color Purple* (1982), Jolley's *Palomino* (1980), *Miss Peabody's Inheritance* (1983), and *The Well* (1986), Dick's *The Shelf* (1984), O'Brien's *The High Road* (1988), DeLynn's *Don Juan in the Village* (1990), Byatt's *Possession* (1990), Brown's *The Terrible Girls* (1990), and Winterson's *Oranges Are Not the Only Fruit* (1985), *The Passion* (1987), and *Written on the Body* (1992).

tor is recollecting a magical day spent with Delores on the boardwalk on the Jersey shore. With vendors selling fried clams and the Marvelettes' "Please Mr. Postman" audible in the background, they had entered an old-fashioned photo booth and taken a strip of four shots. "The first three," says the narrator, "were black-and-white with Delores sitting on my lap. But, at the last minute, she grabbed my face between her hands and kissed it so deeply in front of the camera that my face got drawn into her face. When the pictures came out of the little slot she snatched the strip right away, tore off the three posed ones and threw them in the garbage, handing me the kiss. 'Here,' she said, being nobody's fool. 'I want you to have this one' " (122).

Is it going too far to see conjured up in this visionary moment— reilluminated, as it were, by photo-imaginative flash—the two faces of Mrs. Veal and Mrs. Bargrave, leaning into one another, and into that ghostly kiss so long awaited and so long foresworn? Three hundred years too late perhaps, but as in the terrible old joke, better latent than never. As Schulman's narrator herself says, caught up in the ardor of memory, "That was it. There was no more beating around the bush. No more pretending" (122).

Why, since the eighteenth century, this phantasmagorical association between ghosts and lesbians? And why the seductive permutation of the metaphor in the twentieth century? The answer, it seems to me, is not far to seek. The spectral figure is a perfect vehicle for conveying what must be called—though without a doubt paradoxically—that "recognition through negation" which has taken place with regard to female homosexuality in Western culture since the Enlightenment. Over the past three hundred years, I would like to suggest, the metaphor has functioned as the necessary psychological and rhetorical means for objectifying—and ultimately embracing—that which otherwise could not be acknowledged.

Psychoanalytic theory offers an interesting analogy. Freud, in his famous essay on negation (published three years before *The Well of Loneliness*) argued that the most important way in which repressed thoughts entered into individual consciousness, paradoxically, was through disavowal. To seek to negate an idea—as when one says of an unknown person in a dream, "it was *not* my mother"—was in fact, according to Freud, to affirm the truth of the idea on another level:

The ghost of a desire: *The Kiss* by Clarence
White, 1904. *Courtesy of the Library
of Congress.*

We emend this: so it *was* his mother. In our interpretation we take the liberty of disregarding the negation and of simply picking out the subject-matter of the association. It is just as though the patient had said: "It is true that I thought of my mother in connection with this person, but I don't feel at all inclined to allow the association to count."[36]

Precisely "by the help of the symbol of negation," Freud concluded, "the thinking-process frees itself from the limitations of repression and enriches itself with the subject-matter without which it could not work efficiently."[37]

One might think of lesbianism as the "repressed idea" at the heart of patriarchal culture. By its very nature (and in this respect it differs significantly from male homosexuality) lesbianism poses an ineluctable challenge to the political, economic, and sexual authority of men over women. It implies a whole new social order, characterized—at the very least—by a profound feminine indifference to masculine charisma. (In its militant or "Amazonian" transformation lesbianism may also, of course, be associated with outright hostility toward men.) One might go so far as to argue—along with Adrienne Rich, Gayle Rubin, and others—that patriarchal ideology necessarily depends on the "compulsory" suppression of love between women.[38] As Henry Fielding put it in *The Female Husband*, the vehemently antilesbian pamphlet he published anonymously in 1746, once women gave way to "unnatural lusts," there was no civil "excess and disorder" they were not liable to commit.[39]

Beginning in Western Europe in the eighteenth century, with the gradual attenuation of moral and religious orthodoxies, the weakening of traditional family structures, urbanization, and the growing mobility and economic independence of women, male authority found itself increasingly under assault. And not surprisingly, with such far-reaching social changes in the offing, the "repressed idea" of love between women—one can speculate—began to manifest itself more threateningly in the collective psyche. Eighteenth- and nineteenth-century ideologues were at once fascinated and repelled by the possibility of women without sexual allegiance toward men.[40] And ultimately a backlash set in—characterized as we have seen in the writings of Diderot, Gautier, James, and others, by an effort to derealize the threat of lesbianism by associating it with the apparitional.

From one angle this act of negation made a sort of morbid sense; for how better, one might ask, to exorcize the threat of lesbianism than by turning it into a phantom? The spectral metaphor had useful theological associations: witches, after all, dealt in spirits, and the witchcraft connection could be counted on to add an invidious aura of diabolism to any scene of female-female desire. ("Oh we wouldn't have stood a chance in that time," says Matt in Duffy's *Microcosm*, thinking of the Middle Ages; "sure sign of a witch to love your own sex" [271].) But more important by far was the way the apparitional figure seemed to obliterate, through a single vaporizing gesture, the disturbing carnality of lesbian love. It made of such love—literally—a phantasm: an ineffable anticoupling between "women" who weren't there.

—Or did it? As I have tried to intimate, the case could be made that the metaphor meant to derealize lesbian desire in fact did just the opposite. Indeed, strictly for repressive purposes, one could hardly think of a *worse* metaphor. For embedded in the ghostly figure, as even its first proponents seemed at times to realize, was inevitably a notion of reembodiment: of uncanny return to the flesh. "This image obsesses me, and follows me everywhere," says the narrator in Gautier's *Mademoiselle de Maupin*, "and I never see it more than when it isn't there" (180). To become an apparition was also to become endlessly capable of "appearing." And once there, the specter, like a living being, was not so easily gotten rid of. It demanded a response. It is precisely the demanding, importuning aspect of the apparitional that Radclyffe Hall depicted to such striking allegorical effect in the last pages of *The Well of Loneliness*.

Though in the course of this essay I have, for rhetorical purposes, implied a break between older "homophobic" invocations of the apparitional lesbian and later revisionist ones, it is perhaps more useful in the end to stress the continuity between them. If it is true that the first stage of recognition is denial, then the denial of lesbianism—through its fateful association with the spectral—was also the first stage of its cultural recognition. In the same way that the act of negation, in Freud's words, "frees the thinking process from repression," so the spectral metaphor provided the very imagery, paradoxically, through which the carnal truth of lesbianism might be rediscovered and reclaimed by lesbian writers.

This process of "recognition through negation" may have something to do, finally, with one of the most intriguing features of modern lesbian-themed literature—its tendency to hark back, by way of embedded intertextual references, to earlier works on the same subject. I mentioned in passing Stephen Gordon's "haunted" reading of Krafft-Ebing in *The Well of Loneliness* and Maureen Duffy's lengthy citation from Charlotte Charke's 1755 *Life* in *The Microcosm*, but other examples abound. In both Colette's *Claudine à l'école* and Lillian Hellman's *The Children's Hour*, the characters are reading Gautier's *Mademoiselle de Maupin*; in Brigid Brophy's *The Finishing Touch*, the main character not only invokes Gautier but also Renée Vivien's *Une Femme* *m'apparut* and Proust's *Sodom et Gomorrhe*. In Christine Crow's *Miss X*, the narrator quotes (with irony) from Baudelaire's "Femmes damnées" and jokes compulsively about Radclyffe Hall's *Well of Loneliness*. In Sarah Schulman's *After Delores*, one of the narrator's friends is reading—and rewriting—Renault's *The Friendly Young Ladies*. For the reader attempting to proceed logically, as it were, through the canon of lesbian writing, such rampant intertextuality can bring with it an unsettling sense of déjà vu—if not a feeling of outright "possession" by the ghosts of the lesbian literary past.*

Yet the haunted nature of modern lesbian writing attests directly, I think, to the process by which lesbianism itself has entered into the imaginative life of the West over the past two centuries. It is a curious fact that for most readers of lesbian literature, at least until very recently, it has seldom mattered very much whether a given work of literature depicted love between women in a positive or negative light: so few in number have such representations been over the years, and so intense the cultural taboo against them, that virtually any novel or story dealing with the subject has automatically been granted a place in lesbian literary tradition. (Thus even such negative-seeming works as Diderot's *La Religieuse*, James's *The Bostonians*, or Renault's *The Friendly Young Ladies* continue to hold an acknowledged, if not exactly esteemed, place in the underground lesbian literary canon.[41]) Like the analyst, who, in Freud's words, "takes the liberty of disregarding [any] negation," interested readers have tended simply to "pick out the subject-matter" of lesbianism, regardless of surrounding context, in order to retrieve it for their own subversive imaginative ends.

In the case of the apparitional lesbian, twentieth-century lesbian writers have been able for the most part to ignore the negative backdrop against which she has traditionally (de)materialized. By calling

---

*The passage in Schulman's *After Delores* is exemplary in this respect. Beatriz is describing a screenplay she is writing based on *The Friendly Young Ladies*. In Beatriz's new version, Leo and Helen are lesbians but do not acknowledge the fact to one another until an American woman seduces one of them. Then they are forced to confront the truth of their lives. As Beatriz says to the narrator, "You see, it forces them to confront the lie in their relationship and their complicity in that lie, a lie that has consumed ten years of their lives" (54). The effect of this embedded invocation, even with Beatriz's critical reenvisioning of the plot, is to break down boundaries between Renault's novel and Schulman's own—to make the reader feel suspended, as it were, within a single lesbian Ur-text, replete with plots and counterplots, conjurings and reconjurings.

her back to passionate, imbricated life—by invoking her both as lover and beloved—they have succeeded in transforming her from a negating to an affirming presence. But they have altered our understanding of the homophobic literature of the past as well. For once apprised of the apparitional lesbian's insinuating sensualism—and her scandalous bent for return—we can no longer read, say, the novels of Diderot or James without sensing something of her surreptitious erotic power. Indeed, like Mrs. Veal, she may haunt us most when she pretends to demur. For even at her most ethereal and dissembling, as when seeming to "wave off" the intrusive pleasures of the flesh, she cannot help but also signal—as if by secret benediction—that fall into flesh which is to come.

4

SYLVIA

TOWNSEND

WARNER

AND THE

COUNTERPLOT

OF LESBIAN

FICTION

W h a t i s a lesbian fiction? According
to what we might call the "Queen Victoria Principle" of cultural analysis, no such entity, of course, should even exist. The reader will recollect the instance of regal *faiblesse* I mentioned in my introduction:
how when Queen Victoria was asked by her ministers in 1885 whether the recently legislated Criminal Law Amendment Act outlawing
homosexual acts between men should be made to apply to women as
well, she is supposed to have expressed disbelief that such acts between women were physically possible. Desire between men was
conceivable, indeed could be pictured vividly enough to require

policing. Desire between women was not.[1] The love of woman for woman, along with whatever "indecency" it might entail, simply could not be represented. According to this primal (il)logic, it would follow, therefore, that "lesbian fiction" is also inconceivable: a nonconcept, a nothingness, a gap in the meaning of things—anything but a story there to be read.

We pride ourselves nowadays on having made some intellectual advances on the Victorian position. We know that lesbian fiction, like lesbianism itself, exists; we may even be able to name a few celebrated (or reviled) lesbian novels—*The Well of Loneliness, Nightwood, Orlando, The Desert of the Heart, The Female Man*, and so on. And yet, on what theoretical basis do we make such denominations? What characteristics inform our definition of "lesbian fiction" itself? Is a "lesbian novel" simply any narrative depicting sexual relations between women? If this were the case, then any number of works by male writers, including Diderot's *La Religieuse*, for example, or some of the other pornographic or semipornographic texts of male voyeurism, would fall under the rubric of lesbian fiction. Yet this does not feel exactly right. Would a lesbian novel be a novel, then, written by a lesbian? This can't be the case, or certain of Willa Cather's novels, say, or Marguerite Yourcenar's, would have to be classed as lesbian novels, when it is not clear that they really are. "A novel written by a lesbian depicting sexual relations between women" might come closer, but relies too heavily on the opacities of biography and eros, and lacks a certain psychic and political specificity.

The concept of "lesbian fiction," one has to conclude, remains somewhat undertheorized. It remains undertheorized, paradoxically, even in those places where one might expect to see it brought under the most intense scrutiny—in critical studies specifically dealing with the subject of homosexual desire in fiction. To date, the most provocative and influential study on this theme has undoubtedly been Eve Kosofsky Sedgwick's *Between Men: English Literature and Male Homosocial Desire* (1985). This brilliant meditation on "homosociality" in literature, which Sedgwick wrote, as she recounts in her introduction, out of a specifically "antihomophobic and feminist" position, can justly be said to have galvanized the world of gay literary studies, at least as far as that world is presently constituted in the United States.[2]

And yet how is the question of lesbian fiction handled in this book? The answer, simply, is not at all. To be fair to Sedgwick, she is aware of the omission and candidly acknowledges it in her introduction. "The absence of lesbianism from the book," she writes, "was an early and, I think, necessary decision, since my argument is structured around the distinctive relation of the male homosocial spectrum to the transmission of unequally distributed power relations."[3] In other words, the very terms of Sedgwick's argument do not allow for any consideration of lesbian desire or its representation. But how can this be so?

Put in the most basic form, Sedgwick's thesis (which will already be familiar to many readers) is that English literature, at least since the late seventeenth century, has been structured by what she calls the "erotic triangle" of male homosocial desire. Drawing on the work of René Girard, Claude Lévi-Strauss, and especially Gayle Rubin, whose classic feminist essay, "The Traffic in Women," underpins much of the thinking here, Sedgwick argues that just as patriarchal culture has traditionally been organized around a ritualized "traffic" in women—the legal, economic, religious, and sexual exchange of women between men (as in the cherished institutions of heterosexual love and marriage)—so the fictions produced within patriarchal culture have tended to mimic, or represent, the same triangular structure. English literature is "homosocial," according to Sedgwick, to the extent that its hidden subject has always been male bonding—the bonding mediated "between" two men through, around, or over, the body and soul of a woman. In fiction as in life, the "normative man," she writes, uses a woman "as a 'conduit of a relationship' in which the true *partner* is a man" (26).

In a series of bravura readings, Sedgwick traces the persistence of the male-female-male "homosocial paradigm" in English writing from Shakespeare and Wycherley through the novels of Sterne, Hogg, Thackeray, Eliot, and Dickens. What she discovers along the way is that homosociality also has its discontents. These arise, not unexpectedly, from the ambiguous relationship between homo*sociality* and homo*sexuality*. The system of male domination, according to Sedgwick, depends on the maintenance of highly charged attachments between men. "It is crucial to every aspect of social structure within the exchange-of-women framework," she writes, "that heavily freighted bonds between men exist, as the backbone of social form or forms" (86). At the same time, she points out, when these male-male attachments become *too* freighted—that is, explicitly sexual—the result is an ideological contradiction of potentially crippling magnitude. If a man can become "like" a woman in the act of homosexual intercourse, what is to distinguish such a man from any woman? By doing away with the "female middle term" and blurring the putative difference between "male" and "female," the overt eroticization of male bonds undermines the very conceptual distinction on which modern patriarchy is founded.

How then to separate "functional" male bonds—those that bolster the structure of male domination—from those that weaken it? In Sedgwick's insinuating rereading of patriarchal cultural history, literature itself has been a primary means of resolving, or of attempting to resolve, this potentially disruptive ideological problem. Its solution has been to emphasize, with an almost paranoiac insistence, the necessity of triangulation itself—of preserving the male-female-male "erotic paradigm" precisely as a way of fending off the destabilizing threat of male homosexuality. The plots of classic English and American fiction, according to Sedgwick, are blatantly, often violently, homophobic: in Hogg's *Confessions of a Justified Sinner* or Dickens's *Our Mutual Friend*—to take two of her more memorable examples—the homoerotic desire of man for man is shown to lead, as if by Gothic compulsion, to morbidity, persecution, mania, and murder. By activating what she calls the standard plot mechanisms of "homosexual panic," these novels, along with many others, reveal themselves as none too subtly disguised briefs on behalf of the mediated eros of male homosocial desire. The triangular male-female-male figure returns at the conclusion of each story—triumphantly reinstalled—as a sign both of normative (namely, heterosexual) male bonding and of a remobilization of patriarchal control.

The obsession with vindicating male homosociality at the expense of male homosexuality has not been confined, writes Sedgwick, to the works of the English literary tradition. Indeed, in the most ambitious formulation of her argument, she asserts that the entire European literary canon since the Renaissance might be considered a massively elaborated (and ultimately coercive) statement on male bonding. What makes a literary work "canonical," in her view, is precisely in fact the degree of its absorption in the issue of male homosociality. She makes this provocative claim in a crucial passage—once again from the introduction—in which she explains the somewhat idiosyncratic assortment of texts to which individual chapters of *Between Men* are dedicated:

> The choices I have made of texts through which to embody the argument of the book are specifically *not* meant to begin to delineate a separate male-homosocial literary canon. In fact, it will be essential to my argument to claim that the European canon as it exists is already such a canon, and most so when it is most heterosexual. . . . I have simply chosen texts at pleasure from within or alongside the English canon that represented particularly interesting interpretive problems, or particularly symptomatic historical and ideological modes, for understanding the politics of male homosociality.   (17)

Literature canonizes the subject of male homosociality; in return, it would seem, the subject of male homosociality canonizes the work of literature.

Within such a totalizing scheme, with its insistent focus on relations "between men," what place might there be for relations between women? Sedgwick is aware, or at least half-aware, that her theory in some way fails "to do justice to women's own powers, bonds, and struggles" (18). She freely acknowledges that her reluctance to distinguish between what she calls "ideologizing" and "de-ideologizing" narratives may have led her to present "the 'canonical' cultural discourse in an excessively protean and inescapable . . . form." Yet at the same time she makes it clear that she can offer little in the way of comment on "women's own cultural resources of resistance, adaptation, revision, and survival." She is content to send out a somewhat perfunctory appeal to her readers for "better analyses of the relations between female-homosocial and male-homosocial structures" (18).

If the subject of female bonding sets up a kind of intellectual or emotional "blockage" in Sedgwick's argument, the specialized form of female bonding represented by lesbianism seems to provoke in her, interestingly enough, even deeper resistance. In the one or two somewhat strained paragraphs of *Between Men* that Sedgwick *does* devote to women's bonds, she more or less summarily dismisses *lesbianism* as a useful category of analysis. In contrast to the spectacularly polarized arrangement she finds in the realm of male desire, she can see no real cultural or ideological distinction, in the case of women, between homosociality and homosexuality:

> The diacritical opposition between the "homosocial" and the "homosexual" seems to be much less thorough and dichotomous for women, in our society, than for men. At this particular historical moment, an intelligible continuum of aims, emotions, and valuations links lesbianism with the other forms of women's attention to women: the bond of mother and daughter, for instance, the bond of sister and sister, women's friendship, "networking," and the active struggles of feminism. The continuum is crisscrossed with deep discontinuities— with much homophobia, with conflicts of race and class—but its intelligibility seems now a matter of simple common sense. However agonistic the politics, however conflicted the feelings, it seems at this moment to make an obvious kind of sense to say that women in our society who love women, women who teach, study, nurture, suckle, write about, march for, vote for, give jobs to, or otherwise promote the interests of other women, are pursuing congruent and closely related activities. (2–3)

Lesbians, defined here, with telling vagueness, only as "women who love women," are really no different, Sedgwick seems to imply, from "women promoting the interests of other women." Their way of bonding is so "congruent" with that of other women, it turns out, that one need no longer call it homosexual. "The adjective 'homosocial' as applied to women's bonds," she concludes, *"need not be pointedly dichotomized as against 'homosexual'; it can intelligibly denominate the entire continuum"* (3; my emphasis). By a disarming sleight of phrase, an entire category of women—lesbians—is lost to view.

In the face of these rhetorically tortured and—for Sedgwick— uncharacteristically sentimental passages, one's immediate impulse may be to remark, somewhat uncharitably, that she has not "gotten the point," so to speak, of pointedly dichotomizing lesbian from straight existence. What may appear "intelligible" or "simple common sense" to a nonlesbian critic will hardly seem quite so simple to any female reader who has ever attempted to walk down a city street holding hands with, let alone kissing or embracing, another woman. The homosexual panic elicited by women publicly signaling their sexual interest in one another continues, alas, even "at this particular historical moment," to be just as virulent as that inspired by male homosexuality, if not more so.[4] To obscure the fact that lesbians are women who have sex with each other—and that this is not exactly the same, in the eyes of society, as voting for women or giving them jobs—is, in essence, not to acknowledge the separate peril and pleasure of lesbian existence.

Are we then simply to blame Sedgwick for succumbing, albeit belatedly, to the Queen Victoria Principle? I think not—for what I am calling, perhaps too tendentiously, the "blockage" in her theory, is intimately related, paradoxically, to its strength. It is precisely because Sedgwick has recognized so clearly the canonical power of *male-male* desire—and has described so well its shaping role in the plots of eighteenth- and nineteenth-century English and American literature— that she does not "get the point" of *female-female* desire. For to do so would mean undoing, if only imaginatively, the very structure she is elsewhere at such pains to elaborate: the figure of the male homosocial triangle itself.

To theorize about female-female desire, I would like to suggest, is precisely to envision the taking apart of this supposedly intractable patriarchal structure. Female bonding, at least hypothetically, destabilizes the "canonical" triangular arrangement of male desire, is an affront to it, and ultimately—in the radical form of lesbian bonding—displaces it entirely. Even Sedgwick's own geometrical model intimates as much. As the figure below suggests, the male-female-male erotic triangle remains stable only as long as its single female term is unrelated to any other female term. Once two female terms are conjoined in space, however, an alternative structure comes into being, a female-male-female triangle, in which one of the male terms from the original triangle now occupies the "in between" or subjugated position of the mediator.

Within this new *female* homosocial structure, the possibility of male bonding is radically suppressed: for the male term is now isolated, just as the female term was in the male homosocial structure.

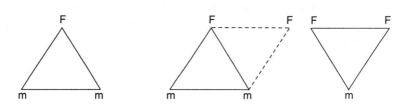

But one can go still further. In the original male-female-male configuration, we may recollect, the relationship between the dominant
male terms was not static. Indeed, this was the inherent problem in
the structure from the patriarchal perspective: that the two male
terms might hook up directly, so to speak, replacing the heterosexual
with an explicitly homosexual dyad. Yet exactly the same dynamism
is characteristic of the female homosocial triangle. In the most radical
transformation of female bonding—i.e., from homosocial to *lesbian*
bonding—the two female terms indeed merge and the male term
drops out. At this point, it is safe to say, not only is male bonding
suppressed, it has become impossible—there being no male terms
left to bond.

A pleasing elaboration of the Sedgwickian model, perhaps—but
does it have any literary applications? If we restrict ourselves, as
Sedgwick herself does, to the canon of eighteenth- and nineteenth-
century English and American fiction, the answer would have to be
no, or not really. Indeed, one might easily argue that just as the major
works of realistic fiction from this period constitute a brief against
male homosexuality (Sedgwick's point), so they also constitute, even
more blatantly, a brief against female homosociality. Even in works in
which female homosocial bonds are depicted, these bonds are inevitably shown giving way to the power of male homosocial triangulation.
In Charlotte Brontë's *Shirley*, for example, a novel that explicitly the-
matizes the conflict between male and female bonding, the original
female homosocial bond between Shirley Keeldar and Caroline
Helstone (a bond triangulated through the character of the mill owner
Robert Moore) is replaced at the end of the novel by not just one, but
two interlocking male homosocial triangles, symbolized in the marriages of Robert with Caroline and of Robert's brother Louis with

Shirley. True, *Shirley* represents an unusually tormented and ambivalent version of the male homosocial plot: but even Brontë, like other Victorian novelists, gives way in the end to the force of fictional and ideological convention.[5]

But what if we turn our attention to twentieth-century writing? Are there any contemporary novels that undo the seemingly compulsory plot of male homosocial desire? It will come as no surprise that I am about to invoke such a work, and that I propose to denominate it, without further ado, an exemplary "lesbian fiction." The work I have in mind is Sylvia Townsend Warner's 1936 *Summer Will Show*, a historical fiction set in rural Dorset and Paris during the revolution of 1848. What makes this novel paradigmatically "lesbian," in my view, is not simply that it depicts a sexual relationship between two women, but that it so clearly, indeed almost schematically, figures this relationship as a breakup of the supposedly "canonical" male-female-male erotic triangle. As I shall try to demonstrate in what follows, it is exactly this kind of subverted triangulation, or erotic "counterplotting," that is in fact characteristic of lesbian novels in general.

Summer Will Show is not, I realize, a well-known piece of fiction—indeed quite the opposite. Even among Townsend Warner devotees it is still a relatively unfamiliar work, despite a Virago reprint in 1987. Townsend Warner's earlier novel *Lolly Willowes* (1926) remains generally better known; later works, such as the novel *The Corner That Held Them* (1948), the biography of T. H. White (1967), and the short story collection *Kingdoms of Elfin* (1977) have attracted more critical attention.* What notice *Summer Will Show* has received has tended to

---

*Townsend Warner's brilliant and varied writings, many of which touch on the theme of homosexuality, have been sorely neglected since her death in 1978—not least by gay and lesbian readers and critics. Her most enthusiastic admirer, somewhat unexpectedly, remains George Steiner, who in the pages of the *Times Literary Supplement* (December 2–8, 1988), pronounced *The Corner That Held Them* a "masterpiece" of modern English fiction. Claire Harman's biography, *Sylvia Townsend Warner*, will no doubt help to rectify this curious situation, as should Wendy Mulford's *This Narrow Place*, a superb study of the relationship between Townsend Warner and the poet Valentine Ackland, her lover of thirty years. Also of great interest is Townsend Warner's correspondence, edited by William Maxwell. Besides displaying Townsend Warner's matchless wit and unfailingly elegant style, the letters also demonstrate that she was capable of imagining Queen Victoria's sex life, even if Queen Victoria could not have imagined hers (see letter to Llewelyn Powys, December 7, 1933).

be condescending in nature: because Townsend Warner wrote the
novel during the period of her most passionate involvement with the
British Communist party and intended it in part as an allegory of the
Spanish Civil War, it has often been dismissed as a "Marxist novel"
or leftist period piece. While not entirely an *un*read work of modern
English fiction, *Summer Will Show* is at the very least an *under*read
one.

Yet some of the resistance the work has met with must also have to
do, one suspects, with its love story, which challenges so spectacularly the rigidly heterosexual conventions of classic English and American fiction. This story begins deceptively simply, in a seemingly rec-
ognizable literary landscape: that of nineteenth-century fiction itself.
The tall, fair-haired heroine, Sophia Willoughby, is the only daughter of wealthy landed gentry in Dorset, the heiress of Blandamer
House (in which she resides), and the wife of a feckless husband,
Frederick, who, after marrying her for her money and fathering her
two small children, has abandoned her and taken a mistress in Paris.
At the start of the novel, Sophia is walking with her children, a boy
and a girl, on a hot summer's day to the limekiln on the estate, in the
hope that by subjecting them to a traditional remedy—limekiln
fumes—she can cure them of the whooping cough they have both
contracted.

Already in these opening pages, given over to Sophia's reveries on
the way to the limekiln, we have a sense of her proud, powerful, yet
troubled nature: like another Gwendolen Harleth or even a new Emma
Bovary, she broods over her unhappy marriage and yearns ambiguously for "something decisive," a new kind of fulfilment, some "moment when she should exercise her authority" (11).[6] While devoted to
her children, she also feels constricted by them and infuriated at her
husband for leaving them entirely to her care. As for Frederick himself, she harbours no lingering romantic illusions there, only "icy disdain," mixed with a sense of sexual grievance. It is not so much that
she is jealous—their marriage has been devoid of passion—but that
she resents his freedom and his predictably chosen "bohemian"
mistress:

> For even to Dorset the name of Minna Lemuel had made its way. Had
> the husband of Mrs. Willoughby chosen no other end than to be scan-

dalous, he could not have chosen better. A byword, half actress, half strumpet; a Jewess; a nonsensical creature bedizened with airs of prophecy, who trailed across Europe with a tag-rag of poets, revolutionaries, musicians and circus-riders snuffing at her heels, like an escaped bitch with a procession of mongrels after her; and ugly; and old, as old as Frederick or older—this was the woman whom Frederick had elected to fall in love with, joining in the tag-rag procession, and not even king in that outrageous court, not even able to dismiss the mongrels, and take the creature into keeping. (31)

At the same time, however, Sophia feels an odd gratitude to the other woman: thanks to Minna, Sophia reminds herself, she is "a mother, and a landowner; but fortunately, she need no longer be counted among the wives" (20).

All this is to change as a result of the limekiln visit itself. With Sophia looking on, the limekiln keeper—a silent, frightening-looking man with sores on his arms—suspends each of the children over the kiln. Though terrified, they inhale the fumes and Sophia takes them home. In the next few weeks, her attention is distracted by the arrival of her nephew Caspar, the illegitimate mulatto child of an uncle in the West Indies. At her uncle's request, she takes Caspar to Cornwall to place him in a boarding school. Returning home, she finds her own children mortally ill: the limekiln keeper was in fact carrying smallpox and has infected both children. Sophia delays writing to her husband to inform him; yet Frederick comes anyway, having been recalled by a letter written by the doctor who is attending the children.

At once Sophia senses a subtle change in her husband, a mystifying new refinement, which she attributes—balefully, yet also with growing curiosity—to the influence of his unseen mistress. Listening to him repeat the words "*Ma fleur*" over his dying daughter's sickbed, it seems to Sophia as if a stranger were speaking through him: someone possessed of "a deep sophistication in sorrow." The intrusive cadence, she reminds herself angrily, must be copied from "that Minna's Jewish contralto." Yet afterward, when both of the children are dead and Frederick has gone back to Paris, Sophia finds herself haunted by a memory of the voice—one that seems, "according to her mood, an enigma, a nettle-sting, a caress" (83).

With the death of Sophia's children, the crucial action of the novel commences. Distraught, grief-stricken, yet also peculiarly obsessed with her husband's other life, Sophia decides to seek him out in Paris, for the purpose (she tells herself) of forcing him to give her more children. Yet, as if driven by more mysterious urgings, she finds herself, on the very evening of her arrival, at the apartment on the Rue de la Carabine where Minna holds her salon. Entering the apartment unobserved, Sophia joins the crowd of guests (including Frederick himself) who are listening to their hostess tell a story.

The story, which is presented as an embedded narrative, is a hypnotic account of Minna's childhood in Eastern Europe—of the pogrom in which her parents were killed, of her own escape from the murderers, and of her eventual rescue by a vagrant musician. The experience of persecution has made her an artist, a storyteller, a romantic visionary, and a political revolutionary. As Sophia listens, seemingly mesmerized by the Jewish woman's charismatic "siren voice," she forgets entirely about Frederick and the putative reason why she has come. Suddenly the tale is interrupted—barricades are being put up outside in the streets; the first skirmishes of what will become the February Revolution are about to begin. Minna's listeners, mainly artists and intellectuals who support the revolt, depart, along with Frederick, who has not yet seen his wife. And Sophia, still as if under a spell, finds herself alone in the room with Minna.

She is utterly, heart-stoppingly, captivated. Not by Minna's beauty—for Frederick's mistress is a small, dark, and sallow woman, with "a slowly flickering glance" and "large supple hands" that seem to "caress themselves together in the very gesture of her thought" (127). Yet something in this very look, "sombre and attentive," alive with tenderness and recognition, ineluctably draws Sophia to her. ("I cannot understand," Sophia finds herself thinking, "what Frederick could see in you. But *I* can see a great deal" [154].) Minna in turn seems equally delighted with her lover's wife. Together they look out on the barricades: Frederick is below and now sees Sophia; he is piqued when she refuses his offer of a cab. Minna also ignores him, so he leaves. Minna then confides in Sophia her hopes for the success of the insurrection. Sophia, entranced yet also exhausted, falls asleep on Minna's sofa. When she awakens the next day, her hostess is sitting beside her. Inspired by the strange "ardour" of the Jewish woman's attention, the normally reticent Sophia suddenly finds herself overcome by an urge to recount the story of *her* own life. As if freed from an invisible bondage, she finds herself talking for hours. When Frederick returns that afternoon, he is momentarily "felled" to discover his wife and mistress "seated together on the pink sofa, knit into this fathomless intimacy, and turning from it to entertain him with an identical patient politeness." For "neither woman, absorbed in this extraordinary colloquy, had expressed by word or sign the slightest consciousness that there was anything unusual about it" (157).

Nor, might it be said, does Townsend Warner. The attraction between Sophia and Minna is treated, if anything, as a perfectly natural elaboration of the wife-mistress situation. The two women, it is true, separate for several weeks, in part because Sophia is afraid of the depth—and complication—of her new attachment. While the political turmoil in the city grows, she stays with her wealthy, superannuated French aunt, Léocadie, who tries to reconcile her with Frederick. Yet she is drawn back into Minna's orbit soon enough, when she hears that Minna has given away almost all of her money to the striking workers and is destitute. Outraged with Frederick for "casting off" his mistress (which is how Sophia describes the situation to herself), she determines to fulfill his "obligations" herself. She returns to the now-shabby apartment on the Rue de la Carabine, and finding Minna weak with cold and hunger, decides to stay and care for her. As her absorption in the other woman grows—and is reciprocated— Sophia gradually feels her old identity, that of the heiress of Blandamer, slipping away. As if "by some extraordinary enchantment," she is inexorably caught up in Minna's world and in the revolutionary activity in which Minna is involved.

Meanwhile Frederick, incensed by the alliance between his wife and his (now) ex-mistress, cuts off Sophia's allowance in order to force her to return to him. Yet his machinations serve only to intensify— indeed to eroticize—the intimacy between the two women. When Sophia tells her friend that Frederick has told the bank not to honor her signature "as he is entitled to do being my husband," they suddenly comprehend their desire for what it is:

"You will stay? You must, if only to gall him."

"I don't think that much of a reason."

"But you will stay?"

"I will stay if you wish it."

It seemed to her that the words fell cold and glum as ice-pellets. Only beneath the crust of thought did her being assent as by right to that flush of pleasure, that triumphant cry.

"But of course," said Minna a few hours later, thoughtfully licking the last oyster shell, "we must be practical."   (274)

Townsend Warner, to be sure, renders the scene of their passionate coming together elliptically—with only a cry (and an oyster) to suggest the moment of consummation—yet the meaning is clear: Sophia has severed all ties with the past—with her husband, her class, and with sexual convention itself.[7]

In the final section of the novel, spring gives way to summer; the popular insurrection, dormant for several months, flares once again. Inspired by her new-found love for Minna, Sophia throws herself into political activity, becoming a courier for a group of communists who are collecting weapons in preparation for open civil war. Her last contact with her husband comes about when her nephew Caspar suddenly turns up in Paris, alienated and sullen, having run away from the school in Cornwall: Sophia is forced to ask Frederick for money to pay for the youth's schooling in Paris. Without her knowledge, Frederick, who now cynically supports the government, instead buys Caspar a place in the Gardes Mobiles, the force opposing the now-imminent June rebellion.

Returning from one of her courier missions, Sophia finds that street fighting has begun in the neighbourhood around the Rue de la Carabine. Minna is already on the barricades. Together they join in the battle, loading and reloading the workers' rifles. The Gardes Mobiles launch an attack on the barricade and Sophia, to her surprise, recognizes Caspar in their midst. He plunges a bayonet into Minna, who falls, apparently mortally wounded. Sophia shoots Caspar in retaliation, but is herself captured and taken away with some other prisoners to be executed, only to be freed the next day because she is a woman. She searches frantically for Minna but cannot discover if she is alive or dead. The revolt has been put down and the workers' hopes seemingly destroyed. Returning to Minna's apartment, yet still harboring a hope that her lover will return, Sophia opens one of the pamphlets that she had been delivering the previous day. It is Marx's *Communist Manifesto*. As she settles down to read—exhausted but also arrested by its powerful opening words—the novel comes ambiguously to an end.

I will return to this somewhat curious denouement in a moment: I would like to draw attention first to the more obviously revisionist aspects of Townsend Warner's narrative. For *Summer Will Show*—as I hope even my highly compressed account of its characters and incidents will have indicated—is a work obsessed with "revising" on a number of counts. In the most literal sense the novel is a kind of revisionist fantasia: in recounting the story of her pseudo-Victorian heroine, Sophia Willoughby, Townsend Warner constantly pastiches— yet also rewrites—Victorian fiction itself. The opening scene at the limekiln, for example, both recalls and traduces the episode in *Great Expectations* in which Pip is dangled over a limekiln by the infamous Orlick: the "great expectations" here belong, ironically, to the observer, Sophia herself. The early episodes involving the mulatto Caspar and the uncle in the West Indies likewise rework and subvert elements from *Wuthering Heights* and *Jane Eyre*. After Sophia's arrival in Paris, a curiously erotic scene in which Minna shows her her duelling pistols (154–6) is an almost direct parody of a similar moment in *Shirley:* Minna's guns are about to be given up to the striking workers of Paris: the guns that Caroline Helstone shows to Shirley Keeldar are their protection *against* the striking workers of Briarfield. Minna herself is a kind of revolutionary variant on a George Eliot heroine. Her Jewishness and political radicalism bring to mind characters and situations from *Daniel Deronda* and *Felix Holt;* her appearance—and passionate intelligence—may be modeled on Eliot's own. Yet she is far more deviant than any Eliot heroine is ever allowed to be. Tellingly, her very name appears to originate in the famous passage in *The Mill on the Floss* in which Maggie Tulliver declares her wish to "avenge" all the unfortunate dark-haired heroines of English literature— "Rebecca, and Flora MacIvor, and Minna, and all the rest of the dark unhappy ones."[8] Maggie's Minna is the hapless heroine of Sir Walter Scott's *The Pirate*, abandoned by her lover on a frigid Scottish beach.

By contrast, Townsend Warner's Minna—with her freedom from convention, her sexual charisma, and survivor's instinct—is at once a satirical rewrite of the first Minna and a more resilient version of Maggie herself.

But it is not only English fiction that Townsend Warner is rewriting in *Summer Will Show*. In a somewhat tongue-in-cheek note composed in the 1960s, she revealed that in order to write the book she "re-read Berlioz's *Mémoires*, and with an effort put the French novelists out of my mind."[9] Berlioz is certainly there, but so too are the French novelists. The scenes at Minna's Parisian salon have the flavour of Staël and Hugo as well as of Stendhal and Balzac; Sophia's right-wing aunt Léocadie, along with her egregious confessor Père Hyacinthe, are straight out of *La Comédie humaine*. But it is Flaubert, obviously, and *his* novel of 1848, that Townsend Warner is most deeply conscious of displacing. Anyone who doubts the subterranean importance of *L'Éducation sentimentale* to *Summer Will Show* need only consider the name Frédéric—or Frederick—and the parodistic relationship that exists between Flaubert's antihero, Frédéric Moreau, and Townsend Warner's comic villain, Frederick Willoughby.*

To invoke Flaubert's masterpiece, however, is also to return—with a vengeance—to the Sedgwickian issue of erotic triangulation. For what is *L'Éducation sentimentale* if not a classic work, in Sedgwick's terms, of male homosocial bonding? Flaubert's Frédéric, we recall, acts out his emotional obsession with his friend Arnoux by falling in love first with Arnoux's wife, then with his mistress. Townsend Warner's Frederick, by contrast, not only has no male friend, his wife and his mistress fall in love with each other. In the very act of revising Flaubert—of substituting her own profoundly "anticanonical" fiction in place of his own—Townsend Warner also revises the plot of male homosocial desire. Indeed, all of her revisionist gestures can, I think, be linked with this same imaginative impulse: the desire to plot

---

*Frederick Willoughby is condemned by his name on two counts of course: if his first name recalls the stooge of Flaubert's *L'Éducation sentimentale*, his last he shares with the unprincipled villain of Austen's *Sense and Sensibility*. In Austen's novel, we recall, the more hapless of the two heroines is abandoned by (John) Willoughby in favour of a rich heiress. To the extent that (Frederick) Willoughby—now married to his rich heiress—is himself abandoned by wife and mistress both, one might consider Townsend Warner's novel a displaced sequel to Austen's: a kind of comic postlude, or "revenge of Marianne Dashwood."

against the seemingly indestructible heterosexual narrative of classic European fiction.

This work of counterplotting can best be figured, as I suggested at the outset, as a kind of dismantling or displacement of the male homosocial triangle itself. Granted, at the beginning of *Summer Will Show*, the hoary Sedgwickian structure still seems firmly in place: Sophia is more or less mired in the "in between" position that patriarchal society demands of her. As the only heiress of Blandamer, "the point advancing on the future, as it were, of that magnificent triangle in which Mr. and Mrs. Aspen of Blandamer House, Dorset, England, made up the other two apices" (3), she has functioned, we are led to deduce, as the social mediator between her own father, who has been forced to give her up in marriage in order to perpetuate the Aspen family line, and Frederick, the son-in-law, who has enriched himself by allying himself with the Aspen patrimony.

Yet instabilities in this classic male-female-male triad soon become apparent. The deaths of Sophia's children are the first sign of a generalized weakening of male homosocial bonds; these deaths, we realize, are not just a transforming loss for Sophia, but for Frederick also, who loses, through them, his only remaining biological and symbolic connection to Sophia's dead father, his partner in the novel's original homosocial triangle. Significantly, perhaps, it is the son who is the first of the children to die: in a way that prefigures the symbolic action of the novel as a whole, the patrilineal triangle of father-mother-son here disappears, leaving only a female-male-female triangle, composed of Sophia, Frederick, and their daughter. Even at this early stage, one might argue, Townsend Warner represents the female-dominant triangle as "stronger," or in some sense more durable, than the male-dominant one.

Yet other episodes in the first part of the novel suggest a disintegration of male homosocial structures. When Sophia delays writing to Frederick during the children's illness, her doctor, thinking the absence of her husband a scandal, writes to him without her knowledge. The letter is intercepted by the doctor's young wife, who brings it to Sophia and offers to destroy it. "Why should all this be done behind your back?" exclaims the outraged Mrs. Hervey, "what right have they to interfere, to discuss and plot, and settle what they think best to be done? As if, whatever happened, you could not stand alone, and judge for yourself! As if you needed a man!" (72). Admittedly, Sophia decides in the end to let the letter be sent, but the intimation here of an almost conspiratorial bonding between the two women—against *both* of their husbands—directly foreshadows the more powerful bonding of Sophia with Minna. And as will be true later, a strong current of erotic feeling runs between the two women. "She might be in love with me," Sophia thinks after Mrs. Hervey "awkwardly" embraces her during one of their first meetings. Now, as she looks at the letter "lying so calmly" on Mrs. Hervey's lap, it suddenly seems only a pretext: "some other motive, violent and unexperienced as the emotions of youth, trembled undeclared between them." Later, they walk hand in hand in a thunderstorm, and Sophia briefly entertains a fancy of going on a European tour with Mrs. Hervey—"large-eyed and delighted and clutching a box of watercolour paints"—at her side (78).

With the love affair between Sophia and Minna, one might say that the male homosocial triad reaches its point of maximum destabilization and collapses altogether. In its place appears a new configuration, the triad of *female* homosocial desire. For Frederick, obviously, is now forced into the position of the subject term, the one "in between," the odd one out—the one, indeed, who can be patronized. Sophia and Minna do just this during their first supper together, following the memorable colloquy on the pink sofa. Sophia takes it upon herself to order the wine, a discreetly masculine gesture that inspires Minna to remark, "How much I like being with English people! They manage everything so quietly and so well." Sophia, catching her drift, instantly rejoins, "And am I as good as Frederick?" "You are much better," Minna replies. After a short meditation on Frederick's shortcomings, the two women subside into complacent amity. "Poor Frederick!" says one. "Poor Frederick!" says the other (161–62).

We might call this the comedy of female-female desire: as two women come together, the man who has brought them together seems oddly reduced, transformed into a figure of fun. Later he will drop out of sight altogether—which is another way of saying that in every lesbian relationship there is a man who has been sacrificed. Townsend Warner will call attention to this "disappearing man" phenomenon at numerous points, sometimes in a powerfully literal way.

When Sophia returns, for example, to the Rue de la Carabine to help the poverty-stricken Minna, only to find her lying chilled and unconscious on the floor, she immediately lies down to warm her, in "a desperate calculated caress." Yet this first, soon-to-be eroticized act of lying down with Minna also triggers a reverie—on the strangeness of the season that has brought them together, on the vast distance each has traversed to arrive at this moment, and on the man "between them" who is of course not there:

> It was spring, she remembered. In another month the irises would be coming into flower. But now it was April, the cheat month, when the deadliest frosts might fall, when snow might cover the earth, lying hard and authentic on the English acres as it lay over the wastes of Lithuania. There, in one direction, was Blandamer, familiar as a bed; and there, in another was Lithuania, the unknown, where a Jewish child had watched the cranes fly over, and had stood beside the breaking river. And here, in Paris lay Sophia Willoughby, lying on the floor in the draughty passage-way between bedroom and dressing-closet, her body pressed against the body of her husband's mistress. (251)

The intimacy, here and later, is precisely the intimacy enjoined by the breakup of monolithic structures, indeed, by the breakup of triangulation itself. For what Sophia and Minna discover, even as they muse over "poor Frederick," is that they need him no longer: in the draughty passageway leading to a bedroom, the very shape of desire is "pressed" out of shape, becoming dyadic, impassioned, lesbian.[10]

What is particularly satisfying about Townsend Warner's plotting here is that it illustrates so neatly—indeed so trigonometrically— what we might take to be the underlying principle of lesbian narrative itself: namely, that for female bonding to "take," as it were, to metamorphose into explicit sexual desire, male bonding must be suppressed. (Male homo*social* bonding, that is; for lesbian characters in novels can, and do, quite easily coexist with male homo*sexual* characters, as Djuna Barnes's *Nightwood*, or even *Orlando* in its final pages, might suggest).[11] Townsend Warner's Frederick has no boyhood friend, no father, no father-in-law, no son, no gang, *no novelist on his side* to help him retriangulate his relationship with his wife—or for that matter, with his mistress either. To put it axiomatically: in the absence of male homosocial desire, lesbian desire emerges.

Can such a principle help us to theorize in more general ways about lesbian fiction? Obviously, I think it can. It allows us to identify first of all two basic mimetic contexts in which, in realistic writing, plots of lesbian desire are most likely to flourish: the world of schooling and adolescence (the world of premarital relations) and the world of divorce, widowhood, and separation (the world of postmarital relations). In each of these mimetic contexts, male erotic triangulation is either conspicuously absent or under assault. In the classically gynocentric setting of the girls' school, for example, male characters are generally isolated or missing altogether: hence the powerfully female homosocial/homosexual plots of Colette's *Claudine à l'école*, Clemence Dane's *Regiment of Women*, Dorothy Strachey's *Olivia*, Antonia White's *Frost in May*, Christa Winsloe's *The Child Manuela* (on which the film *Mädchen in Uniform* is based), Lillian Hellman's *The Children's Hour*, Muriel Spark's *The Prime of Miss Jean Brodie*, Catharine Stimpson's *Class Notes* or more recently, Jeanette Winterson's *Oranges Are Not the Only Fruit*, in which the juvenile heroine woos her first love while attending a female Bible study group.

Yet the figure of male homosociality is even more pitilessly compromised in novels of postmarital experience. In the novel of adolescence, it is true, male homosocial desire often reasserts itself, belatedly, at the end of the fiction: the central lesbian bond may be undermined or broken up, usually by having one of the principals die (as in *The Child Manuela* or *The Children's Hour*), get married (as in *Oranges Are Not the Only Fruit*), or reconcile herself in some other way with the erotic and social world of men (as in *Claudine à l'école* or *The Prime of Miss Jean Brodie*). We might call this "dysphoric" lesbian counterplotting. To the extent that it depicts female homosexual desire as a finite phenomenon—a temporary phase in a larger pattern of heterosexual *Bildung*—the lesbian novel of adolescence is almost always dysphoric in tendency. [12]

In post-marital lesbian fiction, however, male homosocial bonds are generally presented—from the outset—as debilitated to the point of unrecuperability. Typically in such novels, it is the very failure of the heroine's marriage or heterosexual love affair that functions as the pretext for her conversion to homosexual desire. This conversion is radical and irreversible: once she discovers (usually ecstatically) her passion for women, there is no going back. We might call this "euphoric" lesbian counterplotting: it is an essentially comic, even utopian plot pattern. A new world is imagined in which male bonding has no place. Classic lesbian novels following the euphoric pattern include Jane Bowles's *Two Serious Ladies*, Jane Rule's *The Desert of the Heart*, and Patricia Highsmith's *The Price of Salt*, as well as numerous pulp romances of recent vintage, such as Ann Bannon's *Journey to a Woman* and Katherine V. Forrest's *An Emergence of Green*. In that it too begins with a failed marriage (that of Robin Vote and Felix Volkbein), even such a baroquely troubled work as *Nightwood*, paradoxically, might be considered euphoric in this respect: though its depiction of lesbian love is often malign, the novel takes for granted a world in which female erotic bonds predominate—so much so that the very possibility of male homosociality seems negated from the start.*

With its insouciant, sometimes coruscating satire on male bonding, *Summer Will Show* typifies the postmarital or conversion fiction: its energies are primarily comic and visionary. It is a novel of liberation. As Minna says to Sophia at one point: "You have run away. . . . You'll never go back now, you know. I've encouraged a quantity of people to run away, but I have never seen any one so decisively escaped as you" (217). Yet is this the whole story? Given that the novel concludes with Minna herself apparently slain on the barricades, a victim of Caspar (who in turn is the pawn of Frederick), how com-

---

*The reader may object, rightly, that the most famous lesbian novel of all, Radclyffe Hall's *The Well of Loneliness*, does not seem to fall clearly into either the euphoric or the dysphoric category. It may well be that we need to devise a new category—that of "lesbian epic"—to contain Hall's manic-depressive extravaganza. True, in that it manages to work unhappy variations on both the premarital and the postmarital plot types (Stephen's first love, Angela, is a married woman who refuses to leave her husband; her second, Mary, leaves Stephen in order to marry a male friend), *The Well of Loneliness* often leans in a dysphoric direction. Yet the introduction midway through the novel of the Natalie Barney character, Valérie Seymour, and Hall's tentative limnings of a larger lesbian society in Paris, also seem to promise an end to Stephen's intolerable "loneliness"—if only in some as yet ill-defined, unknown future. With its multiplying characters and subplots, constant shifts in setting and mood and powerfully "ongoing" narrative structure, *The Well* seems more a kind of Homeric or Tennysonian quest-fiction—a lesbian *Odyssey*—than a novel in the ordinary sense.

plete, finally, is what I am calling, perhaps too exuberantly, its "undoing" of the classic male homosocial plot?

That the ending of *Summer Will Show* poses a problem cannot be denied: Wendy Mulford, one of Townsend Warner's most astute critics, calls it an unconvincing "botch"—though not, interestingly, for any purely narratological reason. For Mulford, Minna's bayoneting by Caspar is symptomatic of Townsend Warner's own emotional confusion in the 1930s, over whether to devote herself to her writing or to revolutionary (specifically Marxist) political struggle. To the extent that Minna, the storytelling romantic, represents the potentially anarchical freedom of the artist, she has to be "sacrificed," Mulford argues, in order to "free the dedicated revolutionary" in Sophia, who functions here as a stand-in for the novelist herself. At the same time, Mulford conjectures, "[Townsend Warner's] unconscious was unable to consent to such a move"—hence the novel's descent into bathos and melodrama at this point.[13]

Yet Mulford already oversimplifies, I think, in assuming without question that Minna is dead. Granted, Minna seems to be dead (during the onslaught on the barricade Sophia sees Caspar's bayonet "jerk" in Minna's breast), yet, in a curious turnabout in the novel's final pages, Townsend Warner goes out of her way—seemingly gratuitously—to hint that she may in fact still be alive. Though unsuccessful, Sophia's attempts to locate Minna's body raise the possibility that her lover has survived: a witness to the scene on the barricades, Madam Guy, concedes that Minna was indeed alive when she was dragged away by soldiers; her daughter confirms it (397–98). Later visits to "all the places where enquiries might be made" turn up nothing, but the man who accompanies Sophia reminds her that the officials in charge may be misleading her on purpose—the implication being that her friend may in fact be held prisoner somewhere (399). The ambiguity is hardly resolved even at the last. When Sophia returns to Minna's apartment and takes up the *Communist Manifesto*, her peculiarly composed attitude seems as much one of waiting as of tragic desolation: far from being traumatized by seeing "the wine that Minna had left for her" or Minna's slippers on the floor, she merely sits down to read, as though Minna were at any moment about to return. The utopian tract she peruses in turn hints symbolically at the thematics of return: if we take seriously the analogy that Townsend

Warner has made throughout the novel between her heroine's political and sexual transformation, the inspiriting presence of the *Manifesto* here, with its promise of revolutionary hope resurrected, may also portend another kind of resurrection—that of Minna herself.

The novelist here seems to test how much implausibility we are willing to accept—for according to even the loosest standard of probability (such as might hold, say, in Victorian fiction) the possibility that Minna should survive her bayoneting by Caspar, an event which itself already strains credibility, must appear fanciful in the extreme. Yet it cannot be denied that Townsend Warner herself seems drawn back to the idea—almost, one feels, because it *is* incredible. Having offered us a plausible (or semiplausible) ending, she now hints, seemingly capriciously, at a far more unlikely plot turn, as if perversely determined to revert to the most fantastical kind of closure imaginable.

Without attempting to diminish any of the ambiguity here, I think Warner's restaging of her conclusion—this apparent inability to let go of the possibility of euphoric resolution however improbable such a resolution must seem—can tell us something useful, once again, about lesbian fiction. By its very nature lesbian fiction has—and can only have—a profoundly attenuated relationship with what we think of, stereotypically, as narrative verisimilitude, plausibility, or "truth to life." Precisely because it is motivated by a yearning for that which is, in a cultural sense, implausible—the subversion of male homosocial desire—lesbian fiction characteristically exhibits, even as it masquerades as "realistic" in surface detail, a strongly fantastical, allegorical, or utopian tendency. The more insistently it gravitates toward euphoric resolution, moreover, the more implausible—in every way—it may seem.

The problem with Townsend Warner's novel—if in fact it is a problem—is not so much that it forfeits plausibility at the end but that it forfeits it from the start. There is nothing remotely believable about Sophia Willoughby's transformation from "heiress of Blandamer" into lover of her husband's mistress and communist revolutionary, if by "believability" we mean conformity with the established mimetic conventions of canonical English and American fiction. The novelist herself seems aware of this, and without ever entirely abandoning the framing pretense of historicity (the references to real people and events, the "Berliozian" local color), often hints at the artificial, "as if" or hypothetical nature of the world her characters inhabit. Metaphorically speaking, everything in the novel has a slightly suspect, theatrical, even phantasmagorical air. Revolutionary Paris resembles a stage set: the rebels near Minna's house are arrayed like "comic opera bandits" (177), a bloody skirmish in the streets is a "clinching raree-show" (171). Trying to convince her to return to her husband, Sophia's aunt Léocadie becomes a "ballerina," with Frederick "the suave athletic partner, respectfully leading her round by one leg as she quivered on the tip-toe of the other" (203). Elsewhere Frederick is a "tenor" plotting with the "basso" Père Hyacinthe (192). The captivating Minna, in turn, is a "gifted tragedy actress" (217), a "play-acting Shylock" (212), or someone "in a charade" (268). Sometimes Minna leaves the human realm altogether, metamorphosing into something from fairy tale or myth—a "Medusa," a "herb-wife," a "siren," a "sorceress"—or a creature out of beast fable or Grandville cartoon. She is a "macaw," Sophia thinks, a "parrot," "some purple-plumaged bird of prey, her hooked nose impending," or perhaps the "sleekest" of cats (326). Her passion for Minna, Sophia concludes, is like the poet's—"of a birth as rare / As 'tis of object strange and high . . . begotten by despair / Upon impossibility" (289).

These built-in intimations of artifice and romance, of delight and high fakery, present on almost every page of *Summer Will Show*, work against the superficial historicism of the narrative, pushing it inexorably towards the fantastic. Of course a hankering after the fantastic is present elsewhere in Townsend Warner's writing: *Lolly Willowes*, we recall, begins as a seemingly straightforward tale about a spinster in an ordinary English village, but swerves abruptly into the marvellous when the spinster joins a coven of witches led by the Devil. Indeed the development of Townsend Warner's writing career as a whole suggests a progressive shifting away from realism toward the explicitly antimimetic modes of allegory and fable: in her last published stories, collected in *Kingdoms of Elfin*, she dispensed with human subjects entirely, choosing to commemorate instead the delicate passions of a race of elves.

Yet the fantastical element in *Summer Will Show*, is not, I think, simply a matter of authorial idiosyncracy. Other lesbian novels display the same oscillation between realistic and fabulous modes. One need only think again of *Orlando* or *Nightwood*, or, indeed, of Joanna Russ's *The Female Man*, Elizabeth Jolley's *Miss Peabody's Inheritance*, Lois Gould's *A Sea-Change*, Sarah Schulman's *After Delores*, Margaret Erhart's *Unusual Company*, Michelle Cliff's *No Telephone to Heaven*, or any of Jeanette Winterson's recent novels, to see how symptomatically lesbian fiction resists any simple recuperation as "realistic." Even as it gestures back at a supposedly familiar world of human experience, it almost invariably stylizes and estranges it—by presenting it parodistically, euphuistically, or in some other rhetorically heightened, distorted, fragmented, or phantasmagoric way. In the most extreme manifestation of this tendency, the pretence of mimesis collapses completely. In Monique Wittig's *Les Guérillères* or Sally Gearheart's *The Wanderground*, for example, two explicitly utopian lesbian novels, the fictional world itself is fantastically transfigured, becoming a kind of sublime Amazonian dream space: the marvellous inversion, in short, of that real world—"between men"—the rest of us inhabit.[14]

What then *is* a lesbian fiction? Taking Sylvia Townsend Warner's *Summer Will Show* as our paradigm, we can now begin to answer the question with which we started. Such a fiction will be, both in the ordinary and in a more elaborate sense, noncanonical. Like Townsend Warner's novel itself, the typical lesbian fiction is likely to be an underread, even unknown, text—and certainly an underappreciated one. It is likely to stand in a satirical, inverted, or parodic relationship to more famous novels of the past—which is to say that it will exhibit an ambition to displace the so-called canonical works that have preceded it. In the case of *Summer Will Show*, Townsend Warner's numerous literary parodies—of Flaubert, Eliot, Brontë, Dickens, and the rest—suggest a wish to displace, in particular, the supreme texts of nineteenth-century realism, as if to infiltrate her own fiction among them as a kind of subversive, inflammatory, pseudo-canonical substitute.

But, most important, by plotting against what Eve Sedgwick has called the "plot of male homosociality," the archetypal lesbian fiction decanonizes, so to speak, the canonical structure of desire itself. Insofar as it documents a world in which men are "between women" rather than vice versa, it is an insult to the conventional geometries of fictional eros. It dismantles the real, as it were, in a search for the not-yet-real, something unpredicted and unpredictable. It is an assault on the banal: a retriangulating of triangles. As a consequence, it often looks odd, fantastical, implausible, "not there"—utopian in aspiration if not design. It is, in a word, imaginative. This is why, perhaps, like lesbian desire itself, it is still difficult for us to acknowledge—even when (Queen Victoria notwithstanding) it is so palpably, so plainly, there.

5

THE

DIARIES OF

ANNE LISTER

The question of whether or not women in earlier centuries engaged in sexual relations with one another continues, happily, to bedevil the historians of sexuality. How many times have we been informed—seemingly with ponderous finality—that while various eighteenth- and nineteenth-century women may have had impassioned friendships with one another, may even have slept for years in the same bed with a beloved "companion" or "darling" or "sweet love," lesbian eroticism As We Know It Today (the kind presumably involving soft lighting, old Dusty Springfield records, multiple orgasms, and so on) was still very much A Thing of The Future? Only with the rise of sexology and new categories of sexual deviance in the late nineteenth and early twentieth centuries, has it been argued, did physical love between women become a conceptual possibility or, indeed, a part of real women's lives. And yet the past itself—or so some recent archival discoveries suggest—may have other and more provocative tales to tell.

Consider the celebrated case of Lady Eleanor Butler and Sarah Ponsonby, better known as the "Ladies of Llangollen," who eloped to Wales together in 1778 and lived in a cottage there in seemingly virginal bliss for over fifty years. Ponsonby and Butler might be said to emblematize the kind of depressingly chaste female-female bonding modern social historians have become so fond of discovering in past epochs. Indeed so often has their story been trotted out as proof of the noncarnal nature of eighteenth- and nineteenth-century female friendships, one might almost speak of them as the official "mascots" of the no-sex-before-1900 school. Writes Elizabeth Mavor in *The Ladies of Llangollen: A Study in Romantic Friendship* (1971), the "obvious Freudian interpretation" is a "blunt instrument" for understanding tender attachments like that between the Ladies: the conventions of female friendship in the late eighteenth and early nineteenth century "allowed for a dimension of sympathy between women that would not now be possible outside an avowedly lesbian connection." Such relationships could remain innocent—even "Edenic"—because they had not yet been "biologically and thus prejudicially defined."[1] Other writers, such as Lillian Faderman in *Surpassing the Love of Men: Romantic Friendship between Women from the Renaissance to the Present* (1981), have concurred; according to Faderman, who refers to them as "the great 'success story' of romantic friendship," the Ladies whiled away their days together receiving visitors, arranging flower bouquets, translating Tasso, and pottering about in the garden, without—she implies—ever getting down and dirty.[2]

In a sense, of course, the Ladies themselves ("those abnormally self-advertised old frumps," as one later nineteenth-century writer called them) are partly responsible for their mascot standing in the literature of female romantic friendship. Virtually from the moment their relationship became public knowledge—the *General Evening Post* published a somewhat prurient description of their "sweet retreat" at Plas Newydd in 1790—the Ladies engaged in a discreet public relations campaign, a sort of back-and-fill operation, designed to diffuse any air of scandal and sexual innuendo hovering about them.

Beginning with the letter they wrote to the Tory politician Edmund Burke asking for advice about how to prosecute the *General Evening Post* for its "libels" on their relationship, Ponsonby and Butler worked hard at presenting their intimacy to the world as the veritable epitome of celibate devotion—not least by cultivating friendships with those likely to defend them in print. These efforts paid off: in 1796 their friend Anna Seward published a poetical tribute, *Llangollen Vale*, eulogizing the "vestal lustre" of their "sacred Friendship"; and later, in a sonnet dedicated to them in 1824, no less a figure than William Wordsworth celebrated that blessed "Vale of Friendship"

> where, faithful to a low roofed Cot
> On Deva's banks, ye have abode so long;
> Sisters in love, a love allowed to climb
> Even on this earth, above the reach of Time![3]

And indeed the myth of Ponsonby and Butler's "sisterly" attachment has proved extraordinarily durable over time. In the well-known essay she published about them in *Ces Plaisirs* (*The Pure and the Impure*) in 1932, the French writer Colette not only reiterated the traditional view of the Ladies as "two faithful spinsters," untouched by any form of "Sapphic libertinage," but offered their story as a paradigm of that "unresolved and undemanding sensuality" characteristic (she hoped to convince her readers) of love between women. Such "perilously fragile" desire, wrote Colette, typically sought (and found) its consummation in a mere "exchange of glances, an arm laid on a shoulder, and is thrilled by the odor of sun-warmed wheat caught in a head of hair." Eleanor Butler's monotonous, reverential journal reminiscences about her "darling Beloved" (collected in a memorial volume in 1930) offered, Colette argued, the perfect illustration of this ascetical brand of passion: the Ladies' delight in one another was at bottom complacent, narcissistic, and "nourished on very little":

How marvelously compact the repetition of days, repeated like the reflections of a lamp in a perspective of mirrors! Perhaps this love, which according to some people is outrageous, escapes the changing seasons and the wanings of love by being controlled with invisible severity, nourished on very little, permitted to live gropingly and without a goal, its unique flower being a mutual trust such as that other love can never plumb or comprehend, but only envy; and so great is such a love that by its grace a half century can pass by like "a day of delicious and exquisite retirement."[4]

In this placid obliviousness to "the feverish pleasures of the senses," Colette concluded, the Ladies of Llangollen were the exemplary "Sapphic" couple—basking in their "pure but irregular passion" in a manner "as gentle as tame doves."[5]

And yet doubts remain. For those of us who continue to wonder what this insufferable pair *really* did in bed (and whether it may not indeed be time to revise the often cloying "romantic friendship" model) it is both amusing and enlightening to discover that at least one contemporary was similarly bothered. Here is Anne Lister (1791–1840), author of a set of voluminous diaries recently unearthed in an obscure Yorkshire archive, speculating about the sex life of the Ladies in an entry from 1822:

> Foolscap sheet from M—. . . . She seems much interested about Lady Eleanor Butler & Miss Ponsonby and I am agreeably surprised (never dreaming of such a thing) at her observation, "The account of your visit is the prettiest narrative I have read. You have at once excited & gratified my curiosity. Tell me if you think their regard has always been platonic & if you ever believed pure friendship could be so exalted. If you do, I shall think there are brighter amongst mortals than I ever believed there were . . . " I cannot help thinking surely it was not platonic. Heaven forgive me, but I look within myself & doubt. I feel the infirmity of our nature and hesitate to pronounce such attachments uncemented by something more tender still than friendship. (210)[6]

Wrote Lister after visiting Plas Newydd—where she was struck by a "*je ne sais quoi*" in the manner of the sixty-seven year-old Ponsonby—there was indeed "something in their story & in all I have heard about them here that, added to other circumstances, makes a deep impression" (201).

Lister had reason to be excited—for she was herself more than a little acquainted with that "something" other than friendship of which she (fleetingly) suspected the Ladies. The unmarried daughter of provincial gentry, who for many years led an outwardly respectable life at the family seat, Shibden Hall, in West Yorkshire, Lister had been embroiled from adolescence onward in a series of passionate physical relationships with women. These she described at length—and on occasion lubriciously—in a secret "crypt hand," or code, in her diaries. Discovered in 1981 by the researcher Helena Whitbread, who subsequently transcribed them and published a selection from them in 1988 and a second volume of extracts in 1992, Lister's journals cast an altogether new light on the "romantic friendship" issue. Not only do her often ticklish revelations challenge assumptions about the supposed sexual "innocence" of women in earlier centuries, they offer a spectacular rebuke to the no-lesbians-before-1900 myth. Whether or not the Ladies of Llangollen were the pristine beings of historiographic fantasy (and the jury is still out on *them*) Anne Lister most decidedly was not—and in the gaiety and explicitness of her divergence commands attention.

The story told in the diaries is indeed a startling one—not least because Lister's world seems at first glance so familiar: very much the cosy domestic universe of a Jane Austen novel. In the diaries composed between 1817 and 1824, for example, the years available to us in Whitbread's first volume, we see Lister engaging in all the conventional ladylike pursuits one associates with Austen heroines: she visits with local Halifax gentry, plays backgammon and whist with her aunt and uncle Lister (with whom she lives), does needlework, practices the flute, and attempts to teach herself Euclidean geometry. Like Emma Woodhouse, Lister is a terrific snob, and enjoys recording in her journal the various failings of close friends and acquaintances. The Misses Greenwood and their friends are "a vulgar set" from whom she is glad to escape; one Miss Fairfax is "very handsome, but shockingly disfigured with out-of-curl ringlets literally almost 1/2 yd long, & an awkward dancer with elbows like skewered pinions" (173). The unfortunate Staveleys are a "bold, boisterous, vulgar" lot, and Mrs. Staveley "slatternly," with eccentricities that fail to amuse the ever-social-climbing Lister: "Met her walking one day in the town with her hands under her petticoat & she pulled out 2 great muffins" (226).

But one is soon aware of a kind of surreal slippage out of the ordinary. In one entry from 1818, Lister mentions in passing "how the people generally remark, as I pass along, how much I am like a man." Out on an evening walk (to the evocatively named Cunnery Lane) she is harassed by some laborers: "three men said, as usual, 'That's a man' & one axed [*sic*] 'Does your cock stand?' " (48–49). She is melancholy afterwards—"I know not how it is but I feel low this evening"—but is later is comforted (as they lie in bed) by her friend M—, who in "speaking of my manners, owned they were not masculine but such was my form, voice & style of conversation, such a peculiar flattery & attention did I shew [to young women], that if this sort of thing was not carried off by my talents & cleverness, I should be disgusting" (116). Her demeanor is "not all masculine," Lister herself comments a few entries later, "but rather softly gentleman-like. I know how to please girls" (136).

Portrait of Anne Lister (1781–1840). *Courtesy of Calderdale Museums, Yorkshire.*

She becomes obsessed with a pretty young woman named Miss Browne, whom she romantically rechristens "Kallista," after the character played by Mrs. Siddons in Rowe's *The Fair Penitent*. "Slept very ill last night. Did nothing but dream of Miss Browne; of being at their house; hearing her play on the piano & witnessing the vulgarity of her mother. I wish I could get the girl out of my head" (42). Since she is loath to invite Miss Browne to Shibden Hall (their families are not on visiting terms) Lister takes to lingering in a lane near Miss Browne's house and accompanying her to church. On one of these occasions she asks Miss Browne if she likes the poetry of Lord Byron. "Yes, perhaps too well," is the coquettish reply, after which Lister contemplates sending "the fair charmer" an anonymous "Cornelian heart, with a copy of his lines on the subject" (42). "I could soon be in love with the girl," she confides to her journal, and fantasizes making some favorable "impression on her in the amatory way" (75).

Miss Browne appears to respond: "she said she had thought of me last night," Lister records in February of 1819, "but so much that it prevented her sleeping & she must not think so much of me after going to bed in the future" (77). Indeed, during one particularly involved conversation (outside the Halifax lending library), Miss Browne confesses to having "strange thoughts" and to wishing Lister were a "gent" (78). Before long, the pair are taking lengthy walks on the moor and engaging in heavy flirtation—complete with some inventive fetish-play involving one of Lister's protobutch sartorial accouterments:

> She mentioned on the moor my taking off the leather strap put through the handle of my umbrella, which made it look like a gentleman's. I said I would do it if she asked me but not otherwise. She asked & I did it instantly. Surely she must like my society & would be more or less than woman were she unmoved & unpleased by my attentions. (80)

"I must mind I do not get into a scrape," writes Lister in a flush of erotic confidence; "wishing I was a gent; I can make her believe anything, etc; bespeaks my influence, & a few more walks & perhaps she will understand her feelings better" (79).

This particular "scrape," however, was not to be. Though Lister succeeded on one occasion in kissing her would-be inamorata "on her lips, a very little moistly," she was dismayed when Miss Browne abruptly announced her engagement to a certain Mr. Kelly. The lovely "Kallista," Lister concluded, was rather "stupidish" after all, and except for her "good looks & character for amiability" had little to say for herself (72). When the two met again after Miss Browne's marriage, Lister was polite and noncommittal, though noted with secret pleasure that the new Mrs. Kelly still "now & then rather coloured when I spoke to her" (192).

Lister took the disappointment with equanimity, one suspects, because she was hardly at a loss for other company. Throughout the period of her flirtation with Miss Browne, as numerous remarks in her diary make clear, she was also embroiled in several other dalliances, including three full-blown (if intermittent) sexual affairs. The most casual of these seems to have been with Anne Belcombe, who appears in several (somewhat cryptic) entries in November and December 1820, when she and Lister are both guests at Langton Hall, the country home of a mutual friend. At one point during this bizarre sojourn (the house party seems entirely made up of unmarried young women flirting wildly with one another), Lister installs herself in Belcombe's bedroom and proceeds to act "rather lover-like, reminding her of former days." Belcombe feigns displeasure, contending that such sex-play is "wrong," but nonetheless lets Lister kiss her breasts. Alas, notes Lister in her journal, "neither she nor her room seemed very sweet to my nose." By the next night, however, matters have improved: coming again to Miss Belcombe's room, the amorous Lister tells her that she has "a pain in her knees" ("my expression to her for desire") and the two, amid giggles, are surreptitiously united (139–41).

Far more important to Lister, however, were two other lovers—Isabella Norcliffe ("Tib") and Anne Belcombe's sister Marianne ("M—"). By 1817 Lister had already been involved with both in long-standing and clearly physical relationships. The affair with "Tib," a frequent visitor to Shibden Hall, seems to have been relatively untroubled, despite Tib's predilection for drink and snuff and staying in bed until mid-afternoon. Tib was devoted to Lister (despite Lister's obvious inconstancies), and in November 1819 professed a willingness to marry her "in disguise at the altar" (105). (One presumes that what is meant—in this somewhat obscure yet intriguing entry—is that the masculine-looking Lister would have disguised herself as a man during the ceremony.)[7] But at the same time the relationship seems to have lacked a certain erotic piquancy. "A kiss of Tib, both last night & this morning," writes Lister in October 1821, "but she cannot give me much pleasure & I think we are both equally calm in our feelings on these occasions" (170).

100

THE DIARIES OF
ANNE LISTER

Not so the liaison with the ambiguously seductive "M—," a married woman with whom Lister had been passionately embroiled since 1812. Lister's descriptions of their numerous sexual contacts (all carried on, apparently, without the knowledge of M—'s husband) are indeed remarkably charged, once one gets used to the diarist's sometimes curious Regency lingo. Lister speaks of being "on the amoroso," having "the erotics," or feeling "in the amatory way" with M—: a "kiss" is her codeword for an orgasm. "Went to M—but somehow did not manage a good kiss. Refused to promise till I had really felt that she was my wife. Went to her a second time. Succeeded better" (159). "Two kisses last night, one almost immediately after the other, before we went to sleep" (194). "We drew together, made love & had one of the most delightfully long, tender kisses we have ever yet had" (293).*

M—, for her part, seems to have been skilled at saying the right thing at the right time. Witness Lister's entry for November 18, 1819:

> From the kiss she gave me it seemed as if she loved me as fondly as ever. By & by, we seemed to drop asleep but, by & by, I perceived she would like another kiss & she whispered, "Come again a bit, Freddy." For a little while I pretended sleep. In fact, it was inconvenient. But soon, I got up a second time, again took off, went to her a second time &, in spite of all, she really gave me pleasure, & I told her no one had ever given me kisses like hers.   (105)

And again: "Two last night: M—spoke in the very act. 'Ah,' said she, 'Can you ever love anyone else?' She knows how to heighten the pleasure of our intercourse. She often murmurs, 'Oh, how delicious,' just at the very moment. All her kisses are good ones" (351).

Sex apart, however, the relationship was hardly a satisfying one. Though pledging loyalty to "Fred" (as she called Lister), M—worried aloud that their liaison was "unnatural" and was perpetually afraid of being found out. She was troubled by her lover's masculine

---

*A skeptical reader might object that here, as in the famous song, "a kiss is just a kiss." But consider Lister's entry for December 14, 1822: "I had a very good kiss last night. Tib had not a very good one. . . . I have been perpetually in horrors for fear of infecting Tib. I wonder whether the discharge is at all venereal or not?" (230). Here both the unusual syntax and Lister's train of thought—moving directly from the "kiss" to the possibility of venereal infection—offer strong evidence, it seems to me, for the code meaning I have suggested. In addition, Lister knew French well, and would undoubtedly have known the double sense of the verb *baiser*, which means both to kiss and to fuck.

appearance and resisted Lister's subtle yet persistent efforts to separate her from her husband. In turn, Lister (who was as romantic as
she was concupiscent) sometimes found M—short on sensibility.
"The want of a thousand little delicate notices in her letters, of what I
have written & of what she might know I have felt," she writes in one
low mood, "often makes me fear she has not that fineness, that romantic elegance of feeling that I admire. . . . Perhaps I require
too much. It must be an elegant mind joint with a heart distilling tenderness at every pore that can alone make me happy" (265). In 1821,
both women became infected with a venereal disease M—(they believed) had received from her husband; Lister, in turn, gave the infection to the hapless Tib. (Lister's fruitless search for a cure for this
affliction—both for herself and for her lovers—makes for one of the
more somber undercurrents of the diary.) After 1824, when Lister
began a series of solitary European travels (the point at which the first
volume of diaries end), both relationships waned.

What to make of such sensational goings on? Regarding what she
referred to as her "oddity," the fact that she could not live happily
without the emotional and sexual "rousing" that women supplied
her, Lister seems to have been remarkably self-aware and guilt-free.
She and M—, it is true, sometimes fretted over the legality of their
sensual relation—usually before or after a particularly gratifying
"kiss." "No soffistry [sic]," wrote Lister in 1819, after a feverish night
with M—, "could gloss over the criminality of our connection" (104).
But it is interesting to note that the "crime" Lister had in mind at such
moments was usually adultery rather than homosexuality: "I felt that
she was another man's wife." And even then, or so she often tried to
convince M—, she thought their liaison justified by the fact that M—'s
unhappy marriage was no more than "legal prostitution" (104).

Regarding love between women in general, Lister was beyond
even these minor scruples. In her diary she frequently observed that
the love of men was not for her: "I love, & only love, the fairer sex &
thus beloved by them in turn, my heart revolts from any other love
than theirs" (145). A great reader of Rousseau—she often quotes the
Confessions—she was convinced that her passion for women, while
certainly unusual, was nonetheless sanctioned by nature. Her yearning for female company was not "taught" or "fictitious"—i.e.,
learned out of books—but something altogether "instinctive" and
"natural" (297). "I do not like to be too long estranged from you some-

times," she wrote to M—in 1821, "for, Mary, there is a nameless tie in
that soft intercourse which blends us into one & makes me feel that
you are mine. There is no feeling like it. There is no pledge which
gives such sweet possession" (145–46). The heart, Lister believed,
followed its own sacred laws.

At the same time, a modern reader cannot help but be struck by
some of the more complicated aspects of Lister's attempts at self-
definition. Her masculine identification was intense—manifest not
only in an idiosyncratic appearance (she dressed entirely in black and
early on adopted what she called her "gentlemanly" manners) but
also in astonishingly direct sexual fantasies: "Foolish fancying about
Caroline Greenwood, meeting her on Skircoat Moor, taking her into
a shed that is there & being connected with her. Supposing myself in
men's clothes and having a penis, tho' nothing more" (151). Working
with her gardener and some boys in the grounds around Shibden
Hall, she notes that "all this ordering & work & exercise seemed to
excite my manly feelings. I saw a pretty young girl go up the lane
& desire rather came over me" (267). And in an entry from 1823, musing over the relationship between two women friends, she wonders
somewhat salaciously whether one of them has ever used a "phallus"
on the other. A highly self-conscious penis envy—to put it most
provocatively—seems to have shaped Lister's sexual personality, as it
has indeed shaped much of the secret history (and transgressive pleasure) of lesbian eroticism down through the centuries.[8]

Similarly, for all of Lister's sense of the "untaught" nature of her
yearnings, her sexual career was richly mediated by cultural influ-
ences. Classical literature, particularly the satires of the Roman writers Juvenal and Martial (which she had taught herself to read in Latin), supplied her with a useful knowledge of ancient homosexual acts
and a historic precedent for her own behavior.[9] It also functioned for
her as a sort of secret language or semaphor. In one of the most interesting sequences in the diaries, Lister makes the acquaintance of a
neighborhood bluestocking named Miss Pickford, who, like herself,
is masculine in looks and sentimentally attached to a young woman, a
Miss Threlfall. Somewhat in the way that two lesbians today meeting
for the first time might make coy "testing" allusions to Jodie Foster,
say, or Joan Armatrading, in order to confirm one another's sexual
orientation, Lister and Pickford carry on long euphemistic discus-

sions about the meaning of certain lubricious passages in the Latin classics. Lister never reveals the extent of her own homosexual activity explicitly, but she and "dear Pic" (who also goes by the name of "Frank") reach an understanding: "Miss Pickford has read the Sixth Satyr of Juvenal. She understands these matters well enough" (268).

The poetry of Byron was another important if paradoxical source of self-knowledge. The scandalous *Don Juan* was a special erotic talisman; Lister was gratified to hear that even the high-minded Miss Ponsonby (of the aforementioned Ladies of Llangollen) had confessed to reading the first canto.[10] Much of Lister's compulsive sexual adventurism seems to have been unconsciously modeled on Byron's; she identified with him both in his role as arch-romantic and as the most notorious womanizer of the early nineteenth century. (Ironically, like most of her contemporaries, she knew Byron only as the heterosexual rake; our current view of him has been richly complicated by new evidence of his own lifelong homoeroticism.) Lister's often melodramatic travails with the "fair sex," her all-black clothing and, later, the self-imposed exile and journeying to exotic lands (she died of a fever in the Caucasus in her fiftieth year) all bespeak this subliminal Byronic fixation.

Lister's fascination with Byron was not of course unique (the poet was after all at the height of his fame in the early 1820s) but it points up nonetheless an important theme in lesbian cultural history. One could compile a fat book on the (mostly) unacknowledged role that Byronic posturing has played in lesbian self-fashioning over the past two centuries—from Lister's romantic borrowings to the flamboyant dandyism of George Sand, Radclyffe Hall, Vita Sackville-West, or the painter Gluck, through to the more stylized and subversive chic of a Marianne Moore or a Janet Flanner. Certainly by the early twentieth century a sort of "fetishized" Byronism had become a constituent element in lesbian visual iconography: witness the dark hair, moody good looks (complete with scar), and tailored men's clothing of Radclyffe Hall's heroine Stephen Gordon in *The Well of Loneliness* (1928). (Stephen even shares Byron's last name.) In our own day the hidden archetype has surfaced once again—sometimes curiously overlaid with the image of Elvis Presley—in singer k.d. lang's brooding, enigmatic profile, and in those potent images of virile, dark-haired butches gracing the pages of *On Our Backs*.[11]

The power of the Byronic archetype, or so Lister's story suggests, may lie in its usefulness as a sort of enabling erotic fiction. Heterosexual male rakery and lesbian desire have often been covertly connected in the lesbian imagination; even today, figures such as Byron, Don Juan, Casanova, and Lothario crop up constantly—in varying guises—in sexually themed lesbian writing. (One thinks of the Don Juanish female narrator of Jane DeLynn's 1990 *Don Juan in the Village*, haunting the lesbian bars of New York City in search of pickups, or of the main character in Jeanette Winterson's 1992 *Written on the Body*, who though apparently a woman, is named Lothario.) Lister herself identified not only with Byron but also—in the studied pursuit of "Kallista"—with both Lothario and Lovelace, the famous seducer in Samuel Richardson's *Clarissa*.*

Such cross-gender self-mythologizing, and, in particular, the symbolic assumption of the identity of the male libertine, has had a shaping role to play, I would argue, in the cultural evolution of female homosexual identity. In a society that typically ghosts or occludes images of women desiring women, the homosexually inclined woman will inevitably be attracted to the next best thing: to images of *men* desiring women. In the transgressive figure of the rake, whose obsession with women is so great as to put him at odds with his society—he has no "job" or social function other than his lust and often breaks the law in order to achieve his ends—the lesbian finds, as it were, her heterosexual twin: the outlaw male whose subversive longing in some way mirrors and licenses her own. Precisely by drawing on the myth of a Byron or Don Juan, of the man ruled by his desire for women, inventive nineteenth-century women like Anne Lister found a way "into" their own transgressive desire: the one kind of sexual unorthodoxy sanctioned the other.[12]

Which leads us back, by a sort of roundabout, to the point at which we began—the Ladies of Llangollen and the issue of romantic friendship.

---

*In choosing the name Kallista for Miss Browne, Lister was implicitly associating herself with Lothario, Kallista's lover in Rowe's *The Fair Penitent* (1703). (Given Lister's familiarity with the Roman poets, she may also have associated the name, if only unconsciously, with the gender-bending story of Callisto, attendant to the goddess Diana, who in book 2 of Ovid's *Metamorphoses* is raped by Jupiter in the shape of Diana.) Elsewhere, Lister's habitual use of the epithet "fair charmer" to refer to Miss Browne recalls Lovelace's use of the same epithet to refer to Clarissa.

A basic assumption of the no-lesbians-before-1900 school, as I noted at the outset, is that it took the rise of nineteenth- and twentieth-century sexology, with its morbidifying categories, to give the lesbian a sense of sexual identity. As Lillian Faderman puts it in *Odd Girls and Twilight Lovers: A History of Lesbian Life in Twentieth-Century America*, "the sexologists were certainly the first to construct the conception of the lesbian, to call her into being as a special category." Only in the twentieth century, she claims, "through the legacy of Freud and all his spiritual offspring" have we become so "hyper-sophisticated concerning sex" that "whether or not two women who find themselves passionately attached choose to identify themselves as lesbians today, they must at least examine the possibility of sexual attraction between them and decide whether or not to act upon it. Such sexual self-consciousness could easily have been avoided in earlier eras."[13]

Yet the conventional notion that most women remained blissfully ignorant about sex before Freud and his ilk came along may be worth challenging. As far as lesbianism goes, there are many routes through which one may arrive at self-understanding. Certainly in Lister's imaginative appropriation of various conventional erotic models—including the model of male libertinism—we sense an erotic self-awareness and intentionality as "modern-seeming" in its own way as anything on offer in the twentieth century. Indeed, for all her romantic posing, one often detects a waggish irony in Lister's manner—a self-conscious delight in stratagem and role-playing and giving it back to the girls with the "speaking eyes" (232). "Oh, women, women!" she exclaims gaily in 1824; "I am always taken up with some girl or other" (346).

Lister seems, moreover, to have shared this sophisticated attitude with many of her female acquaintances—and not only the various Yorkshire Circes who fell gladly or madly into bed with her. One of the most striking things about reading Lister's diaries—once one gets over the first shock of their sexual frankness—is the degree of acceptance with which Lister's friends and associates appear to have regarded her, despite her obvious mannishness and eccentricity. She seems to have been surrounded by people who not only recognized her peculiar emotional makeup but took it discreetly in stride. Her aunt Lister is an interesting figure in this regard. Living with Lister at Shibden Hall, she seems to have known exactly what was going on between Lister and M—, for example, and was even aware of her

niece's venereal disease. Yet never once, to judge by Lister's affectionate entries about her, did she express anything other than genial toler-
ance of Lister's behavior. Similarly, when Lister records a laughing
conversation with one of her aunt's friends—"Mrs. Priestley said she
always told people I was natural, but she thought nature was in an
odd freak when she made me" (347)—one has the sense of a female
culture rather more worldly and comprehending than one might expect to find in the dark ages before sexology.

Lister, it is true, was not always likeable. Her politics were reactionary, her taste absurd (she doted on Thomas Moore's *Lalla Rookh*),
and she often treated her lovers disingenuously—especially the long-
suffering Tib. She could be comically vain and hypochondriacal:
"Three walnuts after dinner must have disagreed with me. About 7
1/2, felt a universal sensation of pricking & swelling, & went in a hurry to bed. Crimson all over me. Every feature double its size & much
pain in my head & stomach. Lay till 10 1/2 . . . (tho' still very crimson & swell'd)" (67). And yet she becomes in her own way a woman
compelling respect—precisely on account of her sexual urgency and
the honesty and immediacy with which she recorded it:

'Tis high time to go to bed. I have been musing this hour past, & it is
just one. There is one thing that I wish for. There is one thing without
which my happiness in this world seems impossible. I was not born to
live alone. I must have the object with me & in loving & being loved, I
could be happy.   (250)

Rediscovered after nearly two hundred years, the story of this human need—and the energetic way Lister sought to satisfy it—is
nothing short of a revelation. Here indeed an alternative to the Ladies
of Llangollen and the lugubrious myths of lesbian asexuality. Here
indeed (as if we needed it) another proof that truth is stranger than
fiction. As a character in a recent lesbian novel observes, "When you
love women the way I do, when your life has been built around the
pursuit of women's love, there are a hundred moments bathed in
shadows cast from a fire or candle or the strange yellow light of an old
kitchen."[14] What Anne Lister's diaries suggest is that such grateful
pursuit is not new—that the embodied love of woman for woman has
been a part of life far longer than many have assumed, and that we
have only now begun to uncover its remarkable, lyrical history.

6

MARIE

ANTOINETTE

OBSESSION

What might it mean to suffer from Marie Antoinette obsession? In the approved manner of the late nineteenth-century sexologists, Krafft-Ebing, say, or Havelock Ellis, let us begin anecdotally, with several case histories.

In 1900 the Swiss psychologist Theodore Flournoy, professor of psychology at the University of Geneva, published *From India to the Planet Mars*—an investigation of the case of "Hélène Smith," a celebrated spirit medium active in Genevan spiritualist circles in the 1890s. While in a state of hypnotic trance Smith claimed to have had three previous incarnations—as a fourteenth-century Indian princess named Simandini, as an inhabitant of the planet Mars, and as Marie Antoinette, the doomed queen of France. During her se-

Portrait of Marie Antoinette by Elisabeth Vigée-Lebrun.
Courtesy of Wildenstein and Co.

ances, which she conducted with the help of a mysterious "control" from the spirit world named Leopold, who communicated by rapping on a table, Smith was able to "relive" these past lives in precise, often bizarre detail. Flournoy, an experimental psychologist with an interest in spiritualism and the occult, began observing Smith's trances in 1894, and in his book offered an account of these visionary "cycles" while also speculating along Freudian lines about their psychological origins.[1]

The "Hindoo" and "Martian" cycles were outlandish enough: in fourteenth-century India, Smith revealed, she had lived at the court of a ruler named Sivrouka; on Mars, she had been an individual named Pouzé Ramié. While entranced, she was able to produce long passages of automatic writing—sometimes in a language resembling Sanskrit (of which she claimed no conscious knowledge) and sometimes in a so-called Martian dialect. Flournoy devotes several chapters of meticulous philological analysis to these fascinatingly cryptic compositions.[2] Yet the Marie Antoinette cycle was, if anything, even more colorful. Were one to give it an attention proportionate to its importance in Smith's "somnambulic life," Flournoy observed, a hundred pages would not suffice.[3]

Smith's royal "romance" typically began with a communication from Leopold, her spirit control. Leopold, it was revealed, was an otherworldly manifestation of the eighteenth-century Italian magician Joseph Balsamo, otherwise known as Cagliostro, who had once—at least according to Smith—been passionately in love with Marie Antoinette. While under Leopold's spiritual control, which she experienced as a kind of possession, Smith spoke in "the deep bass voice of a man," used masculine gestures, and frequently professed her love for the ill-fated French queen in an Italian accent. Soon, however, she progressed to reincarnating the spirit of Antoinette herself. At such moments, she would pantomime with a handkerchief or an imaginary fan, pretend to take snuff, mimic the action of throwing back a train, and address those present as though speaking to members of a court. On one occasion, she identified two male sitters as "Philippe d'Orléans" and "Mirabeau" and engaged them in conversation on eighteenth-century political matters. At another seance in 1896, Flournoy reports, Smith addressed "touching exhortations to a lady present whom she took for the Princesse de Lamballe." This poignant encounter, "Leopold" later informed witnesses, was a "reproduction of the last evening which the unhappy queen, sustained by her companion in captivity, passed in this world."[4]

Admittedly, Smith's royal incarnation had its ludicrous aspects. Spectators sometimes caught out "Her Majesty" in peculiar anachronisms. At one seance attended by Flournoy in 1896, Smith accepted a cigarette from the man she called "Philippe," despite the fact that she did not smoke in ordinary life. "But the remarks of the persons present upon the historical untruthfulness of this feature," Flournoy notes, "must have registered, and bore fruit, since at the following seances she did not seem to understand the use of tobacco in that form; she accepted, on the other hand, with eagerness, a pinch of imaginary snuff, which almost immediately brought about by auto-suggestion a series of sneezes admirably successful."[5] When participants spoke of such things as telephones or bicycles, Smith-as-Antoinette would at first seem to comprehend their meaning, then (observing "the smile of the sitters") would somewhat suspiciously feign "sudden ignorance and astonishment in regard to it."[6] Even the skeptical Flournoy, however, was forced to admit that Smith's embodiment of the queen was often convincing, if not moving. "When the royal trance is complete," he wrote, "no one can fail to note the grace, elegance, distinction, majesty sometimes, which shine forth in Hélène's every attitude and gesture."

> She has verily the bearing of a queen. The more delicate shades of expression, a charming amiability, condescending hauteur, pity, indifference, overpowering scorn flit successively over her countenance and are manifested in her bearing, to the filing by of the courtiers who people her dream. . . . Every thing of this kind, which cannot be described, is perfect in its ease and naturalness.[7]

However deeply rooted in hysteria, he concluded, it was all a most "sparkling romance."

Seven years after the publication of *From India to the Planet Mars*, in June 1907, a writer in the British *Journal of the Society for Psychical Research* described a similar fantasy having to do with Marie Antoinette. Under the heading "Dream Romances," the anonymous author—who allowed herself to be identified only as someone of "strongly developed artistic sensibilities"—confessed how she had been haunted since youth by an apparition that she believed to be the ghost of the French queen. The haunting had begun in early childhood, when a "strange woman" in a long, old-fashioned dress, with "masses of grey hair, done up in a fashion quite unlike to the people I was accustomed to see," appeared in her bedroom and tenderly caressed her face as she lay in bed.[8] Her mother's attempts to convince her that there was no such woman failed: in fact, the apparition returned even when her mother kept watch in the room. Soon the writer came to look upon her nightly visitor as a "secret friend," and especially admired her beautiful kindly face and deep blue eyes. These last, she says, were "brilliant like stars, though at times the lids looked very heavy, as though she had been crying." The apparition never spoke to her, she recollected, but this seemed natural to her at the time: "I *felt* that we understood one another."[9]

Gradually the conviction came over her that her spectral visitor was none other than Marie Antoinette. Espying her mother dressing one evening for a masquerade ball, she recognized her mother's costume—"of the Louis XVI period"—as identical to that of her silent friend. She became obsessed with reading about the French Revolution and developed a private cult around the queen's memory. In her teens, she says, she "spent hours at the South Kensington Museum, gazing at Marie-Antoinette's bust, examining her toilet-table with its little rouge pots, etc." "I can honestly say my happiest hours were spent in contemplating these treasures, though it was always with an emotion bordering on tears that I faced the bust of the queen."[10]

Later on, though the night-time visits gradually ceased, she continued to have fantastic dreams and waking visions in which she saw the woman she believed to be Marie Antoinette performing characteristic actions—playing cards, for example, "with Louis XVI and Madame Elizabeth," or listening to music, seemingly "in a palace or else a park." Once, while in a hotel room at Margate, she had a vision of the queen imprisoned in the Conciergerie in the final days of her life—her expression "haggard and agonized," her hair entirely white, and her eyes fixed in "a strange, glassy look." When the writer rushed forward to embrace her, the apparition abruptly vanished. A few years later, upon visiting Versailles for the first time, the writer experienced an eerie sense of déjà vu and a dreadful "choking sensation" upon entering the queen's former apartments.

During these hallucinatory episodes, the writer says, she sometimes saw herself as well, though oddly enough as a boy, "never as a girl." Her most terrifying vision of this kind came one night at a hotel in Paris on the rue St. Honoré. There she dreamed that she saw a huge crowd assembled outside the window and Marie Antoinette passing by in a tumbril. Then she saw herself in male guise, "struggling frantically to push my way through and shouting incessantly: 'The queen! Let me get to the queen! I must get to the queen!'" Then again: "I was under the scaffold, stabbing furiously at the legs of the executioner to prevent him from doing his gruesome work, while the crowd jostled me back. Then I gave a horrible shriek . . . and that was the end of my dream." To this day, she added, she was unable to walk down the rue St. Honoré or across the Place de la Concorde (former site of the guillotine) without a horrible sensation of fear and revulsion.[11]

The writer of "Dream Romances" confessed that she had learned to be reticent about her strange experiences: since childhood, she admitted, friends and relations had laughed at her royal fancies, and she feared further humiliation once her case became widely publicized. Nonetheless, she concluded her brief memoir with a tremulous appeal for understanding. At times, she opined, she felt herself "on the point of reconstructing a consecutive remembrance of some former existence while in France, but no sooner do I seem to hold the thread I lose it, which is a very painful sensation." Lacking such remembrances, she could think of no other "plausible explanation" for her visions. Yet she remained hopeful that on returning to France she would solve her haunting mystery once and for all.[12]

Four years after the publication of "Dream Romances," yet another case of Marie Antoinette obsession came to public attention—perhaps the most outré of all. In a book entitled *An Adventure*, published by Macmillan's in 1911, two English spinsters identified only as "Miss Morison" and "Miss Lamont" described how, during a sightseeing tour of the gardens at Versailles near the Petit Trianon in 1901, they had encountered the apparition of the queen and several members of her court. The story was not a hoax: the misses "Morison" and "Lamont," it was subsequently revealed, were in fact two eminently respectable female academics, Charlotte Anne Moberly and Eleanor Jourdain, the principle and vice-principal, respectively, of St. Hugh's College, Oxford. Not only were they in earnest; for the next fifteen years they continued to enlarge upon their tale, often in the face of exquisite public ridicule.

Their "adventure" had been as follows. On the afternoon of August 10, 1901, after touring the main palace of Versailles (which neither had visited before), the two ladies had gotten lost somewhere in the surrounding grounds while looking for the Petit Trianon, the famous rustic retreat of Marie Antoinette. After trying unsuccessfully to get their bearings—or so they maintained—they had encountered a succession of unusual-looking personages: a peasant woman and girl

Portrait of Charlotte Anne Moberly by
W. Lewellyn, 1889. *Courtesy of St. Hugh's College,
Oxford University.*

in picturesque rural costumes, two men in green liveries and three-cornered hats, an ugly and strangely "repulsive" pockmarked man sitting by a kiosk, a running man with buckled shoes, a man dressed like a footman, and finally, a beautiful fair-haired lady in an "old-fashioned" dress and pale green fichu. The latter sat sketching on the lawn near a small building they assumed to be the Trianon. As they walked toward it, both were overwhelmed by a powerful feeling of melancholia and oppression. Once inside the building, however, where a jolly French wedding party was in progress, they recovered their spirits and the rest of their visit passed uneventfully.[13]

Returning to Versailles a few months later, Moberly and Jourdain were unable to retrace their steps, finding much of the scenery around the Trianon mysteriously altered. At the same time—or so

Eleanor Frances Jourdain, c. 1912. *Courtesy of Stanford University Libraries.*

they claimed—they learned that August 10, the date of their first visit, had been the anniversary of the 1792 sacking of the Tuileries, when
Marie Antoinette and Louis XVI had been forced to flee for their
lives and take refuge in the hall of the National Assembly. Shocked
and excited by the coincidence, the two of them gradually evolved the
theory that they had somehow traveled back in time—perhaps by entering "telepathically" into the reveries of Marie Antoinette as she
huddled with Louis XVI and their children in the National Assembly right after the sacking of the royal palace. Under those anxious
circumstances—the two surmised—the queen must have relieved
her spirits by thinking back, nostalgically, to the final happy summer
she had spent at the Petit Trianon in 1789. By some uncanny process,
they concluded, what they had seen in 1901 were those very images

of the Trianon—and of the people associated with it in 1789—that had flitted, phantomlike, through the queen's thoughts in 1792.

Convinced that their theory was correct, Moberly and Jourdain now began an exhaustive—indeed obsessional—search for proof. Between 1901 and 1911, they combed archives and libraries, reading everything they could lay their hands on about Marie Antoinette and the Trianon. They presented their findings in *An Adventure*, complete with footnotes, maps, appendices, and other scholarly looking paraphernalia. As far as they were concerned the mystery had been solved: every person seen in 1901 was precisely identified with someone present at the Trianon in 1789. The two men in green, for example, were identified as members of Marie Antoinette's private *gardes suisses;* such royal guards, Moberly and Jourdain informed their readers, invariably wore liveries of exactly this color while on duty at the Trianon. The sinister pockmarked man was identified with the queen's would-be enemy, the comte de Vaudreuil: the comte's face, according to several old memoirs they had consulted, had been scarred by smallpox. The running man was identified as one of the queen's pages: he wore buckled shoes of exactly the kind fashionable "after 1786"—and so on. The sketching lady, the two maintained, was none other than Marie Antoinette herself. Her "pale green fichu," they wrote, was identical to one they had found described in the notebooks of Mme. Éloffe, the queen's dressmaker, from July 1789. After completing these demonstrations, Moberly and Jourdain concluded *An Adventure* with a lyrical epilogue entitled "A Rêverie: A Possible Historical Clue"—a blatantly fictional stream-of-consciousness account (mostly composed by Moberly) of the supposed thoughts and reflections of Marie Antoinette on August 10, 1792.[14]

Hardly surprisingly, given its bizarre subject matter and the prominence of its authors, *An Adventure* produced a storm of controversy. Among the more scathing attacks on the book was Mrs. Henry Sidgwick's review in the *Journal of the Society for Psychical Research*, in which she accused Moberly and Jourdain of outright folly and self-deception. What they had encountered at Versailles in 1901, she contended, were merely "real persons and things" that they had subsequently "decked out by tricks of memory (and after the idea of

haunting had occurred to them) with some additional details of costume suitable to the times of Marie Antoinette."[15] In *Psychical Research*
(1911), the scientist W. F. Barrett took a similar line: the two ladies'
claims, he thought, were the result of "lively imagination stimulated
by expectancy" and lacked any "real evidentiary value."[16] Such skep-
ticism, however, only prompted Moberly and Jourdain to further as-
severations. In 1913, they published a revised edition of *An Adventure*
with a section entitled "Answers to Questions We Have Been Asked,"
in which they reiterated their belief that they had indeed seen the
queen and members of her court—and not unusually dressed gar-
deners, tourists, film actors, or people in masquerade costume, as
Sidgwick and others had suggested.[17] The controversy ultimately
outlived them. Though Jourdain died in 1924 and Moberly in 1937—
each staunchly maintaining the truth of their story to the end—books
and articles disputing the claims of *An Adventure* continued to appear
well into the 1950s. As late as 1976, the two ladies' literary executor
published her own debunking explanation of the "Trianon ghosts" in
a lengthy essay in *Encounter*.[18]

Why so many apparitions of Marie Antoinette? The simplest answer, of course, may be that some hidden chain of influence links the
three cases. Flournoy's book on Hélène Smith, translated into English in 1901, was well known enough in England in 1907 for the author of "Dream Romances" to have been aware of it; in their introduction to "Dream Romances," the editors of the *Journal of the Society for
Psychical Research* themselves called attention to it.[19] In turn, Moberly
and Jourdain, writing in 1911, could easily have read either Flournoy's book or "Dream Romances" and used one or both as inspiration
for *An Adventure*. Several contemporaries in fact suspected them of
appropriating the Marie Antoinette theme. W. F. Barrett, in his attack on *An Adventure* in 1911, mentioned both *From India to the Planet
Mars* and "Dream Romances" in his remarks and hinted that some act
of conscious or unconscious borrowing had taken place.[20] In *The
Ghosts of Versailles: Miss Moberly and Miss Jourdain and Their Adventure*, a
three-hundred-page "critical study" published in 1957, Lucille
Iremonger, who had been a student at St. Hugh's, argued that since
Eleanor Jourdain read French, she could easily have read Flournoy's
book when it appeared in 1900 in its original language. The book had

been successful and had gone through three editions within a few months.[21]

Yet to posit that some sort of "copycat" syndrome must have been at work in a sense merely restates the original problem. The communication, as if by infection, of delusional ideas from one person to another is of course not unknown to psychologists. One need only think of outbreaks of St. Vitus's dance in the Middle Ages, the witchhunting manias of the sixteenth and seventeenth centuries, the collective hallucinations seen on World War I battlefields, or the UFO and Elvis Presley sightings of our own day to appreciate the contagious power of certain delusional ideas. And yet even allowing for an element of hysterical contagion in the cases under consideration, the basic psychological issue is still left unresolved. To plagiarize someone else's fantasy of seeing Marie Antoinette is, after all, just as peculiar as coming up with such a fantasy on one's own. What was it about Marie Antoinette—and Marie Antoinette alone—that she should become so extraordinarily present, more than one hundred years after her death, to four presumably intelligent, well-educated, and otherwise conventional women?

Flournoy's remarks on Hélène Smith in *From India to the Planet Mars* suggest a way into the problem. Flournoy, who was one of the earliest disciples of Freud, explained Smith's "royal romance" in classic psychoanalytic terms—as the hysterical manifestation of an unconscious hostility toward her parents. Like Anna O. (to whom he compares her), Smith had been born into comfortably bourgeois circumstances, yet grew up feeling misunderstood and unappreciated by her parents—"like a stranger in her family and as one away from home."[22] This emotional isolation led by turns, he hypothesized, to "a sort of instinctive inward revolt against the modest environment in which it was her lot to be born, a profound feeling of dread and opposition, of inexplicable *malaise*, of bitter antagonism against the whole of her material and intellectual environment."[23] As a teenager, Smith expressed this yearning "for a life more brilliant than her own" decoratively, by turning her parents' sitting room into a kind of Beardsleyesque *salon*, complete with Japanese vases, engravings, and miniature hanging lamps. Later, however, in her twenties, she began to manifest her dissatisfaction more eccentrically—by falling into states of "obnubilation" (i.e., hypnotic trance), joining in seances, and indulging in "megalomaniac" reveries.[24]

That Smith should have fixed upon Marie Antoinette as her primary alternative personality made sense, according to Flournoy, on two counts. "The choice of this role," he maintained,

> is naturally explained by the innate taste of Mlle. Smith for everything that is noble, distinguished, elevated above the level of the common herd, and by the fact that some exterior circumstance fixed her hypnoid attention upon the illustrious queen of France in preference to the many other historic figures equally qualified to serve as a point of attachment for her subconscious megalomaniac reveries.[25]

The latter circumstance, he speculated, had been an engraving—first seen by Smith in 1892 or 1893—depicting a scene from Alexandre Dumas's *The Memoirs of a Physician* (1846–48), one of a series of historical romances written by Dumas about life under the ancien régime. In the scene in question, the sixteen-year-old Marie Antoinette, shortly to ascend the throne of France (Dumas's novel is set in 1773), meets the mysterious magician-doctor Joseph Balsamo (Cagliostro), who invites her to look into the future by gazing into the water in a magic decanter. Seeing the terrible fate in store for her, the Dauphiness faints dead away. Soon after being shown the engraving, the entranced Smith announced "through the table" that she was Marie Antoinette and "Leopold," her control, whose spiritual identity had previously been unclear, was Cagliostro. One could only surmise, wrote Flournoy, that the sight of the engraving had somehow "given birth to this identification of Hélène with Marie Antoinette, as well as to that of her secondary personality of Leopold with Cagliostro."[26] As for the melodramatic touches Smith brought to her role as the queen—her parting embrace of the supposed "princesse de Lamballe" for example—these could be explained, he thought, by the intellectual context in which Smith had grown up: sentimental stories having to do with the queen and the French Revolution were, after all, he concluded, among "the classes of facts" best known "in France today."[27]

The central argument here—that Hélène Smith's Antoinette impersonation was a way of getting back at unresponsive parents—strikingly anticipates Freud's argument, of course, in the well-known essay "Family Romances" from 1909. The fantasy of being descended from royalty, Freud thought, had its origins in the unconscious resentment that children felt toward their mothers and fathers. There were "only too many occasions," he contended, "on which a child is slighted, or at least *feels* he has been slighted, on which he feels he is not receiving the whole of his parents' love, and and most of all, on which he feels regret at having to share it with brothers and sisters."[28] In retaliation for such slights, the child was wont to imagine himself a stepchild or adopted child, and to replace his parents in fantasy with others, "occupying, as a rule, a higher social station." For Hélène Smith—whom Flournoy describes as "disgusted" by her "insipid and unpleasant surroundings" and "wearied" by "ordinary, commonplace people"—the act of becoming Marie Antoinette was conceivably simply a convenient means of avenging herself upon "vulgar," uncomprehending parents and of intimating to the world that she had indeed been "born for higher things."[29]

A similar argument, one suspects, could be made about the authors of "Dream Romances" and *An Adventure*. In the case of the "Dream Romances" writer especially, it is difficult *not* to invoke the obvious psychoanalytic allegory. The writer hints that her childhood was unhappy; her mother in particular seems to have neglected her. She speaks of lacking any sense of "those intimate blood-ties that generally exist between members of the same family," and of being reproached by her relations for a want of "esprit de corps." In the fantasy of the secret friend, the beautiful spectral woman who comes at night to give comfort, it is almost impossible not to see an element of symbolic wish-fulfillment. "Many an evening, when my parents were entertaining guests, or had artistes to sing and play, which kept me awake," the writer somewhat broodingly relates, "the presence of my unknown friend comforted me. She remained with me for hours, and sometimes put a cool, slender hand on my head while she bent down to look at my face."[30] Here at last was someone, she insinuates—and a queen no less—to give her the attention she deserved. That her real mother inevitably objected to these "nervous fancies" seems only to have increased their intoxicating power over her: as with Hélène Smith, revenge seems to have played an important role in the larger wish-fulfillment structure.

In the case of Moberly and Jourdain, the biographical picture is more complicated, yet similar psychological factors may have been at work. Both women were members of large families, even by Victorian standards: Moberly was the seventh of fifteen children, Jourdain the first of ten, and each felt overshadowed by siblings. Both had cold and forbidding mothers: Moberly's always wore a "severe matron's cap" and refused to call her husband by his first name; Jourdain's was known for her sarcastic tongue.[31] Both women's fathers, in turn, blatantly preferred sons to daughters. Moberly's father—for many years the headmaster of Winchester and later bishop of Salisbury—did not believe in educating women; Moberly acceded to the principalship of St. Hugh's only after his death, and largely by accident. Jourdain's father, also a clergyman and scholar, seems to have taken little interest in his eldest daughter's academic career, even when she became the first woman to undergo a *viva voce* examination in modern history at Oxford in 1886.[32]

Hostility toward these unsatisfactory parents may have motivated certain aspects of *An Adventure*. Like the "Dream Romances" writer, Moberly and Jourdain both seem to have envisioned Marie Antoinette, at least in part, as a kind of idealized maternal substitute: the obsession with finding her at the Trianon (and later, symbolically, in their researches) could, at a pinch, be read as a search for that "mother love" their real mothers seem not to have supplied. One of the crucial pieces of evidence they put forth in support of their claim that the sketching lady of 1901 was in fact the French queen, interestingly, was the so-called Wertmüller Antoinette, a portrait from the 1780s depicting the young Marie Antoinette with her two children, which they said "brought back" the lady's features exactly. Conveniently enough, the early nineteenth-century memoirist Mme. Campan had declared the Wertmüller portrait the truest likeness of the queen.[33] But the image may have interested them for another reason: with its insistent visual focus on the queen's maternal body (reinforced by the crudely triangular composition), it also satisfied, perhaps, subliminal longings in both women for a compensatory image of maternal tenderness.

Finding a new mother in Marie Antoinette was in turn a way of retaliating against powerful yet impervious fathers. Of course from one perspective Moberly and Jourdain's *Adventure* might be read as a coded plea for paternal *approval:* the elaborate mimicry of scholarly

The Wertmüller portrait of Marie Antoinette, 1785. *Courtesy of the National Swedish Art Museum.*

conventions, the ponderous footnotes and obsessional adumbration of "evidence," all suggest a desire to placate (if only superficially) emotionally distant scholar-fathers. By becoming Oxford dons, and part of the first trail-blazing generation of English women academics, Moberly and Jourdain had from the start not-so-secretly modeled themselves on imposing male parents. And yet one also senses a sub-terranean animosity in *An Adventure*—an urge to show up, as it were, these same authority figures. By using the sober devices of masculine scholarship to tell a decidedly fabulous and "gynocentric" story, Moberly and Jourdain found a way, perhaps, of subtly arraigning those patriarchs—real and symbolic—who seemed to discount them and their achievements.[34]

Suggestive as it may be, however, the standard Freudian model of the family romance still leaves the most puzzling feature in the cases before us unexplained. Psychoanalysis describes the royal fantasy only in negative and generalized terms—as a mode of psychic protest or revenge. And yet, in the peculiar passion with which Hélène Smith, the "Dream Romancer," and Moberly and Jourdain made the Marie Antoinette connection, we sense something more than mere atavistic complaint. There is an idiomatic, loverlike intensity about each woman's fixation, a lyrical-romantic ardor powerfully suffused with what can only be described as homosexual pathos. These, above all, are homoerotic fantasies, in which the queen plays the part of both seductive object of desire and visionary emblem of female-female bonding.

We sense this pathos most strikingly, perhaps, in the case of the "Dream Romances" writer, whose Marie Antoinette fantasies are startling for both their erotic intensity and openly transsexual aspects. The writer's vision of Antoinette, leaning over her bed at night, leaning into her, as it were, to caress and be caressed, is as much a lover's as a child's vision—replete with heterodox possibility. In these hours of voluptuous communion, she notes, "I had full leisure to note every detail of her face, which seemed to me very beautiful." Later she speaks of the queen as "dearer to me than any one in the world."[35] The fantasy of being a boy seems to have licensed these curiously sapphic devotions: the writer betrays no embarrassment at declaring—or embracing—a female love object. At times, it is true, she veils her passion in transvestite melodrama: the dream she describes in which she see herself, in heroic male guise, attempting to save Marie Antoinette from the guillotine has an air about it of sentimental kitsch, though it is perhaps no less compelling for that. The fantasy of gallantry allowed her love to flourish; in erotic self-obfuscation she found release.

Similar themes can be discerned in the visions of Hélène Smith. Smith, as Flournoy notes, was unmarried: indeed she used her psychic gift to resist men and matrimony from an early age. Despite her "profound isolation of heart," she told the psychologist, "I could not make up my mind to marry, although I had several opportunities. A voice was always saying, 'Do not hurry: the time has not arrived; this is not the destiny for which you are reserved.'"[36] Later she personified this "voice" in the figure of "Leopold," her spirit control. Leopold played the role of invisible watchdog in Smith's life— addressing her harshly whenever she allowed herself to be approached by men. Once during her adolescence, she said, Leopold had had "an explosion of wrath" when her middle-aged family doctor (like Herr K. in Freud's case history of Dora) attempted to kiss her.[37] On another occasion, he violently berated her for accepting a rose from a man on a streetcar.[38]

With the evolution of Smith's career as a medium and the development of the "royal romance" in the early 1890s, Leopold came to assume an even more prominent role in her psychic life. Smith at times described feeling herself mysteriously "*becoming* or *being*" Leopold: "This happens most frequently at night, or upon awakening in the morning. She has first the fugitive vision of her protector; then it seems that little by little he is submerged in her; she feels him overcoming and penetrating her entire organism, as if he really became her or she him."[39] As in the case of the "Dream Romances" writer, this alternative male self—bizarrely realized—gave Smith access to a sphere of explicitly homoerotic emotion. Leopold's dramatic assertion "through the table" that he was actually Cagliostro, and in love with Marie Antoinette, became for Smith, one suspects, a phantasmagorical way of signifying her own sexual attraction to the French queen, whom at other moments, of course, she also impersonated. Taken over by the spirit of "the powerful and manly Count of Cagliostro," wrote Flournoy, "[Smith's] eyelids droop; her expression changes; her throat swells into a sort of double chin, which gives her a likeness of some sort to the well-known figure of Cagliostro."[40] Her words, paradoxically addressed to herself (as Marie Antoinette), came forth "slowly but strong" in "the deep bass voice of a man." While one hesitates to label Smith's fantasies as lesbian in any simplistic sense—the "Hindoo" and "Martian" cycles reveal a sexual personality of quite staggeringly polymorphous perversity—there is a strong suggestion here that her "royal romance," so weirdly enacted, was powerfully informed nonetheless by latent homosexual interests.

Compared with these colorful goings-on, Moberly and Jourdain's rather more straightforward hallucination of Marie Antoinette at the

Trianon may seem a bit tame. And yet theirs is in some ways the most homosexual vision of all—as the biographical background to *An Adventure* makes clear. At the time of the fateful excursion to Versailles in August 1901, Moberly and Jourdain were virtual strangers to one another, having met in Paris only a few weeks before. A mutual friend had recommended Jourdain to Moberly for the vacant post of vice-principal at St. Hugh's, where Moberly had served as principal since 1886. The sightseeing trip was in part an experiment to see if the two women could work together compatibly. It was a success in more ways than one. Following the experience at the Trianon, Moberly and Jourdain not only became colleagues at St. Hugh's and collaborators on *An Adventure* but lived together (in a relationship described by one observer as that of "husband and wife") for the next twenty-three years, until Jourdain's death in 1924.[41]

What this sequence of events suggests, of course, is that the vision of Marie Antoinette in some way triangulated—or made possible—Moberly and Jourdain's own lifelong homoerotic attachment. In the months immediately following the Trianon experience, as Lucille Iremonger records in *The Ghosts of Versailles*, the two women became inseparable friends: "The shy woman [Moberly] liked the sociable one [Jourdain]; the plain unfeminine creature warmed to the little charmer, flowery hats, silken ankles and all." The joint obsession with Marie Antoinette seemed to underwrite their courtship: "Soon, too soon, many thought, the vacations which Annie Moberly had once spent with relations . . . were all spent searching for 'proof' for the Versailles 'adventure' in company with Miss Jourdain."* It was as if, indeed, Marie Antoinette had brought them together.

At a deeper level, Moberly and Jourdain seem to have been using the figure of the queen to legitimate, if only unconsciously, their own unorthodox emotional needs. Certainly the story in *An Adventure* can

---

*Though she never once uses the word *lesbian* to describe them, Iremonger's interest in her subjects' emotional predilections often verges on the prurient. Quoting an unnamed St. Hugh's source, she animadverts on Jourdain's "unhealthy" relationships with various students in the college, who reciprocated by falling in love with their principal: "An illuminating punning phrase which had currency at that time was, 'Have you crossed Jordan yet?' In other words, have you fallen under the sway of this woman who is acknowledged to be consciously exercising her charm to bind students to her?" According to the mistress of Girton, Iremonger notes, "a lot of kissing went on"; see *Ghosts of Versailles*, pp. 87–88.

be read as a kind of lesbian legitimation fantasy. In both its details and overall structure, it seems to dramatize a movement away from masculine sexuality toward a world of female-female love and ritual. The pseudonymous "Miss Morison" and "Miss Lamont," lost in a mysterious garden, are questing after the palace of a beautiful queen. After numerous adventures, including a frightening meeting with a "repulsive-looking man" (the kiosk man), they encounter, as if in a vision, the beautiful queen herself. In the guise of the sketching lady, she seems to bring about a kind of mystical marriage between them. Ever after—the two resolve—they will testify together to what they have seen. Their symbolic odyssey ends, fittingly enough, with a real marriage, when they come upon the French wedding party, inside the "female" space of the Trianon itself.[42]

Later, when *An Adventure* met with attack, Moberly and Jourdain defended their claims so fiercely, one suspects, because they were trying in part to maintain this subliminal fiction of legitimation. It was as if they needed the queen in order to justify themselves as "husband and wife"—women living together in a potentially incriminating homosexual dyad—before a hostile and rejecting world.*

Why this recurrent association between Marie Antoinette and female homoeroticism? To get at the meaning of such obsession, it seems to me, we need to look beyond the somewhat specialized fictions of the family romance to something much broader: to what we might call *cultural romance* or the dynamics of collective fantasy. Hélène Smith, the "Dream Romances" writer, and Moberly and Jourdain were not the only women of the later nineteenth century, it turns out, haunted by ghostly dreams of Marie Antoinette. Particularly among women in England, where sympathy for the ancien régime had long been a staple of popular romantic sensibility, Marie Antoinette was in fact a kind of cult figure—the object of a widespread and often curiously eroticized group fixation. A host of hagiographical biographies from the period, such as Henrietta Keddie's

---

*Moberly and Jourdain's wishful use of a supernatural third party to triangulate, and thereby legitimate, their lesbian relationship will not appear so bizarre, perhaps, when one considers other such triangles existing between homosexual women in the period. Radclyffe Hall and Lady Una Troubridge, for example, formed a similar spiritual triangle with Hall's deceased ex-lover "Ladye," Mabel Batten, with whom they communicated regularly through a spirit medium for over twenty years. See Baker, *Our Three Selves*, pp. 84–97.

Marie Antoinette (1883), dedicated to one whose tribulations "will never cease to melt all hearts, so long as manly pity and womanly tenderness endure," bear witness to the phenomenon.[43]

This fixation needs to be differentiated at once, I think, from what might loosely be called the "heterosexual" fascination with the queen traceable in the works of eighteenth- and nineteenth-century male writers. Edmund Burke's famous description of Marie Antoinette in her prime "glittering like the morning-star, full of life, and splendor, and joy," or Thomas Carlyle's romantic paean to the hapless queen, fated to end her life among the most "vicious" of men, or even Charles Dickens's chivalrous asides on "the Widow Capet" in *A Tale of Two Cities*—while laden with historical pathos—nonetheless seldom display the same perfervid intimacy, the clandestine, excitable joy, and the uncanny urge to bring back to life so palpable in the fantasies of her female admirers.[44]

For subtly inspiring the feminine fixation (in all of its strange embodied tenderness), I would like to argue, were shadowy rumors having to do with Marie Antoinette's own purported homoeroticism. That Marie Antoinette was herself a lover of women had been rumored at least since the 1770s, when stories about her scandalous friendships with women had circulated freely in court circles. In the years before the Revolution, antiroyalist propagandists had in turn taken up the rumor, giving it sensational play in a series of widely distributed obscene pamphlets and broadsheets. In an effort to undo the damage done to her reputation by such assaults, the queen's nineteenth-century apologists tried to defend her by emphasizing the "romantic" (and hence platonic) nature of her female friendships. And yet precisely by dwelling on the issue, they also succeeded, paradoxically, in keeping the problem of her sexuality before the public eye. By the end of the century, not only were the rumors about Marie Antoinette's homosexuality still alive, she had become for certain of her female admirers a kind of secret heroine—an underground symbol of passionate love between women. It made sense that Hélène Smith, the "Dream Romances" writer, and Moberly and Jourdain should have used her to underwrite their own homoerotic romances, for she had already been thoroughly coded, as it were, into late nineteenth-century culture as the "sapphic" queen par excellence.

2

How had rumors of Marie Antoinette's homosexuality come to haunt the nineteenth century? Without question the queen herself had something to do with it—though exactly how much is still a matter of debate. Whether Marie Antoinette was "really" a lesbian, if indeed the term can be said to apply under the circumstances, remains in dispute. Stefan Zweig, author of *Marie Antoinette: The Portrait of an Average Woman* (1933) and the first modern biographer to discuss the question with anything resembling frankness, thought that she had indeed had homosexual affairs—if only, as it were, by default. She was at heart, he argued, "a thoroughly natural, an essentially feminine woman, gentle, tender, ready to surrender herself to the embraces of the male." Owing to Louis XVI's mysterious impotence, however, during the first seven years of their marriage—from 1770 to 1777—she had been forced to turn elsewhere in order "to gratify her physiological requirements." "She had need," he affirms, "of someone who would relieve her spiritual and bodily tensions, and since, for propriety's sake, she would not (or would not yet) seek it from a man, Marie Antoinette at this juncture involuntarily turned towards a woman friend."[45] The doting princesse de Lamballe was the first of these intimate friends, only to be supplanted later by the dashing comtesse de Polignac, who inspired in the queen "a sort of superheated falling in love."[46] Only the curing of Louis XVI's impotence in 1777, and Marie Antoinette's subsequent motherhood, Zweig concludes, turned her sexual interests back in a more conventional direction.[47]

Other biographers are more equivocal. Both Dorothy Moulton Mayer in *Marie Antoinette: The Tragic Queen* (1968) and Joan Haslip in *Marie Antoinette* (1987) deny the lesbian allegation; Mayer, in fact, dismisses it as "rubbish." Yet both also linger, somewhat ambiguously, on the subject of Marie Antoinette's unusual interest in other women. During the first years of her reign especially, Mayer writes, when the young queen lived "without hope of any normal sexual life with her husband," she turned for "love and understanding" to various attractive women at court, such as the raven-haired Polignac.[48] Haslip dwells at length on the queen's emotional susceptibility to

Marie-Thérèse Louise, princesse de Lamballe. From
Francis Montefiore, *The Princesse de Lamballe* (London,
1896). *Courtesy of Stanford University Libraries.*

pretty women. In the delicate princesse de Lamballe, with her "huge
blue eyes and long blonde curls," she writes, Marie Antoinette
thought she had found the "ideal companion"; later infatuations included the "exquisite" Lucie Dillon (who became one of the queen's
ladies-in-waiting), an unnamed actress, and the "insinuating" Polignac, who used her position to enrich her large and ambitious family.[49]

Whatever the truth of the matter, it is clear that rumors about Marie Antoinette's homosexuality had begun to spread across France—
and even to England—well before the French Revolution. "They
have been liberal enough to accuse me of having a taste for both wom-
en and lovers," she wrote to her mother, the Empress Maria Theresa
of Austria, in 1775.[50] In the years leading up to the Revolution, antiroyalist propagandists elaborated on the charge in a host of secretly

published pornographic *libelles* designed to inflame public sentiment against her. In the anonymous *Portefeuille d'un talon rouge* (1779) and the *Essai historique sur la vie de Marie Antoinette* (1781), for example, the queen was accused of bringing the vice of "tribadism" with her from Austria into France and of having affairs with the comtesse de Polignac and Mme. Balbi. In the scurrilous *Amours de Charlot et de Toinette* (1779), she was depicted in "criminal" embraces with the princesse de Lamballe. And in the grossly obscene *Le Godmiché royal* (1789), in the guise of the goddess "Junon," she was shown deploying a dildo on her

Portrait of Yolande Gabrielle, comtesse (later duchesse) de Polignac, 1783, by Elisabeth Vigée-Lebrun. *Courtesy of the National Trust, Waddeston Manor, and the Courtauld Institute of Art.*

Marie Antoinette with one of her ladies-in-
waiting. From *La Vie privée de Marie-Antoinette*
(c. 1780). *Courtesy of the Bibliothèque nationale,
Paris.*

female lover "Hébée" (Polignac or Lamballe), after complaining about
her husband's impotence—a motif revived in the equally scandalous
Fureurs utérines de Marie Antoinette, femme de Louis XVI of 1791.[51]

Lesbianism was not the only form of sexual transgression attributed to Marie Antoinette in the *libelles:* it was often alleged that she
had also had adulterous affairs with the king's brother, the comte
d'Artois, and numerous other male figures at court. But the charge of
homosexuality was unquestionably the one that clung most damagingly. At the start of the Revolution, especially abroad, it turned
otherwise sympathetic observers against her. "The queen of France,"

wrote Hester Thrale Piozzi disgustedly in her diary in 1789, "is at the Head of a Set of Monsters call'd by each other *Sapphists*, who boast her example; and deserve to be thrown with the He Demons that haunt each other likewise, into Mount Vesuvius."⁵² Later, when the Revolution turned violent, the "tribadism" accusation seems to explain some of the unusually sadistic actions of the Parisian crowd. After the princesse de Lamballe was brutally murdered and mutilated during the September Massacres in 1792, for example, a screaming and drunken mob carried her head on a bloody pike to the Temple (where Marie Antoinette and her family were imprisoned) with the grotesque demand that the queen be forced to "kiss the lips of her intimate." Only the intervention of a prison governor, who convinced the mob to parade the head through the streets of Paris so that all might enjoy the "trophy" of victory, kept them from imposing this ghastly (yet telling) humiliation upon her.⁵³ In turn, at Marie Antoinette's trial just before her execution in October 1793, the "crime" of her homosexuality was invoked again, mingled with others (including a charge of incest with her own son) and made part of the Revolutionary Tribunal's death-dealing case against her.⁵⁴

Which isn't to say that the rumor went unchallenged. True, during the queen's lifetime, amid the turmoil of insurrection, little could be done to stop the flow of scurrilous *libelles*—thousands of copies of which circulated freely in France up until the time of her execution.⁵⁵ (And even afterwards, one suspects: the lesbian diarist Anne Lister, visiting Paris in 1825, reported hearing from one of her female lovers there that "Marie Antoinette was accused of being too fond of women.")⁵⁶ Nonetheless, following the defeat of Napoleon and the restoration of the monarchy in 1814, a host of royalist apologists and defenders of the ancien régime stepped forth, determined to rehabilitate the queen's reputation. Laying the lesbian rumor to rest as swiftly as possible, obviously, was a crucial part of this revisionist project.

The first of Marie Antoinette's nineteenth-century apologists, the staid Mme. Campan, tried to defuse the lesbian charge by underplaying it as much as possible. In the course of her 450-page *Mémoires sur la vie privée de la reine Marie Antoinette* (1823), the former lady-in-waiting at Versailles referred to the rumor only once, and then only euphemistically. Two "infamous accusations," she allowed, had been made against the queen in her lifetime: "I mean the unworthy suspicions of too strong an attachment for the Comte d'Artois, and of the motives for the tender friendship which subsisted between the Queen, the Princess of Lamballe, and the Duchess of Polignac."[57] After rebutting the first charge in detail, she responded to the second more vaguely, as if to keep her readers from thinking too long about it: "As to the intimate connection between Marie Antoinette and the ladies I have named, it never had, nor could have, any other motive than the very innocent wish to secure herself two friends in the midst of a numerous Court; and notwithstanding this intimacy, that tone of respect observed by persons of the most exalted rank towards majesty never ceased to be observed."[58] Something indeed so "infamous," it seemed, was best passed over as rapidly and obscurely as possible.

Beginning with the Goncourt brothers, however, subsequent defenders of the queen's reputation settled on a far more flamboyant and paradoxical strategy. Instead of obscuring Marie Antoinette's relations with other women, they sought to romanticize them. In their *Histoire de Marie-Antoinette*, the relentlessly hagiographical biography they published together in 1858, the Goncourts presented Marie Antoinette as a tragic heroine brought low by the malignity of fate and of "le peuple," who persistently misrepresented her character and actions. Her friendships with women, they maintained, had arisen simply out of an innocent yet heartfelt desire for intimacy and companionship. In the early part of her reign, oppressed by the alien formality of the French court, she had instinctively gravitated toward companions in whom she could confide freely and tenderly. In the serene princesse de Lamballe, she discovered "la tolérance, la simplicité, l'amabilité, l'enjouement tranquille"; in the enchanting Polignac, "une douceur piquante" and a charming "esprit" that came as refreshment to her often-wearied spirit.[59] Those who later calumniated her, wrote the Goncourts, simply did not understand the purity of feeling that inspired such delicate "tendresse."

Over time and through adversity the heroic nature of these attachments had been revealed. Between Marie Antoinette and the comtesse de Polignac, the Goncourts contended, there had subsisted a devotion so powerful that only the queen's heart-rending command after the storming of the Bastille, that Polignac flee the country for her own safety, convinced her beloved "amie" to leave her side. The grief-filled letters that subsequently passed between them, the brothers enthused, were a veritable "chef d'oeuvre" of female-female love:

> What an incomparable baring of the soul! What delicate matters delicately expressed! And what words, such as women only possess—one alone can evoke a world of feeling! The kindly sob, the sweet sadness resembles the lamentation of a great soul, and sorrow is exalted to the heroism of tears.[60]

As for the tragic bond between Marie Antoinette and the unfortunate princesse de Lamballe, this was from the start one of those "rare and great loves that Providence unites in death"—an almost supernatural-seeming devotion.[61] As with Polignac, the queen had begged her "chère Lamballe" to escape in 1789, but to no avail: the princess had ultimately proved her love by giving up her life for the woman she adored. Following the news of Lamballe's terrible death, wrote the Goncourts, Marie Antoinette sat immobilized in her prison room in the Temple, seeing nothing, like a statue. It was as if, they suggested, she were still in communication with her friend—"as if that ensanguined blonde head behind the curtains were to gaze at her forever!" No more poignant moment, perhaps, was to be found in all the annals of the Revolution.[62]

Between 1860 and 1900, a host of Marie Antoinette biographers followed in the Goncourts' footsteps, elaborating on the heroic friendship theme. In works such as Amélie Lenormant's *Quatres Femmes au temps de la Révolution* (1866), Charles Duke Yonge's *Marie Antoinette* (1876), Julie Lavergne's *Légendes de Trianon, Versailles, et Saint-Germain* (1879), Henrietta Keddie's *Marie Antoinette* (1883), Lord Ronald Gower's *The Last Days of Marie Antoinette* (1885), Pierre de Nolhac's *La Reine Marie-Antoinette* (1890), M. C. Bishop's *Prison Life of Marie Antoinette* (1894), Anna L. Bicknell's *Story of Marie-Antoinette* (1897), and Clara Tschudi's *Marie Antoinette* (1898), one finds the same sentimental motifs cropping up again and again: the queen's "sisterly" tenderness for Lamballe and Polignac, their bravery on her behalf, her terrible grief at separating from them in the darkest days of the Revolution. The gruesome martyrdom of Lamballe made her a special object of fascination, and in numerous works of the period, such as W. R. Alger's *The Friendships of Women* (1872), Sir Francis Montefiore's *The Princesse de Lamballe* (1896), and the pseudonymously authored *Secret*

The death of the princesse de Lamballe, 1792. From Adolphe Thiers, *History of the French Revolution* (London, 1838). *Courtesy of Stanford University Libraries.*

Memoirs of Princess Lamballe (1901), she appears as a full-blown romantic heroine in her own right.[63]

There can be no doubt what message these later nineteenth-century defenders of the queen were *trying* to get across: many of them openly affirmed Marie Antoinette's sexual purity and blasted the "vile falsehoods" perpetrated in her name. "A reciprocity of friendship between a queen and a subject," declaimed one of them, excoriating the "blackest calumny" made against the queen and the comtesse de Polignac in the 1770s,

> by those who never felt the existence of such a feeling as friendship, could only be considered in a criminal point of view. But by what per-version could suspicion frown upon the ties between two married women, both living in the greatest harmony with their respective husbands, especially when both became mothers and so devoted to their offspring? This boundless friendship DID glow between this calumniated pair—calumniated because the sacredness and peculiarity of the sentiment which united them was too pure to be understood by the groveling minds who made themselves their sentencers.[64]

At the same time, however, by the breathless, titillating, even obsessional manner in which they dwelt upon these "sacred and peculiar" attachments, they also managed, paradoxically, to reinfuse them with a curious erotic charge.

The queen's intimacy with the ill-fated princesse de Lamballe (that "ever-regretted angel") seemed especially to invite embellishment of this sort. Consider, for example, the apologists' oddly voluptuous handling of what one might call the "sledge party episode" from Mme. Campan. In her memoir of 1823, Campan had mentioned in passing that during the unusually cold winter of 1775–76, Marie Antoinette, nostalgic for the customs of her Austrian youth, had taken to riding out with friends in sleighs around the snowy country-side outside Paris. It was during these "celebrated sledge parties" (condemned by her enemies at court), wrote Campan, that the queen became "intimately acquainted with the princesse de Lamballe, who made her appearance in them wrapped in fur, with all the brilliancy and freshness of the age of twenty; the emblem of spring, peeping from under sable and ermine."[65]

In her 1883 biography of Marie Antoinette, Henrietta Keddie transformed this brief description into a homoerotic set piece—at once magical and fetishistic. After marveling first over how "the Queen's white horses, blue velvet harness, and gold and silver tin-kling bells startled the Boulevards with a vision from fairyland," she lingered, like a sentimental novelist, on the imagined face of the princess, sensuously pinked by the cold: "Almost rivalling the Queen's face in beauty was another young face rising above the wraps of martin and ermine, with the delicate complexion heightened by the snow-wind."[66] Later on, describing Marie Antoinette's supposed reveries after Lamballe's death, Keddie lovingly evoked the image again: "She [Marie Antoinette] was once more gliding over the snow plain, unspotted by a single drop of blood, and a fair young face, gathering gladness from her own, was close to hers."[67] Nor was Ked-die the only nineteenth-century female biographer to reimagine these romantic excursions: "Marie Antoinette," rhapsodized Anna L. Bicknell in her own biography of the queen from 1897, "delighted to recall the pastimes of her childish days at Vienna, had sledges pre-pared, in which she flew over the frosted ground with the Princesse, who, fair and fresh as a rose under her rich furs, looked like spring itself in mid-winter."[68]

Other writers lingered voyeuristically over episodes from later, more tragic times. During her first separation from the princesse de

Lamballe, wrote Sir Francis Montefiore in his lachrymose 1896 life of
the princess, Marie Antoinette was so anguished by her companion's
absence from court she had her portrait painted "on the looking glass
of the room she most frequented."[69] On another occasion, in 1791,
after the queen and Louis XVI had made their unsuccessful flight
from Paris and had been recaptured at Varennes, she sent the princess
a ring, set with a lock of her now-whitened hair and with the pathetic
words "bleached by sorrow" engraved upon it. The melancholy Lamballe in turn sent the queen a repeater-watch ("to remind her of the
hours we have passed together") and expressed the gallant wish to
"live or die" near her.[70] Among the last possessions taken from Marie
Antoinette on the day of her final removal to the Conciergerie, it was
poignantly noted, had been a tear-stained miniature of the princesse
de Lamballe.[71]

Perhaps the most suggestive of all the post-Goncourtian defenses
was the mawkish *Secret Memoirs of Princess Lamballe*—dedicated once
again to Lamballe and the "saint-like martyred" queen she served.
This blatantly fictionalized work, the real authorship of which remains uncertain, purported to be a selection of extracts from the
princesse de Lamballe's journal up until 1792, edited and annotated
by an Englishwoman, "Catherine Hyde," who claimed to have been
the princess's confidential secretary and secret messenger during the
first years of the Revolution. The relationship between Lamballe and
the queen, Hyde complained, had often been unjustly maligned. By
presenting Lamballe's diary (with which she had supposedly been en-
trusted just before the princess's death), Hyde wished to demonstrate, she said, how "heavenly" the love between "this august, la-
mented, injured pair"—her mistress and the queen—in fact had
been.[72]

What the *Memoirs* is really, however (besides an obvious hoax), is a
maudlin, almost prurient paean to the joys of female bonding. Thus
the "princess's" description of how she and Marie Antoinette first
met, when the queen paid a visit to her and her father-in-law, the duc
de Penthièvres, soon after the death of the princess's young husband
in 1775:

It was amid this gloom of human agony, these heart-rending scenes of
real mourning, that the brilliant star shone to disperse the clouds,

which hovered over our drooping heads,—to dry the hot briny tears which were parching up our miserable vegetating existence—it was in this crisis that Marie Antoinette came, like a messenger sent down from Heaven, graciously to offer the balm of comfort in the sweetest language of human compassion. The pure emotions of her generous soul made her unceasing, unremitting, in her visits. . . . But for the consolation of her warm friendship we must have sunk into utter despair![73]

Not long after, writes the princess, she began dining "*tête à tête* with Her Majesty," who continued to shower her with tokens of affection. During one especially intimate conversation, she recalls, "my tears flowing down my cheeks rapidly while I was speaking, the Queen, with that kindness for which she was so eminently distinguished, took me by the hand, and with her handkerchief dried my face."[74] Then the queen announced her intention to appoint her superintendent of her household at Versailles. With the arrival of the Princess Elizabeth, the queen's sister-in-law, the scene escalated into a rhapsodical three-way communion: "The Queen took me by the hand. The Princess Elizabeth, joining hers, exclaimed to the Queen, 'Oh, my dear sister! let me make the trio in this happy union of friends!'"[75] And soon after, writes the princess, Marie Antoinette embraced her again, exclaiming, "Death alone can separate us!"[76]

In her own numerous commentaries on the princess's narrative, the mysterious "Catherine Hyde" lingers on similar themes. Her own love for the princess, she claims, was as fervent as that of the princess for Marie Antoinette. Nicknamed by her Italian-speaking mistress her "*cara Inglesina*," Hyde often risked her life, she says, by going in boy's clothes to deliver secret messages between the princess and the queen during the first years of the Revolution.[77] So devoted was she to the royalist cause she refused to leave her patroness even in 1792, when Lamballe was confined with the queen in the Tuileries: "I begged [the princess's] forgiveness, and on my knees implored that she would not send me away in the hour of danger."[78] Their eventual parting, which supposedly took place only when Marie Antoinette ordered the unwilling Hyde on a last secret mission to Italy, was almost unbearably poignant: "I took her hand; I bathed it with my tears, as she, at the same moment, was bathing my face with hers. . . . The Princess Lamballe clasped me in her arms. 'Not only letters,' exclaimed she, 'but my life I would trust to the fidelity of my *vera, verissima, cara Inglesina!*'" Witnessing this orgiastic display of emotion, says Hyde, Marie Antoinette was herself wracked by uncontrollable sobs.[79]

At the moment of farewell, Hyde says, the princess seemed to become a radiant, unearthly, almost spectral apparition—"animated by some saintlike spirit, with scarcely a consciousness of its own existence, and with no thought but that of consoling those around, and no desire but that of smoothing their path to those mansions of eternal peace to which she had already, by anticipation, consigned herself." Indeed, her servant recalls, "her countenance beamed with a serenity perfectly supernatural," while "the graces that played about her bespoke her already the crowned martyr of Elysium."[80]

Hyde falls into the language of the apparitional again in the concluding pages of the *Memoirs*, when she describes her grief upon hearing of the terrible death of the princess during the September Massacres—supposedly at the hands of a mulatto whom Lamballe had supported since childhood:

> Words cannot express what a void I felt on returning some years after these horrible calamities to Paris, to find that no trace of the angelic form of my beloved benefactress had been suffered to remain; that no clue had ever been discovered to the sod which enwraps her mutilated body; that there was not even a tombstone to point out the resting place of her mangled frame. There would have been happiness in communing with her spirit over her burial place. What a school for royalty and earthly grandeur! . . . How often have I left the sons of mirth and gayety paying libations to Bacchus to pass an hour at the grave of Marie Antoinette, lamenting I could not enjoy the same consolation, and unburden the anguish of my soul in solemn prayer, over her martyred friend.[81]

In lieu of such intimacy, Hyde is forced to make do with memories—above all, of the "divine" friendship subsisting between her beloved mistress and the same Marie Antoinette, over whose grave she now weeps. That friendship remains, she ends grandiloquently, "an everlasting monument that honors their sex."*

---

*Marie Antoinette's nineteenth- and early twentieth-century biographers frequently used ghostly metaphors to describe her, especially—as one might expect—in melodramatic pas-

What would imaginative contemporaries such as Hélène Smith, the "Dream Romances" writer, or Moberly and Jourdain have made of such spectral romancing? The answer, I think, is not far to seek. Though ostensibly concerned with laying the rumor of her homosexuality to rest, Marie Antoinette's late nineteenth-century biographers found themselves, like the ghost-obsessed author of the *Secret Memoirs*, ineluctably haunted by it, unable to let it go—unable to keep themselves from embellishing obsessively and ambiguously upon it. By idealizing Marie Antoinette's friendships with women, they sought, obviously, to exorcize the specter of her putative lesbianism once and for all. Yet precisely by dilating so ardently on the exalted nature of her same-sex friendships, they succeeded in transforming her into a symbol of homoerotic romance. In the very act of supposedly "delesbianizing" Marie Antoinette they made her over—paradoxically—into a subject for cryptolesbian reverie.

For women such as Hélène Smith, caught up in dreams of homage and desire, the melancholic "Dream Romances" writer, haunted by her ghostly lady, or the jointly besotted Moberly and Jourdain, unable or afraid to act out their homosexual impulses in any other way, the fantasy of occult connection with Marie Antoinette must have seemed a safe yet also powerfully gratifying way of articulating otherwise inadmissible erotic desires. Marie Antoinette was safe, theoret-

---

sages dealing with her last days and death. In *Marie Antoinette*, Clara Tschudi spoke of her "blanched face" and "almost spectral appearance" at her trial (282); in *The Last Days of Marie Antoinette*, Lord Ronald Gower described her as "pale as death" on the way to the scaffold (158). Certainly her appearance deteriorated dramatically while she was imprisoned in the Temple and the Conciergerie; most famously, by the last year of her life, her once-luxuriant blonde hair had gone completely white. The constant uterine hemorrhages from which she suffered at this time undoubtedly contributed to her wraithlike appearance. But one also senses in the persistence with which her biographers describe her appearance as "ghostly" or "unearthly" an impulse to invest her story with uncanny elements. Sometimes a supernatural theme surfaces directly. At the end of her 1897 biography of the queen, Anna L. Bicknell asserted that when Marie Antoinette's executioner displayed her head to the crowd after guillotining her, her face "expressed perfect consciousness, and the eyes looked on the crowd" with an expression of "intense astonishment, as of some wonderful vision revealed" (324–25). In his 1909 biography of the queen, Hilaire Belloc claimed that in Germany on the night of October 16, 1793, just after her execution, her distant cousin, George of Hesse, "saw the White Lady pass, the Ghost without a face that is the warning of the Hapsburgs, and the hair of his head stood up" (394). In the context of such weird ruminations, the apparition-seeing of the "Dream Romances" writer and Moberly and Jourdain is perhaps not as wholly eccentric as it might at first appear.

wise inadmissible erotic desires. Marie Antoinette was safe, theoretically, because she was "innocent." "If the unfortunate Queen," as Catherine Hyde assured her readers, "had ever been guilty of the slightest of those glaring vices of which she was so generally accused, the Princess [de Lamballe] must have been aware of them; and it was not in her nature to have remained the friend and advocate, even unto death, of one capable of depravity."[82] Yet the very fiction of Marie Antoinette's innocence, so feverishly adumbrated in the biographies, facilitated the subversive workings of lesbian romance. It opened up a space for erotic fantasy, made possible a host of spectral encounters. "The Queen of France," wrote one of her fantasists, "had love in her eyes and Heaven in her soul."[83] Imagining such love, indeed basking in its reflected light, the clandestine lover of women might find consolation and secret communion—a ghostly authorization for half-conscious but nonetheless potent desires.

3

In pronouncing Marie Antoinette a code figure for female homoeroticism, even a kind of protolesbian heroine, I run the risk, I realize, of being accused of indulging in a little imaginative projection myself. After all, it might be argued, Marie Antoinette is remembered today mainly for the egregious (and apocryphal) "Let them eat cake"—and the sensational manner of her death—and not for any presumed sexual irregularity.[84] Even if it is true that her biographical image in the nineteenth century was oddly colored by homoerotic elements, and that women such as Hélène Smith, the "Dream Romances" writer, and Moberly and Jourdain covertly fantasized about her as a lover of women, is that enough to declare her, as I have done here, the object of a collective lesbian fixation? To some, the fact that Marie Antoinette's putative lesbianism is *not*, for the most part, common knowledge today may suggest that her nineteenth-century biographers were in fact more successful at suppressing the rumor of her homosexuality than I have allowed.

The most compelling evidence for Marie Antoinette's cult figure status, I would like to suggest by way of coda, is to be found in the lesbian literary cultural tradition itself—especially in works of fiction written by and about lesbians in the first decades of the twentieth century. The homosexuality of Marie Antoinette is in fact a kind of communal topos in lesbian writing of the early twentieth century: a shared underground motif or commonplace. If Hélène Smith, the "Dream Romances" writer, and Moberly and Jourdain used Marie Antoinette unconsciously, so to speak, to symbolize erotic impulses of which they were themselves only half aware, twentieth-century lesbian writers and artists have exploited the queen's image far more artfully and self-consciously—to symbolize, if not glamorize, the possibility of love between women. Indeed, to the extent that they have continued to romanticize Marie Antoinette, modern lesbian writers have taken up where her nineteenth-century biographers left off, but with one crucial difference: they affirm rather than deny the sexual nature of her intimacies with women.

The first English writer to invoke Marie Antoinette specifically as a lesbian icon, as far as I have been able to discover, is the little-known Rose Laure Allatini, whose *Despised and Rejected*, published under the pseudonym "A. T. Fitzroy," appeared in 1918. This remarkable novel (which was immediately banned on account of its powerful antiwar sentiments and homoerotic plot line) is the story of a young woman and a young man who become engaged on the eve of the First World War. Both are pacifists; each is also unconsciously drawn to members of his or her own sex. When the man falls in love with a fellow conscientious objector, he recognizes his homosexuality and breaks off the engagement. The woman is then forced to confront her own homosexual desires. Over the course of the novel, which ends with the man's imprisonment, the two find a new (and surprisingly hopeful) emotional bond in the recognition of their shared nature.

It is not simply that Allatini's heroine's name is Antoinette. (Though brought up in England, she is supposedly the child of French emigrés.) In the opening scene of the novel, a number of guests in a hotel, including Antoinette, are diverting themselves by performing a little costume drama about the French Revolution. The play's author, a somewhat silly young woman named Rosabel, has written it in honor of Antoinette, whom she idolizes. When Antoinette perversely chooses the part of Charlotte Corday instead of that of her namesake, the infatuated Rosabel is sorely tried: "Antoinette, darling, I do think it's such a pity—though of course you know best, and I'm sure you're simply wonderful as Charlotte

Corday—but I did write Marie Antoinette's part on purpose for you—so sweet that you've got the same name, isn't it? And I know I'm no good in the part . . ." Rosabel, the narrator observes, "was ready to lavish great floods of adoration on her friends or on characters in history or fiction. At present the said adoration was equally divided between Antoinette de Courcy and the 'Unhappy Queen.'"[85]

The scene is meant to be satirical of course—with the joke on Rosabel. (Later on when war breaks out, she abruptly switches her affection from Marie Antoinette to the queen of Belgium, whom she sees as "just as unfortunate and more up-to-date.") But it also suggests something about Allatini's heroine. Antoinette. Though opting here for the part of Charlotte Corday, Antoinette cannot escape, as it were, from her fateful name—or from the powerful homoerotic emotion with which it is so obviously associated. In the same hotel is Hester, a mysterious older woman with whom Antoinette herself will soon become wildly infatuated. Though Antoinette resists her feelings for Hester—turning instead to men and hopes of marriage—she is caught out by the end of the novel, when she realizes that she has loved the older woman all along. The elaborately homoerotic invocation of Marie Antoinette at the outset might thus be said to function as a kind of proleptic hint to the reader—as the cipher, or symbolic intimation, of Antoinette's own emerging lesbian desires.

An even more striking invocation of the Marie Antoinette topos occurs in *The Well of Loneliness*, Radclyffe Hall's openly polemical classic of lesbian fiction from 1928. Midway through that novel, Radclyffe Hall's lonely young heroine, Stephen Gordon, who has yet to confide in anyone her tormented knowledge of her own homosexuality, pays a visit to Versailles in the company of Jonathan Brockett, a sympathetic yet oddly effeminate artist friend who has taken her under his wing. Brockett guides her through the rooms of the palace— "repeopling the place for Stephen so that she seemed to see the glory of the dancers led by the youthful Roi Soleil; seemed to hear the rhythm of the throbbing violins, and the throb of the rhythmic dancing feet as they beat down the length of the Galerie des Glaces." But "most skillfully of all," the narrator observes, "did he recreate for her the image of the luckless queen who came after; as though for some reason this unhappy woman must appeal in a personal way to Stephen."[86]

As soon as Stephen and Brockett enter the dead queen's apartments (where Stephen is inexplicably moved), Brockett's comments become even more insinuating:

> Brockett pointed to the simple garniture on the mantelpiece of the little salon, then he looked at Stephen: "Madame de Lamballe gave those to the queen," he murmured softly.
>
> She nodded, only vaguely apprehending his meaning.
>
> Presently they followed him out into the gardens and stood looking across the Tapis Vert that stretches its quarter mile of greenness towards a straight, lovely line of water.
>
> Brockett said, very low, so that Puddle [Stephen's servant] should not hear him: "Those two would often come here at sunset. Sometimes they were rowed along the canal in the sunset—can't you imagine it, Stephen? They must often have felt pretty miserable, poor souls; sick to death of the subterfuge and pretences. Don't you ever get tired of that sort of thing? My God!– I do." But she did not answer, for now there was no mistaking his meaning.[87]

The episode, which concludes with the two of them visiting Marie Antoinette's "Temple de l'Amour," close by to the Petit Trianon, is

94. *Versailles — Trianon – Temple de l'Amour*

The Temple de l'Amour, near the Petit Trianon, Versailles, visited by Stephen Gordon in Radclyffe Hall's *The Well of Loneliness* (1928). From a French postcard, c. 1900. *Author's collection.*

incomprehensible without some knowledge of the homoerotic bio-graphical traditions surrounding the queen in the later nineteenth century. Clearly, Radclyffe Hall expected her lesbian readers to un-derstand the reference to "Madame de Lamballe" and to find in Brockett's cryptic history lesson a consoling, if melancholy, image of homosexual communion. (The subtle parody of Moberly and Jour-dain's *An Adventure* also seems intentional.)* Evoking the love be-tween queen and princess, Brockett manages, as if by a delicate sem-aphor, to communicate to Stephen both the fact of his own homosexuality and his unspoken awareness of her own. In turn, grasping his meaning, she is suddenly able to see her lesbianism in a larger emotional context. Marie Antoinette functions here as a kind of potent ancestor spirit, whose spectral presence at once liberates and affirms Stephen's own half-acknowledged erotic desires. Later on, when Stephen at last finds happiness with a woman lover, she will in fact return to Versailles with her, as if in tribute to her unseen benefactress.[88]

In several other well-known lesbian novels of the twenties and thir-ties, the ghost of Marie Antoinette, though unnamed, hovers dis-creetly behind the scenes. In Virginia Woolf's *Orlando* (1928), memo-ries of Marie Antoinette (and the rosy-cheeked Lamballe) seem to haunt the courtship scenes of Orlando and Sasha, the Russian "Princess," who begin their androgynous romance by riding out in sledges, then skating, over the ice of the frozen Thames. ("And then, wrapped in their sables, they would talk of everything under the sun; of sights and travels; of Moor and Pagan; of this man's beard and that woman's skin; of a rat that fed from her hand at table; of the arras that moved always in the hall at home; of a face; of a feather. Nothing was too small for such converse, nothing was too great.")[89]

---

*That Radclyffe Hall was familiar with *An Adventure* and its authors seems to me likely indeed, given her lifelong interest in occultism and psychical research. Radclyffe Hall and Una Troubridge's twenty-year homosexual relationship paralleled Moberly and Jourdain's in interesting ways; both couples felt themselves deeply susceptible to supernatural influ-ences. In Brighton in 1920, in the company of Troubridge, the novelist saw the apparition of a mutual friend inspecting an automobile in a garage. Like Moberly and Jourdain before them, the two sent an account of their experience to the editors of the *Journal of the Society for Psychical Research*, who published it in the April 1921 issue under the title "A Veridical Apparition."

In *Extraordinary Women* (1928), Compton Mackenzie's comic satire on lesbian expatriate society on Capri in the 1920s, the gallant Anastasia Sarbécoff, an impoverished member of the sapphic colony on the island of "Sirène," "[steps] out as dauntlessly toward an old age of penury as the French nobility stepped forward to the guillotine"; another character presents herself as "deliciously *ancien régime.*"[90] (Though not, obviously, a lesbian himself, the discerning Mackenzie seems to have had a remarkable intuitive understanding of contemporary lesbian tropes.)

Rather more somberly, in a dreamlike passage in Djuna Barnes's *Nightwood* (1936) Robin Vote, the homosexual wife of the luckless would-be aristocrat Felix Volkbein, dresses herself in the magnificent, dilapidated costumes of a woman of the later eighteenth century:

> Her skirts were moulded to her hips and fell downward and out, wider and longer than those of other women, heavy silks that made her seem newly ancient. One day [Felix] learned the secret. Pricing a small tapestry in an antique shop facing the Seine, he saw Robin reflected in a door mirror of a back room, dressed in a heavy brocaded gown which time had stained in places, in others split, yet which was so voluminous that there were yards left to refashion.[91]

Captivated, yet unable to penetrate her uncanny alienation, Felix concedes defeat: "Looking at her he knew that he was not sufficient to make her what he had hoped; it would require more than his own argument. It would require contact with persons exonerated of their earthly condition by some strong spiritual bias, someone of that old regime, some old lady of the past courts, who only remembered others when trying to think of herself."[92]

In Olive Moore's *Celestial Seraglio* (1929), the adolescent heroine's boarding-school beloved, Joyce, holds her head so elegantly after being reprimanded by a teacher she looks like "Marie Antoinette on her way to execution"; in Antonia White's similarly themed *Frost in May* (1933), an older girl the heroine is in love with "[moves] in her haze of charm like Marie Antoinette."[93] And, as we have seen, in Sylvia Townsend Warner's *Summer Will Show* (1936), the heroine Sophia Willoughby's female lover is stabbed on a barricade by a mulatto boy whom Sophia has raised up, in a scene that weirdly recalls the melodramatic demise of the princesse de Lamballe as recounted by "Catherine Hyde" in the anonymous *Secret Memoirs of Princess Lamballe*.[94]

Marie Antoinette's ghost lingers on, finally, even in more recent lesbian writing and iconography. In the 1950s, Lennox Strong published an article in the *Ladder*, the first national lesbian magazine, detailing Marie Antoinette's putative affairs with women; the article was reprinted in a collection of *Ladder* essays in 1976.[95] In 1985 Florence King invoked the memory of the princesse de Lamballe in her lesbian coming-of-age story, *Confessions of a Failed Southern Lady;* a character in Jeanette Winterson's homoerotic historical romance *The Passion* (1987) "still [prays] for the soul of Marie Antoinette."[96] Images of Marie Antoinette likewise continue to crop up in contemporary visual representations of female homosexuality. The cover of a 1974 paperback edition of *The Well of Loneliness* shows two women in quasi-eighteenth-century costume, one of whom wears a cameo of a

Marie Antoinette and Yolande de Polignac. From the lesbian periodical the *Ladder*, c. 1955. *Courtesy of Stanford University Libraries*.

Eighteenth-century-themed cover of *The
Well of Loneliness* (New York, 1974). *Courtesy
of Simon and Schuster.*

woman resembling the queen at her neck. An advertisement for a
women-only dance in the gay and lesbian magazine *Outweek* (1991)
shows another pair of women, one dressed in the rustic-rococo style
adopted by Marie Antoinette in the 1780s. And most amusingly, perhaps, in the rock video "Vogue" (1990), the pop icon Madonna, also
dressed as Marie Antoinette, offers her own ambiguous paean to late
twentieth-century lesbian chic.[97]

From one angle, the lesbian rehabilitation of Marie Antoinette—a
process that I have argued can be traced back to the Goncourt
brothers—might be derided, of course, as hopelessly politically in-
correct. From the late nineteenth century onward, from Hélène

148

"Marie Antoinette" advertisement.
From *Outweek*, 1991.

Smith and Radclyffe Hall to *Outweek* and Madonna, what I have defined as Marie Antoinette "obsession"—her overt or covert celebration as homoerotic icon—might easily be condemned as a distinctly dubious, even reactionary subcultural phenomenon. Since the turn of the century, the queen's numerous acolytes have shown little interest in her actual political beliefs (except, embarrassingly, to defend them) or her scabrous role in some of the events leading up to the French Revolution. Of the feckless, manipulative, often ruthless figure who comes across in more objective histories, those who romanticize her love of women have had virtually nothing to say.[98]

And yet, one cannot help but feel in the end, perhaps, that there is also something bizarrely liberating, if not revolutionary, about the transmogrification of Marie Antoinette into lesbian heroine. It is true that there is a nostalgic element in her cult: women who thought they "saw" her, like Hélène Smith, the "Dream Romances" writer, and Moberly and Jourdain, were in one sense flagrantly retreating into the past, into a kind of psychic old regime. But in the act of conjuring up her ghost, they were also, I think, conjuring something new into being—a poetics of possibility. It is perhaps not too much to say that in her role as idealized martyr (as in *The Secret Memoirs of Princess Lamballe* or *The Well of Loneliness*), Marie Antoinette functioned as a kind of lesbian Oscar Wilde: a rallying point for sentiment and collective emotional intransigence. She gave those who idolized her a way of thinking about themselves. And out of such reflection—peculiar as its manifestations may often look to us now—something of the modern lesbian identity was born.

7

HAUNTED BY

OLIVE

CHANCELLOR

It has long been fashionable—
mirabile dictu—to assert that Henry James's *The Bostonians* (1886) is
not "really" about lesbianism. Despite James's interest in the "un-
wholesome" side of female-female intimacy, declared Oscar Cargill in
a book on James in the 1960s, it was wrong to call *The Bostonians*
"merely a study of Lesbianism."[1] For Walter F. Wright, writing in
1962, it was unnecessary to "encumber" the novel with lesbianism;
"The theme is about something else."[2] James himself, argued Maxwell Geismar a few years later, would have been "horrified" at the
thought of anyone reading his fiction as a study in "lesbian pathol-
ogy."[3] And recent commentators have concurred. Jean Strouse, in

her 1980 biography of James's sister Alice, warns us that it is a "great mistake" to "read lesbianism into *The Bostonians*."[4] Tony Tanner is downright pontifical: "It is irrelevant and limiting," he concludes in a passage on *The Bostonians* in *Henry James* (1987), "to consider it as a study of lesbianism."[5]

Paradoxically, however, James's critics have had no qualms about arguing what might seem a contradictory point: that Olive Chancellor, the character in *The Bostonians* who is in many ways its central moral and psychological presence, is obviously—and at times even excruciatingly—a repressed lesbian. Ever since Lionel Trilling's description of her in *The Opposing Self* as a "deteriorated Minerva, presiding in homosexual chastity over the Athens of the New World," it has been de rigueur to refer to Olive (while also deploring her tastes) as a recognizably "deviant" female type.[6] In the intensity of her doomed passion for the redheaded Verena Tarrant, writes F. W. Dupee, Olive shows herself as "pretty distinctly a case of perverse sexuality."[7] Her unconscious "homosexuality," says William McMurray, "is the biological evidence of a rigid self-centeredness that has blinded itself to the heterogeneous character of reality."[8] According to Irving Howe, by jealously obstructing the bond between Verena and Basil Ransom, the "unnatural" Olive threatens the essential "rhythms of life."[9] She "hates men," writes Tony Tanner, with a "twisted passion" and fails utterly to achieve "any kind of full sexual humanity."[10] For Edmund Wilson, Olive is simply "horrid."[11]

We are confronted here, of course, with an interesting non sequitur. How can James's novel *not* be "a study of lesbianism" if its central character—as many have repeatedly affirmed Olive to be—is in fact a "horrid" lesbian? What else besides such a character, one wonders, would one need? Certainly ordinary readers (including a number of would-be censors) have had no difficulty labeling *The Bostonians* a lesbian novel. As Jeannette Foster observes in the introduction to her classic bibliography, *Sex Variant Women in Literature* (1956):

> No class of printed matter except outright pornography has suffered more critical neglect, exclusion from libraries, or omission from collected works than variant [i.e., lesbian-themed] belles-lettres. Even items by recognized masters, such as Henry James's *The Bostonians* and

Maupassant's "Paul's Mistress," have been omitted from inclusive editions issued by reputable publishers. When owned by libraries such titles are often catalogued obscurely, or impounded in special collections almost inaccessible to the public, or they have been "lost"—most probably stolen—and not replaced.[12]

Whether the exclusion of *The Bostonians* from the comprehensive 1906–10 New York edition of James's works had anything directly to do with its subject matter is perhaps debatable, but it is nonetheless clear that among the general reading public the novel has always had a reputation—as Foster tactfully puts it—for being full of "variant" interest.[13]

Must we then arraign James's critics for a kind of homophobic double-talk? Certainly they often seem to want it both ways. James, the "Master," the argument seems to go, would never have dreamed of writing about anything so crude or clinical-sounding as "lesbianism." But since he did—witness the unpleasant Olive—he must have done so in order to condemn her. Hence the almost universal (and often illogical) vilification of Olive's "unnatural" desires, lack of "full sexual humanity," and so on.

And yet a conscientious reader (even a conscientious lesbian reader) may nonetheless want to rein in the sense of pious indignation. For there still is, if not exactly a problem, certainly an ambiguity about the "lesbianism" of *The Bostonians*. In what, precisely, does "it" consist? Though it may seem clear on the surface that James conceived Olive as a kind of homosexual type, it is not *as* clear, it seems to me, in what sense the novel itself is specifically "about" female homosexuality. Like Jeannette Foster, I happen to think that *The Bostonians is* an important lesbian novel, and should be understood as such, but I am also willing to acknowledge that its *lesbianism* (to isolate the term in all of its offending and awkward grandeur) is often elusive. Wherein does it lie? Through what textual gestures, or representational maneuvers, does it make itself known? In what follows I would like to explore this somewhat opaque issue—along with what we can determine of James's attitudes regarding female homosexuality—with an eye toward ultimately placing *The Bostonians*, explicitly, within a larger lesbian literary tradition.

James and the Specter of Lesbianism: The Case of *Nana*

We must go to the French novel for our ideas.
—James, "An Animated Conversation," 1889

At the risk of being accused of perversity, I would like to maintain at the outset that I think it impossible to understand the homosexual aspect of *The Bostonians* without first turning away, to some extent, from James's own comments about the novel. The jottings James made in his notebook in 1883, while he was preparing to work on *The Bostonians*, are well known, having often been rehearsed by critics. He wished, he declared, "to write a very *American* tale, a tale very characteristic of our social conditions, and I asked myself what was the most salient and peculiar point in our social life. The answer was: the situation of women, the decline of the sentiment of sex, the agitation on their behalf." In depicting the relation between his two main female characters—Olive Chancellor and Verena Tarrant—he desired, he wrote, to delineate "one of those friendships between women which are so common in New England." The "whole thing," James concluded, was to be "as American, as possible, and as full of Boston: an attempt to show that I *can* write an American story."[14]

The emphasis here on the "Americanness" of the novel has frequently been echoed—often with a note of nationalistic fervor—by James's (mostly American) critics. Thus Trilling and Howe and others have marveled at the vivid rendering of the New England "scene," James's attention to local color and detail, his considerable (and sometimes surprising) familiarity with late nineteenth-century American social reform movements, and his sensitive insight—dramatized in the bitter clash between Olive Chancellor, the austere denizen of Charles Street, and Basil Ransom, the displaced and impoverished Southern veteran—into the lingering moral and spiritual divides afflicting the national psyche in the years immediately following the Civil War.[15]

And in similar fashion, most commentators on the novel have followed James in stressing the peculiarly "American" nature of the bond between Olive Chancellor and the beautiful young "oratress,"

Verena Tarrant. Such romantic friendships between single women in late nineteenth-century New England, R. H. Gooder reminds us in a recent introduction to *The Bostonians*, were indeed "common enough to have been called 'Boston marriages.' " Like the bluestocking Olive, the partners in such "marriages" were often intellectually distinguished: Margaret Fuller, Sarah Orne Jewett, Elizabeth McCracken, Charlotte Cushman, and James's own invalid sister, Alice, were among a host of brilliant New England women who spent their lives with devoted female companions. Echoing biographical speculations by Leon Edel and Jean Strouse, Gooder suggests that James's portrait of Olive and Verena's relationship may have been inspired in part by the close attachment that sprang up in 1879 between Alice and Katharine Peabody Loring, the "beloved friend" with whom Alice shared the last twelve years of her life. This attachment, like most Boston marriages, Gooder implies, was more spiritual and emotional than physical in nature.[16]

While I don't dispute the importance of recognizing the New England context of much of *The Bostonians* or the fineness of James's powers of local observation, I think the near-total critical fixation on the book's "American" element has resulted in a certain myopia regarding what one might call its "European" or counter aspect: its subtle reworking of characteristically European literary themes (including that of homosexuality) and its special relationship with several works of later nineteenth-century French fiction in particular. Though James's friendships with Flaubert, Edmond de Goncourt, Maupassant, Zola, Paul Bourget and others are a matter of record—and his debt to the French naturalist school widely acknowledged—little has been made of this linkage specifically in connection with *The Bostonians*.*

---

*This isn't to say the linkage is ignored—on the contrary, no less an authority than Leon Edel, James's biographer, notes that by the early 1880s, under the influence of the French naturalists, James had determined that "his new novels [*The Bostonians* and *The Princess Casamassima*] would 'do' Boston and London as Zola had done his Paris, and was to do the coal mines—by descending into the very heart of his subject" (*Henry James*, p. 105). Other critics elaborate: both Lyall H. Powers, in *Henry James and the Naturalist Movement*, and Robert Emmet Long, in *Henry James: The Early Novels*, notice the "pervasive" influence of Daudet, the Goncourts, and Zola in James's novels of the 1880s. With the exception of Long, however, who limns an important connection with Daudet's *L'Évangéliste* (1883), and Adeline R. Tintner, who, in *The Book World of Henry James*, finds traces of Balzac's *La Fille aux yeux*

With regard to the issue of lesbianism—and in what way it is or isn't "present" in *The Bostonians*—the American emphasis has been especially distracting. It may be true perhaps that Olive and Verena's relationship has a certain loose historical connection with the so-called Boston marriage phenomenon, and with the well-documented friendship between Alice James and Katharine Loring in particular— but to say so, in my view, is not to say very much at all. Indeed, in some ways, the merely local or biographical approach leads one straight into an interpretive dead end. In a crudely literal sense, neither Olive nor Verena bears much resemblance to Alice James or Katharine Loring; and the suggestion, sometimes bruited, that the fictional portrait of Olive owes something to Alice seems to me almost entirely unfounded.[17] James's conscience-ridden, exalted, painfully humorless suffragette (whom Basil Ransom, with some sympathy, recognizes as "a woman without laughter") seems in personality and mental outlook nothing like the sardonic Alice—who by all accounts retained her coruscating and sociable wit to the last days of her life. Nor do we find much of the girlish and flirtatious Verena in the stalwart, unglamorous, even virile Loring. (Alice once referred to Loring as "the excellent but prosaic K."[18]) In sensibility, as in appearance, the two couples could hardly seem more different.

Most important, the relationship between Alice and Loring seems to have lacked utterly that peculiar admixture of hunger, fierceness, and encroaching desperation—inescapably sexual in origin—which so suffuses Olive's feeling for Verena. James's and Loring's was indeed a "Boston marriage" in the classic sense—tenderly affectionate, yet seemingly unruffled by strong erotic undercurrents. Olive's longing for Verena, however, is unmistakably a grand passion, and carries with it all of the agitation, self-heightening, and morbid neurasthenia typically associated with such monumental emotion. There is nothing in the documented relation between Alice James and Katharine Loring to account for Olive's "white-faced" and stricken gaze when she first lays sight on Verena at Miss Birdseye's, her agonized, almost

---

d'or in *The Bostonians*, few critics have sought to uncover specific intertextual linkages. When it comes to a more particularized sort of source hunting, James's commentators have been much more inclined, again, to look for American prototypes—notably in Hawthorne's *The Blithedale Romance* (1852) and Howells's *The Undiscovered Country* (1880).

shuddering ecstasy when Verena agrees to live with her "forever" on Charles Street, or indeed her obliterating sexual despair when the younger woman at last leaves her for Basil Ransom. There is nothing in their relation, in other words, to account for what actually *happens* in *The Bostonians*—where Olive's passion comes from, or why, seemingly so inexorably, it ends in erotic calamity.

From many points of view *The Bostonians* is—as James designed—a "very *American* tale." But in its suggestive handling of the theme of female homosexuality it is also a very "French" tale, in ways that James's own comments, like a kind of patriotic smokescreen, have tended to obscure. "L'amour sapphique," after all, was one of the great imaginative motifs of nineteenth-century French literature— from Gautier's *Mademoiselle de Maupin*, Balzac's *La Fille aux yeux d'or* (1835), and Baudelaire's *Les Fleurs du mal* (1857) to Rachilde's *Monsieur Vénus* (1884), Catulle Mendès's *Méphistophéla* (1890) and Pierre Louÿs's *Chansons de Bilitis* (1894). Of James's familiarity with the rich tradition of French writing on lesbianism there can be no doubt: as a reviewer for the *Nation* and other literary journals in the 1870s and 1880s he wrote extensively about French fiction and the novels of Gautier, Balzac, and Zola in particular.[19] In the works of the French novelists, James found both a precedent and a license for his own homoerotic plot making. And from one novel above all, as I shall argue, he drew special inspiration: Zola's notorious *Nana* (1880)—of which *The Bostonians* is a disguised and ironic transformation. Here, rather than in any real-life model, I think, is to be found the provocation for James's own "sapphic" tale.

This is not to say, of course, that we see in James—ever—any of that would-be salaciousness, shading at times into outright obscenity, so common in the nineteenth-century French literature of female-female desire. There is nothing in *The Bostonians* to match, for instance, the sheer lubriciousness of the following passage from *Mademoiselle de Maupin*, in which Gautier's heroine-in-disguise tells of a love rendezvous with the courtesan Rosette:

> She came to me, sat down on my lap quicker than lightning, put her arms round my neck, clasped her hands behind my head, and her mouth clung to mine in a wild embrace; I felt her breasts, half-naked and aroused, buoyant against my breasts, and her interlaced fingers

tighten in my hair. A quiver ran all through my body, and my nipples stood out.[20]

Or her langorous, Humbert-Humbert-like reverie after she undresses her little female page Ninon and takes her to bed:

Her body was a little marvel of delicacy. Her arms were rather thin, like those of any young girl, and they had an inexpressible suavity of line. Her budding breasts gave such charming promise that no fuller breasts could have borne comparison. She still had all the graces of the child, she already had all the charms of the woman; she had reached that adorable moment of transition from the little girl to the young girl: a fugitive, imperceptible moment, a delightful time when beauty is full of hope, and every day, instead of taking something from your love, adds new perfections to it.[21]

Nor, to look ahead to *Nana* itself, is there anything in James's novel remotely comparing with Zola's sordid picture of Nana and her prostitute-lover Satin, playing out their desire in front of a group of drunken gentlemen—

Satin, having peeled a pear, came and ate it behind her darling, pressing against her shoulders and whispering remarks in her ear at which they roared with laughter. Then she decided to share her last piece of pear with Nana, and presented it to her between her teeth; the two women nibbled at each other's lips, finishing the pear in a kiss.[22]

—or his coarsely titillating views of the Parisian sexual underworld, as in this description of a sapphic *table d'hôte* in the Rue des Martyrs:

There were about a hundred women there, who had seated themselves wherever they could find a vacant place. Most of them were enormous creatures in their late thirties, with bloated flesh hanging in puffy folds over their flaccid lips, but in the midst of all these bulging bosoms and bellies there were a few slim, pretty girls to be seen. These still wore an innocent expression in spite of their immodest gestures, for they were just beginners in their profession, picked up in some dance-hall and brought along to Laure's by one of her female customers. Here the crowd of portly women, excited by the scent of their youth, jostled one another in order to treat them to all kinds of dainties, paying court to them rather as a group of ardent old bachelors might have done. (258)

Not for the creator of Miss Birdseye and Doctor Prance, the corpulent denizens of Café Laure.

For James, it need hardly be said, found overt references to lesbian eroticism, if not repellent, profoundly unsuitable for polite fiction. His taste inevitably rebelled against what he would later call "the failure of fastidiousness."[23] Indeed, were one to judge by his critical comments alone, one might easily be beguiled into thinking that he found the theme itself repugnant. As a reviewer of French writing, he regularly disparaged works containing explicitly lesbian scenes, though always (one must hasten to note) in the most glancing and delicate of terms. Thus, in his otherwise laudatory posthumous tribute to Gautier from 1872, he described *Mademoiselle de Maupin* as that writer's "one disagreeable performance." It was "rather a painful exhibition of the prurience of the human mind," he added, "that, in most of the recent notices of the author's death (those, at least, published in England and America) this work alone should have been selected as the critic's text."[24] Elsewhere, he spoke of the book as a "puerile performance" and dismissed Swinburne's enthusiasm for it as "perversity of taste."[25]

Animadverting in 1878 on the later editions of *Les Fleurs du mal*, to which Baudelaire's famous "interdicted" verses on lesbianism had been restored, James observed that reading such poetry was like "[seeing] a gentleman, in a painful-looking posture, staring very hard at a mass of things from which, more intelligently, we avert our heads."[26] He took a similar line on Maupassant's somewhat squalid short story, "La Femme de Paul" (1881). This tale, in which a young man loses his mistress to a predatory male impersonator at a riverside amusement park, while various onlookers cry out "Lesbos! Lesbos!" was, James opined, a case of genius gone "woefully astray." Like other "gross imperfections" in Maupassant's oeuvre, it was "absolutely unadapted to the perusal of ladies and young persons."[27] And reviewing *Nana* itself in 1880, he spoke, with quaint dismay, of its "monstrous uncleanness" and of the "singular foulness" of Zola's imagination.[28]

And yet it would be a mistake to read too much into these carefully measured reflections, or to see James as put off in some deep way by the subject of female homosexuality per se. As always in James, the apparent prudishness is no more than skin-deep. Even in the *Nana* piece—on the surface the most censorious of his seemingly anti-lesbian statements—his objection is less to any particular subject matter than to Zola's humorlessness and the "melancholy dryness of his execution." Zola's characters simply did not come alive, James complained; indeed, "anything less illusory than the pictures, the people, the indecencies of *Nana*, could not well be imagined." For all her depravities, the bisexual Nana, he thought, was a mere cutout: "the figure of the brutal *fille*, without conscience or soul, with nothing but devouring appetites and impudences, has become the stalest of the stock properties of French fiction, and M. Zola's treatment has here imparted to her no touch of superior verity." The French novelist was welcome, James concluded, "to draw as many figures of the same type as he finds necessary, if he will only make them human."[29]

On the contrary, it was precisely by way of *Nana* that James found an ingenious means of treating the subject of lesbianism in *The Bostonians*. Zola's novel appeared—to much scandal—in January of 1880; James reviewed it a month later. By 1883, when James had begun work on *The Bostonians*, *Nana* remained the most notorious French fiction of its day.[30] By setting up a discreet chain of intertextual connections between Zola's novel and his own, James was able to insinuate the *idea* of lesbianism into *The Bostonians* without—so to speak—openly representing it. The trick is similar to one he would later dramatize in *The Awkward Age* (1899). There, the fact that the young heroine has read a certain scandalous "French novel" (the title of which remains forever unspecified) casts a compromising pall over the way she is regarded by a prospective suitor. The unnamed novel might indeed be said to "haunt" her career on the marriage market.* In *The Bostonians*, it is not so much that any particular character is haunted in this way, but that the novel itself is: for *Nana*, after a fashion, inhabits it. It is there, "within" *The Bostonians*, like a kind of ghostly shadow text, subtly imparting a host of subliminal meanings. In the end, by summoning up *Nana* in this spectral manner (and its lesbian passages in particular), James was able to address the problematic theme of fe-

---

*That the unnamed and "very *awful*" book on which James's heroine's marital hopes are wrecked may in fact be *Nana* is suggested by her own name—Nanda (Brookenham). See *The Awkward Age*, especially book 8, chapter 30.

male homosexuality without doing violence to his notion of literary decorum.

Few of these ghostly connections, I admit, may seem obvious at first glance. What link *can* there be, the skeptic will want to know, between Zola's Second Empire Paris, with its sewers and sensuality and engrossing corruption, and James's austere, reformist Boston? Between golden, outrageous French prostitutes, reeking "of the animal essence of woman," and ascetical beings like Olive, yearning only (or so it seems at first) for the day "she might be a martyr and die for something"? What connection, indeed, between *Nana's* relentless *impudeur*—castigated by one critic as "the incipient erethism of an ambitious and impotent brain maddened by its sensual visions"[31]—and Jamesian ultrarefinement? Though both *Nana* and *The Bostonians* take place in or around 1870, their characters, like their creators, seem to inhabit almost comically disparate physical and emotive worlds.

And yet, as James would write to a friend in 1896, "Zola is awfully *sound*—I have a tenderness for Zola. Not a pennyworth of distinction, but a shopful of *stuff*. What he says is good for you—put on blinders—and jog on the straight road."[32] A clue to just what "*stuff*" James found so useful in *Nana* is suggested by the title James originally gave to *The Bostonians* but later abandoned: *Verena*. For it is precisely through Verena—the "attractive but ambiguous young person" with whom both Olive and Basil fall in love—that the connection with the earlier novel is established. As far as the theme of homosexuality is concerned, the lurking assonance between "Nana" and "Verena" is too important to ignore. By linking Verena from the start with Zola's infamous prostitute-heroine, the "golden fly" who preys on women and men alike, James sets up that subliminal (and somewhat perverse) intertextual backdrop against which the lesbian relationship at the heart of *The Bostonians* will be played out.

In a submerged fashion, a Nana/Verena parallel can be seen to shape much of what goes on in *The Bostonians*—especially in its mainly comic first half. Consider, for example, the opening scenes of each novel. Zola's fiction begins, we may recall, with a *début*: Nana, a courtesan and "high-class *cocotte*," is making her first appearance as Venus, the goddess of love, in a burlesque operetta—*The Blonde Venus*—at the Théâtre des Variétés. Hoping for scandal and entertainment, a crowd of excited spectators have gathered to witness her performance. When Nana finally enters, half-naked and brazen in her mythological guise, her fair red hair "hanging loosely over her shoulders," she proceeds to work up her audience into a paroxysm of collective lust. Trilling out spicy lyrics in a "plebeian" voice, she sends "shivers" through all who listen to her; by undulating back and forth and thrusting out her breasts, she elicits rapturous, sweaty applause. As she moves upstage, exposing a neck "on which her reddish hair looked like an animal's fleece," the clapping and the cries become "positively frantic." By the time she reaches the shocking climax of her act—in which she mimics the goddess rising from the waves ("with no veil save her tresses" and her naked body displayed "in all its foamlike whiteness")—her audience sits breathless, as if "under a spell" (44–45). The tension only breaks when, with Nana "smiling in all the splendour of her sovereign nudity," the curtain falls and the audience relaxes into a final thunderous storm of applause.

Yet *The Bostonians* also opens with a *début*—in a scene that, though superficially more decorous, might be read as a covert parody of Zola's. Like Nana, the redheaded Verena is also making her first appearance—not, to be sure, as the star in a lascivious operetta, but as a "high-class speaker" in the elderly Miss Birdseye's living room. Like Zola's heroine, Verena has risen from the obscure lower depths of society; in the glancing portrait of her father, the odious quack healer and mesmerist, Selah Tarrant, James hints at a background of almost Rougon-Macquart-style racketiness. And like Nana, too, she has an immediate, imponderable *succès fou*. Delivering her speech (on the sufferings of women) like one "peculiarly" possessed, she puts everyone who listens to her "under a charm."[33] At the end, when her mother, Mrs. Tarrant, takes her in her arms and kisses her, the motley audience at Miss Birdseye's is "exceedingly affected" and breaks into vociferous "exclamations and murmurs" (59).

Certain details of the latter scene—all carefully stage-managed—suggest just how closely James had indeed studied his French precursor. Verena's red hair and white skin ("white as women are who have that shade of red hair") are her most obvious physical links with Zola's heroine; her love of candy, remarked upon by Dr. Prance (40), a rather more subtle one. (Throughout Zola's novel, Nana is shown subsisting, out of sickly habit, on daily bags of burnt almonds and sweets made out of "confectioner's jam.") When Verena is introduced to the stately Mrs. Farrinder, the jealous *doyenne* of the lecture circuit, the older woman stares down upon her rival, James says, with "the frown of a Juno." In Zola's novel, a flaccid "Juno" is one of the crude mock Olympians run off the stage during Nana's *coup de théâtre*. And several other characters recall specific individuals from the earlier fiction. The crass young journalist, Matthias Pardon, eager to cash in on Verena's performance, seems closely modeled on the character of Fauchery—the writer from the *Figaro* who becomes both Nana's publicist and one of her many lovers. And when Pardon exclaims, in Basil Ransom's hearing, that "there's money for some one in that girl; you see if she don't have quite a run!" (59)—there is more than a little hint, I think, of that famous (albeit coarse) set piece later on in Zola's novel in which a racehorse named Nana, backed by one of her lovers, wins the Grand Prix de Paris.

But the most important link with *Nana* is James's half-mocking presentation of Verena as a kind of love goddess, who like her vulgar French prototype, produces universal erotic perturbation. Just as Nana's libidinous performance as "Venus" works an unstoppable sensual charm over everyone who watches her (and all of the men and women who will later in the novel become her lovers are present at her *début*) so Verena, by her speech, inspires a barely suppressed collective "contagion" (60). To see her is, as it were, to cathect upon her. This dubious triumph, James hints, has more to do with her "free young attitudes," of course, than with anything she actually says. For Basil Ransom, deep-dyed misogynist and connoisseur of "little variety actresses," her effect is decidedly nonintellectual: "to *his* starved senses she irresistibly appealed" (56). Her odd theatricality is part of her power: with her hypnotic voice and entrancingly "supple" figure, she exudes an air "of being on exhibition, of belonging to a troupe, of living in the gaslight" (53). She is a seductress, a "half-bedizened damsel," whose rich tresses, gathered into a serpentine coil, seem to glow with the mysterious "brightness" of her nature (54). For Olive Chancellor, watching her performance as if stunned—like the Comte Muffat watching Nana—Verena is simply "very wonderful" (73).

At several points James comes close to giving away his hand entirely. Basil, listening to Verena's vague quasi-feminist importunings, yet "steeled against the inanities she uttered," blames her conniving father for making her speak such "trash." She does so, he thinks, simply out of a yearning for approval:

> For the necessity of her nature was not to make converts to a ridiculous cause, but to emit those charming notes of her voice, to stand in those free young attitudes, to shake her braided locks like a naiad rising from the waves, to please every one who came near her, and to be happy that she pleased. (57)

That the "naiad rising from the waves" image can be read as a slyly embedded allusion to Nana's spectacular emergence from the foam at the climax of *The Blonde Venus* seems to be verified at the telling conclusion of Verena's speech. The cynical Basil can only marvel at "the sweet grotesqueness of this virginal creature's standing up before a company of middle-aged people to talk to them about 'love,' the note on which she had closed her harangue. It was the most charming touch in the whole thing, and the most vivid proof of her innocence" (58–59). Verena winds up with the topic of "love" because like Nana, iconographically speaking, she *is* Love—and of a distinctly fleshly sort.

It would be possible of course to extend the Nana/Verena parallel forward in numerous directions—to see, for example, how the interesting theme of prostitution, neatly smuggled in from Zola, shapes certain elements in James's plot. (The scene in which Selah Tarrant more or less "sells" his daughter to Olive Chancellor is only one among many in which James appears to be importing directly from the grosser thematic stores of his French precursor.) But the point I want to make has more to do with what one might call the "aura" of *The Bostonians*: the way in which James's insistent allusions to *Nana* work to instill by indirection an oddly voluptuous, even carnal atmosphere in his own text—even when nothing overtly "sexual" seems to be happening. Verena is, as it were, contaminated by her resemblance to Nana; the vice of the one shadows over the virtue of the other.

This phenomenon (almost a kind of intertextual pollution) has what one might call its heterosexual manifestations—most noticeably in those scenes, such as the *début* itself, or that of Verena's speech at Mrs. Burrage's, in which we see Verena primarily through Basil's eyes. In the crowd at Mrs. Burrage's, for example, when Basil, momentarily overwhelmed by Verena's sensual presence ("amid lights and flowers . . . like an actress before the footlights"), finds himself becoming dizzy ("the room wavered before his eyes, even Verena's figure danced a little" [258]), it is difficult not to think, perhaps, of the vertiginous effect Nana has on her minions at the Théâtre des Variétés: "the whole house seemed to be swaying, seized by a fit of giddiness in its fatigue and excitement" (46). Or of the sexy, claustrophobic sensation she induces in the Comte Muffat, when he visits her backstage: "He needed air, and was leaving with a dizzy feeling produced by that dressing-room, a scent of flowers and female flesh which choked him" (68). In turn, when Basil—jealously observing Verena's effect on "the thick outer fringe of intently listening men" who surround her—notices that their attention has become "anything but languid" (253), the "Zolafied" reader may be reminded, again, of Nana's rather more coarsely galvanizing effect on *her* admirers:

> A wave of lust was flowing from her as from a bitch on heat, and it had spread further and further until it filled the whole house. Now her slightest movements fanned the flame of desire, and with a twitch of her little finger she could stir men's flesh. Backs arched and quivered as if unseen violin-bows had been drawn across their muscles; and on the nape of many a neck the down stirred in the hot, stray breath from some woman's lips. In front of him Fauchery saw the truant schoolboy half lifted out of his seat by passion. Curiosity led him to look at the Comte de Vandeuvres, who was very pale, with his lips pursed; at fat Steiner, whose face was apoplectic; at Labordette, ogling away with the astonished air of a horsedealer admiring a perfectly proportioned mare; and at Daguenet, whose ears were blood-red and twitching with pleasure.   (46)

The effect, in each case, is of a kind of hallucinatory "bleed through," of an obscene leakage from one fiction to the other. If Nana "is" Verena, then what Nana is to men, Verena is too.

Yet even more striking is the way in which the Zola connection works to sexualize—obliquely yet persistently—the relationship between Verena and Olive. Nana's potent female charm not only excites men, obviously: a good part of Zola's novel is devoted to the desire she provokes in Satin—the conniving lesbian prostitute with whom she becomes involved soon after her triumph in *Blonde Venus*. Yet Verena's appeal is similarly ambisexual, as Olive's infatuation for her quickly discloses. ("Nature," writes James, "had given her a beautiful smile, which fell impartially on every one, man and woman, alike" [114].) By setting up a train of discreet yet compromising intertextual links between Verena and Nana on the one hand, and Olive and Satin on the other, James manages to suggest the *effect*, if not exactly the reality, of a reciprocal lesbian desire. To the degree that Verena and Olive seem unconsciously to mimic their indecent French counterparts— at times even appear to be "possessed" by them—so their relationship itself comes to seem haunted by a ghostly Zolan carnality.

Once again one has a sense of backhanded parody. Each liaison starts in the same way: Satin materializes ("like a lady paying a call") in Nana's crowded dressing room and tries, amid the hubbub, to make a date with her (138); Olive, in ludicrous parallel, approaches Verena amid the crush of admirers at Miss Birdseye's and shyly invites her to Charles Street (63). Satin is "pale" and "tall" and bitterly hostile toward men (138); so too—as Basil Ransom will imminently discover—is Olive Chancellor. By appearing in Nana's room, Satin is of course blatantly angling for professional and sexual favors, while Olive longs, more mystically, for "a friend of her own sex with whom she might have a union of soul" (75). But for all her high-mindedness, James suggests, Olive is hardly less predatory. When she cogitates later over how best to draw the younger woman into her orbit ("Olive wished more and more to extract some definite pledge from her; she could hardly say what it had best be as yet; she only felt that it must be something that would have an absolute sanctity for Verena and would bind them together for life" [105–6]), she seems to follow Satin's method exactly: the goals are ostensibly different, but the premeditation (and resulting, successful, "pickup") are the same.

Olive, it is true, has a noble view in mind for her new protégée: convinced of Verena's burgeoning "genius," she intends to turn her into a feminist Joan of Arc, a maiden-warrior in the glorious struggle for women's rights. Her own role, she imagines, will be that of tutor and intellectual mentor. Thus those long Charles Street winter nights, "secure from interruption," during which she lectures to Verena on "masculine grossness" and "the history of feminine anguish," while the lamplight outside casts its strange "pink flushes on snow" (168–74).

Yet here too one has the sense of James rewriting—and in a most slyly insinuating fashion. Satin also is a pedagogue of sorts—concerned with "educating" Nana (who cares little for women at first) in the ways of homosexual vice. This she accomplishes by initiating her into the sapphic underworld at the Café Laure and constantly harping on the "swinishness" of men. She first seduces Nana in fact, expeditiously, after Nana comes to her one night in distress after being beaten by a male lover. In a small hotel room on the Rue Laval, where the two have shut themselves in against the chill night air, Satin adopts the part of outraged ally, "railing against the male sex even more indignantly than her friend." These sisterly consolations, neatly laced with antimale abuse, lead inevitably to sex:

> "Let's go straight to bed, pet. We'll be better off there. . . . Oh, how silly you are to get all worked up! I tell you, they're dirty swine! Forget about them . . . I'm here, and I love you. Don't cry now—just to please your little darling."
>
> And, once in bed, she took Nana in her arms straight away to comfort her. . . . Little by little her gentle embrace persuaded Nana to dry her tears. She was touched, and returned Satin's caresses. When two o'clock struck the candle was still burning, and the sound of muffled laughter was mingling with words of love. (279)

Nana in turn proves an eager pupil: not only is she violently "overwhelmed and excited" by the lovemaking with Satin, she soon takes a wicked pleasure in flaunting her liaison before jealous male lovers, such as the sadly obsessed Comte Muffat (343).

In James's novel, all that is lacking, one may feel, is the actual consummation. The late-night, cocoonlike atmosphere is the same; so too the tender, obsessional colloquy on the iniquities of men:

> They read a great deal of history together, and read it ever with the same thought—that of finding confirmation in it for this idea that their sex had suffered inexpressibly, and that any moment in the course of human affairs the state of the world would have been so much less horrible (history seemed to them in every way horrible), if women had been able to press down the scale. (168)

And Verena, too, is a quick study—full of her own happy "suggestions" and a strange, unerring "facility" at which the enraptured Olive can only marvel: "[Verena's] share in the union of the two young women was no longer passive, purely appreciative; it was passionate, too, and it put forth a beautiful energy" (160). While the snow floats delicately down outside, muffling every sound, the room on Charles Street, like the room on the Rue Laval, becomes a curiously boudoirlike retreat, a place where "ruddy" shadows dance on the walls and the thick warm air itself seems to inspire "enlarged and intensified vision" (168). By the time that James—in the guise of coyly reticent narrator—acknowledges that Olive, lost in adoration, "was more and more happy to think that their cause should have the services of an organization so rare," the sense of creeping double entendre—and of Zolaesque sexual titillation—is almost inescapable (169).

Elsewhere, James will compromise Olive and Verena further by surrounding them, sometimes laughably, with various objects and "props" associated in *Nana* with deviance and homosexual love. In Zola's novel, Satin and Nana carry on their liaison in Nana's decadently appointed Paris apartment on the Avenue de Villiers, amid the stereotypical paraphernalia of fin de siècle sapphic libertinism— ottomans and Persian rugs, "pink silk hangings," tiger skins and bearskins, "bronzes and Chinese vases full of flowers," and "armchairs as wide as beds" (312–13). (In one lubricious scene Satin and Nana actually have sex on the pile of animal skins.) On the rare occasions the intoxicated twosome venture outside, they bring with them all the lascivious charm "of an Oriental bazaar let out into the open street" (271).

Yet again as if elaborating a private joke, James often places Verena and Olive in similarly suggestive surroundings. Though Olive claims to abhor "French ideas," she has a distinct hankering, even on respectable Charles Street, after *le luxe et la volupté*. "Miss Chancellor," writes James, "had no difficulty in persuading herself that persons doing the high intellectual and moral work to which the young ladies in Charles Street were now committed owed it to themselves, owed it to the groaning sisterhood, to cultivate the best material conditions" (166). She likes flowers and draperies and luxurious upholstery; Olive's parlour, Verena boasts to her mother, "is a regular dream-like place to sit" (94), and even Basil is struck by Olive's "cushioned feminine nest" (14). Most comically, perhaps, Olive enjoys creating odd

Nana-like effects around her protégée: "She's going to have a tree in," Verena tells Mrs. Tarrant, "she says she wants to see me sitting under a tree." "I believe it's some oriental idea," Verena charmingly explains; "it has lately been introduced into Paris" (94).

At one point Olive will take Verena to Paris literally, of course—in the hope that living on a "continent of strangers" will make them "cleave more closely still to each other" (164). It is fitting, I think, that their relationship is at its homoerotic zenith, or appears to be, while they reside in the city of Nana and Satin. Asked by Basil about this mysterious sojourn later, the ingenuous Verena will say only that she and Olive saw "some wonderful contagious types" and heard "much that was suggestive" (216–17). But to Basil's cynical eye, both women seem to exhibit a disturbing new sensuality after their Parisian adventure. Seeing them together at Mrs. Burrage's for the first time after their return, he cannot help but notice (with mixed emotions) how the golden-haired Verena "drops" down upon a sofa like "a nymph sinking on a leopard-skin" (214).

Perhaps the most incriminating of all of James's Zolan allusions comes near the end of *The Bostonians*, after the relationship between the two women has begun—according to its own inexorable rhythm—to self-destruct. The scene is Marmion, the idyllic summer house on Cape Cod to which Olive (in desperation) has brought Verena, along with Miss Birdseye and Dr. Prance, in an attempt to get away from Basil. Yet even here, in the seemingly desexualized world of James's feminine pastoral, certain crude Zolan truths are waiting to be revealed. At the end of Zola's novel, we may recall, Satin is ultimately undone by Nana's unrepentant profligacy: when Nana betrays her repeatedly with other lovers, Satin gives way to "mad" outbursts of jealousy in the flat on the Avenue de Villiers (433). After wearing herself out with these "frenzies of love and anger," she leaves Nana to the Comte Muffat and goes off in disgust—only to die a short time later, having "ruined her health so completely" (448). Her death is followed, with melodramatic swiftness, by Nana's own—of a particularly ghastly strain of smallpox. Zola's novel ends, notoriously, with a grotesque description of Nana's face, corrupting in death into a "shapeless pulp, in which the features had ceased to be discernible," but around which "the hair, the beautiful hair, still blazed like sunlight and flowed in a stream of gold" (470).

Yet when Basil arrives at Marmion and, to Olive's horror, begins to woo Verena in earnest, James uses the identical image—of the grossly decomposing face—to insinuate once again an atmosphere of homosexual longing. On Basil's final day at Marmion, when he and Verena fail to return from a sailing expedition, Olive, who has been walking on the shore, fantasizes in an access of hysterical panic that Verena has been drowned at sea: "She saw the boat overturned and drifting to sea, and (after a week of nameless horror) the body of an unknown young woman, defaced beyond recognition, but with long auburn hair and in a white dress, washed up in some far-away cove" (397). The reference here is unmistakable—almost as if Olive, somewhat surreally, knew Zola's book herself. Down to the monstrous wreath of red-gold hair, Verena and Nana seem to blend ghoulishly together here, even, paradoxically, as their "features" collapse into unrecognizability. Overcome by terror, Olive rushes wildly back to the summer house, crying aloud for her faithless friend.

The vision of Verena, "defaced beyond recognition," might easily be read as the sign of Olive's wish to punish the younger woman for her now-imminent defection. Yet as in Zola's final description of Nana, in which charnel house voyeurism is wedded to a certain perverse eroticism, it also suggests a savage and undiminished sensuality. Verena may in fact be akin to a prostitute—a new "Bostonian" Nana—but Olive, like an addict, craves her nonetheless. Indeed, as Olive waits helplessly for Verena's return, the fantasy of obliteration abruptly modulates into unadulterated physical yearning: "then it was, above all, that she felt how *she* had understood friendship, and how never again to see the face of the creature she had taken to her soul would be for her as the stroke of blindness." As the shadows around Marmion lengthen and Verena still does not return, Olive's frightful wrenching sobs convey "only a wild personal passion, a desire to take her friend in her arms again on any terms, even the most cruel to herself" (397).

James refines on Zola, of course: in the description of Olive's brief, morbid fantasia there is nothing of Zola's schoolboyish absorption in the symptomology of dissolution. ("One eye," Zola writes gleefully of Nana's dead face, "had completely foundered in the bubbling purulence, and the other, which remained half open, looked like a dark, decaying hole"). Instead, what James counts on is a kind of intertextual ghost effect to supply his own want of sensational detail. The image of Nana haunts the image of Verena like a grisly overlay, evoking both pity and terror, while the "face" of James's narrative itself remains pure and pristine and cool—untouched by any overt (juvenile or French) vulgarity.

Yet this, I am suggesting, is James's method throughout *The Bostonians*: to insinuate *through* Zola, as it were, a host of provocative effects, while at the same time never breaking with a certain self-appointed decorum. When it came to broaching the taboo subject of lesbianism, *Nana* provided James with the necessary shorthand, a bag of intertextual tricks, through which otherwise unassimilable connections—literary and sexual—could be made. Nothing is ever *said* in *The Bostonians*; yet because (it seems) Olive is to Verena as Satin is to Nana, anything may be *imagined*. The reader is caught up in the resulting paradox: though we can't see what exactly is "going on" between Olive and Verena, "it," nonetheless, seems to stare us brazenly in the face.

The "now you see it, now you don't" technique may go some way toward explaining the paradox with which we began: the assertion by numerous modern critics that while Olive is "clearly" a lesbian character, and her desire for Verena undoubtedly a homosexual one, *The Bostonians* is not itself "about" lesbianism. For in one sense James's ploy succeeds almost too well. By default, it makes room for a certain kind of *hypocrite lecteur* who enjoys extemporizing on female homosexuality (and freely abominating it) while also pretending not to recognize it. Given that lesbianism is no more than a ghost in *The Bostonians*—a spectral effect rather than something lavishly embodied—any reader wishing to deny its presence in the narrative can easily do so, especially since Verena so blithely traduces Olive in the end.

And yet it is hard to believe—the traditional prejudices of criticism notwithstanding—that this is exactly what James had in mind: that the question of female same-sex desire be ruled out of court simply because Olive and Verena's relationship ends badly. Olive is the key figure here, of course: a specter who refuses to disappear. She haunts us and moves us—just as she haunted and moved James himself, I think—in part because of her melancholia (which seems at bottom unassuageable) and in part because of her sheer intransigence: her refusal to let go—or relax her grip—even when her hands are already empty. Even the sanctimonious Basil, though appearing to carry the day at the Music Hall, is haunted by her in the end. In the last bitter moment between them, as he moves in to take Verena away from her for good, "the expression on [Olive's] face," James writes, "was a thing to remain with him forever." Transfixed by her haggard face, the eyes "straining forward, as if they were looking for death," Ransom "had a vision, even at that crowded moment, that if she could have met it then and there, bristling with steel or lurid with fire, she would have rushed on it without a tremor, like the heroine that she was" (432). Like the uncanny passion she symbolizes, Olive Chancellor is in fact inescapable, a stark "vision" impressed upon the mind's eye—forever.

Ironically, Olive's metamorphosis here into English and American literature's first lesbian tragic heroine—for that is how I think she must ultimately be regarded—is in no way Zolaesque. On the contrary: though I have pointed to the shadowy connection with *Nana*'s Satin, there is in fact no *true* precedent for Olive—at least as she appears in James's final vision—in Zola's painfully antiheroic fictional world. And herein, I grant, lies the paradox of my own argument. Though James exploits the connection with *Nana* often, even comically at times, to insinuate Olive's sexual "morbidity," he nonetheless breaks with his precursor in his final attitude toward her.[34] He doesn't let her die out, like Satin, in some Bostonian version of Zolan venereal squalor; nor, at the last, is she made to seem contemptible. Indeed, Olive is too noble a presence altogether, James seems to hint at the end, to be contained within such a demeaning and sordid intertextual framework. In the space remaining, I would like turn to this ultimate Jamesian swerve *away* from Zola—and Olive's tragic apotheosis—as a way of approaching a more significant issue: how to situate *The Bostonians* more exactly in the tradition of Anglo-American lesbian writing.

Olive Never Lets Go

Least of all was she a "thing"; she was intensely, fearfully, a person.
—*The Bostonians* (89)

The canny reader will perhaps have anticipated this about-face in the argument; for in all of the most telling respects—it need hardly be said—Olive is as *unlike* Zola's trashy Satin as anyone could possibly be. Satin is, after all, a fairly minor character in *Nana*, and one ends up caring very little about her, in part because she cares so little about anyone herself—Nana included. Despite the jealous tantrums she throws near the end of the novel, Satin commonly treats Nana with the same ruthlessness that Nana displays toward her, and at odd moments their roles even seem to blur confusingly. In one scene, for instance, soon after she comes to live with Nana on the Avenue de Villiers, Satin abruptly "scampers" off to the Café Laure, to take up with an old lover, Madame Robert, and Nana is forced to go there to find her. "After that," writes Zola, "the same thing happened again and again. A score of times Nana, a tragic figure filled with all the fury of a jilted woman, went off in pursuit of that slut, who kept running away on impulse, bored by the comforts of the big house" (327–28). With Nana and Satin here temporarily exchanging roles—Satin becoming the betrayer and Nana the betrayed—any straightforward parallel with Olive and Verena obviously breaks down.

Indeed, the only character in *Nana* who comes close to matching Olive in degree of feeling—and fearsome capacity for suffering—would have to be the tormented Comte Muffat, the pious, painfully repressed aristocrat who becomes Nana's lover, throws over his marriage and fortune for her, and is ultimately ruined by his sexual obsession with her. His passion is as lonely and fanatical as Olive's, and, as with Satin, there are certain occult physical resemblances. When the journalist Fauchery scans the crowd during Nana's performance at the Théâtre des Variétés and turns around to look at the Muffat box, he is "astounded" by what he sees—for "behind the Countess, who looked pale and serious, the Count was sitting bolt upright, his mouth agape and his face mottled with red" (46). There is more than a hint of this passage, I think, in James's description of Olive, when Basil glances over at her during Verena's debut: "[she] showed him an extraordinary face, a face he scarcely understood or even recognized. It was portentously grave, the eyes were enlarged, there was a red spot in each of the cheeks, and as directed to him, a quick, piercing question, a kind of leaping challenge, in the whole expression" (62).

The association here between Olive and Muffat is a paradoxical one, however, in that it also points up just how radically James breaks with Zolan convention. The Muffat-Nana story is the prototype, of course, for a host of later nineteenth- and early twentieth-century "femme fatale" narratives, in which a supposedly good or respectable man is destroyed by his obsession with a wicked showgirl-prostitute: Theodore Dreiser's *Sister Carrie* (1900), Frank Wedekind's *Lulu* plays (1903), and a host of early cinematic melodramas, such as G. W. Pabst's 1929 *Pandora's Box* (adapted from Wedekind) and Josef von Sternberg's *The Blue Angel* (1930) and *Blonde Venus* (1932)—the title of which directly echoes *Nana*—all replay the basic Zolan scenario in different ways. Included among the stock figures in such works is almost always a lesbian character—like Satin, slightly to one side of the main action—who shares the male protagonist's erotic interest in the femme fatale. The Countess Geschwitz in *Lulu* is perhaps the classic example: she openly competes with the Muffat character, Dr. Schön, for Lulu's sexual favors. In fact much of the pathos surrounding the male protagonist in the stereotypical femme fatale narrative—for he invariably comes to seem emasculated and pathetic—has to do with the fact that his lover not only betrays him with other men but with women as well.*

James's first and most startling break with convention, obviously, is to shift attention away from the male to the female lover—indeed, to do away with the Muffat figure entirely. (If such a character can be said to survive at all in *The Bostonians*, it is only vestigially—as in the figure of the mother-dominated Henry Burrage, Verena's wealthy, yet ultimately ridiculous "Harvard" suitor.) Olive in effect usurps the place of the Muffat character, drawing toward her all of the pathos and pity-evoking charisma that, in a more conventionally ordered fiction, would normally be assumed by the male heterosexual protagonist.

But by changing the sex of the Zolan "victim" from male to female, James also works a kind of generic transformation in his fiction as well. It is impossible to speak of the Muffat-Nana story as tragic—so predictably does it deteriorate into mere coarse and alienating burlesque. Burlesque is of course the dominant mode in *Nana*: from the

---

*Much of Marlene Dietrich's conspicuous success as a cinematic femme fatale had to do, I think, with her sophisticated understanding of the way in which the hint of bisexuality intensifies the femme fatale's mesmerizing power over her victims: the shocking kiss on the lips that Dietrich gives another woman in the cafe scene in *Morocco* (1930)—while a group of bemused spectators look on—might be considered one of the signal moments in Dietrich's consolidation of her own persona as "fatal" female.

very beginning, with the performance of *Blonde Venus*, in which the gods and goddesses of Olympus are shown descending to earth and cavorting ignominiously in Parisian brothels and stews, the novel stages—relentlessly—the spectacle of "great things" brought low. Muffat himself will mimic this descending action in one of his sex scenes with Nana, when he crawls on all fours before her and barks like a dog (441). Similar scenes of degradation occur in the later femme fatale narratives as well: the pitiful fate of the Emil Jannings character in Von Sternberg's *The Blue Angel*—reduced by his craving for Lola (Marlene Dietrich) to a sodden alcoholic wreck in clown makeup—suggests a strong downward pull, in the genre as a whole, toward bathos and the antiheroic.

Yet James, by replacing Muffat with a female character, somehow restores a tragic dimension to the femme fatale plot, thereby fundamentally altering its nature. This is not to say that James never lampoons Olive; on the contrary, the connection with Satin is itself a sort of extended intertextual burlesque—for Olive is made to seem by it less "sublime" than she thinks herself. He debunks her in other ways too: in the famous scene in which, almost "panting" with excitement, she asks Verena whether she knows the celebrated line from *Faust*, *"Entsagen sollst du, sollst entsagen!"* and then exhorts her, like the German wizard, to "renounce, refrain, abstain!" the overweening absurdity of the entreaty is matched only by her blanket self-deception regarding her own motives (81).

And yet, though her defeat at the end of the novel is presented as devastating, Olive is never reduced to a state of complete moral or psychic abjection. We sense her residual grandeur even in the midst of fiasco. Something of this felt power undoubtedly arises from the fact that at various points in the novel James has already shown his sympathy for her in an unexpected yet effective manner: by having Basil—of all people—notice in her a certain potential for magnificence. At their first meeting, it is Basil who sees "in a flash that no one could help her: that was what made her tragic" (9). And later, like a fighter respectful of the strength of his opponent, he acknowledges her "strenuous" capacity for "taking things hard" and fearless, almost soldierly sense of duty (15). Such tokens of esteem, hinting as they do at Olive's heroic potential from the start, seem all the more meaningful coming from Basil, who by temperament, taste, and politics (not to mention the sexual rivalry between them) should be the character in the fiction perhaps least likely to admire anything about her.

Nor does James hesitate to suggest, in a manner that also works subtly to ennoble her, a larger tragic fatality at work in Olive's destiny. Unlike Muffat, whose final humiliation seems oddly mechanical, a matter of crude biological "impulses" taking their inevitable debilitating toll, Olive seems caught in the coils of some implacable power—some baffling unseen entity (authorial or Providential) determined to turn her most cherished hopes to ashes. One of the striking aspects of Olive's suffering is precisely, from one perspective, how *un*-motivated it seems—how easily, in fact, everything that she is forced to endure might have been avoided. If James's plot has any superficial flaw, it is precisely this: that Olive's invitation to Basil to accompany her to Miss Birdseye's—the impulsive gesture on which everything else in the novel depends—is, psychologically speaking, the fiction's least plausible action. James goes to some lengths to account for it: though shy and almost pathologically afraid of strangers, Olive acts ostensibly out of a desire to be "generous" to her impoverished Southern cousin in the way that her dead mother would have wished her to be (9–11). But her action remains a puzzling and somewhat arbitrary one—the sort of grotesque "accident" or tragic mistake, like Oedipus's slaying of Laius, in which one senses the directing hand of some invisible cosmic ironist. Olive herself seems aware at times of some unseen power bent on her mortification: her frequent "previsions" and presentiments—such as her "mystical foreboding" that Basil will somehow interfere in her relationship with Verena (265)—seem at once to relieve her of personal responsibility and to surround her story with an inexplicable yet luminous tragic aura. [35]

And, at the last, James is careful to show Olive "upright in her desolation"—despite the staggering psychic blow Basil and Verena together conspire to deal her. This moment of transcendence does not come without a struggle: when Basil first breaks into the waiting room at the Music Hall where she and Verena and Verena's parents have been sequestered, while the impatient mob waiting for Verena's speech howls and stamps in the auditorium next door, he finds Olive "prostrate" and "fallen over," her head "buried in the lap of Verena's mother"—as if through some magical fleshly metonymy, the older woman might substitute for the younger (425). When Mrs. Tarrant in turn extends herself, sobbing weakly on the sofa, leaving Olive to face Basil alone, Olive seems briefly to contemplate launching herself downward for good—if only he will spare her: "I'll do anything—I'll be abject—I'll be vile—I'll go down in the dust!" (429). But, only a second or two later, she is on her feet—and "as soon as Ransom looked at her he became aware that the weakness she had just shown had passed away" (432). When Mrs. Farrinder enters the room, loudly berating her for Verena's nonappearance at the podium, Olive—now ignoring her persecutors entirely—flies out of the room toward the platform herself. And there, had it been possible for Basil to observe her, James concludes—

> it might have seemed to him that she hoped to find the fierce expiation she sought for in exposure to the thousands she had disappointed and deceived, in offering herself to be trampled to death and torn to pieces. She might have suggested to him some feminine firebrand of Paris revolutions, erect on a barricade, or even the sacrificial figure of Hypatia, whirled through the furious mob of Alexandria. (433)

In this imagined moment of "fierce expiation"—with its hint of sacrificial pathos and spiritual transfiguration—Olive attains a level of heroic sublimity undreamed of in Zola, and in so doing lifts *The Bostonians* itself up and out of the tainted realm of antilesbian burlesque into the authentic space of tragedy.

In the introductory (and freely polemical) essay in this volume, the reader will perhaps recall, I not-so-delicately impugned the author of *The Bostonians* for what I saw as his retracing of a familiar homophobic story: of a woman turned to vapor on account of her love for another woman. Olive Chancellor, I suggested there, was ultimately no different from countless other lesbian "phantoms" inhabiting nineteenth-century male fantasy—was indeed simply a new version of those familiar sapphic wraiths, like Delphine and Hippolyte in Baudelaire's "Femmes damnées," doomed to wander the earth forever with morbid longings unassuaged. When in the novel's last pages she appears before Basil as a pale-faced "presentment" of "blighted hope and wounded pride," she seems—I wrote—to forfeit her flesh before our eyes, to sicken and fade into the air, even as she forfeits her passionate claim on Verena and runs away from the scene. She becomes—or seems on the verge of becoming—that sexual cipher that Basil so desperately wants her to be (432).*

This gloomy picture needs qualifying, however, when we place James's novel in a wider literary context. As I intimated earlier, a certain "homophobic" reading of *The Bostonians* will always be possible: James, the master of multivalence, does nothing in fact to suppress it. There will always be readers, I suspect, for whom Verena's "healthy heartlessness" toward Olive is her saving grace, and who are capable of asserting—while also pretending to liberal fairmindedness—that "if we don't at first think of Basil Ransom as a threat to Verena's liberty no less dangerous than Olive, that is because we are so anxious for Ransom to win the struggle."[36]

And yet the importance of James's literary experiment in *The Bostonians* should not be underestimated. He is the first major modern writer—and here the contrast with Zola and the French school is most instructive—to open a space for a sympathetic reading of a lesbian character. Not only is Olive the first woman in mainstream Anglo-American writing to desire another woman and survive: in her own awkward, purblind fashion she is the first to approach the heroic.† This isn't to say that James enforces the "tragic" reading on us; he simply makes it possible—one choice among others. We are free to regard Olive as morbid or unnatural if we wish, to deride her yearning as anathema or pollution, but James allows for a more humane response as well. Indeed, the very fact that he so seldom proselytizes openly on Olive's behalf, and then only elliptically, will make her for some an even more compelling figure. Secreted within a mass of otherwise sardonic commentary, an isolated authorial remark such as "in reality Olive was distinguished and discriminating" (185)—buried in

---

*The spiritualist theme in *The Bostonians* is a major one and intersects frequently (yet also ambiguously) with the novel's sexual themes. Though it is Olive who is most explicitly figured as a sort of ghost or apparition, Basil and Verena too are also powerfully "infected" by the novel's spectral thematics. For an examination of the spiritualism issue—and James's intricate deployment of supernatural metaphors throughout *The Bostonians*—see Banta, *Henry James and the Occult*, pp. 96–100 and 178–83, Kerr, *Mediums, and Spirit-Rappers, and Roaring Radicals*, pp. 190–222, and Wolstenholme, "Possession and Personality."

†I distinguish her here from characters such as Gautier's Mademoiselle de Maupin, who, though a "hero" of sorts, hardly qualifies as a realistic psychological portrait.

a paragraph devoted to Olive's sister Mrs. Luna—can take on, in the moment of reading, an impressive moral force.

It would be interesting, were this a biographical study, to examine the particular psychological determinants that brought James to this imaginative breakthrough: this opening up, as it were, of lesbian tragic space. Here, undoubtedly, the story of Alice James and Katharine Loring would have some bearing—may indeed have been the real-life emotional configuration that prompted the realization in James that the love of woman for woman might be a source of memorable human drama. In turn, one would also want to look at James's own sexuality—or what can be deciphered of it—in order to pursue the important question whether his own covert homoeroticism in fact predisposed him to a kind of imaginative identification with Olive Chancellor. That it may have done so is borne out, I think, by one of the most striking passages in *The Bostonians*: in which Olive is described, soon after her meeting with Verena, as having "taken Verena up, in the literal sense of the phrase, like a bird of the air," spreading over her "an extraordinary pair of wings," and carrying her "through the dizzying void of space" (73). ("Verena liked it, for the most part; liked to shoot upward without an effort of her own and look down upon all creation, upon all history, from such a height.") Ignoring the bird, James's critics have traditionally glossed the passage as an allusion to book 11 of *Paradise Lost*—in which the angel Michael walks with Adam to the top of a high hill after the Fall and sets before him a vision of human history until the Flood.[37] The Miltonic echo may indeed be there, but what the image much more directly and vividly recalls is the preeminent classical instance of male homosexual desire, Zeus's rape of Ganymede while in the shape of an eagle. The passage could in fact be said to mark a kind of allegorical "crossing point" or junction at which the thematics of male and female homosexuality coincide. That James, whether consciously or no, sets up such a linkage may indeed reveal something about the degree of his own emotional investment in Olive's final suffering and reversal.

I would like to conclude, however, by calling attention to some of the strictly literary historical ramifications of the Jamesian move toward the tragic. If *The Bostonians* stands, in my reading, as the first and perhaps most haunting "lesbian tragedy" in modern English and American literature, and Olive Chancellor (potentially) as the first lesbian tragic heroine, neither one is the last. Indeed the influence of James's novel on later writers—and Anglo-American lesbian writers in particular—has been far greater, I think, than is generally recognized. Well into the twentieth century, Olive's betrayal by Verena lingers on in the lesbian literary imagination—as the subliminal pattern, even mythic archetype, of the sort of erotic misfortune to which the "inverted" woman is prone and must somehow strive to transcend.

Radclyffe Hall—I am sure—follows James in the first half of *The Well of Loneliness*, for example, when she describes the emotional manhandling of her heroine, Stephen Gordon, by the flirtatious yet treacherous married woman, Angela Crossby. As a transplanted American and former variety actress, Angela is a strange mixture of Jamesian and Zolan elements. She is the daughter, she tells Stephen, of an impoverished Southerner who lost his estate in the Civil War and was forced to go north to New York to seek work—a Basil Ransom-like odyssey on which she accompanied him. When he died penniless, she was forced to go on the stage, and soon began letting various men support her in exchange for sexual favors. (Angela's history combines and recombines—bizarrely—aspects of Basil's, Verena's, *and* Nana's story) The wealthy Ralph Crossby saved her from a sordid end ("my health was crocking; lots of our girls ended up in the hospital wards") by marrying her and taking her back to his English country estate.[38]

Like Olive, Stephen craves a "union of souls" with Angela (who is estranged from her husband) yet will be bitterly disappointed. Her excited, embarrassed appeal at the start of their relationship (" 'I want very much to be your friend if you'll have me' ") subtly echoes Olive's doom-laden opening speech to Verena (" 'Will you be my friend, my friend of friends, beyond every one, everything, forever and forever?' "); and her eventual humiliation—after Angela abandons her for the mustachioed Roger Antrim—has a similar freakish Jamesian pathos. "All the loneliness that had gone before was as nothing to this new loneliness of spirit. An immense desolation swept down upon her, an immense need to cry out and claim understanding for herself, an immense need to find an answer to the riddle of her unwanted being."[39] Radclyffe Hall does not stay in this purely dysphoric register, of course: when Stephen becomes a writer and (unlike Olive) finds consolation later with another lover, one sees her creator trying to move out of the severely "end-stopped" Jamesian narrative paradigm. But the Angela episode nonetheless remains a crucial one—not least because it establishes Stephen for the first time as a kind of martyr to homosexual love, one who will never fully escape the stigma of her "unwanted" sexuality, yet whose recurrent anguish is clearly meant, like Olive's, to evoke our pity and compassion.[40]

One could find similar traces of James in many other early twentieth-century lesbian novels. Dorothy Strachey's *Olivia*, as the name of its central character suggests, is yet another somewhat more subtle reworking of the Olive/Verena story. The connection, I grant, may appear attenuated here: the schoolgirl Olivia's ill-fated passion for her teacher, Mademoiselle Julie, seems to have little on the surface to connect it with Olive's for Verena—except that both are equally star-crossed. Yet in the heroine's very forlornness, in her morbid shock when Julie abandons her for another, there is a strong emotional echo, I think, of Olive's suffering in *The Bostonians*. One might think of Strachey's hapless "Olivia" as Olive Chancellor in a younger incarnation—as an Olive learning, as it were, for the first time, the pattern of rhapsody and betrayal.*

But let me close with perhaps the greatest and most "Jamesian" lesbian novel of them all: Djuna Barnes's *Nightwood* (1936). From its clamorous, baffled beginnings to its surreal and shocking end, Barnes's novel is nothing less, I think, than a sort of modernist rewrite of *The Bostonians*—an uncanny "return of Olive Chancellor," in which the story of Olive and her betrayal is replayed, over and over again, like a kind of nightmarish marionette show, in the fateful affair between

---

*Worth noting is the prevalence of the Olive/Olivia "marker" in twentieth-century lesbian-themed writing: "Olivia" is one of Stephen Gordon's middle names; one thinks also of Woolf's "Chloe liked Olivia" from *A Room of One's Own* (1929). And "Olive" returns, hauntingly, in one of the catalogues of amazonian female names in Monique Wittig's *Les Guérillères* (1969):

AUBIERGE CLARISSA PHAEDRA
EUDOXIA OLIVE IO MODESTA
PLAISANCE HYGEIA LOUISA
CORALIE ANEMONE TABITHA
THELMA INGRID PRASCOVIA
NATALIE POMPEIA ALIENOR

See Wittig, *Les Guérillères*, p. 37.

Nora Flood and Robin Vote. For who indeed is Barnes's Nora, if not
Olive Chancellor startlingly reembodied? Like Olive, whose Charles
Street home is notoriously a haunt for "witches and wizards, mediums, and spirit-rappers and roaring radicals" (3), Nora (before her
move to Paris), we learn, keeps "the strangest 'salon' in America":

> It was the "paupers" salon for poets, radicals, beggars, artists, and
> people in love; for Catholics, Protestants, Brahmins, dabblers in black
> magic and medicine; all these could be seen sitting about her oak table
> before the huge fire, Nora listening, her hand on her hound, the fire-
> light throwing her shadow and his high against the wall. Of all that
> ranting, roaring crew, she alone stood out. The equilibrium of her na-
> ture, savage and refined, gave her bridled skull a look of compassion.
> She was broad and tall, and though her skin was the skin of a child,
> there could be seen coming, early in her life, the design that was to be
> the weather-beaten grain of her face, that wood in the work; the tree
> coming forward in her, an undocumented record of time.[41]

And like Olive, Nora ("the early Christian") is a masochist of extravagant, almost fantastic proportions: "Nora had the face of all people who love the people—a face that would be evil when she found
out that to love without criticism is to be betrayed. Nora robbed herself for everyone; incapable of giving herself warning, she was contin-
ually turning about to find herself diminished" (51). Of Olive we
learn that "the prospect of suffering was always, spiritually speaking,
so much cash in her pocket" (105); of Nora, that "wandering people
the world over found her profitable in that she could be sold for a
price forever, for she carried her betrayal money in her own pocket"
(52).

In Nora's love for the elusive Robin, Barnes conjures a ghostly simulacrum of Olive's love for Verena. For Robin—who like Verena, exhibits a strange, almost obscene receptivity to the unseen—is preoc-
cupied with something "other" than the tall and awkwardly reticent
woman who desires her. Humming weird music hall songs in a mesmerizing, delinquent voice, "songs of the people, debased and haunting, songs that Nora had never heard before, or that she had never
heard in company with Robin," Robin becomes inaccessible in a way
that prefigures the sexual betrayal to come: "When the cadence
changed, when it was repeated on a lower key, [Nora] knew that Rob-

in was singing of a life that she herself had no part in; snatches of harmony as tell-tale as the possessions of a traveller from a foreign land; songs like a practised whore who turns away from no one but the one who loves her" (57). (Through a strange kind of intertextual default, Nana too, one notes, haunts such passages.)

Nora's doom will be sealed in Jamesian metaphor. When in despair over Robin's treacheries, Nora arrives at Dr. Matthew O'Connor's squalid walk-up in the famous chapter "Watchman, What of the Night?" Barnes's imagery recalls James's as well as Isaiah's: Olive's vision of the terrible "suffering of women" (the vision she mistakenly presumes Verena to share) comes to her "in the watches of the night," and references to "watching" and "watchmen" pervade James's novel.[42] Later, when Nora tells O'Connor of finding a doll on the bed in the room of the woman Robin has been unfaithful to her with—a doll identical to one Robin once gave to her—and then lapses into her own spooky, sybilline reverie ("we give death to a child when we give it a doll—it's the effigy and the shroud; when a woman gives it to a woman, it is the life they cannot have, it is their child, sacred and profane; so when I saw that other doll—" [142]), we see Barnes, at her most sublime, turn a passing Jamesian sarcasm—Mrs. Farrinder's contemptuous dismissal of Olive's love for Verena as "a kind of elderly, ridiculous doll-dressing" (157)—into an unnerving metaphysical set piece on lesbian desire.

But it is Barnes's representation of Nora's erotic suffering, perhaps, that most starkly recalls James—the agony of the one who must wait, as in the most frightful of anxiety dreams, for the wasting blow to strike. "Listening to the faint sounds from the street, every murmur from the garden, an unevolved and tiny hum that spoke of the progressive growth of noise that would be Robin coming home,"

> Nora lay and beat her pillow without force, unable to cry, her legs drawn up. At times she would get up and walk, to make something in her life more quickly over, to bring Robin back by the very velocity of the beating of her heart. And walking in vain, she suddenly would sit down on one of the circus chairs that stood by the long window overlooking the garden, bend forward, putting her hands between her legs, and begin to cry, "Oh, God! Oh, God! Oh, God!" repeated so often that it had the effect of all words spoken in vain. (61)

In such moments of all-consuming "night"—which Nora will strive heroically to live through, with the bitter succor of Matthew Mighty-Grain-of-Salt O'Connor's Tiresian transvestite wisdom ("You thought you knew, and you hadn't even shuffled the cards"), Olive Chancellor indeed comes to haunt Barnes's novel—thin like the air, yet full of a cryptic human majesty, inviting thoughtful and endless remembrance.

A Private Coda: Two Versions of the Same Face

Two versions of the same face hover in a ghostly fashion over this essay. The first (which will perhaps come as no surprise) is the face of Vanessa Redgrave, whose transcendent portrayal of Olive Chancellor in an otherwise mediocre film version of *The Bostonians* from 1984, constitutes, quite simply, one of the great cinematic performances of the century. As one commentator noted when the film first appeared:

> We cannot mock her as she runs sobbing on the beach at Cape Cod searching for her lost love who is somewhere on the water in a boat with Ransom, and we understand—horrified but participating—the ambiguity of her visions of Verena's drowning. When she returns later and falls into Verena's arms we do not dare to despise her, though both scenes verge on the ludicrous. Redgrave has made her performance the heart of the film and lifted the character to the height of tragedy.[43]

The image of Redgrave-as-Olive (as in the still reproduced below) epitomizes for me the heroic element in James's novel and has shaped, almost talismanically, I realize, my own reading of it. Redgrave is the last inheritor in our own time of the tradition of Rachel, Bernhardt, and Duse—a tragic muse.

By one of those strange freaks of association that come without prompting, however, the Redgrave/Olive face has ineffably blended in my mind's eye with another: that of the noble and sublime Maria Falconetti, in Dreyer's celebrated silent film *La Passion de Jeanne d'Arc* (1928). The same haunted look is there—of wonderment and terror, yearning and despair—caught forever in rhapsodic, emotional close-up. With her close-cropped head and silent, evolving gaze, Falconetti seems the archetype behind Redgrave's searching portrayal: the em-

Two versions of the same face: Vanessa Redgrave in *The Bostonians*, 1984; Maria Falconetti (with Maurice Schutz) in *La Passion de Jeanne d'Arc*, 1928. *Courtesy of Photofest and the Museum of Modern Art.*

bodiment of some as-yet undiscerned human tragedy one longs to call lesbian.

What to do with such a connection? Joan of Arc travels through time as a peculiarly sapphic heroine: Vita Sackville-West wrote a book about her; Radclyffe Hall wanted to. The lesbian actress Eva Le Gallienne played her, in Paris in 1925, in a play written for her by her lover, Mercedes de Acosta. And James's Olive Chancellor is an acknowledged, sometimes quivering, member of her cult. Olive wants to see Verena (achingly) as a new Joan: Verena's "sharp, inspired vision" of female suffering—Olive fools herself into thinking—is just like "Joan of Arc's absolutely supernatural apprehension of the state of France" (115). But Verena is neither martyr nor saint, being content to live out her days as an "ordinary pusillanimous, conventional young lady." It is Olive herself, of course, who most recalls the lost heroine of France—the one who wore men's clothes, spoke with God, and was betrayed. When Olive cries out, in the glow of Verena's first enchantment of her heart, "I should like to be able to say that you are my form—my envelope. But you are too beautiful for that!" (149), she converses in the unaltered tongue of the mystic. And thus perhaps the haunting power of the face: from Olive to Redgrave to Falconetti to Joan to Olive: we intuit a new sort of heroine—one who loves her brilliant phantoms in the way that other women love men.

8

THE

GAIETY OF

JANET

FLANNER

History was made at the *New Yorker* recently when, in the course of a review of the work of the late Robert Mapplethorpe, the gifted photographer whose explicitly homoerotic images have excited the wrath of bigots and would-be censors far and wide, the art critic Ingrid Sischy used the occasion, gracefully and courageously, to come out in print. She'd first seen, and been moved by, Mapplethorpe's photographs "at a time in my life when I was afraid of what might happen—and worried about how my parents would feel—if I said I had a girlfriend, not a boyfriend." It was a relief, she acknowledged, to find Mapplethorpe addressing the subject of homosexuality "in an unqueasy, honest, and often beautiful way."[1] What was memorable about Sischy's own moment of candor was precisely its context. Though the *New Yorker* has always been hospitable to homosexual writers—and especially lesbian writers—this was the first time, surely, that one had spoken up as one in its pages.

One cannot help wondering what Janet Flanner—for fifty years the Paris correspondent for the *New Yorker* and herself a lover of women—would have made of Sischy's revelation. Like most lesbians of her generation, Flanner believed in keeping her emotional life private: in her famous "Letter from Paris," published regularly in the *New Yorker* from 1925 to 1975, she invariably used the decorous, sexually ambiguous pseudonym *Genêt* and sought to avoid any obvious self-revelation. As Brenda Wineapple notes in a recent biography, Flanner disdained the first-person singular.* "The trick is never to say 'I,'" she told a friend in the 1960s; "You're safer with one or it. 'I' is like a fortissimo. It's too loud."[2] Certainly it would never have occurred to Flanner to make a public profession of her homosexuality, least of all in the pages of the magazine to which she remained proudly devoted throughout her long and distinguished career.

Such reticence was partly prudential, of course. Flanner was without question the best-known American woman journalist of her epoch, and her prominent position demanded a certain discretion. In the cruel 1950s, especially, Flanner would have been a fool to make an obvious point of her sexual persuasion. But her biographer suggests that this circumspection was also symptomatic—was indeed the sign of an essentially secretive and "compartmentalizing" sensibility. From the start, argues Wineapple, Flanner's personality was shaped by an impulse toward evasion and self-obfuscation. Her life was "an eminently private one, devoted to concealment, not revelation, and the conscious crafting of an identity."[3] "Genêt" was only the most visible mask, says the biographer, behind which Flanner hid the idiosyncracies of a passionate but often conflicted nature.

And yet despite the element of truth here, one may balk at such easy, quasi-therapeutic generalizations. Surely the "fortissimo 'I'" is not the only means by which a lesbian spirit may reveal itself? And surely in the case of the dashing, mannered, supremely ironical Flanner—who once described herself to a colleague as "a gentleman of the press in skirts"—there was more going on than wary self-

---

Genêt: A Biography of Janet Flanner (1989).

concealment? We are accustomed nowadays to biographers dealing frankly with the sex lives of their subjects, and would probably find unusual or remiss any biographer who did not. (It is a tribute to the degree to which in the late twentieth century we have accepted Freud's view of sexuality as being at the core of personality that such expectations arise.) Though Flanner's biographer offers a chronicle of this "full disclosure" sort, making no bones about her subject's homosexual orientation, she nonetheless manages to miss something essential—a certain complicating, uninhibited, even loverlike gaiety—in both the life and the work. One is forced to conclude, albeit unwillingly, that a kind of ghosting of the lesbian subject can occur, paradoxically, even when the fact of homosexuality is acknowledged. As long as a biographer remains imaginatively untouched by the sensual life of his or her subject—deficient in what might be termed a sort of amorous empathy—the result will indeed be pale and wraithlike: a mere shadow of what might have been.

Who was Janet Flanner? Later in life, Flanner liked to claim that she had "no biography" before the 1920s, when she moved to Paris, established herself in the bohemian and expatriate circles of the Left Bank, and began writing for Harold Ross's fledgling *New Yorker*. Regarding her early life, she was, admittedly, inclined to be disingenuous—in part, one suspects, because of the pain the subject caused her. Born in 1892 into a stolidly bourgeois Indianapolis family, the second (and wittiest) of three daughters, Flanner grew up in comfortable, progressive surroundings. But there were disquiets under the surface. When pressed for information about her parents, Flanner typically said that her father had made his fortune in real estate, but his actual profession, Wineapple reveals, was that of a high-class undertaker. (As late as 1972, at the age of eighty, Flanner was still trying to convince a cousin to remove the name "Flanner" from the family business, Flanner and Buchanan.)

Flanner also tended to suppress the fact of her father's suicide, in his own mortuary in 1912. It was an event that left the Flanner daughters solely responsible for their demanding, often histrionic mother. Between 1912 and 1921, Flanner made a series of increasingly desperate attempts to escape the oppressive maternal orbit. Hoping to become a novelist, she attended the University of Chicago for a year (she never received a degree), worked briefly as a drama critic for the *Indi-*

anapolis Star, and finally, on impulse, married a man named William
Rehm, with whom she moved to Greenwich Village in 1918.

The marriage was not a success—the two separated almost
immediately—but the three-year New York sojourn turned out to be
fateful. For there, while working on her only novel (later published as
The Cubical City in 1926) and mingling with members of the Algon-
quin Club, Flanner met the sloe-eyed, exotically named Solita Solano, the first of the three women with whom she was to be erotically
and emotionally involved for the rest of her life. Solano was a reporter
for the *New York Tribune*, spoke numerous languages, and was active
in artistic and suffragist circles. She was (notes Wineapple) "given to
large enthusiasms," and idolized, among others, the actress Sarah
Bernhardt, whose tear-soaked handkerchief she made off with after a
performance of *Camille* and treasured until her death.

Like Flanner, Solano, whose real name was Sarah Wilkinson, had
things to hide. She hated her middle-class background (she had re-
named herself after a mythical Spanish grandmother), and she too,
had recently fled an unhappy marriage—literally, by climbing out a
window. Sharing a distaste for the philistinism of postwar American
life, Flanner and Solano felt an immediate accord. When Solano received an assignment from *National Geographic* to report on political
affairs in Greece and Turkey, it seemed only natural that the two
women—who were also now lovers should pool resources and go to
Europe.

Asked later why she had chosen to live in France, Flanner explained that she had "wanted Beauty, with a capital B. . . . I was
consumed by my own appetite to consume—in a very limited way, of
course, the beauties of Europe."[4] Her biographer paints a more complicated picture. Flanner was unquestionably glad to get away from
her fractious mother, whom she had left—for good, as it turned
out—in the care of her younger sister. Paris provided a kind of sensual, emotional, and intellectual fulfillment that all of her years in the
Midwest—and even the time in New York—had failed to supply.
Soon after settling in Paris in 1922, Flanner and Solano entered into
the salon life of the city: their homosexuality, far from being a hin-
drance, provided a crucial entrée into the most fashionable literary
and artistic coteries, the majority of which were dominated by
wealthy English and American lesbians.

Flanner became friendly not only with Gertrude Stein and Alice B. Toklas, for whom she felt a lifelong affection, but also with Natalie Barney, the renowned author, hostess, and sapphic seductress, whose house on the Rue Jacob featured a small "Temple de l'Amitié" around which she would dance with her female guests. (Other decidedly "lesbic" acquaintances of the twenties included Djuna Barnes, Sylvia Beach, Romaine Brooks, Margaret Anderson, Georgette Leblanc, and Dolly Wilde—stylish niece of Oscar—who sometimes masqueraded as her celebrated uncle.) Expatriation, Flanner discovered, was a paradoxical sort of homecoming: after the glum appurtenances of Indianapolis, "Paris, France" seemed to welcome her, she wrote, with "an old girl's countenance, shaded by a trollop's gay wig."[5]

She also discovered her vocation. In 1925, when Jane Grant, writing on behalf of her husband, Harold Ross, asked Flanner to contribute an occasional "Letter from Paris" to Ross's new magazine, the *New Yorker*—something that would include "incidental stuff on places familiar to Americans" along with "dope on fields of the arts and a little on fashions"—Flanner, recognizing that her old dream of becoming a novelist had faded, jumped at the chance. Her first Paris letter (to which Ross himself appended the byline "Genêt," imagining it to be the Frenchified version of Janet) was an immediate success. She was soon writing regular thousand-word dispatches, delighting in her new life, and posing for photographs. In the famous studio portrait taken of her by Berenice Abbott in 1927, Flanner stares out at the camera unflinchingly—a handsome and incalculable presence, her strange Merlin-like white hair aglow. Though clad, outlandishly enough, in a dinner jacket, striped pantaloons, and dandified top hat—the last festooned with a black and a white mask—the new foreign correspondent looks imperturbably chic. That Genêt, at thirty-five, had a last found a world sentient enough to contain her was evident: nor would she soon relinquish what she had found.

Flanner's "Letter from Paris" was a fortnightly testament to her love affair with her adopted city. The basic format of the letters never altered, though Flanner's journalistic interests evolved and deepened as the decades passed. Her pieces from the 1920s—devoted mainly to scandals, exhibitions, musical events, the doings of the smart set—tended to be lighthearted and gossipy in nature, befitting an enchanted epoch. She often drew on friends and acquaintances for ma-

Portrait of Janet Flanner by Berenice Abbott,
1927. *Courtesy of Commerce Graphics*.

terial: Picasso, Stein, Joyce, Loie Fuller, Nancy Cunard, Josephine
Baker, Virgil Thomson, Beach, Isadora Duncan, Colette, Radclyffe
Hall, and Mistinguett all make their appearances against a backdrop
of cafés and salons, first nights and fancy-dress balls. And already the
hallmarks of the famous Flanner style were present: the ironic flour-
ishes, the polysyllabic wit, the taste for glittering, catachrestic, sometimes macabre description.

Attracted by anything theatrical, outré, or baroque, Flanner per-
fected a prose to match—full of spectacular figures, mordant turns of
phrase, adamantine alliteration, and a sinuous, burnished beauty.
Thus Isadora Duncan, Flanner wrote, had, "with her heroic sculp-
tural movements," arrived in Paris "like a glorious bounding Minerva
in the midst of a cautious corseted decade," but ended her career in
neglect, "dropped by the wayside, where she lay inert like one of the
beautiful battered pagan tombs that still line the Sacred Way between
Eleusis and the city of the Parthenon."[6] Of Diaghilev's dancers she

noted that they had "psychology in their muscles as well as in their
minds"; a performance of Prokofiev's *Le Fils prodigue* (choreography
by the young Balanchine) featured "not only Lifar but the witty,
graceful, brutal, burlesquing, intellectual legs of the Russian Ballet."[7] Alice B. Toklas, according to Flanner, welcomed guests at the
Rue de Fleurus like a "praying mantis among strawberry leaves."[8]
The delicate, tiny-voiced chanteuse Yvonne George (whose forte was
nautical songs) "sang of sailing ships, which her tenderness reduced
to the size of the little barks retired sailors imprison in bottles."[9]

Flanner was delighted by idiosyncracy in any form. Colette, she
mock-seriously informed her readers, was the first "dendrophile" of
French letters: she brought her Parisian audience "news of nature"
with "the strangeness of a traveler who tells of an unknown land."[10]
The celebrated *grande horizontale* Liane de Pougy wore emerald rings
on her toes, but "only when in bed."[11] Barbette, the Texan-born ac-
robat who performed on the high wire at the Cirque Médrano in female costume, liked to adorn himself with "fifty pounds of white os-
trich plumes" along with a diaphanous white skirt: against the blue
background of the Médrano, his "fabulous *chute d'ange* fall" had "the
mythical quality of a new Phaethon deserting the sky."[12] Describing
Sarah Bernhardt in old age ("a one-legged, insoluble mystery on a lit-
ter, muffled beneath wigs, false teeth, furs, veils, leopard skins, and
make-up"), Flanner noted that the eccentric actress had made for herself "a museum of all the false limbs manufacturers sent her on approval, and planned to buy a park to try them out in, but forgot."[13]

Such ceremonial, absurdist turns (modeled, perhaps, on her idol,
Gibbon) were a Flanner speciality. But she never let the blandish-
ments of style overpower her commitment to truth. At the end of the
Bernhardt piece, amid a dazzle of prose rivaling Bernhardt's own
legendary refulgence, Flanner's admiration for her subject shone
through:

> At her last dinner parties, she was brought in after her guests, was
> propped up at the end of her table like a painted mummy, alternately
> simulating fright, shyness, and loss of memory, though forgetting
> nothing, seeing all—an amazing old actress and female, still rich in
> wit, revenge, surprise, chatter, contempt of and hunger for the hu-
> man comedy.[14]

Beginning in the 1930s, with the gradual darkening of the European situation, the Paris letters began to take a more somber, populist note. An ardent believer in Lincolnian democracy—a legacy of her Midwestern upbringing that she never repudiated—Flanner viewed the international rise of "nauseating fashionable fascism" with unmitigated disgust. In her journalism from the thirties, on inflation, bread riots in the streets of Paris and Berlin, the rise of Hitlerism, refugees from Spain, the Munich crisis, and so on, she revealed an unexpected gift for political and economic commentary.

Still, she never lost her interest in the quirks, vital or malign, of human character. In the devastatingly Swiftian (and prescient) profile of Hitler that she published under the title "Führer" in February and March 1936, she used her standard satiric technique—the accumulation of small, perverse, homely details—to underline her loathing for the demagogue and his politics:

> Dictator of a nation devoted to splendid sausages, cigars, beer, and babies, Adolf Hitler is a vegetarian, teetotaler, non-smoker, and celibate. He was a small-boned baby and was tubercular in his teens. He says that as a youth he was already considered an eccentric. In the war, he was wounded twice and almost blinded by mustard gas. Like many partial invalids, he has compensated for his debilities by developing a violent will and exercising strong opinions. Limited by physical temperament, trained in poverty, organically costive, he has become the dietetic survivor of his poor health. He swallows gruel for breakfast, is fond of oatmeal, digests milk and onion soup, declines meat, which even as an undernourished youth he avoided, never touches fish, has given up macaroni as fattening, eats one piece of bread a meal, favors vegetables, greens, and salads, drinks lemonade, likes tea and cake, and loves a raw apple. Alcohol and nicotine are beyond him, since they heighten the exciting intoxication his faulty assimilation already assures.[15]

The deceptively neutral manner is typical. Hitler's bleak digestive regimen, exposed here in almost clinical detail, becomes the metaphor of a poisonous hatred of life. Against such soul-destroying asceticism—the costiveness of the moral or political fanatic—Flanner waged a life-long, eloquent battle.

Flanner spent the war years in Manhattan, having fled Paris in

September 1939; but she returned to France immediately following the liberation. Her postwar dispatches, on the bombed-out cities, the newly discovered concentration camps (she was one of the first journalists to enter Buchenwald), and the slow rebuilding of European society, contain some of the most incisive and heartfelt writing she ever did. She continued to write extensively about politics in the fifties and sixties, reporting in detail on the vicissitudinous career of de Gaulle (whom she admired), the bloody and protracted Algerian crisis, the fluctuating French economy, and at the last, the tragicomic events of May 1968.

In turn, her achievements as a journalist received international acclaim. In 1948 Flanner was made a knight of the Légion d'Honneur for "services to France"; in 1959 she was elected a member of the National Institute for Arts and Letters; and in 1966, when her Paris letters from 1944 to 1965 were republished as a book (edited by William Shawn), she won the National Book Award. *Paris Was Yesterday*, a collection of her *New Yorker* writings from the twenties and thirties, was published, also to great acclaim, in 1972. She died in 1978, having written her valedictory "Letter from Paris" in 1975.

Her biographer seems most comfortable with Flanner in her later years—indeed, with Flanner the much-decorated public figure. Wineapple is at her best describing the externalities of her subject's life: Flanner's financial and living arrangements (she spent most of her time in Paris in rooms at the Hotel Continental and the Ritz), her relations with editors and publishers, the glamorous international milieu in which she lived and worked. Yet one cannot help feeling that something about Flanner—the private woman—has eluded her.

The problem, it must be said, has to do with Flanner's lesbianism, a topic with which Wineapple often seems uncomfortable. True, she gives a more or less straightforward account of the two women with whom Flanner became involved after she and Solita Solano gradually moved apart in the 1930s: Noel Haskins Murphy, an American widow and former opera singer living at Orgeval, outside Paris, whom Flanner met in 1932, and Natalia Danesi Murray, the Italian journalist and Rizzoli executive, with whom she fell in love while in New York during the Second World War. But she seems unwilling to dwell very deeply on the embodied side of Flanner's passions.

She seldom refers, for example, to Murray's moving collection of

Flanner's love letters, *Darlinghissima: Letters to a Friend* (1985), despite the remarkable, often lyric revelations contained there. "I found in my papers a Kodak picture of you in a white long skirt on the back porch of the Fire Island house"—Flanner wrote to Murray in the 1970s:

> It must have been taken by me, I suppose, in the first week of our new love for each other. How we burned and so publicly. I could report on each motion of our bodies. I recall them all so vividly. Poor John [Mosher] so choked at the waste of oil in the lamp that I let burn all night when we lay awake. [16]

Elsewhere, as in the letters she wrote to Murray during their many transatlantic separations, Flanner sought to conjure up her lover's bodily presence through a sort of verbal-sensual legerdemain:

> Oh, my fine, intelligent, good darling friend, my true and sweet generous friend, I send you over the ocean like a cloud moving from this continent to you, on whatever pavement you are standing or in whatever address with its particular chair where you are sitting, I send you my heart beat, my head beat, my beating of my soul against time; I send you my message of attachment. . . . Touch it, take it; you have touched me with your words; they touch me like your thoughts, as if they had a form one could feel with one's skin or hands. [17]

Flanner and Murray were lovers for almost thirty years. But the Flanner capable of such "tender love achievements"—the investor in the treasury of physical passion—is almost entirely missing from Wineapple's pages.

More troubling, the biographer is inclined to exaggerate what she thinks of as Flanner's "conflict" over her homosexuality. "Genêt," Wineapple is convinced, became over the decades a disguise behind which she hid her sexuality from the world. Posing as an "androgynous, anonymous, invented" being not only gave Flanner a needed sense of "security" and "legitimacy" but also left her, according to Wineapple, guilty and ill at ease. Wineapple points to Flanner's notorious perfectionism—she fretted over each of her *New Yorker* essays and constantly worried that she was losing her gift—as a symptom of this inner turmoil. Impersonating "Genêt," the biographer hints darkly, "may well have robbed [Flanner] of her own voice." [18]

Yet this is far too bleak and simplistic a view. So taken up is Wine-apple with the notion of Flanner's guilt, which she associates with her lesbianism, that she is unable to recognize how *gay* in every sense Flanner's *New Yorker* writings really are. Granted, Flanner's "Genêt" style is arch and impervious, like any code. And, like any great stylist, Flanner struggled perpetually with the intractability of words. But for anyone who can read the code—for a homosexual reader, perhaps—her Paris letters are a veritable trove of emotional information.

It is not merely that Flanner chose to write so often about homosexual subjects. (Her meditations on Proust, Stein, Cocteau, Colette, Bricktop, Radclyffe Hall, Gide, Thomas Mann, Ravel, Violette Leduc, and others constitute a kind of ongoing brief on behalf of modern Anglo-European homosexual sensibility.) The manner itself is gay, often to the point of blithe and outright camp. Thus, recollecting Radclyffe Hall, whose scandalous lesbian novel *The Well of Loneliness* (banned in England) was published in France in 1929, Flanner remembered her "beautifully tailored suits" and "perfect haircut"—along with the comical inadequacies of her fiction. "The Paris Latin Quarter denizens first met her at a tea (with wonderful cucumber sandwiches) at Miss Natalie Barney's, heavily attended, since *The Well of Loneliness* had aroused a great deal of curiosity, if very little admiration as a literary or psychological study."[19] Here, a succession of discreet yet unmistakable cues (perfect haircuts, Miss Natalie Barney, cucumber sandwiches) function as a kind of witty semaphor, clueing in the reader that the author herself knows whereof she speaks.

At times Flanner's writing verged on the palpably homoerotic, especially when she came to describe, as she often did, women's voices and bodies. She took a Saint-Simonian pleasure in female beauty. Early in her career she celebrated Josephine Baker's "caramel-color body," the charms of La Goulue ("a pretty, full-fleshed blonde of the mortal Olympian type popular with gay Edwardians the world over"), and Tiana Lemnitz's "handsome" Octavian in a 1930s *Rosenkavalier*—her favorite (and the most sapphic) of modern operas.[20] Writing about Wallis Warfield Simpson during the abdication crisis, Flanner gave an ironic yet subtly appreciative itemization of Mrs. Simpson's most attractive features, ending up at her "small and elegant" feet, with their "classically separated toes and rouged nails," which—as she dryly noted—"in these days of Riviera sunbathing, are well-known."[21]

Later on, in the sixties, she mused memorably over the flickering vision of Brigitte Bardot on French color television, "casting on the screen the image of her sensual flesh, the long, yellow straight stream of her ocher hair, and the odd, nacreous shading of her personality, with something intimate about it, like the inside of a seashell."[22] In turn, in perhaps her most overtly erotic piece of writing ever—a ravishing account of the dazzling Ingres retrospective in Paris in 1968—Flanner dwelt rhapsodically on the bather in the foreground of *Le Bain turc*: that "isolated, splendid female nude, seated on a carpet and fully displaying that superb, naked, idle, womanly back—that perfectly fleshed view, with averted face, that over time has become Ingres's chaste anatomical trademark." The sight of this and the other gloriously "bare-backed" women in Ingres's paintings, Flanner observed, had been without question the "major pleasurable event" of the year.[23]

Flanner's biographer is oblivious to this not-so-cryptic kind of self-revelation, as she is to the virile, appreciative beauties of the Flanner style. (Of the Ingres piece, Wineapple notes only that Flanner wrote "lovingly" of the pictures she had seen.) The result is a curiously morose, even misguided, portrait of her subject. Wineapple's Flanner is a vaporish, dull, somewhat neurotic figure who never quite seems to match up with the vibrant and magnificent presence revealed in photographs. She lacks the real Flanner's heft and fleshliness—her sheer physical joy in the richness and variety of human life.

What lesson to draw here? Perhaps that the biographer must be a lover as well as a diagnostician. Certainly, he or she must have a power of sympathetic feeling broad enough to encompass and bring to life, not only the so-called dark side but also the distinctive pleasure-world of his or her subject. This is no less true of the biographer of a lesbian subject—however difficult it may sometimes be (given the aura of taboo with which such things are usually enshrouded) to communicate the more sensuous and celebratory aspects of lesbian experience. In the case of a writer like Flanner, it is impossible to understand the woman without adopting, after a fashion, her own uniquely susceptible and homosexually inflected response to the world. If only temporarily, one has to let oneself become that tender, idiosyncratic, woman-enchanted commentator on life—a sort of lesbian Eustace Tilley—that she herself took delight in being.*

I am not suggesting, by any means, that only a biographer who is herself lesbian can do justice to a lesbian subject. Some of the most compelling recent biographies of lesbian writers and artists have not, in fact, been written by lesbian authors. I think here of Hilary Spurling's mordantly insightful life of Ivy Compton-Burnett, of Victoria Glendinning's richly sympathetic biography of Vita Sackville-West, or of Claire Harman's adventurous, intelligent life of Sylvia Townsend Warner.[24] One of the very best, surely, among recent lesbian biographies is Michael Baker's life of Radclyffe Hall—a masterpiece of civilized understanding that, for all its wit and forthrightness, never once condescends to its somewhat intractable subject.[25]

But what a biographer must undoubtedly have is a willingness to recognize joy—gaiety—when it is there. Janet Flanner was not a "typical" lesbian, if we take *typical* to mean (as many apparently still do) withdrawn, depressive, sexually frustrate, unstylish, or lacking in humor. She militated, utterly, against the "well of loneliness" stereotype—being neither lonely nor particularly unhappy. She lived at the center of her world, and while loving, and loving deeply, against the grain, maintained an essentially comic, urbane, and optimistic outlook on life.

Disappointingly, the charmed homosexual being known as "Genêt" has yet to find her ideal biographer-lover: the one who can match

---

*Flanner, sporting a monocle and comically fastidious air, posed for a photograph as the *New Yorker* mascot Eustace Tilley in the 1930s. The photo is reproduced in Brendan Gill, *Here at the New Yorker*. Tilley, it is worth noting, seems to have been coded with lesbian significance from the moment of his invention in 1925. In an aside on the monocle as lesbian "signifier" in *Vested Interests: Cross-Dressing and Cultural Anxiety*, Marjorie Garber quotes me as saying—in a conversation we had in 1989—"that Janet Flanner in a monocle is the model of, and for, the signature portrait of Eustace Tilley on the cover of the *New Yorker*, so that the *New Yorker* is in some sense 'originally' a lesbian magazine, however that identity was masked" (p. 155). This is not, I fear, strictly accurate. What I think I said (!) was that I thought that pictures of *Radclyffe Hall* had inspired the image of Tilley. Numerous caricatures of Radclyffe Hall in monocle and wing collar appeared in the sophisticated Anglo-American popular press around the time of the *New Yorker*'s founding, and I think it likely indeed that Rea Irvin, the artist who invented Tilley, was aware of them. Flanner's impersonation, therefore, would be a sort of second-order imitation, but one that also neatly reinscribes, obviously, the original "lesbian" visual subtext.

her word for word, pleasure for pleasure. But perhaps—in the end—she doesn't need to. If, in her magical letters from Paris, Janet Flanner never revealed her sexuality in so many words, what she did share with her readers—her ineradicable, coruscating delight in the world—was in its own way a perfect coming out.

9

IN PRAISE OF

BRIGITTE

FASSBAENDER

(A MUSICAL

EMANATION)

To "come out" as the fan of a great diva is always an embarrassing proposition—as difficult in its own way, perhaps, as coming out as a homosexual. For what can be more undignified than confessing one's susceptibility to a thrilling female voice? As Brigid Brophy has observed, in *Mozart the Dramatist*, the "listening" role is by its very nature regressive: the audience at an opera must "renounce the power of speech" and can only signify pleasure "by the infantile methods of inarticulate cries and hand-clapping."[1] Even after the performance, though one's powers of ut-terance may return, the baby mood often continues, resulting in effusions of a typically absurd and cloying sort. Witness, for example, the painfully empurpled prose of James Huneker, music critic for the *New York Times*, commenting on a performance by the famous Scottish-American diva Mary Garden in 1926:

> Nuance, which alone makes art or life endurable, becomes an evocation with Miss Garden. I lament that she is not in a more intimate setting, as the misted fire and rhythmic modulations of her opaline art and personality are lost in such a huge auditorium as the Lexington Theatre. I saw her, a slip of a girl, at Paris, early in this century, and framed by the Opéra Comique, of whose traditions she is now the most distinguished exponent. She was then something precious: a line of Pater's prose, the glance of one of Da Vinci's strange ladies; a chord by Debussy, honey, tiger's blood, and absinthe; or like the enigmatic pallor we in Renaissance portraits; cruel, voluptuous, and suggesting the ennui of Watteau's L'Indifférent. . . . One can't praise the art of Mary Garden without loving the woman![2]

At best, the diva-worshipper is a kind of parody adult, a maker of silly sounds and fatuous conceits—a sort of gurgling, burbling semi-idiot.

How much more embarrassing, then, to have to come out as a *female* diva-worshipper. For if Brophy once again is correct, the female fan is not only abject but perverse. The great diva's appeal is intrinsically erotic in nature, Brophy argues; through prodigies of breath control and muscular exertion—virtuoso feats easily reinterpreted as "metaphors of virtuoso performance in bed"—she stimulates repressed sexual memories in her listeners. Declares Brophy, deliciously embellishing on Freud: "[The prima donna's virtuosity] is of a kind precisely calculated to figure to the unconscious as a metaphor of sexual virtuosity, since the fluctuation of lovers' breathing is the indication of sexual intercourse which children most commonly contrive to eavesdrop."[3] In particular, by evoking a sound-memory of one's mother having sex, the diva reawakens the infantile fantasy of having sex *with* the mother. For female fans, the implication is obvious: to enthuse over the voice is, if only subliminally, to fancy plumping down in bed with its owner.

None of which makes any easier my principal task in this essay— to bear witness, without seeming too hopelessly fixated, to the peculiar power that one opera singer in particular (the superlative German mezzo Brigitte Fassbaender) has for some time exerted over my own imagination. I am conscious that in coming out in this way, as a female fan, as a victim of *Schwärmerei*, I risk giving too much away— and that the "coming out" will appear just that, a coming out. Perhaps one of the reasons that the most vocal diva admirers of the past two hundred years have tended to be homosexual men is that it is the least embarrassing for them—of all the modern sexual subgroupings— to enthuse in public over the female singing voice: the libidinal element inspiring the enthusiasm is there, by happy circumstance, most artfully disguised and displaced.[4]

Given the risks of self-revelation, it is comforting to discover that, unlike Stephen Gordon in *The Well of Loneliness*, one is not the only one ("like Cain . . . marked and blemished!"), and that, even in the realm of perversity, one can find compatriots and companions-at-arms. Though seldom advertised as such, there is in fact a long tradition of "sapphic" diva-worship in the world of opera: a history of female-to-female "fan" attachments as intense, fantastical, and sentimental as any ever enacted on the fabled isle of Lesbos. From Catalani, Malibran, Melba, and Mary Garden to Sutherland, Baker, Horne, and Von Stade, the greatest divas have always excited ardor in their female as well as male fans—and an ardor often implicitly tinged, if not openly charged, with homoeroticism. The otherwise sober-minded feminist film critic who recently admitted in the pages of the *Village Voice* to a stupefying crush on Jessye Norman (with whom she had once shared an elevator) was—though perhaps without realizing it—reviving a tradition of awe, delight, and comic self-abasement as old as the opera itself.[5]

That such a tradition should exist makes sense, of course, especially when we turn back the clock. Particularly for women of ninety or a hundred years ago, when the expression of passionate interest in one's own sex was inhibited by a host of cultural taboos, it must have been curiously exhilarating to enter an alternate universe—the opera house—in which many of the more restrictive norms governing ordinary female-female experience were temporarily suspended. Where else but in the plush darkness of Covent Garden, the Met, or the Opéra Comique, say, might a respectable woman of the nineteenth century have spent two or three hours staring raptly at another through binoculars? Before very recent times, the opera house (along with the theater) was one of only a few public spaces in which a woman could openly admire another woman's body, resonate to the penetrating tones of her voice, and even imagine (from a distance) the blood-warmth of her flesh—all in an atmosphere of heightened emotion and powerful sensual arousal. It is no wonder that for women whose erotic interest in other women was strong—the young Willa Cather, for example—the opera house should become almost a holy site, a kind of Temple of Love, or Venusberg of the homoerotic.[6]

Not every woman—admittedly—automatically fell under the spell: Virginia Woolf's jaundiced comment to a friend after attending a performance at Bayreuth ("Imagine a heroine in a nightgown, with a pigtail on each shoulder, and watery eyes, ogling heaven") suggests a certain intellectual resistance—at the very least—to the opera's peculiar pansexual magic.* Yet Woolf may be the (wary) exception proving the rule. What has always attracted women to opera, or so the unsung history of female diva-worship would appear to suggest, is precisely its homosexual dimension—the space that it allows for "loving" another woman, if only from afar. Before turning to my own perhaps too-transparent infatuation with *die Fassbaender*, I would like to offer a brief history of this tradition—not so much to exculpate myself, but as a way of diluting, as it were, some of the inevitable mortifications of self-exposure.

1

One could do worse than to begin with Queen Victoria—the ranking female diva lover of the nineteenth century. Victoria's adolescent passion for the Italian soprano Giulia Grisi is well-documented: after first hearing Grisi at the King's Theatre in 1834 in the role of Donizetti's Anna Bolena, the fourteen-year-old princess (who was a singer

---

*Virginia Woolf, letter to Vanessa Bell (August 16, 1909), in *The Letters of Virginia Woolf* 1:407. Not all of Woolf's comments on opera, it must be said, are so disdainful. Though unimpressed by what she saw at Bayreuth in 1909, she became a frequent, even avid opera-goer in the 1930s. Gluck and Mozart were particular favorites; Gluck's *Orfeo*, she wrote in 1933, was "the loveliest opera ever written." On June 12, 1935, she attended a Glyndebourne performance of Mozart's *The Magic Flute* in which the part of Papageno was sung by none other than Willi Domgraf-Fassbaender, the father of Brigitte Fassbaender. See *The Letters of Virginia Woolf*, 5:259 and 400.

Drawing of Giulia Grisi in *I Puritani* by the
young Victoria, 1834. From George Rowell,
Queen Victoria Goes to the Theatre (London, 1978).
Courtesy of Stanford University Libraries.

herself and already something of a connoisseur of voices) began filling
her diaries and letters with effusive paeans to her new idol. "She is a
most beautiful singer and actress and is likewise very young and pretty," she wrote after Grisi's debut; "she sang *beautifully* throughout but
particularly in the last scene when she is mad, which she *acted* likewise *beautifully*."[7] Hearing her as Desdemona a week later, the enraptured princess wrote that "she *sang* and *acted* quite beautifully! and
looked lovely."[8] And again, the following week: "Desdemona, Mdlle.
Grisi, who looked BEAUTIFUL and sung MOST EXQUISITELY
and acted BEAUTIFULLY. She personates the meek and ill-treated
Desdemona in a most *perfect* and *touching* manner."[9] Not even the
charismatic, ill-fated Maria Malibran could dislodge the Italian prima
donna from her place in the young princess's affections: when both
divas sang at Kensington Palace for Victoria's sixteenth birthday celebration, she wrote (somewhat heartlessly) afterward that Malibran

was "shorter than Grisi and *not nearly so pretty* . . . Her low notes are *beautiful*, but her high notes are thick and not clear. *I* like *Grisi by far better* than her."[10]

After her accession and marriage Victoria directed her attention toward other celebrated female singers—Pauline Viardot-Garcia, Emma Albani, and most famously, the so-called Swedish Nightingale, Jenny Lind, who became the object of extensive royal patronage in the 1840s and 1850s. At Lind's London debut in Meyerbeer's *Robert le Diable* in 1847, or so her biographers recount, "an incident occurred . . . illustrating in a remarkable manner the effect produced in the Royal box by Jenny Lind's transcendent talent":

> When the fair *cantatrice* was summoned before the curtain, Her Majesty cast a superb bouquet, which lay before her in the Royal box, at the feet of the *debutante*. The incident—certainly unparalleled on any former occasion in this country—was unobserved by the great majority of the audience; but the gracious act of condescension did not escape the fair songstress, and a profound curtsey acknowledged the Royal recognition of her success.[11]

In the succeeding months, Lind was invited several times to sing at Buckingham Palace, "where the purity, the sweetness and softness of her voice were much dwelt upon by the Queen, as well as the charming and unpretending grace of her manners."[12] Included among the tokens of favor the queen subsequently bestowed on her were a finely worked jewel bracelet and a Pekingese dog from the royal kennels.

Later in life, despite retiring from public operagoing after the death of Prince Albert, Victoria was still giving way to these regal diva enthusiasms. In her autobiography from 1922 the French singer Emma Calvé (creator of the leading role in Massenet's *Sapho*) describes being approached by the queen's sculptor cousin, the Countess Theodora de Gleiken, who had been commissioned by Victoria to make a portrait bust of Calvé as Santuzza in *Cavalleria Rusticana*. The bust was subsequently installed in the queen's private suite at Windsor Castle. After Victoria's death, when Calvé asked Princess Beatrice, the queen's daughter, what had become of it—assuming that it had been relegated to some attic storeroom—the princess assured her she was mistaken: "We have gathered together all our mother's favourite possessions, portraits, statues, mementos of all kinds, and placed them in a room known as the Victoria Room. There they will remain as long as the castle stands."[13]

Yet for all her sentimental connoisseurship, Victoria cannot be considered the typical diva-worshipper. Her high status gave her unusual powers (such as the right to command private performances), while her celebrated devotion to husband and children effectively disguised whatever element of latent homoeroticism may have been present in her obsessions with certain singers. More typical of the phenomenon of "sapphic" diva-worship—especially in the later nineteenth and early twentieth century—were those young, usually anonymous female fans who pursued their idols from opera house to opera house, much in the manner of modern groupies chasing after a rock star. The notorious "Gerry-flappers" who waited every night at the stage door of the Met for Geraldine Farrar in the teens and twenties, casting flowers and love notes in her direction when she emerged, exemplify this more humble yet fanatical kind of fan devotion; so too those impassioned student girls who signed on as supers for a performance of *Dinorah* with the Italian soprano Galli-Curci in 1918, so that they might steal glimpses of their heroine at close range from behind the scenery.[14]

It is true, of course, that not every diva attachment carries with it exclusively romantic-erotic meanings: many of the most fervent diva-worshippers of the past have been budding divas themselves, for the simple reason that young singers often find in older singers technical and personal attributes worth emulating. It is a standard feature of "diva autobiography," for example, for the singer-author to eulogize a prima donna from her youth who functioned as a model and inspiration. Thus Frida Leider, the great Wagnerian soprano, on her girlhood devotion to Geraldine Farrar: "She seemed to me the most elegant and bewitching creature, and I used to colour all the sepia postcards which showed her in a long evening gown, a little diadem of pearls in her gently waved hair, with long white kid gloves, her head gracefully rested on one hand."[15] Farrar herself described being bowled over as a child by "the fascinating Calvé" ("the supreme and daring French woman never to be forgotten once heard!"), while Galli-Curci remembered spending hours in her teens dwelling reverently on the fact that her own name—Amelita Galli—contained

The Gerry-flappers: Geraldine Farrar's female fans, 1920s.
Courtesy of Stanford University Libraries.

the same number of letters as Adelina Patti's.[16] In one of the most ludicrous of such anecdotes, the sublime Rosa Ponselle, an admirer in her adolescence of Tetrazzini, Calvé, and Melba, claimed to have quarreled with the priest at her confirmation when he refused to let her take "Melba" as her saint's name.[17]

Yet it hardly seems a coincidence that so many of the distinguished women of the past who have recorded obsessions with opera singers have been bisexual or lesbian in emotional inclination. Some, like George Sand, who adored Maria Malibran and found the inspiration for her romantic novel *Consuelo* in the singing of Malibran's sister, Pauline Viardot-Garcia, are well known; others, such as Anne Lister, the nineteenth-century womanizer of chapter 5, who kept a coded diary both of her concertgoing and of her numerous lesbian love affairs (she heard Catalani in York in 1823), are, if obscure, no less interesting.[18] Indeed, one could almost speak of diva-worship as an "objective correlative" of female homoeroticism in the nineteenth and early twentieth century—so obviously and so often, especially among women of a certain class and educational background, were its rhapsodies and exaltations the token of a deeper emotional and physical yearning after the feminine.

Witness Sand, for example, writing to her husband in 1831 after abandoning him in order to take up a bohemian life in Paris: "I saw Madame Malibran in *Otello*. She made me weep, shudder, and suffer as though I had been watching a scene from real life. This woman is the foremost genius of Europe, as lovely as a Raphael madonna, simple, energetic, naive, she's the foremost singer and foremost trage- dian. I'm mad about her."[19] The "madness" for Malibran was in part responsible for Sand's notorious adoption of male dress at this time: she first assumed her androgynous top-hatted costume, she later maintained, precisely in order to procure cheap standing-room tick- ets (available only to men) at the Théâtre des Italiens where Malibran was performing.[20] Malibran inspired one of Sand's first short stories—*La Prima Donna*—as well as her subsequent love affair with the actress Marie Dorval, who bore a striking resemblance to the Spanish singer. Writes Sand's biographer, "like Maria Malibran, Marie Dorval was anything but handsome, being too small and frail to have a commanding stage presence. . . . But what she lacked in natural attributes was more than matched by a passionate intensity and a lack of theatrical artificiality which had made her the darling of the Romantics."[21] In Sand's infatuation with her "dear loved one" ("Never did Erinna reply to Sappho in a more caressing voice") there is more than a little hint that she wished to recreate in the flesh the idealized passion for Malibran.[22]

A bit later, across the channel, the lesbian composer and conductor Ethel Smyth was another flagrant diva-worshipper. In *Impressions That Remained*, her engaging autobiography from 1919, Smyth (whose later infatuations would include the elusive Virginia Woolf) described holding a love-struck vigil while a teenager, her "heart beat- ing furiously," outside Jenny Lind's house in London in the early 1870s. "From allusions to her triumphs in old volumes of *Punch*, and my mother's descriptions of her supreme art, she had long been one of my heroines, and if anyone had told me that one day I should become fairly intimate with this striking and terrifying personality I should have gone off my head on the spot."[23] Later, while studying composi- tion in Leipzig, Smyth conceived a passion for the celebrated operetta singer Marie Geistinger, who came to epitomize for her "all the heroines I loved and pitied . . . Maria Stuart, Adrienne, Phèdre, Hermione (in *Winter's Tale*), and others." Indeed, Smyth recollected, "I was quite mad about the Geistinger, and after the performances used to stand for long half hours in snow or slush to see her muffled form shoot out of the stage door into her fly."[24] When "the Geistinger" responded with an invitation to visit her at home, the "shock of seeing Maria Stuart at close quarters, in a tight-fitting dark blue satin bodice covered with spangles, rouged up to the eyes, and wearing a fluffy light wig," Smyth wrote, "produced a commotion in my breast as when the tide turns against a strong wind."[25] Though the relationship soon petered out—Geistinger being absorbed in her needlework and dogs and accompanied by a skulking husband—Smyth subsequently named her next musical composition, a somewhat turgid Brahmsian pastiche, the "Geistinger Sonata."[26]

Certain famous turn-of-the century divas seem to have inspired such homoerotic emotion as a matter of course. Nellie Melba's numerous female admirers included both Vita Sackville-West and Violet Trefusis: when forced by her hypocritical family to marry—precisely in order to cover up the scandal of her affair with Sackville-West—the unregenerate Trefusis demanded that Melba sing at the wedding.* Janet Flanner was an ardent Mary Garden fan: in a letter to Natalia Danesi Murray in 1961, she recalled how during her college years in Chicago she braved the freezing winds coming off Lake

---

*See Trefusis, *Violet to Vita*, p. 110. Like Olive Chancellor, who takes Verena Tarrant to *Lohengrin* in the hope that the shared experience of listening to Wagner's music will strengthen the younger woman's love for her, Trefusis used opera, like a kind of magic talisman, to keep the moody Sackville-West under her spell. In a love letter to "Dmitri" (her nickname for Vita) from 1918, one finds the following:

> My sister is playing Prince Igor—the part that is so like my Dmitri . . . I shall take you to hear "Khouantchine" which is of all music the most sensuous, the most "bariolé," the most abandoned, and the most desolate. . . . One day I shall write a book on the baleful influence music has had on my life. (78)

Elsewhere she opines to Vita, "Oh my sweet, how I miss you. How I *longed* for you at the opera" (125). Though we know a good deal about opera's aphrodisiac role in heterosexual culture (especially in literature: think of the opera scenes in Flaubert, Stendhal, Tolstoy, or Edith Wharton), a study has yet to be written on the interesting part opera plays in the mediation of homosexual and especially lesbian relations. In *The Queen's Throat* (1993), Wayne Koestenbaum makes a brilliant start, but the focus—with a few suggestive exceptions—is almost exclusively male.

Michigan just to hear her idol sing in Prokofiev's *The Love of the Three Oranges*.[27] And in *My Thirty Years' War* (1930), Margaret Anderson, the founder of the avant-garde *Little Review*, described how she and Jane Heap, her first lover, once wangled a meeting with Garden by writing a series of adulatory articles about her. "The air was charged with an animal magnetism that one rarely has the pleasure of feeling," wrote Anderson, recollecting the event; "the challenge of Mary Garden's presence is one of the most thrilling human experiences I remember."[28]

Garden, who cultivated an air of sexual ambiguity quite brazenly— she created the lesbian role of Chrysis in Erlanger's *Aphrodite* in 1906

Mary Garden (1874–1967). "The challenge
of Mary Garden's presence," said Margaret
Anderson, "is one of the most thrilling
human experiences I remember." *Courtesy of
the Bettmann Archive.*

Mary Garden as Salomé, 1908. *Courtesy of
Stanford University Libraries.*

and sang the *tenor* part of the Jongleur in Massenet's *Le Jongleur de
Notre-Dame* in 1908—inevitably provoked strong feminine reactions.
In 1913, following a Garden performance in Philadelphia, a hysterical young woman named Helen Newby killed herself after being refused admittance to Garden's hotel room. Newby, reported the *New
York Times*, had "fallen in love" with Garden after seeing her photograph two years earlier, and suffering from a delusion that the singer
was Queen Cleopatra and she herself her slave, worshipped her "as a
heathen worships his idol." Newby was found dead clutching Garden's picture to her breast.* (Garden, although shaken, managed to

---

*The hapless Newby, a Bryn Mawr student and daughter of a wealthy Pennsylvania busi-
nessman, was found in the woods near her home on February 17, 1913, having shot herself
in the head. Garden, who mentions the incident briefly in the autobiography she
coauthored with Louis Biancolli, *Mary Garden's Story,* subsequently maintained she hadn't

sing Thaïs at the Met the following evening.) And in James Huneker's *Painted Veils*, a scandalous *roman à clef* about the opera world published in 1920, the Mary Garden character is shown pursuing and being pursued by a wealthy lesbian admirer in men's clothes ("a crazy-cat but a jolly girl") who later pays her way to Europe. In her pioneering bibliography *Sex Variant Women in Literature*, Jeannette Foster hints that the admirer may have had her counterpart in real life.*

Even more enthralling to female fans than Garden, however, was the great Swedish-American soprano, Olive Fremstad, who sang Isolde, Kundry, Brünnhilde, and other leading Wagnerian roles at the Met between 1903 and 1914. Given the sheer number and distinction of her women admirers—not to mention the Garbo-like eccentricities of her personal life—Fremstad might be considered the sapphic "cult" diva par excellence. Fremstad's most famous devotee was the novelist Willa Cather: Cather befriended the diva in 1913 after inter-

---

known about Newby's desire to meet her but would have agreed to see her had she been aware of her distress. (She nonetheless hinted to friends that she believed Newby had wanted to kill her too, in a kind of murder-suicide.) The Newby story appears on the front page of the *New York Times* for February 18, 1913. Other accounts of the incident—some more colorful than others—can be found in the *New York Herald*, *New York Tribune*, *Chicago Daily Tribune*, *Philadelphia Inquirer*, *Philadelphia Record*, and *Harrisburg Patriot* for the same date.

*Thus Huneker's description of Allie Wentworth, who pursues the heroine, Easter, after meeting her at her singing teacher's house:

> Allie Wentworth was a masculine creature, who affected a mannish cut of clothes. She wore her hair closely cut and sported a hooked walking stick. Her stride and bearing intrigued Easter, who had never seen that sort before. All of Wentworth's friends were of the sporting order. All smoked, and, a shocking deviation from the conventionality of that time, they drove their own motor-cars. Easter thought them rather free in their speech, and too familiar. Allie was always hugging her when alone. She drank liqueurs with her coffee and wasn't ashamed to avow the habit. She invited Easter to visit her and Madame Frida gave her consent. They are immensely wealthy, she confided to her pupil and may be of use to you some day. Allie is a crazy cat but a jolly girl.

Huneker is fairly explicit regarding the lesbian aspects of the relationship: when Easter returns from Europe with Allie, where she has become a singing sensation, she taunts a jealous male admirer with her newfound love of Gautier and Zola: "That girl helped me over some rough places in Europe. I shall never give her up, never. . . . I love sumptuous characters. That's why I love to read *Mlle. Maupin*. Also about that perverse puss Satin in *Nana*. She reminds me of Allie and her pranks—simply adorable, I tell you! Toujours fidèle." See *Painted Veils*, pp. 67 and 257. For Foster's remarks on the novel see *Sex Variant Women in Literature*, pp. 265–66 and 316.

viewing her for *McClure's* and later used her as the model for Thea
Kronberg, the austere yet curiously compelling heroine of *The Song of
the Lark*, the novel Cather published in 1915 about the coming of age
of a celebrated singer. When Fred Ottenburg, Thea's would-be suitor
in that novel, tries to describe the special quality of her vocalism, it is
not difficult to read into his sensual, almost libertine appreciation
something of Cather's own powerfully eroticized feeling for
Fremstad:

> "The people who chatter about her being a great actress don't seem to
> get the notion of where *she* gets the notion. It all goes back to her origi-
> nal endowment, her tremendous musical talent. Instead of inventing a
> lot of business and expedients to suggest character, she knows the
> thing at the root, and lets the musical pattern take care of her. The
> score pours her into all those lovely postures, makes the light and
> shadow go over her face, lifts her and drops her. She lies on it, the way
> she used to lie on the Rhine music."[29]

"With Mme. Fremstad," wrote Cather elsewhere, "one feels that the
idea is always more living than the emotion; perhaps it would be near-
er the truth to say that the idea is so intensely experienced that it becomes emotion."[30]

Less familiar, however, may be the case of Mary Watkins Cushing,
who began by worshipping Fremstad from afar and ended up living
with her for a number of years as a sort of private secretary-
companion. In her amusing though also somewhat reticent 1954
memoir, *The Rainbow Bridge*, Cushing described becoming infatuated
at nineteen with Fremstad after hearing her debut as Brünnhilde at
the Met. The performance had been an unusual one: tortured in the
past by the traditional "steel bodices of Bayreuth," Fremstad had
chosen to wear for the occasion "a mere bandeau slung to her shoulders with leather straps," an Amazonian cloak and kirtle, and sandals
with leather thongs—a boyish and athletic costume in which her
youthful admirer, gazing through binoculars, unabashedly delighted. Desperate to meet the "goddess" who had so entranced her,
the enterprising Cushing (who was an art student) drew a sketch of
Fremstad in her new costume and sent her a letter describing it.
Fremstad responded with an invitation to tea—an event for which
Cushing, "speechless with joy," prepared herself by taking a per-
fumed bath and shampooing herself "to a high degree of elegance." "I

Sketch of Olive Fremstad as Brünnhilde, 1903, by Mary Watkins
Cushing. From *The Rainbow Bridge* (New York, 1954). *Courtesy of Stanford
University Libraries*.

felt like a medieval esquire in vigil on the eve of knighthood. I was a foolish and star-struck girl, but I had a vague and disturbing sense of fate in operation, and wished to meet it in a state of grace."[31]

Fate was indeed operating, because Fremstad—besides being enchanted by the sketch—was taken enough with her new fan to ask her, not long after, to accompany her on a European tour. With her parents' grudging permission (they were clearly cowed by the impetuous diva) Cushing did so, and for the next eight years lived with Fremstad in the capacity of lady companion and self-described "buffer" against the world.[32] The relationship lasted until 1918, when Cushing, in a fit of patriotism, joined a women's ambulance corps going out to France. (It was seeing a pickled human head, cut in half lengthwise, that Fremstad used to demonstrate the physiology of the vocal organs to her singing students which convinced Cushing, she said later, that she had the psychological stamina to cope with the horrors of war.) The two women remained close, however, and Cushing was with Fremstad at the singer's death in 1951.[33]

Whether Cushing's relationship with Fremstad should be characterized as a homosexual one is questionable: there is no evidence to suggest that the two women were ever actually lovers. Among sophisticated contemporaries, however, it is clear that their intimacy aroused gossip and speculation. In Marcia Davenport's *Of Lena Geyer* (1936)—the mock biography of a fictitious Wagnerian diva modeled largely, like Cather's Thea Kronberg, on Fremstad—the relationship between the singer, Lena Geyer, and her companion Elsie deHaven closely parallels that between Fremstad and Cushing, though with its homoerotic element rather more plainly spelled out. (Davenport, daughter of the soprano Alma Gluck and an opera commentator for the National Broadcasting Company in the 1940s, was herself no stranger to the intoxications of diva-worship.)[34] "Miss deHaven" first appears in Davenport's novel as a mysterious black-clad young heiress of "strange" and "morbid" disposition who follows Geyer across Europe from opera house to opera house, always sitting alone in the same seat in the sixth row. When she begins sending Geyer gigantic flower bouquets, the singer's jealous French lover, the Duc de Chartres, tries to shield her from deHaven's "unnatural" obsession. "I felt as if a cold hand, nay, the fin of a cold-blooded creature of the sea, had swept over my heart," he says after being introduced to her; "her wor-

Olive Fremstad as Isolde, early 1900s. *Courtesy of
Stanford University Libraries.*

ship of my darling Lena could be construed only in the most horrible
light; and I boiled with fiery determination never to allow the two to
meet."[35]

The duke's efforts notwithstanding, Geyer becomes secretly fascinated with her new admirer, and after a performance of *Le Nozze di
Figaro* (a change from her usual Wagnerian fare), invites deHaven
backstage. There, "goggle-eyed with wonder," the smitten heiress is
allowed to watch while the singer proceeds to divest herself somewhat provocatively of the heavily brocaded gown she has worn as
Mozart's Countess. "Madame Geyer stood up and shook herself," de-
Haven recollects later:

> The whole thing slipped off around her feet, leaving her in a high-
> busted corset and a pair of lacy cambric drawers. I must have shown

the question in my mind—how could she sing in such stays? She answered by remarking that she was about ready to throw them all into the fire and start a vogue for natural lines on the stage. The sequel is that she did. Dora unlaced her, and removed the harness. As she did so, Madame Geyer groaned and stretched delightedly, then slipped a dressing gown over her shoulders and sat down again while Dora took off her white wig.[36]

Reclothing herself in a glamorous silk-lined cloak and "velvet carriage boots," Geyer then sweeps the younger woman off to her hotel room for an intimate late-night supper of "favorite Mozart dishes," including eggballs and a *Himmeltorte*. When the love-struck deHaven, trembling, like a sort of Cherubino-in-training, confesses her infatuation, Geyer enfolds her in a voluptuous embrace. "I was so unnerved by the emotions of the past twenty-four hours," deHaven says later, "I could not regain control of myself. For the first time in my life I was freely and utterly giving way to deep feeling. Lena Geyer pressed my head against her shoulder and murmured to me in German, tender broken phrases that one would use to a child. I felt as if I should die for love of her."[37] Geyer, it is now revealed, has tired of the duke, and finding all other men "brutish," longs for a faithful female companion with whom to share her life. Over the next few weeks the duke—to his mortification—is phased out, and the adoring deHaven (who asks nothing more of life "than the privilege of living with Lena Geyer and of acting as companion, secretary, housekeeper, amanuensis, and confidante") joyfully takes her place as the singer's unofficial consort. "I cannot imagine what Lena saw in me," she remarks later, after Geyer's death; "we will have to let it go as the same sort of mystery that holds a forceful, handsome, desirable man to a homely little shadow of a wife."[38]

Davenport's novel might be said to encapsulate the most narcissistic, and even absurd, of sapphic fan fantasies—that of being "taken up" (recognized, petted, and adored in turn) by the one whose voice enthralls. Yet as Davenport's barely disguised reworking of the Fremstad-Cushing story suggests, it was a fantasy that could on occasion come true. More than one fan in the annals of female diva-worship has, like Mary Watkins Cushing or the fictional Elsie deHaven, ended up "marrying" her favorite singer. The most famous of English lesbian novelists, Radclyffe Hall, lived for nine years with

Mabel Batten, a well-known lieder singer and concert performer of the Edwardian era; they met in Homburg in 1907 and were lovers until Batten's death in 1916.[39] And Margaret Anderson—the same Margaret Anderson who enthused in her youth over Mary Garden—lived for twenty-one years with the celebrated French opera singer Georgette Leblanc, the first Mélisande and widow of Maeterlinck. Anderson and Leblanc shared their ménage (a romantic lighthouse in Normandy) with a Belgian woman named Monique Serrure, who had herself given up a career as a schoolteacher many years earlier after hearing Leblanc sing Thaïs at the Opéra de la Monnaie in Brussels. Merely listening to Leblanc's voice, Serrure said, had made her want to serve her—which she did, as cook and housekeeper, for the next forty years.[40]

It would be easy enough, I imagine, to find examples of similar fan devotion in more recent times; for despite the incursion of new and more up-to-date forms of mass entertainment, both operagoing and its colorful corollary, sapphic diva-worship, continue to flourish. Indeed, thanks to the proliferation of cheap recordings and videotapes and what one might call the privatization of the operatic experience, more of such worship may in fact be going on—behind closed doors—than ever before. Unless I am utterly mistaken, numerous postwar divas (and Kathleen Ferrier, Joan Sutherland, Jessye Norman, Janet Baker, Frederica Von Stade, and Tatiana Troyanos are among those who come immediately to mind) retain same-sex followings at least as large—if not always as comically conspicuous—as those inspired in an earlier age by Lind and Fremstad and Garden.* Although hysterical fan "hunting packs" of the sort that carried Geraldine Farrar aloft down Broadway after her farewell performance at the Met may no longer exist (except perhaps in Japan, where same-sex performer worship continues to take unusual and extravagant forms), the rituals of adoration, to judge by ticket sales and fan club subscriptions, still entice the susceptible.[41]

At the same time, with the gradual change in social attitudes toward homosexuality, it has become possible—or nearly possible—to

---

*Witness the following in the advertisement section of a recent *Gramophone*: "GUNDULA JANOWITZ DEVOTEE wishes to correspond with others to exchange views and music. Vivienne Rendall, 88 Newton Road, Great Ayton, North Yorkshire."

acknowledge the libidinal element in such veneration. As early as 1956, Brigid Brophy—in her novel *King of a Rainy Country*—depicted a tender lesbian scene between diva and female fan.[42] The homoerotic impulse animating much diva-worship of the past has been, as it were, desublimated: to the point that certain singers have become popular icons within a newly enfranchised female homosexual subculture. (Ferrier was perhaps the first major modern singer to inspire a visibly lesbian following; Norman, Von Stade, Brigitte Fassbaender, Anne Sofie von Otter, Cecilia Bartoli, and Hildegard Behrens are among the more recent sapphic cult divas.) Nowadays it is hard to attend an opera in a city like San Francisco, for instance, with its large and vocal lesbian population, without becoming aware—however subtly—of the various female claques attracted by certain charismatic divas.[43]

Rather than trace out any of these fan networks in more detail, however, I would like to turn instead to my own case—to explore the question of diva-worship, as it were, from within. The purely sociological approach can, perhaps, only take us so far. My hope is that by disclosing as fully and shamelessly as possible the extent of my own partisanship for the aforementioned Fassbaender, I can illuminate some of the more subjective aspects of the phenomenon. I confess to some lingering apprehension—the thought of being lampooned as a "Briggy-flapper" gives pause—but in the interests of scholarship, I proceed.

2

We "Octavians" get some very peculiar fan mail.
—Brigitte Fassbaender, 1991[44]

The obvious question, perhaps, though also a perplexing one, is why Brigitte Fassbaender? There are singers whose voices—as instruments—I find more beautiful; there are singers, even among the rather inglorious cohort currently active, who possess a demonstrably superior technique. (Marilyn Horne would certainly be among the latter: though she and Fassbaender are both dramatic mezzos with fairly heavy, rich voices, Horne's strength and agility—

bordering at times on the superhuman—are considerably greater.) There are, moreover, *singers I have actually heard*. The most paradoxical aspect of my fixation is its curious ineffability. It is not just that I have never once cast a bouquet of roses in Fassbaender's direction or waited patiently in the slush by a stage door in order to watch her getting into a taxi cab; despite nearly twenty years of opera and recitalgoing, I have never—strangely enough—seen and heard her sing in the flesh. Fassbaender remains for me a singing simulacrum: a creation of digital and analog and video tape, a sort of auditory hallucination, or disembodied (though always musical) electronic emanation.

The way that my attachment evolved will perhaps account for this peculiar state of affairs. I first became aware of Fassbaender almost ten years ago, as a result of reading a squalidly entertaining Anne Rice novel, *Cry to Heaven* (1982), about the life and loves of a sex-crazed castrato in eighteenth-century Italy. There, in an afterword, Rice confessed that she had written one of the novel's many bizarre love scenes "to music"—namely, to a 1964 Deutsche Grammophon recording of Alessandro Scarlatti's chamber cantata *Il Giardino d'Amore*, featuring Brigitte Fassbaender as Venus and the American soprano Catherine Gayer as Adonis.[45] Intrigued by this odd admission—the central relationship in Rice's novel is a curious affair between the bisexual castrato and a depraved old cardinal—I acquired the same recording myself a short time later.

Though impressed by Fassbaender's strange androgynous timbre and the precocious skill with which she and Gayer wove their seductive vocal lines (Fassbaender was only twenty-four at the time), I can't say I was immediately struck by *un coup de foudre*. Indeed, for the next seven or eight years, though I continued to collect the odd Fassbaender disc here and there (a *Così* highlights album, some Schubert masses), my attention was drawn to more flamboyant divas such as Callas and Horne, and then to a succession of historical singers, including Lehmann, Flagstad, Ponselle, Elisabeth Schumann, and the glorious, all-too-short-lived Conchita Supervia. Nor did I become aware of Fassbaender's achievements on stage: despite going to the opera as often as possible—first on a graduate student's, then on an assistant professor's salary—I never happened to see her "by accident," as it were, though I was fairly often in places in which she had sung: San Francisco, London, and New York.

A couple of years ago two events snapped me out of my semistupor. The first was the reissue of the Scarlatti cantata on compact disc; the second was an interview with Fassbaender in the music magazine *Gramophone*. To hear Fassbaender's Venus in the new "silver" format, with the sound immeasurably cleaned up and the voice projected with a presence so direct and intimate as to be startling, was a revelation. Here, I realized—listening to her lilting, dignified, yet amorous traversal of Venus's *"Care selve, amati orrori"*—were *portamenti* to be reckoned with. This miniature epiphany (as I now think of it) was loosely akin to those moments in Iris Murdoch novels when two characters who have known one another for years—without feeling the slightest emotional attraction—suddenly fall wildly and improbably in love. Apathy gave way to emotion; cool diffidence to a sudden aching, acute attentiveness.

But the interview, devoted to Fassbaender's then just-released recording of Schubert's *Winterreise* (1990), was in its own way equally galvanizing. Long considered the most profound and difficult of Schubert song cycles, the *Winterreise* has traditionally been "off limits" to women singers on account of its (seemingly) intractable heterosexual premise: the speaker—inevitably presumed to be a man—wanders despairingly through a bleak winter landscape, lamenting the loss of a female beloved. To have a woman perform the songs, or so it has usually been felt, is to complicate—rather uncomfortably—an otherwise familiar (if gloomy) romantic scenario. So intense and potent are the sexual yearnings expressed in Schubert's settings, so *neurotic* the dramatic situation, the use of a female singer inevitably "perverts" the desired aesthetic effect—precisely (it is implied) by raising the problematic specter of lesbianism.*

---

*Nowhere is the implication more flagrant, perhaps, than in Matthew Gurewitsch's lengthy denunciation of Fassbaender's *Winterreise* in the *New York Times*—"Can a Woman Do a Man's Job in Schubert's 'Winterreise?' " The answer, according to Gurewitsch, is no. So "irreducibly confessional" is the Schubert cycle, it remains intractably "unsuitable" material for a woman singer. His elaboration is at once coy and knowing:

> Oh, sure, a chanteuse in a cabaret can purr "Lili Marlene" to the soldiers. But in the usual course of things, men don't sing "Bill" or "My Man," and women pass up "Maria" and "Man of La Mancha" and "Just Like a Woman." No one needs to tell you why. [. . .] Except for purposes of travesty, where the lyrics call for a man rather than a woman or the other way around, what the lyrics say goes. The sexes are equal but separate, and *vive la différence*.

Along with displaying numerous vocal flaws ("savage timbres, wild wobbles, sobs fetched—heaved—from the chest") Fassbaender's version is one in which "nothing

The handful of female singers brazen enough to sing the cycle in the past, such as Elena Gerhardt and Lotte Lehmann, have typically defended themselves against charges of unnaturalness and impudence by stressing the "universality" of the cycle. "This most beautiful cycle of songs," wrote a pious Gerhardt in her autobiography, "can well be interpreted by a woman. It expresses unhappy love, despair and a complete resignation to the fact that life may not hold anything more worth living for. Why should a woman, who is capable of understanding these emotions, not be able to perform it? For me, the psychology of this cycle is that of unhappy love in general, and does not depend on a particular masculine or feminine approach."[46]

Yet Fassbaender, I was intrigued to see, avoided any such diplomatic cant. Indeed, responding to her interviewer's (to my mind) subtly loaded question—"Had she always wanted to sing the *Winterreise?*"—she seemed instead to accentuate, albeit obliquely, the subversiveness of the endeavor. Yes, she replied, though she hadn't "dared" to until she had spent three months working on it with an accompanist in New York. Then, she said, she had premiered it in a little church somewhere outside the city. "The old ladies in the church all sat there eating their cake and sipping coffee, then slowly they began to stop and listen, and they listened more and more! That was, as it were, the performance in secret. Then I brought it to Europe and sang it at Hohenems."[47] In the comical image of a claque of elderly females, mesmerized, cake in hand, by this mysterious "secret" performance, Fassbaender seemed—to me at least—to acknowledge the sexual politics involved in her choice of repertoire and the covert (if eccentric) homoeroticism with which it might be associated. The "old ladies," or so I fondly imagined, had put their authorizing seal on the performance—had in fact, despite coffee and crumbs, called it forth into sensuous life. I quickly sought out the Schubert disc and, like them, was at once transfixed by its uncanny, transsexual beauty.

Struck now with a sense not only of a magnificent voice but also with Fassbaender's idiosyncratic, even daredevil musical personality,

---

works," says Gurewitsch—not least because the singer herself fails to grasp that " 'Winterreise' belongs uniquely to men, for reasons that lie not in principles but in the nature of the work."

Brigitte Fassbaender. "There is no more
vibrantly characterful Lieder-singer
today, man or woman" (Ivan March).
Courtesy of Werner Neumeister.

I immediately embarked on a search for other Fassbaenderiana.
Within a month I had acquired a 1986 collection of Mahler and Berg
songs, a Loewe recital, a recording (with Giulini) of *Das Lied von der
Erde*, and a second Schubert disc, complete with a cover photograph
of the sloe-eyed singer sitting moodily in a graveyard. Yet with each
new purchase the compulsion to hear *more* became greater. And soon
enough, I am embarrassed to say, I found myself haunting local record stores, shuffling through CD racks, and perusing *Opus* catalogues with the eager tremulousness of the addict.

My new habit was hardly an inexpensive one. Not only was Fassbaender's discography from the 1970s and 1980s large, she had been
involved from the start of her career in some rather plush projects.
(She has held long-term contracts with EMI, Deutsche Grammophon, London, and Philips.) In one frightening two-week period,
soon after starting in on her operatic recordings, I greedily bought
up whole boxed sets of Mozart's *La Clemenza da Tito* and *La Finta*

Giardiniera, Strauss's *Die Fledermaus*, Berg's *Lulu, and* Schoenberg's *Gurrelieder*, all simply in order to sample my idol's contributions. Fate seemed to be working obscurely to intensify my fixation: the Loewe disc, for example, which quickly became a special favorite, I uncovered by accident while twiddling—as if impelled by invisible forces—through a remainder bin at Tower Records.

Had I known at the peak of my obsession where to see Fassbaender "live"—whether Bayreuth or Tokyo, Buenos Aires or Sydney—I would probably, madly, have tried to get there. (I was unaware then, in late 1991, that she had already retired several of her most famous roles.)[48] In a belated attempt to catch up with her stage career I did the next best thing, and began raiding the opera video racks. The fact that I didn't own a VCR didn't deter me: I immediately got one. I first "saw" Fassbaender, somewhat anticlimactically, in one of her goofier trouser roles—as a pop-eyed Hänsel, complete with baggy lederhosen, in Humperdinck's *Hänsel und Gretel*. But before long, I had taken her in in an array of more sophisticated parts: as a farouche, tuxedo-clad Orlovsky in *Fledermaus*, as a sensuous yet implacable Charlotte in Massenet's *Werther*, and most fearsomely, as a lurching, makeup-encrusted, get-your-ya-ya's-out Klytemnestra in Strauss's *Elektra*. This scopophilic compulsion finally came to a head one day when I found a Laserdisc version of *Der Rosenkavalier* with Fassbaender as Octavian—her most celebrated part—and spent most of an afternoon exulting over it like a voyeur in a soundproof concrete cubicle at the Stanford University audiovisual center. Seldom has the Presentation of the Rose taken place in less salubrious quarters.

Still, one may ask, Why this riot of fondness over one particular singer? The answer that comes first to mind is a simple one: low notes. I confess to being what Marilyn Horne has termed a "chest nut" (as in "chest notes for chest nuts"), and invariably thrill to Fassbaender's voluptuous command of the reverberant mezzo/contralto register. I share this predilection for the low voice, I find, with numerous female diva-worshippers of the past. Willa Cather cherished Fremstad for her swooping low notes; Ethel Smyth describes Marie Geistinger's voice as "deep and thrilling."[49] And in Marcia Davenport's *Of Lena Geyer*, we discover the following:

> [Geyer] had almost a contralto range; its quality, all in her chest, was thrilling beyond description. In some ways her low voice was more

thrilling than her fiery middle and high one, and in later days the critics used to go wild looking for terms in which to describe it. It was
pure earth, female, sex if you want to call it that. You might say that
where her high tones were enchanting to the imagination, her low
ones warmed the body like an embrace.⁵⁰

Even among diva-worshippers who go in for sopranos rather than
mezzos, it's the bottom notes, one finds, that count: in *Così fan tutte*,
writes Brigid Brophy, it is the "astonishing low notes" sung by Fior-
diligi that suffuse her arias with their almost unbearable emotional
plangency.⁵¹ In Fassbaender's case, the velvety richness of the lower
register—what her admirers refer to as her "smoky" or "dark" or
"chocolate" tone—comes across especially well in recordings, creating unparalleled effects of shading, depth, and sensuality. (Witness,
for example, the vertiginous downward plunges in "Gefrorne
Tränen" in the *Winterreise*, or the ravishing *gravitas* with which she
imbues the Wood Dove's bottom notes in Schoenberg's *Gurrelieder*.)

Yet just as compelling, if not more so, is the style in which the
notes are produced. Fassbaender's manner is typically noble, extro-
verted, even virile. She is not a recessive or shyly self-effacing mezzo,
content to lurk in the background, murmuring little bits of advice to
the soprano. On the contrary, there is a boldness and edge, almost a
"butchness" to her singing—even in lieder, where her interpretations
are often highly unorthodox. This "butch" element (if one may call it
so) may have something to do with the fact that she was trained exclusively by her father, Willi Domgraf-Fassbaender, a prominent
Mozart baritone of the 1930s and 1940s. Music journalists have made
much of this interesting Oedipal connection. A 1981 *Opera* profile devoted to Fassbaender began, in fact, with the following:

> An unidentified author of sleevenotes for an Acanta album of Willi
> Domgraf-Fassbaender concludes his description of the baritone in the
> incomparable Glyndebourne recordings of *Così fan tutte* and *Le Nozze
> di Figaro* as follows: "The greatness of this artist lay in his ability to use
> singing as a means of expressing tangible human emotions. His char-
> acter portrayals were natural and convincing; his diction precise even
> in the most lyrical of phrases and his intelligent approach to the dra-
> matic action gave all that he did a penetrating intensity. Seldom have
> words and music, language and song, been in such agreement." It is
> no coincidence that these same words, put into the present tense and
> substituting "her" and "she" for "his" and "he" could be the perfect

description of Brigitte Fassbaender, mezzo soprano: she happens to be his daughter, and her only vocal studies were with him; from her Nuremberg Conservatory days (1958–61), until his death in February 1978 she went over her roles and Lieder with him.[52]

One hesitates to say that Fassbaender "sings like a man" (though the reviewer here comes close), yet there's an element of truth to the observation: the sound produced is often a curiously unfeminine one. Fassbaender's attack is typically forthright, almost guttural—and not only when she is singing in German. In Don Ramiro's "jealousy" aria in act 3 of *La Finta Giardiniera*, for example, every *t* cuts and every *p* explodes. (She makes the same exaggerated *t* sound at the end of words too, as in the brutal "Ewigkeit" at the end of the Countess Geschwitz's Adagio in *Lulu*.) The breath control is that of the proverbial athlete. Like many mezzos, Fassbaender takes very audible breaths, yet never to distracting effect: she somehow manages to make the intake of breath an integral part of the emotional statement. At times, as in some of the more savage *Winterreise* songs—"Rückblick" or "Die Krähe"—she seems almost to gnaw on, or bite into, the air as she sings, gulping it down, like one craving for sustenance, yet also capturing perfectly the engulfing desperation of Schubert's mad wanderer. But Fassbaender's timbre itself can often sound oddly masculine—to the point that critics have on occasion been confounded by what they hear. Assessing a recent recording of *Die Fledermaus* in which Fassbaender appears as Prince Orlovsky, a writer for *Classic CD*, while marveling at her performance, questioned whether it could really be she delivering Orlovsky's "astonishingly deep" spoken dialogue.[53]

Yet the spell that Fassbaender casts cannot simply be reduced to a matter of sound or technique. Maria Callas, after all, had low notes, power, awesome virtuosity—and even, one might argue, a similar "masculine" forwardness to her singing. Yet while I admire Callas— fiercely—I do not adore her. It's a matter of role-playing: with Callas, the unambiguously heterosexual persona gets in the way—the sense she projected, both onstage and off, of being in thrall to, and exclusively concerned with, a world of men. Dynamic though she is, one seldom has a sense of Callas singing "to" or "for" another woman: the implied auditor is almost always a man. Her most famous parts—

Norma, Tosca—merely reinforce what might be called the hetero-vocalism of her singing: it is an address to a male beloved.

In Fassbaender's case, the address—what one might term the directionality of the vocal appeal—is completely different. Fassbaender seems by contrast acutely aware of female listeners, and to include precisely where Callas seems to exclude. The distinctive virility of Fassbaender's singing may be less a matter of vocal technique, in other words, than a matter of theatricality, of a certain attitude toward her audience. Indeed, she often gives the illusion of singing "for" women and women alone—of conceiving her roles, and projecting them outward, in a manner carefully designed to appeal to an attending, if invisible, cohort of female fans. Where Callas is heterovocal, Fassbaender is homovocal.*And yet, the cynic will object, might not such an effect simply be attributed to the fact that Fassbaender—as a mezzo—has had out of necessity to sing a particularly large number of trouser roles? Given that so many of the standard mezzo parts nowadays—from Sesto in *La Clemenza da Tito* and Arsace in *Semiramide* to Orlovsky in *Fledermaus* and Octavian in *Rosenkavalier*—require the singer literally to sing in drag (and often very passionately) to another woman, is it really so surprising that Fassbaender's onstage persona should seem more homosexually inflected than Callas's? Had Fassbaender had to make a career out of Violettas or Butterflys, matters might be very different.

Indisputably, the present-day mezzo repertoire has a lot to do with what I am calling the "homovocality" of Fassbaender's stage presence. At this point in operatic history, it is indeed the mezzo or contralto

---

*Which is not to say that Callas has ever lacked for lesbian admirers. Witness Janet Flanner's exuberant paean to the diva in the *New Yorker* (March 10, 1965) after hearing her sing Tosca in Paris in 1965:

> Her tragic top notes, sung *mi-voix*, as if to herself, are loudly covered by the orchestra, but the middle and lower registers are unique in their physical loveliness and in their ministrations to her genius for emotive acting—for magnificently incarnating the musical melodrama in which Sardou and Puccini perfectly met on the same desperate, passionate human level. In her duality as actress and singer, Callas has seemed doubly unrivalled. In the opening act, in the church, when, thin and agitated, she enters in full voice and in full love, one does not know which complete concentration of the senses to offer her—whether of the ears or of the eyes—so prodigious is her performance.

It is my impression, however, that Callas does not function *specifically* as a lesbian icon. Her most fervent admirers have usually been men—and homosexual men in particular.

Kathleen Ferrier in *Orfeo*, Covent Garden, 1953. *Courtesy of the Houston Rogers Collection, Theatre Museum, London.*

who is most likely to become a homoerotic icon—precisely because so many of her roles will be travesty parts. This was not always the case. At the turn of the century, apart from Mozart's Cherubino, very few of the standard roles for the mid-to-low female voice were in fact transvestite roles. And, as a consequence, the divas with the largest female followings tended not to be mezzos at all, but heavy dramatic sopranos, like Olive Fremstad, whose speciality was Brünnhilde. (Brünnhilde was in its own day of course the most boldly androgynous of the soprano parts.) Only with the mid-twentieth-century revival of *opera seria* and *bel canto*, in which low-lying travesty roles proliferate, have the majority of sapphic "cult" divas tended to come from the mezzo or contralto ranks. Ferrier was luminous in the trouser part of Orfeo, and Horne, Troyanos, Von Stade, Baker, and Fassbaender have all carried on the distinguished "mezzo-in-drag" tradition.

What separates Fassbaender, however, even from some of her most gifted peers, is the almost shocking intensity with which the transvestite illusion—in all of its giddying psychological complexity—is brought off. Fassbaender is not afraid to identify with the male role, and to identify completely. One critic, describing her controversial *Winterreise*, put the matter this way:

> Any woman who sets out to perform *Winterreise* must decide whether she is going to *be* the young man singing the songs or merely a reciter of his words, and then she must somehow make her point of view clear to her audience. Ludwig [i.e., the German mezzo Christa Ludwig, who sang the cycle in the 1970s] seems to take the more aloof, empathic approach. Her readings are almost maternally consoling. She feels the sentiments deeply, but at second-hand. Fassbaender goes beyond empathy to identify completely with the boy himself, stepping into his boots with such peremptory conviction that we forget a woman is singing. . . . This is Schubert's forlorn wanderer standing in the flesh before us, sounding a little younger than usual and all the more pitiable because of it.[54]

Yet even this may be an oversimplification. If the writer here (who is male) errs in any point, it is in his assertion that Fassbaender *en travesti* makes us "forget a woman is singing." For the very opposite, I think, is in fact the case. It is true, as he implies, that Fassbaender often seems driven from within, possessed by a kind of dramaturgical daemon—to the point that she can sometimes appear to merge, eerily, with her roles, as in the case of Schubert's unhappy wanderer or Strauss's Octavian. But the male persona is only that: a persona, a narrative fiction. Brilliant though "he" is, no one I think ever seriously confuses Fassbaender's Octavian, for example, with a seventeen-year-old boy. What we see before us—in the intoxicating boudoir scene at the start of *Rosenkavalier*—is Fassbaender, the diva, draped langorously across another, making passionate love to her. No matter how artfully "true to life" the boyish gestures, Fassbaender-in-drag fools no one: the fact that the body is female, that the voice is a woman's voice, remains inescapable.

The effect (on this listener at least) is both stirring and paradoxical—like something out of a dream. Precisely to the degree that Fassbaender seems to enter "into" her male roles, precisely as I watch her approach (though without ever reaching) a kind of "zero degree masculinity," I find myself becoming more and more acutely aware of, and aroused by, her femininity. The very butchness with which she tackles, say, a role like Octavian—the sheer, absolutist bravado of the impersonation—infuses it with a dizzying homosexual charge. The more dashingly Fassbaender pretends, the more completely she fails—with the result that a new stage illusion takes shape: that of a woman robustly in love with another woman. When Fassbaender-as-Octavian, singing of her passion for the Marschallin, takes her fellow diva in her arms, I find it difficult not to take *her* literally—to read "past" the narrative fiction toward what I am actually seeing: a woman embracing a lover, even as she pantomimes the part of an impetuous boy. The very deftness of the pantomime prompts a kind of lesbian chauvinism: this is a woman (we are invited to imagine) who is as good as, if not better than, any man.[55]

What exactly is Fassbaender conveying at such moments? Fassbaender's great theme—the emotion she communicates onstage better, I think, than any other living diva—is gynophilia: exaltation in the presence of the feminine. She is unsurpassed at conveying adoration: of female voices, bodies, and dreams. This is true whether she is herself playing a woman or a man, a tragic or a comic part. Her female roles are as strongly homovocal in conception as her male roles. When asked in a recent interview, for example, about her favorite Wagnerian part—Brangaene, Isolde's lady-in-waiting in *Tristan und Isolde*—Fassbaender said that what she found most "riveting" about it psychologically was precisely the ardent tenderness that Brangaene displays toward Isolde:

> Brangaene is the intermediary, the mother substitute who, out of love for Isolde, substitutes the death for a love potion. In doing that she assumes a crucial part in the unfolding of events and her maternal love and anxiety find full expression in the finale.[56]

Brangaene is—after a fashion—as fixated as Tristan. And indeed to listen to Fassbaender's rapturous, no-holds-barred traversal of *"O Süsse! Traute! Teure! Holde! / Goldne Herrin! Lieb' Isolde!"* (O sweetest, dearest, fairest, / golden lady! Beloved Isolde!) is to sense more powerfully than ever the note of wild, almost idolatrous devotion in Brangaene's love for her doomed mistress.

In the case of the Countess Geschwitz in Berg's *Lulu*, the gynophilia is explicitly weighted, of course, with homosexual feeling. Yet here, too, Fassbaender is unafraid to get at the passionate core of the character. At the beginning of that opera's second act, for example, when Geschwitz expresses her delight that the prostitute Lulu, with whom she is besotted, has agreed to attend a lesbian ball that she is hosting, Fassbaender catches (in the line *"Sie glauben nicht, wie ich mich darauf freue, Sie auf unserm Künstlerinnenball zu sehn"*) both the character's awkward, misplaced chivalry and the urgent sexual longing behind it. In turn, when Geschwitz, gazing raptly at a portrait of Lulu as Pierrot, murmurs, as if in a dream, *"Hier sind Sie wie ein Märchen"* (Here you are a fairy-tale creature), Fassbaender's voice seems almost to bend around the words, caressing each syllable with voluptuous precision. And in the famous Adagio in act 3, after Lulu has been murdered offstage by Jack the Ripper, and Geschwitz herself is bleeding to death from the stab wound he has dealt her, the singer's wrenching delivery of Geschwitz's death cry, the voice veering crazily upward on the word *einmal* then plunging down again—*"Lulu! Mein Engel! Lass dich noch einmal sehn!"* (Lulu! My angel! Appear once more to me!)—achieves an effect of erotic pathos no less striking for its brevity and compression.[57]

Yet it is in the trouser roles, and the comic ones especially, that

Fassbaender's skill at enacting such exaltation is most vividly apparent. She has been described, rightly, as the greatest of modern-day Orlovskys, and part of what makes her so outstanding in this difficult role—as the film version of the 1987 Munich *Fledermaus* makes clear—is the panache with which she enters into "his" somewhat bibulous brand of *galanterie*. In the celebrated ball scene in act 2, for example, when the vodka-loving prince first meets the buxom chambermaid Adele (who has sneaked in disguised as an "artiste"), Fassbaender's slyly inflected delivery of his line, "*Ich liebe Künstlerinnen*" (I *love* artistes), conveys perfectly Orlovsky's droll, well-mannered, somewhat alcoholic sexual appreciation.

Later on, when Adele boasts in song about her "Grecian profile" and attractive figure, Fassbaender's mouth droops open salaciously, even as she continues to appraise, with politely vulpine connoisseurship, the particular features in question. Yet most telling, a few moments later, are her scene-stealing antics when Rosalinde, the opera's heroine, arrives at the ball disguised as a Hungarian countess and proceeds to sing a wild romantic "Csárdás" about the beauties of her supposed homeland. While Rosalinde (sung here by Pamela Coburn) undulates seductively at center stage, Fassbaender-as-Orlovsky—seated on an overstuffed sofa behind her and clearly smitten with the new arrival—mimes a kind of half-tipsy sexual ecstasy: writhing in suppressed pleasure, swaying back and forth to the music, gesturing feebly in awe and wonderment. At one point during the song, which grows slowly more and more frenzied, Fassbaender actually picks up a feather boa Coburn has discarded and buries her face in it, only to slump weakly backwards after inhaling its (apparently) intoxicating scent. Seldom, one might say, has diva-worship, hetero or homo, been given a more direct—or suggestive—onstage representation.

Fassbaender's most ravishing study in gynophilic rapture undoubtedly remains, however, her Octavian—the part with which she has always been most closely identified and her undisputed masterpiece of cross-sexual characterization. Which isn't to say (as videotapes of her performances again reveal) that she underplays any of the humor in Strauss's often farcical confection. In the scenes with Baron Ochs, when Octavian is forced by his lover, the Marschallin, to masquerade as her servingmaid "Mariandel" and then has to fight off the baron's crudely pawing embraces, Fassbaender excels in the somewhat mind-boggling physical comedy involved. Commenting on the role, she has remarked that much of the pleasure she derives from it has to do precisely with these uncanny moments of double drag—when she is "a woman singer playing a man who in turn must impersonate a woman."* Tromping ludicrously across stage in Mariandel's bonnet and petticoats, or attempting to wriggle brusquely away from the baron, Fassbaender manages through body language alone to convey every giddying twist in Octavian's sexual charade.

In the opera's great love scenes, however—the opening dialogue with the Marschallin, the ethereal Presentation of the Rose, the ecstatic trio and duet in act 3—Fassbaender becomes by turns tender, noble, fervent, even sublime. She has said that after performing Octavian so many times onstage—she debuted the part in 1967—she gradually reached a point "of feeling completely under his skin."[58] Certainly to judge by the noted 1979 production under Carlos Kleiber, with Gwyneth Jones as the Marschallin and Lucia Popp as Sophie, the metaphor is appropriate. In the opening scene in the Marschallin's bedroom, when Fassbaender as Octavian, disheveled from his night of passion, reaches over to kiss his still-beautiful older mistress, marveling softly how "*das Ich vergeht in dem Du*" (this "I" is lost in this "you"), Fassbaender's mode is passionate and uninhibited—her very body moulding itself to Jones's as they first embrace, then kiss.

---

*Matheopoulos, *Diva*, p. 273. Because of its blatantly erotic gender-bending and heady "girl games" atmosphere, *Der Rosenkavalier* has always been something of a talisman in lesbian culture. In "Der Rosenkavalier," a poem in her *Collected Poems: 1949–1984*, the lesbian poet and novelist Maureen Duffy writes of "learning" how to love an older woman by watching Octavian—

> No pride shall spur me
> Out of sight. I will not leave that room:
> The casket cannot hold my petalled heart.
> I am too old to play she loves me not.

—while in a poem of the same name, in Joan Nestle's *The Persistent Desire*, Pam A. Parker uses the opera and its metaphors to calibrate the pleasures of a "butch" sexuality and sensibility ("embrace her, take hold the way / a woman who fucks women does"). Rather more comically, in a recent issue of the *Los Angeles Reader* (May 12, 1992), the lesbian conceptual artist Linda Montano confessed that a new performance piece—in which she sat for three days and nights on a sawhorse next to some campus horse statues at the University of Texas—was inspired by a childhood fantasy of "running away to Texas and riding a horse while listening to Richard Strauss's *Der Rosenkavalier*."

(Kiri Te Kanawa has described the first five minutes of this scene as "the most awkward to perform in any opera."[59]) There is none of that fleeting physical embarrassment which mars Sena Jurinac's otherwise perceptive performance in the 1962 Karajan *Rosenkavalier*: Fassbaender lets her body itself exemplify delight, even as she invests Octavian's melting *Sprechgesang* with its full measure of boyish charm and provocation.

During the Presentation of the Rose, when Octavian first meets and falls in love with Sophie, Fassbaender (clad in breathtaking silver-white coat and pantaloons) catches with unerring delicacy the exact moment of his transformation: as he watches Sophie breathe in the heavenly "drop of attar" in the silver rose and gives way to love-struck adoration. (While Popp's voice soars upward at the line "*Wie himmlische, nicht irdische, wie Rosen*" [Like roses of heaven, not of earth] Fassbaender closes her eyes, blissfully, like one overcome by some mystical vision.) In turn, when Octavian himself, lost in joyful bafflement, begins singing softly, "*Wo war ich schon einmal und war so selig?*" (Where and when have I been so happy?), Fassbaender leans in, as it were, to the emotion—conveying by look and gesture, as well as by her liquid, delving vocal tone, Octavian's rapture at his newfound passion.

And finally, in the concluding moments of the opera, when Octavian realizes that the Marschallin has already forgiven him for his unfaithfulness and that she wishes him well with his new love, Fassbaender captures to the fullest his astonished gratitude—modulating swiftly into tender reverence—at her goodness and generosity of spirit. Here Fassbaender is inspired: imbuing the famous line, "*Marie Theres, wie gut Sie ist*" (Marie Theres, how good you are) with all of its turbulent layers of emotion, even as she turns toward the audience—hand softly clenched to heart—to join in on the famous trio. When, at the last, after the Marschallin has made her departure and Octavian enfolds Sophie in an embrace, Fassbaender sustains the mood of exaltation by giving Popp a ravishing soul kiss at the end of their final duet: full on the mouth, dignified yet sensual. Nor is the mood broken at the curtain call: here, as if still half in character, Fassbaender can be seen glancing over at one point at Gwyneth Jones, fixing her with a look of piercing admiration, even as she squeezes her hand in quiet triumph.

Fassbaender at the Metropolitan Opera as Octavian in
Strauss's *Der Rosenkavalier*, 1980s. *Courtesy of
Winnie Klotz.*

Is it wrong to celebrate such artistry? There will always be those, I
suppose, who find the frank display of female-to-female adoration
freakish—even when it is presented, as in *Der Rosenkavalier*, under the
legitimating rubric of the dramaturgical. For some, the fact that Fassbaender is playing a young man in Strauss's drama will be no excuse:
to see someone carry on in such a way, even in the most stylized or
refined fashion, is still embarrassing and unsettling. (An elderly
psychoanalyst—heterosexual—once told me, with some contempt,
that she found *Der Rosenkavalier* the most infantile opera ever written.)
Yet this is exactly what for me is so moving: Fassbaender's ability to
give voice to her pleasure, to reveal herself onstage, without shame or
self-censoring, as a *fan* of other women.

What Fassbaender provides is a sensual reminder that the love of woman for woman is not only possible but cherishable—and not only for the recipient. Some perceptive remarks by Willa Cather spring to mind here. Writing, in 1913, in *McClure's* about the great American soprano Geraldine Farrar, Cather spoke insightfully about the crucial importance in the singer's career of her youthful "capacity to admire."

> The best thing that ever happened to Miss Farrar—and insofar as luck goes, she has been the very darling of the gods—was that her parents had courage enough to borrow money and take her abroad to study *early,* before her self-confidence became too confident. Once she got to Paris, the finest thing in her, her capacity to admire, was aroused. Her photographs, taken after a year in Paris, look like another girl. Not that she was humbled. The peculiar note of her personality is that she has never been humbled, but quickened.[60]

It was precisely Farrar's wish to pay tribute to the woman she had come to idolize (her teacher Lilli Lehmann) that made her, according to Cather, what she was: a singer of brilliance, with "an impulsive and tender sympathy with human life." Admiration, Cather affirms, is necessary for growth.[61]

Intellectuals, on the whole, are not used to thinking of the "capacity to admire" as a valuable human quality; indeed, so profound are our modern prejudices against anything smacking of enthusiasm or emotional excess, we are more likely to take such receptivity to others as a sign of moral and intellectual weakness. As I suggested at the outset, coming out as a fan can be an embarrassing business, especially if one wants to continue to be regarded by friends and associates as a normally functioning member of society. Being grown-up, maintaining a properly critical and self-conscious attitude toward the world—or so the ideologues teach us—requires self-control: the rooting out, the rationalization, the analyzing away, of all exaggerated feeling. To "worship" someone (and especially someone as frivolous as a diva) is to be a victim of illusion and false consciousness.

Nor is it only among gloomy leftover Marxists and dour Freudians that such views hold sway: one of the enduring negative stereotypes in tabloid journalism since the late nineteenth century has been that of the "deranged fan"—the person so demented by his love for someone famous he commits an outrage either against himself or the per-

son he reveres. Hero-worship, we are admonished, leads to mania—
to violence or its threat.[62]

But it may also be possible—indeed worthwhile—to try to rehabilitate such emotion. Not that I mean to redeem fans like Mary Garden's suicidal admirer Helen Newby: as long as we live in a culture in
which certain individuals are marketed as celebrities and surrounded
with an aura of confounding wealth, prestige, and power, there will
always be those maddened—sometimes horrifyingly—by their adoration. Yet for every diva-worshipper like Newby, one could find, I
am convinced, hundreds of thousands of others, "quickened" (as
Cather puts it) by their infatuations: enriched and nourished, made
more happy and alive, made more conscious of who they are.

The nourishing power of admiration lies precisely in its connection with the imagination. Since the eighteenth century, opera and
diva-worship—that soaring, numinous love of the woman who
sings—have been inextricably linked with the gynophilic imagination. It is no accident that the burgeoning of opera in eighteenth-
century Europe coincided with the rise of modern feminism—as
Brigid Brophy has pointed out, both opera and feminism reflect the
new Enlightenment respect for and fascination with the female
voice.[63] But in the rush toward generalities, we should not ignore the
powerful and inspiriting role that diva-worship has played in the lives
of actual women. From Malibran to Fremstad, from Fremstad to
Fassbaender, the diva has always offered special consolation to wom-
en who love and cherish their own sex. For lesbian opera fans in particular, the diva's passion is a mirror: a fluid, silvery form in which
desire itself can at times be recognized. By the liberating way that *she*
desires—by the bold ardor of her own "homovocal" exaltation—a
singer like Fremstad or Fassbaender becomes a collective emblem: a
poignant, often thrilling token of homoerotic possibility.

In relating the history of my own infatuation I have adopted, I
find, a somewhat facetious tone, mainly in hopes of avoiding that
"purple" quality which so often creeps into the literature of sapphic
diva-worship. (To those who, nonetheless, still find my expressions
of devotion tasteless, I can only say that I have tried to be as *tastefully*
tasteless as possible.) And yet such defensiveness, I also realize, is
perhaps misplaced. In the same way that in a perfect world no shame

would ever attach itself to the desire of woman for woman, no shame attaches—or should attach itself—to the adoration inspired by a passionate female voice. If I have, however crudely, inspired a desire to hear, or hear again, the singing of Brigitte Fassbaender, I am glad: in the presence of such brave and tender artistry, there is nothing in the end to fear, and much—oh, so very much—to love.

NOTES

1. A Polemical Introduction

1. See de Acosta, *Here Lies the Heart*, and Daum, *Walking with Garbo*. Note the following sample of Garbo's conversation recorded by Raymond Daum, who met the actress in the 1960s, and, over the course of a twenty-year friendship, often transcribed her remarks:

> I always wanted to see *Becket* again, but they put it on television so late at night that I can't watch it, because I'm a limited man. I saw it once in a movie the-ater. I was in a trance—I thought it was absolutely beautiful, in a haunting way. It's obviously homosexual between the two men. I always wanted to see it again, but television will have to change before that can happen. Oh, what a funny man I am.

See *Walking with Garbo*, p. 210.

2. Wittig, "One Is Not Born a Woman," in *The Straight Mind*, p. 13.

3. "Using God as a Cudgel."

4. This isn't to say that female homosexual acts, when detected, have gone unpunished by civil authorities. As Louis Crompton documents in "The Myth

of Lesbian Impunity," women in early modern Europe were sometimes sentenced to death for "crimes against nature" under existing sodomy statutes. A German woman named Catharina Margaretha Linck was hanged and burnt in 1721, for example, for dressing as a man and having "sodomitical" relations with another woman. Yet such dire punishments were rare. In England in 1746, the notorious "female husband" Mary Hamilton—accused of deceiving several women into marriage and sexually penetrating them with an implement "not fit to be mentioned"—was sentenced only to six months in Bridewell. Bets Wiebes, accused in Amsterdam in 1792 of lying with another woman "in the way that a man is used to do when he has carnal conversation with his wife," was sentenced to exile, but ended up spending only a few months in jail. For further discussion of these and other cases, see Crompton, "The Myth of Lesbian Impunity," Eriksson, "A Lesbian Execution in Germany, 1721," Castle, " 'Matters Not Fit to be Mentioned'," and Van der Meer, "Tribades on Trial."

5. The comments made by various MPs during debates over the amendment are revealing. Lesbianism was a terrible danger, one warned, because it "sapped the fundamental institutions of society," destroyed marriages and families, and caused the race to "decline." Yet at the same time its dangers were best left unpublicized. Said Lord Birkenhead, the lord chancellor, speaking out against the amendment: "I would be bold enough to say that of every thousand women, taken as a whole, 999 have never even heard a whisper of these practices. Among all these, in the homes of this country . . . the taint of this noxious and horrible suspicion is to be imparted." Lord Desart seconded his view: "You are going to tell the whole world that there is such an offence, to bring it to the notice of women who have never heard of it, never thought of it, never dreamed of it. I think that is a very great mischief." Lieutenant Moore-Brabazon argued that there were three ways of getting rid of such "perverts"—one could kill them, lock them up, or "leave them entirely alone." He found the latter method the most effective:

> That is the method that has been adopted in England for many hundred years, and I believe that it is the best method now, these cases are self-exterminating. They are examples of ultra-civilisation, but they have the merit of exterminating themselves, and consequently they do not spread or do very much harm to society at large. . . . To adopt a Clause of this kind would harm by introducing into the minds of innocent people the most revolting thoughts.

See Weeks, *Coming Out*, pp. 106–7, Jeffreys, *The Spinster and Her Enemies*, pp. 113–15, and Edwards, *Female Sexuality and the Law*, pp. 43–45. Similar fears may have kept Nazi officials in the 1930s from amending Paragraph 175—the infamous statute prohibiting male homosexuality—to include lesbianism as a punishable offense. See Plant, *The Pink Triangle*, pp. 114–16.

6. The association between lesbianism and the spectral crops up in Hollywood cinema as well; witness the 1963 psychological thriller *The Haunting*, in which (to quote the inimitable Vito Russo) Claire Bloom "gets her psychosexual jollies by hugging Julie Harris and blaming it on ghosts." See Russo, *The Celluloid Closet*, p. 158. Typically, in Hollywood films, spectral plot elements are used to add a certain homosexual frisson to otherwise conventional heterosexual love plots. In the recent romantic comedy *Ghost* (1991), for example, starring Whoopi Goldberg and Demi Moore, Goldberg plays a psychic, Oda Mae, who must convince Moore's character, Molly, that the spirit of Molly's dead lover Sam wants to communicate with her through Oda Mae. When Sam indeed begins "speaking through" Oda Mae, professing his love, the effect is peculiarly homoerotic: as if Oda Mae were speaking for herself instead of the ghost. The fiction of ghostly return, in other words, somehow licenses an uncanny "bodying forth"— onscreen—of female-female eroticism. And in the Blake Edwards comedy *Switch* (1992), starring Ellen Barkin, the link between ghostliness and pseudo-homoerotic spectacle is even more striking. After Steve, an abusive misogynist, is killed by three women and ends up in Purgatory, he is informed by God that if he wants to leave Purgatory and enter heaven, he will have to return to earth and find a woman willing to love him. The "switch" of the title, engineered by the devil at the last minute, is that he is reincarnated as a woman, Amanda, played by Barkin. In the comic scenes that follow, we watch Steve/Amanda attempt to seduce various women (including a lesbian played by Lorraine Braco) in an attempt to find one who will in fact redeem him/her—with the predictably titillating onscreen results.

7. "Dry, desperate, rigid, she yet wavered and seemed uncertain," writes James, "her pale, glittering eyes straining forward, as if they were looking for death." See *The Bostonians*, p. 432.

8. The self-protective "retreat from the world" can sometimes backfire, of course. After eloping together to a cottage in Wales in 1778, the so-called Ladies of Llangollen, Lady Eleanor Butler and Miss Sarah Ponsonby, became instantly famous, and for the next fifty years had to fend off hordes of curious visitors, eager for a glimpse of them in their rural retreat. Garbo's exit from public life after her last film in 1941 was similarly paradoxical: precisely by demanding to be "alone"—or so gay film critic Michael Bronski has argued—Garbo actually fed the many rumors about the unorthodoxy of her private life. See Bronski, "She Really Did 'Want to be Alone,' " pp. 20, 15.

9. Hall, *The Well of Loneliness*, p. 437.

10. Lillian Faderman—whose pioneering study, *Surpassing the Love of Men: Romantic Friendship and Love Between Women from the Renaissance to the Present*, has profoundly influenced lesbian scholarship over the past decade—is undoubtedly the best-known and most eloquent proponent of the sexological model. Faderman recently reaffirmed the "no lesbians before 1900" hypothesis in *Odd Girls and Twi-*

1. A POLEMICAL INTRODUCTION

light Lovers: A History of Lesbian Life in Twentieth-Century America, the sequel to *Surpassing the Love of Men*:

> It was to a large extent the work of the sexologists, which was disseminated slowly to the layman but finally became part of popular wisdom after World War I, that accounts for the altered views of women's intimacy with each other. It may be said that the sexologists changed the course of same-sex relationships not only because they cast suspicion on romantic friendships, but also because they helped to make possible the establishment of lesbian communities through their theories, which separated off the lesbian from the rest of womankind and presented new concepts to describe certain feelings and preferences that had before been within the spectrum of "normal" female experiences. Many early twentieth-century women who loved other women rejected those new concepts as being irrelevant to them because they could still see their feelings as "romantic friendship." But by the end of World War I the tolerance for any manifestations of what would earlier have been considered "romantic friendship" had virtually disappeared. . . . Subsequent generations of women who loved other women soon came to have no choice but to consider themselves lesbians or to make herculean efforts of rationalization in order to explain to themselves how they were different from real lesbians. (35)

Other scholars have made similar arguments: see Sahli, "Smashing," and Smith-Rosenberg, "The Female World of Love and Ritual." Yet Faderman's sexological model has also provoked dissent. In "From Sexual Inversion to Homosexuality," George Chauncey, Jr., points out some of the contradictions in the sexological writings on lesbianism and argues that writers like Krafft-Ebing and Ellis may have had less influence on actual women than Faderman supposes. And, more recently, both Van der Meer, in "Tribades on Trial" (see note 5), and Trumbach, in "London's Sapphists," find traces of an emerging "lesbian identity" much earlier, among the so-called tribades and Sapphists of seventeenth- and eighteenth-century Europe. For an excellent overview of recent scholarship on the identity question, see Vicinus, " 'They Wonder to Which Sex I Belong.' "

11. All of the foregoing terms, with the exception of the early twentieth-century coinages *dyke* and *bull dagger*, were in use long before the 1880s and 1890s. As Van der Meer has pointed out, both *tribade* (from the Latin *faemina tribades*) and *fricatrice* appear in seventeenth- and eighteenth-century legal documents, along with the related terms *subigatrix* and *clitorifant*. *Sapphist*, *amazon*, *freak*, and *tommy* occur in various eighteenth- and early nineteenth-century sources. Hester Thrale Piozzi condemns Marie Antoinette as a "Sapphist" in a diary entry from 1789; Maria Edgeworth uses *amazon* and *freak* to hint at the sexual deviance of a female character in her novel *Belinda* (1801). In *A Sapphic Epistle from Jack Cavendish to Mrs. D***** (1782), an anonymous pamphlet attacking one Mrs. Damer, notorious in the 1780s for her sexual pursuit of other women, Sappho is described as "the first Tommy the world has upon record." Writes Randolph

Trumbach: " 'Tommy' was probably the popular libertine term for a sapphic woman"—a female "equivalent" to *molly*, the slang term given to male homosexuals since the early eighteenth century. See "London's Sapphists," p. 132.

12. I am thinking here especially of the recent work of Trumbach and Van der Meer, as well as that of Elaine Hobby, who is currently writing a study of seventeenth-century lesbianism.

13. When an editor at the *Women's Review of Books* gave me the first volume of Lister's diary, edited by Helena Whitbread, to review in 1989, she mentioned the hoax rumor to me and asked me to judge while reading the diary if the rumor could be true. I rapidly determined that it was not—despite Whitbread's occasionally slapdash editorial procedures. (To a suspicious mind Whitbread's failure to describe the "crypt hand" in which the erotic parts of the diary were written— or the way the code was ultimately deciphered—might well have given pause.) It was nonetheless a relief to discover some time later a scholarly essay from twenty years earlier dealing with the diary, Phyllis M. Ramsden's "Anne Lister's Journal (1817–1840): An Unusual and Valuable Contemporary Record." Relief turned to bemusement, however, when it turned out that Ramsden, who had discovered and decoded the diary in 1958 with her colleague, "the late Miss Vivien M. Ingraham, B.A.," had entirely obscured its sensational sexual contents. Of her subject's personal life, Ramsden said only that Lister "showed little inclination for marriage" and sought sentimental friendships "among her own sex." Regarding the lubricious "crypt" passages, she was positively sly:

> The presence of the "crypt"-alphabet may have deterred some prospective readers in the past, for it is natural to assume that the secret passages are of some special significance and must be deciphered at all costs. Fortunately this is not at all the case. With very few exceptions the passages in "crypt"- alphabet are of no historical interest whatever. Miss Lister used her journal for three quite distinct purposes—first, as a factual record of her actions and interests, second (after her business responsibilities increased), as a business day-box, and third, as a personal diary of her health, her relationships with relatives and friends, her own personal ups and downs. Virtually all the "crypt" passages fall into this last and least rewarding category. Certainly she used it for discretion's sake, for some of the entries referred to family and financial matters, but these passages can usually be identified by their context and are generally short enough to be quickly deciphered. Apart from this the "crypt" passages had to be purely personal, and it can be taken for granted that the longer the passage the less it is worth the tedium of decoding. (10)

Thus the perennial ghosting of the lesbian—here in the name of supposedly honorable scholarship.

14. Sedgwick, *Between Men*, p. 2.

15. The speaker in this case was the Indonesian Muslim leader Hasan Basri. See "World View." Yet similar views appear to flourish among certain members

of the San Francisco police force, who have insisted on wearing latex gloves when arresting lesbian protesters during civil rights demonstrations. On the relative rarity of HIV transmission between women, see Ann Japenga, "Gay Women and the Risk of AIDS," *Los Angeles Times*, April 2, 1986, and S. Chu et al., "Epidemiology of Reported Cases of AIDS in Lesbians, United States, 1980–89," *American Journal of Public Health* (November 1990) 80:1380–81.

16. See "Identity Crisis: Queer Politics in the Age of Possibilities."

17. In keeping with the polemical tone of my introduction, I foreshorten, of course, many of the issues involved in the current academic debates over queer theory. For a more extended discussion of the nomenclature question and some of its theoretical implications, see Teresa de Lauretis's introduction to the special "Queer Theory" issue of *Differences*. In the same issue, in "Tracking the Vampire," Sue-Ellen Case offers some interesting reflections on the word *queer* and on the vexed relationship between "queer theory," on the one hand, and "lesbian theory" on the other. In the entertaining study of the lesbian vampire that follows—a being whom Case identifies as "queer" precisely to the degree that she challenges "the Platonic parameters of Being—the borders of life and death"—Case describes a "kissing cousin," so to speak, of my own figure of the apparitional lesbian.

18. Judith Butler, "Imitation and Gender Insubordination," p. 15.

19. I am aware that my assurance here may still irk some readers—those inclined to see lesbian sexuality as an intractable philosophical problem, ever "shifting, difficult, contradictory," and ultimately impossible to define. To such readers I can only recommend, by way of palliative, Judith Roof's eloquent meditation on the issue of definition in *A Lure of Knowledge*. Roof, like Judith Butler, is deeply perplexed by what it means to say one is a lesbian:

> Identifying as a lesbian already requires a circle where experience and representation define one another. There is no "pure" place unaffected by language and culture that tells me what sexuality or identity are in the first place; any concept of sexuality I have is necessarily a composite of social imperatives, theoretical deliberations, and various philosophical, emotional, and libidinal choices.

And yet at a certain point, she herself admits, one simply has to go on—leaving the philosophical issue on one side and trusting brazenly (if narcissistically) to one's instincts:

> Even if I don't know precisely what lesbian is, I look for the lesbian in the text, for what happens rhetorically to eroticized relations among women, finding, perhaps narcissistically, their catalytic function in feminist theories of writing and reading. I begin with this perspective probably because reading, even academic reading, is stimulated, at least for me, by a libidinous urge connected both to a sexual practice and to the shape of my own desire. (120)

Roof and I speak different critical idiolects, but I admire her candor and follow her entirely when she says, "I don't think I am where I began, but it seems I've always been here."

20. Quoted in Lebrecht, *The Maestro Myth*, p. 147.

21. Or perhaps not. Many doubt that the much-touted affair ever took place. "Garbo was a lesbian," Stokowski's biographer, Oliver Daniel, told Norman Lebrecht, "I very much doubt they were anything beyond good friends." According to a second biographer, Abram Chasins, "Stokowski was unable to give or receive sexual satisfaction and probably never laid a finger on the forbidding Ice Queen." See Lebrecht, *The Maestro Myth*, pp. 145–47.

22. Said, "The Politics of Knowledge," p. 28.

23. Trefusis, *Don't Look Round*, p. 219.

24. Winterson, *Oranges Are Not the Only Fruit*, pp. 47–48.

25. Spoto, *Blue Angel*, p. 105n.

3. The Apparitional Lesbian

1. Daniel Defoe, *A True Relation of the Apparition of one Mrs. Veal* (London, 1706; rpt. William Andrews Clark Memorial Library, 1965), p. 3. Notations in parentheses refer to page numbers in this edition.

2. On the hints of lesbianism in *Roxana* (1724), see my "'Amy, Who Knew my Disease.'"

3. To sample some of the critical controversy see, for example, Vivienne Mylne, "What Suzanne Knew: Lesbianism and *La Religieuse*," Jack Undank, "An Ethics of Discourse," Rita Goldberg, *Sex and Enlightenment*, pp. 169–204, Walter E. Rex, "Secrets from Suzanne," and Eve Kosofsky Sedgwick, "Privilege of Unknowing."

4. Cf. Goldberg, in *Sex and Enlightenment*, on Diderot's distaste for the lesbian mother superior: "Her sexual desire is so easily stimulated that we are meant to think of it as a kind of disease. . . . She is, in fact, an example of the dreaded *homme-femme*, with the desires of a man and the body and supposed emotional weakness of a woman" (197–98).

5. Diderot, *The Nun* (Penguin, 1974), p. 85. All references are to this edition.

6. The pornographic representation of lesbianism may nonetheless have influenced so-called mainstream representation more often—and more profoundly—than is commonly acknowledged. In a subsequent essay in this book ("Marie Antoinette Obsession"), I argue that various pornographic works written at the time of French Revolution depicting the supposed lesbian relationships of the French queen, Marie Antoinette, contributed directly—albeit covertly—to her incarnation in the nineteenth century as an icon of romantic female-female love. The distinction I make in the present essay between polite discourse and its pornographic "shadow," is in one sense an artificial one: from Diderot and Gautier to Zola and Djuna Barnes, mainstream writers taking up

the theme of lesbianism have often, in fact, drawn upon the motifs and stock situations of pornographic discourse.

7. Gautier, *Mademoiselle de Maupin* (Penguin, 1981), p. 304. All further references are to this edition. Richardson's assertion in her introduction to the novel, that "the story is the least important part of the book," is characteristic, alas, of the way in which the majority of commentators have dealt with Gautier's cryptolesbian plot line. For a somewhat less repressive view, see Sadoff, *Ambivalence, Ambiguity, and Androgyny.*

8. Baudelaire, "Femmes damnées (Delphine et Hippolyte)," lines 45–48. The poem was one of those excluded, on grounds of indecency, from the 1861 edition of *Les Fleurs du mal.* It is reprinted in Baudelaire's *Oeuvres complètes* (Gallimard, 1975), pp. 152–55. All French citations are to this edition. The English translation here is by Aldous Huxley, rpt. in Marthiel and Jackson Mathews, eds., *The Flowers of Evil*, pp. 115–23.

9. Swinburne, "Faustine," lines 125–132, in *The Complete Works of Algernon Charles Swinburne* (William Heinemann, 1925), 1:238–43. All references are to this edition.

10. Crowley, "The Lesbian Hell," lines 6–15, in Coote, *The Penguin Book of Homosexual Verse* (1983), pp. 273–75. All references are to this edition.

11. James, *The Bostonians* (Oxford University Press, 1984), p. 325. All references are to this edition.

12. Mackenzie, *Extraordinary Women* (Hogarth, 1986), p. 86. All references are to this edition.

13. Renault, *The Friendly Young Ladies* (Pantheon, 1984), p. 144. All references are to this edition.

14. "Olivia" [Dorothy Strachey], *Olivia* (Virago, 1987), p. 63. All references are to this edition.

15. A similar interchangeability seems to be at work in Shirley Jackson's classic tale of ghostly possession, *The Haunting of Hill House* (1959). Here, four people—two men and two women—come to investigate reports of poltergeist activity in an old New England house once occupied by a late nineteenth-century spinster and her female companion. When one of the women, herself an alienated spinster, falls in love with the other one, the strange forces inhabiting the house begin to harass them both with nightmarish horrors. In the final scene, when the spinster, Eleanor, tries to escape the mansion, her car veers weirdly off into a ditch and she is killed. In Robert Wise's sensational film version of the novel—*The Haunting* (1963)—the lesbian element is even more explicit. See Patricia White's provocative essay, "Female Spectator, Lesbian Specter: *The Haunting.*"

16. Witness the narrator's exclamation, after falling in love with the mysterious Vally, "I saw you today for the first time and already I am the shadow of your shadow." Later she refers to her as "the pale friend of my dreamless past," an "adored image [rising] against the darkness." See Vivien, *A Woman Appeared to Me*, pp. 2–3 and 23–24.

17. Trefusis, *Violet to Vita* (Methuen, 1989), p. 151. All further references are to this edition.

18. Woolf, *The Letters of Virginia Woolf*, 3:396.

19. Woolf, *Letters*, 3:428.

20. Hall, *The Well of Loneliness* (Anchor, 1990), p. 81; all further references are to this edition. Clinicians writing about female homosexuality in the 1940s and 1950s sometimes took passages such as these as evidence of the morbid nature of lesbian desire. In *Female Homosexuality: A Psychodynamic Study of Lesbianism* (1954), the American psychiatrist Frank S. Caprio observed that "lesbians are basically unhappy people. Many admit their unhappiness but others are deceived by their pseudoadjustment to life. They regard themselves as being 'different,' and as pointed out in *The Well of Loneliness*, that they were born that way. In general their attitude toward themselves is a negative one." Among Caprio's gloom-and-doom case histories, interestingly enough, is one involving a suicidal young woman—"Jessie"—who typically "covered her eyes with her arm when she began to talk of her problem." See Caprio, *Female Homosexuality*, pp. 176–80.

21. On Radclyffe Hall's spiritualism and its relation to the *The Well of Loneliness*, see Baker, *Our Three Selves*, pp. 83–98. The intriguing relationship between spiritualism and lesbian proclivities—especially among Englishwomen at the turn of the century—has yet to be explored. The two women who wrote together in the 1890s under the names "Somerville and Ross" are a case in point. After the death in 1915 of Violet Martin ("Martin Ross"), her lifelong companion and erstwhile collaborator, Edith Somerville not only communicated with her through a spirit medium, but claimed to have written subsequent books with her dead friend's aid. "She is gone," wrote Somerville many years later, "but our collaboration has not ended." Edith Lees Ellis, the wife of Havelock Ellis and "Case History XXXVI" in Ellis's *Sexual Inversion* (1897) was another believer: she became addicted to spiritualism after the death of her lover, Lily, in 1903, and "spoke" with her repeatedly during numerous seances. See Collis, *Somerville and Ross*, pp. 176–84, and Grosskurth, *Havelock Ellis*, pp. 211–12.

22. Cited in Baker, *Our Three Selves*, p. 311. The lover in question was Evguenia Souline, with whom Radclyffe Hall became infatuated in the 1930s. On another occasion, Radclyffe Hall warned her that "if you were in my flat at this moment, I would not protect you at all—I'd kill you with love—I'd kiss you until you asked for mercy. I'd kiss you all over that dear body of yours—I'd make that body of yours desire me until your desire of me was as pain" (Baker, *Our Three Selves*, p. 308).

23. In Jolley's haunting fiction, two women—the older in love with the younger—accidentally hit a man in the darkness with their car. In a panic they throw his body down a well on their property. When they hear a voice emanating from the well they realize that he is still alive. Kathy, the younger woman, becomes fascinated by his voice and wishes to marry him. In the Poe-like penultimate scene, her jealous friend—for whom the idea of "that man, touching or han-

dling [Kathy's] perfectly made and childlike body was repulsive"—has the well permanently sealed.

24. Woolf, *Orlando* (Harcourt Brace Jovanovich, 1956), pp. 66–67. All references are to this edition.

25. Letter from Sackville-West to Woolf (October 11, 1928) in the appendix to Woolf, *Letters*, 3:573.

26. Djuna Barnes, *Nightwood* (New Directions, 1946), p. 55. All references are to this edition.

27. The foregoing are all titles of English or American novels listed in Barbara Grier's bibliography, *The Lesbian in Literature*.

28. Witness, for instance, Gale Wilhelm's pulp classic *We Too Are Drifting*. After Victoria, one of the main characters, confesses her love for the boyish Jan, Jan finds herself later "[walking] slowly back and forth with the ghost of the amazing thing Victoria had said that afternoon. She went to bed and lay awake for a long time looking at the ghost in the dark groove of the ceiling" (80). The next day Victoria complains that Jan is gazing at her "as if I were a ghost" (81). That night, however, after they make love for the first time, Jan looks once more up at the ceiling and finds "there was no ghost now"—then sinks blissfully into Victoria's arms (85).

In Paula Martinac's recent lesbian romance, *Out of Time* (1990), the "sex with ghosts" idea is comically literalized. After finding an old scrapbook from the 1920s containing photographs of four mysterious women, the heroine is visited by the ghost of one of them, who comes into her bedroom and proceeds to make love to her.

29. Duffy, *The Microcosm* (Viking Penguin, 1989), p. 5. All references are to this edition.

30. Duffy, "Afterword," *The Microcosm*, pp. 289–90.

31. See Duffy, *The Microcosm*, pp. 70–98. At the end of the sequence Duffy appends the note, "Account of a visit to Mrs. Charlotte Charke by Mr. Samuel Whyte of Dublin; Taken from Baker's *Biographia Dramatica* (I, p. 106), 1812." Much of what appears, however, is actually a phantasmagorical adaptation of several chapters of Charke's own *A Narrative of the Life of Mrs. Charlotte Charke*, recast in the third person, with the name "Charles" (Charke's alias while in male disguise) substituted for the pronoun "I."

32. This is necessarily a somewhat simplistic account of an extremely complex fiction, and some readers may object to the straightforwardly optimistic cast I give to the book here. Matt, one could argue, often seems bemired in a gloomy introspection that is hard to reconcile with any kind of joyous acceptance of lesbian identity. And yet even Matt is capable of comic insight, as in her Joycean reverie on Vicky, who, after a fling with a man, has returned to the House of Shades:

> Others come crowding too, some simply pleased to see her again for herself, some glad to see her bear out their words that she wouldn't be able to keep

away. Jealous as amazons at a rite profaned, a priestess fled from the vestal
temple, once a girl guide always a girl guide, Euridice escaped from the house
of shades up into the light, the outcast crossing the tracks; confirmed in their
way of life by her return, the campus spreads its welcome mat and the doors
close behind her. I watch her dancing, held close in affection and the stifling
folds of Judy's arms. She slips back into place as if she had never been away.
     "Oh it's good to be back. I've missed this place."   (18)

At such moments of embrace—however "stifling" the embrace appears to
Matt—Duffy conveys an authentic sense of the peculiar homecoming her characters feel when returning to the secret yet regenerative space of the women's bar.

     33. Erhart, *Unusual Company* (New American Library, 1987), p. 5. All refer-
ences are to this edition.
     34. Crow, *Miss X, or The Wolf Woman*, p. 58.
     35. Schulman, *After Delores* (Dutton, 1988), p. 1. All references are to this
edition.
     36. Freud, "Negation," p. 235.
     37. Freud, "Negation," p. 236.
     38. See Rich, "Compulsory Heterosexuality and Lesbian Existence," and
Rubin, "The Traffic in Women." Society demands the suppression of same-sex
love, argues Rubin, because such love destroys the distinction between "genders" on which patriarchal authority depends:

> Gender is not only an identification with one sex; it also entails that sexual
> desire be directed towards the other sex. The sexual division of labor is impli-
> cated in both aspects of gender—male and female it creates them, and it cre-
> ates them heterosexual. The suppression of the homosexual component of hu-
> man sexuality, and by corollary, the oppression of homosexuals, is therefore a
> product of the same system whose rules and relations oppress women.
>
>   See Rubin, "Traffic in Women," p. 180.

     39. Fielding, *The Female Husband*, p. 29.
     40. On the paradoxical male attitude toward lesbianism in the eighteenth cen-
tury, see my "Matters Not Fit to be Mentioned." On nineteenth-century re-
sponses, see Faderman, *Surpassing the Love of Men*, especially pp. 277–94, and
Katz, *Gay American History* and *Gay/Lesbian Almanac: A New Documentary, passim*.
     41. All three of these novels are featured prominently, for example, in Jean-
nette Foster's classic bibliographic study, *Sex Variant Women in Literature*.

4. Sylvia Townsend Warner and the Counterplot of Lesbian Fiction

     1. To judge by how frequently it is repeated, the story of Queen Victoria's
pronouncement has taken on, alas, the status of cultural myth—the "truth" of

which is that lesbians don't really exist. Whenever it is retold—even seemingly jokingly, by antihomophobic historians and critics—it almost always prefigures the erasure of lesbianism from the discourse that is to follow, usually through some equation of homosexuality with male homosexuality only. For an example of this phenomenon, see Richard Ellmann's *Oscar Wilde*, p. 409n., in which lesbianism—and Queen Victoria's views thereupon—are mentioned in a footnote, then never referred to again.

2. Theoretical writing on lesbian fiction has been sparse until very recently. Jane Rule's somewhat impressionistic *Lesbian Images* avoided theoretical speculation altogether; Catharine Stimpson's " Zero Degree Deviancy: The Lesbian Novel in English," while ahead of its time, focused only on a few fairly well-known books—*The Well of Loneliness*, *Nightwood*, Rita Mae Brown's *Rubyfruit Jungle*. With the recent burgeoning of interest in lesbian and gay writing, however, some interesting new studies have begun to appear. Bonnie Zimmerman's *The Safe Sea of Women: Lesbian Fiction, 1969–1988*—on structural and thematic patterns found in post-Stonewall lesbian fiction—is one such study; Judith Roof's *A Lure of Knowledge: Lesbian Sexuality and Theory*—on the "symptomatic configurations" of lesbian desire in modern culture—is another. Both Zimmerman and Roof offer close readings of several works, as do Elaine Hobby and Chris White in *What Lesbians Do in Books*. Valuable shorter studies have recently appeared in various edited collections: see, for example, essays by Valerie Miner, Lee Lynch, SDiane A. Bogus, Elizabeth Meese, Marilyn R. Farwell, Judith Fetterley, Jane Marcus, and Shari Benstock in *Lesbian Texts and Contexts: Radical Revisions;* by Judith Mayne and Michèle Aina Barale in *Inside/Out: Lesbian Theories, Gay Theories;* by Sherron E. Knopp and Clare Whatling in *Sexual Sameness: Textual Differences in Lesbian and Gay Writing;* and by Katie King, Sally Munt, Hilary Hinds, and others in *New Lesbian Criticism: Literary and Cultural Readings*. The most useful bibliographic studies of lesbian fiction remain Jeannette Foster's classic *Sex Variant Women in Literature* and Barbara Grier's supplement to Foster, *The Lesbian in Literature*.

3. Sedgwick, *Between Men*. Page numbers of citations are noted in parentheses. Since the publication of *Between Men*, it is true, Sedgwick has begun to explore the subject of lesbianism (and of lesbian authorship) more fruitfully, notably in relation to what she calls "the epistemology of the closet"—the peculiar way in which the reality of homosexuality is at once affirmed and denied, elaborated and masked, in modern cultural discourse. Two of her recent essays are especially relevant here: "Privilege of Unknowing" (on Diderot's *La Religieuse)* and "Across Gender, Across Sexuality: Willa Cather and Others." Even in these seemingly more encompassing pieces, however, Sedgwick's unwillingness to separate herself from the spectacle of male bonding is still in evidence. In the Diderot essay, Sedgwick chooses a work that can be labeled *lesbian* only problematically, if at all: as Sedgwick herself says at one point, "because of the mid-eighteenth-century origin of the novella and because of its conventual venue, the

question of lesbian sexual desire—*is* what is happening sexual desire, and will it
be recognized and named as such?—looks, there, less like the question of The
Lesbian than the question of sexuality *tout court.*" This may be true, but Sedgwick's immediate and seemingly reflexive transformation of the "lesbian sexual
desire" she admits to seeing in *La Religieuse* into a figure for "sexuality *tout
court*"—the site at which the "privilege of unknowing" is manifest—might also
be taken as a symptom of a certain "unknowingness" regarding lesbianism itself:
whatever *it* (lesbianism) is, Sedgwick implies, it is not worth bothering about in
and of itself; it is simply a metaphor for other things that can't be talked about,
such as (no surprise here) *male* homosexuality. Having disposed, at least theoretically, of any lesbian element in *La Religieuse*, Sedgwick then proceeds to slot
the novel comfortably back into the framework of male homosocial desire. Citing
approvingly Jay Caplan's observation that "this novel has the form of a message
addressed by one father to another about their symbolic (and hence, absent)
daughter," Sedgwick concludes that *La Religieuse* displays the "distinctively patriarchal triangular structure" of male homosocial bonding (119)—thus foreclos-
ing any more complex reading of its erotic relations. Tellingly, Sedgwick wonders at one point whether her own resistance to lesbian desire may perhaps have
limited her understanding of the novel, but decides that this can't be so: "it would
not be enough," she assures her reader, "to say that it is my fear of my own sexual
desire for Suzanne [Diderot's heroine] that makes me propulsively individuate
her as an 'other' in my reading of this book" (120). In the Cather piece, Sedgwick's resistance to lesbianism manifests itself less openly but is still palpable:
she is interested in Cather, whom she refers to as "the mannish lesbian author,"
primarily to the extent that Cather exemplifies a "move toward a minority gay
identity whose more effectual cleavage, whose more determining separatism,
would be that of homo/hetero*sexual* choice rather than that of male/female *gender*" (65–66). In choosing in the story "Paul's Case" to depict a young homosexual
man sympathetically, argues Sedgwick, Cather at once performed an act of symbolic contrition for writing a hostile editorial in her youth about Oscar Wilde
("cleansing," in Sedgwick's lurid phrasing, "her own sexual body of the carrion
stench of Wilde's victimization") and provided a wholesome model of "cross-
gender liminality." That Sedgwick prefers such "liminality" to what she disdain-
fully labels "gender separatism" (of which lesbian separatism is a subcategory) is
obvious: Cather is praised, because like "James, Proust, Yourcenar, Compton-
Burnett, Renault" and others she is part of the "rich tradition of cross-gender
inventions of homosexuality of the past century" (66). Sedgwick concludes with a
swooning paean to Cather's *The Professor's House*, that "gorgeous homosocial romance of two men on a mesa in New Mexico" (68). Lesbian authors, it seems, are
valuable here exactly to the extent that they are able to imagine and represent—
what else?—male homosocial bonding. Thus the elevation of Cather, Yourcenar,
Compton-Burnett, and Renault (significant choices all) to an all-new lesbian pantheon: of lesbians who enjoy writing about male-male eros, triangulated or other-

wise, more than its female equivalent. What is missing here is any room for the lesbian writer who *doesn't* choose to celebrate men's "gorgeous homosocial romances"—for whom indeed such romances are anathema, precisely because they get in the way, so damagingly, of women's homosocial romances.

4. Witness one of the findings of a survey conducted by lesbian sex therapist Joanne Loulan among 1,566 lesbians between 1985 and 1987. While 80 percent of all lesbians surveyed reported that they liked to hold hands with their partners, only 27 percent said they felt able to hold hands in public. This "poignant" finding, writes Loulan, is "a statement about the oppression of lesbians in our culture. Heterosexuals assume they have the right to hold hands with their partner in public; most lesbians do not." See Loulan, *Lesbian Passion*, p. 205.

5. The "interlocking male homosocial triangles" at the end of *Shirley* can be visualized as follows:

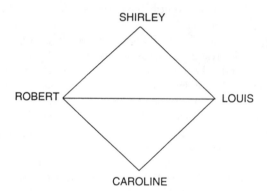

Here the line linking Robert and Louis separates Caroline and Shirley. One can imagine, of course, some hypothetical renewal of erotic bonding between the two women that would recross, so to speak, the line of male bonding; but one would be on the way then to writing a lesbian "postmarital" sequel to Brontë's novel.

6. Townsend Warner, *Summer Will Show* (Virago, 1987). All page numbers noted parenthetically refer to this edition.

7. Since I wrote these words in 1989, two scholars have taken issue—on rather different grounds—with my "decisive" sexualization of the Sophia/Minna relationship. In "Celibate Sisters-in-Revolution: Towards Reading Sylvia Townsend Warner," Robert L. Caserio argues that Townsend Warner intended Sophia and Minna to be seen as chaste "sisters in revolution," akin to the celibate feminists Rhoda Nunn and Mary Barfoot in George Gissing's *The Odd Women* (1893) and Sophia and Constance Baines in Arnold Bennett's *Old Wives' Tale* (1908). And in "Ideology, *Écriture*, 1848: Sylvia Townsend Warner Unwrites Flaubert," Sandy Petrey suggests that the "oyster" passage I cite as a sign of erotic communion is at the very least cryptic and "equivocal" about what is going on between

Sophia and Minna, and should be regarded instead as an instance of Townsend Warner's predilection for ambiguity and "semiotic flux." While intrigued by these criticisms, I remain convinced that Townsend Warner intended the "oyster" episode and following ellipsis to signify the sexual consummation of Sophia's and Minna's relationship. I am left unpersuaded in the end by Caserio's somewhat prim literary historical interpretation: given Townsend Warner's subversive comic outlook and her own exuberantly physical relationship with Valentine Ackland, I think it makes more sense to read *Summer Will Show* as a joyful send-up of the whole pious "celibate sisterhood" tradition. (Wrote Townsend Warner after her first lovemaking with Ackland: "I had not believed it possible to give such pleasure, and to satisfy such a variety of moods, to feel so demanded and so secure, to be loved by anyone so beautiful and to see that beauty enhanced by loving me. The nights were so ample that there was even time to fall asleep in them." [See Harman, *Sylvia Townsend Warner*, p. 108.]) If any couple served as an immediate "model" for Sophia and Minna, it was not, I propose, the chaste Rhoda Nunn and Mary Barfoot, or the sisterly Sophia and Constance Baines, but the decidedly sexy and unsisterly Sylvia Townsend Warner and Valentine Ackland.

As for Petrey's rather more philosophically oriented claims about "semiotic flux," I can respond best by pointing up a hidden paradox in his argument. It may well be, as Petrey suggests, that we need not assume in the case of the oyster passage a "crippling Puritanical blindness in the reviewers who do not seem to have understood the two women's flushes of pleasure and triumphant cries the way we do." The oyster in the scene, after all, as he points out, may be just an oyster. Yet I find it significant that no sense of such "semiotic flux" impairs Petrey's conviction that Minna and *Frederick* have been lovers. He takes it for granted that the heterosexual pair have at one time or another had sexual intercourse, though strictly speaking, the text provides no more "proof" of this than it does for my (admittedly brazen) reading of the scene between Sophia and Minna. (One could conceivably argue that the whole purported liaison between Minna and Frederick is merely Sophia's paranoid fantasy.) Typically, it is lesbian lovemaking that evokes the hermeneutic doubt (is it there?) while ambiguities connected with heterosexual lovemaking go unmentioned.

8. George Eliot, *The Mill on the Floss*, book 5, chapter 4.

9. Townsend Warner, *Letters*, p. 40. Townsend Warner seems to have had Berlioz in mind—and his despairing comment on the hardships suffered by artists and musicians during the 1848 revolution—when she created the character of Guitermann, the impoverished Jewish musician befriended by Sophia late in the novel. See *The Memoirs of Hector Berlioz*, pp. 44–45.

10. A very similar plot twist occurs, interestingly, in a novel that Townsend Warner certainly knew—and paid homage to in *Summer Will Show*—Colette's *La Seconde*, first published in 1929 and translated into English (as *The Other One*) in 1931. In Colette's novel as in Townsend Warner's, a wife and mistress discover to

their mutual delight that they vastly prefer each other's company to that of the man they are supposedly competing for. Colette, it is true, does not eroticize the relationship between her two women characters as explicitly as Townsend Warner does, but her depiction of their alliance (scandalous to the husband) is exhilarating none the less. The Colettian "wife-husband-other woman" configuration turns up again in Townsend Warner's writing, in the slyly comic short story "An Act of Reparation." Here a divorced woman named Lois accidentally meets the young, somewhat befuddled new wife of her former husband while out shopping. After the young woman confesses her anxiety about cooking, Lois goes home with her and shows her how to make oxtail stew. The husband, returning home, smugly concludes that Lois is trying to win him back by showing off her superior culinary skills; but Lois herself knows she is merely performing an "act of reparation" to the young wife, whom she now pities, with unexpected tenderness, for being stuck with the boorish ex-husband.

11. That overtly lesbian and gay male characters often end up inhabiting the same fictional space makes a kind of theoretical as well as mimetic sense: if the imperative toward heterosexual bonding in a fictional work is weak enough to allow one kind of homosexual bonding, chances are it will also allow the other. Two lesbian novels lending support to this idea are May Sarton's *Mrs. Stevens Hears the Mermaids Singing* and Jane Rule's *Memory Board*, both of which include important male homosexual characters.

12. I borrow the euphoric/dysphoric distinction from Nancy K. Miller, who in *The Heroine's Text* uses the terms to refer to the two kinds of narrative "destiny" stereotypically available to the heroines of eighteenth- and nineteenth-century fiction. A euphoric plot, Miller argues, ends with the heroine's marriage, a dysphoric plot with her death or alienation from society. That the terms undergo a dramatic reversal in meaning when applied to lesbian fiction should be obvious: from a lesbian viewpoint, marriage can only be dysphoric in its implications; even death or alienation—if only in a metaphoric sense—may seem preferable.

13. Mulford, *This Narrow Place*, pp. 121–22.

14. That lesbian novelists have been drawn to science fiction should come as no surprise; to the degree that science fiction itself is a form of utopian fantasy, one that posits a fictional world radically different from our own, it lends itself admirably to the representation of alternative sexual structures.

5. The Diaries of Anne Lister

1. Mavor, *The Ladies of Llangollen*, p. xvii.

2. "We do not know whether their relationship was genital," Faderman acknowledges, though it is clear on which side of the question she herself stands:

Their generally rigid, inhibited, and conventional views regarding undress and evidence of sexuality suggest that it is unlikely that as eighteenth-century women, educated in the ideal of female passionlessness, they would have sought genital expression if it were not to fulfill a marital duty. Since they had no sexual duty to a husband, who, as they would have seen it, would be "driven" by his male nature to initiate the sex act, they were probably happy to be oblivious to their genitals.

See Faderman, *Surpassing the Love of Men*, pp. 120–25.

3. Wordsworth, "To the Lady E. B. and the Hon. Miss P., Composed in the Grounds of Plass Newydd, near Llangollen, 1824" in *The Poetical Works of William Wordsworth*, 3:43. On Wordsworth's friendship with the Ladies see Mavor, *The Ladies of Llangollen*, pp. 93 and 185.

4. Colette, *The Pure and the Impure*, pp. 113–14.

5. Colette, *The Pure and the Impure*, p. 118.

6. Whitbread, ed., *I Know my Own Heart*, p. 210. All quotations are from the Virago edition; I have indicated page numbers parenthetically after each quotation. Since I wrote this chapter, *I Know my Own Heart* has been reprinted in an American edition by New York University Press (1992), along with a volume of Lister's later diaries (also edited by Whitbread) entitled *No Priest But Love: The Journals of Anne Lister from 1824–1826*. Pagination is the same in both the Virago and New York University editions.

7. Transvestism crops up at several points in the diary, reinforcing the notion put forth by modern social historians that female homosexuality was frequently linked with cross-dressing in earlier centuries. Lister's masculine-looking friend Miss Pickford tells her at one point "of putting on regimentals & flirting with a lady under the assumed name of Captain Cowper." True to the conventions of contemporary comic drama, "it did not seem that the lady ever found it out but thought the captain the most agreeable of men" (290). For further discussion of the connections between masquerading and homosexual behavior, see my essay "The Culture of Travesty," and longer study *Masquerade and Civilization*, pp. 45–50.

8. There is no indication in the 1817–24 diaries that Lister herself ever used a prosthesis, though she may of course have considered it, given her familiarity with the idea here. She could have known about such implements, possibly, from studying eighteenth-century bawdy writing: both the mock epic *Dildoides* (1706), attributed to Samuel Butler, and the anonymous *Monsieur Thing's Origin; or Seignor D–'s Adventures in Britain* (1722), a comic poem on the pleasure that an ambulatory French dildo, "Monsieur Thing," brings to various English ladies and girls (including a pair of lesbians), were reprinted numerous times throughout the century. And in Henry Fielding's 1746 pamphlet *The Female Husband*, based on a true-life case, the cross-dressing heroine employs an implement "not fit to be mentioned" on a female companion. On the popularity of contemporary dildo literature, see Peter Wagner, "The Discourse on Sex—or Sex as Discourse," and my essay " 'Matters not Fit to be Mentioned.' "

9. Consider lines 300–11 from Juvenal's Sixth Satire:

> What conscience has Venus drunk? Our inebriated beauties
> Can't tell head from tail at those midnight oyster suppers
> When the best wine's laced with perfume, and tossed down neat
> From a foaming conch-shell, while the dizzy ceiling
> Spins round, and the tables dance, and each light shows double.
> Why, you may ask yourself, does the notorious Maura
> Sniff at the air in that knowing, derisive way
> As she and her dear friend Tullia pass by the ancient altar
> Of Chastity? and what is Tullia whispering to her?
> Here, at night, they stagger out of their litters
> And relieve themselves, pissing in long hard bursts
> All over the Goddess's statue. Then, while the Moon
> Looks down on their motions, they take turns to ride each other,
> And finally go home.

From *Juvenal: The Sixteen Satires*, p. 138. Victorian translators, not surprisingly, often obscured the meaning of *inque vices equitant ac luna teste moventur* (Then, while the Moon looks down on their motions, they take turns to ride each other): in his Juvenal edition of 1873, John Delaware Lewis discreetly translated the line as "and by turns indulge in their wanton practices." But even modern translators sometimes give way to prudishness. In a highly regarded version of the satires from 1958, Rolfe Humphries translated the offending line as "*It's my turn now! Let's play horsy!* So in the light of the moon they are moved to the nastiest limits." See Lewis, *D. Junii Juvenalis Satirae. With A Literal English Prose Translation and Notes* (London: Trubner, 1873), p. 69, and *The Satires of Juvenal*, p. 75.

10. See Lister's entry for July 23, 1822.

11. Sandra Gilbert and Susan Gubar briefly discuss Byronic elements in Radclyffe Hall's novel and the paintings of Romaine Brooks in volume 2 (*SexChanges*) of their tripartite study of modern women's writing, *No Man's Land*, pp. 350–53.

12. The psychic process may be similar to that described by Esther Newton in "The Mythic Mannish Lesbian." For Radclyffe Hall and other "mannish" New Women of the early twentieth century, Newton argues, the adoption of a masculine style of dress and manner was a way of "laying full claim" not simply to homosexuality but to sexuality *tout court*: "For bourgeois women, there was no developed female sexual discourse; there were only male discourses— pornographic, literary, and medical—*about* female sexuality. To become avowedly sexual, the New Woman had to enter the male world, either as a heterosexual on male terms (a flapper) or as—or with—a lesbian in male body drag (a butch)" (573). Lister, in the absence of any model of female behavior that might have allowed her to act openly on her sexual impulses, seems—like Radclyffe

Hall—to have appropriated the role of male libertine without too much psychological difficulty.

13. Lillian Faderman, *Odd Girls and Twilight Lovers*, p. 4.

14. Sarah Schulman, *After Delores*, p. 63.

6. Marie Antoinette Obsession

1. Flournoy, *From India to the Planet Mars*. The work was almost immediately translated into English by Daniel B. Vermilye.

2. See, for instance, Flournoy's speculations on the relationship between Smith's "Hindoo" language and Sanskrit, *From India to Mars*, pp. 314–36. Among the experts Flournoy consulted regarding Smith's linguistic productions was his colleague at the University of Geneva, the renowned philologist and founder of semiology, Ferdinand de Saussure.

3. *From India to Mars*, p. 342.

4. Ibid., p. 349. "Leopold," as Flournoy notes, seems here to have gotten his chronology wrong: Marie Antoinette actually outlived the princesse de Lamballe by over a year.

5. Ibid., p. 352.

6. Ibid., p. 354.

7. Ibid., p. 346.

8. "Dream Romances." The author of the narrative has not been identified. According to the editors of the *Journal*, the account was forwarded to them by an associate of the society, a Mrs. Stapleton, of 46 Montagu Square, London, W. Mrs. Stapleton, they said, claimed she had known the writer intimately for many years, and believed her report of her experiences to be a "literally accurate one."

9. Ibid., p. 92.

10. Ibid., p. 93.

11. Ibid., p. 96.

12. Ibid.

13. See Charlotte Anne Moberly and Eleanor Jourdain, *An Adventure* (2d ed.), pp. 1–25. In synopsizing here and elsewhere the complicated background to *An Adventure*, I have drawn on Lucille Iremonger's *Ghosts of Versailles* and Joan Evans's "An End to *An Adventure*." For a closer look at some of the psychobiographical issues involved in the Trianon case, see my related essay "Contagious Folly."

14. During her fictional reverie, the musing Marie Antoinette "sees" the very objects and persons seen by Moberly and Jourdain in 1901—with one amusing addition. Thinking back to her last day at the Trianon, and how she sat sketching on the lawn, she suddenly remembers "two strangers" who walked past her onto the terrace. Thus, presumably, did Moberly and Jourdain, imagining the doomed queen imagining them, seek to lend "telepathic" credibility to their own richly phantasmagorical vision.

15. Mrs. Sidgwick's anonymous review appeared in the June 1911 supple-

ment to the *Proceedings of the Society for Psychical Research*. It is also reprinted in full in chapter 12 of Iremonger's *Ghost of Versailles*.

16. Barrett, *Psychical Research*, p. 201.

17. Moberly and Jourdain, *An Adventure*, pp. 100–20. *An Adventure* went through four editions in all—in 1911, 1913, 1924, and 1955. Each edition was also reprinted. The different editions vary considerably; some, for instance, include the appendixes and "A Rêverie," while others do not.

18. The first book devoted to debunking *An Adventure* was J. R. Sturge-Whiting's *The Mystery of Versailles: A Complete Solution*. It was followed not long after by David Landale Johnston's *The Trianon Case: A Review of the Evidence*. A spate of critical essays on *An Adventure* appeared in the 1950s: W. H. Salter's "'An Adventure': A Note on the Evidence," W. H. W. Sabine's "Is There a Case for Retrocognition?" and Léon Rey's "Une Promenade hors du temps," the first French essay on the subject. (An annotated French translation of *An Adventure*, complete with preface by Jean Cocteau and critical introduction by Robert Amadou, appeared under the title *Les Fantômes de Trianon* in 1959.) The most exhaustive critique of *An Adventure*, however, was undoubtedly Iremonger's 1957 *Ghosts of Versailles*. Iremonger devoted much of her book to an *ad feminam* attack on Moberly and Jourdain themselves, whom she suspected of outright double-dealing. Joan Evans's *Encounter* piece of 1976, "An End to *An Adventure*," while also skeptical in essence, was in part an attempt to defend Moberly and Jourdain against Iremonger's no-holds-barred personal attack.

19. "Dream Romances," p. 90.

20. Barrett, *Psychical Research*, p. 201.

21. Iremonger, *Ghosts of Versailles*, p. 180.

22. Flournoy, *From India to Mars*, p. 27.

23. Ibid., p. 26.

24. See ibid., pp. 48–75, for a detailed clinical assessment of Smith's "spontaneous automatisms" and trance states. Throughout his study Flournoy emphasizes the hysterical nature of Smith's symptoms, referring to them at one point as "eruptions from the subliminal volcano."

25. Ibid., p. 342.

26. Ibid., p. 342–43.

27. Ibid., p. 406.

28. Sigmund Freud, "Family Romances" (1909), in *The Complete Psychological Works of Sigmund Freud*, 9:237–38.

29. "The emotional disposition which I have depicted," writes Flournoy in one particularly florid passage,

> which is one of the forms under which the maladaptation of the organism, physical and mental, to the hard conditions of the environment, betrays itself, seems therefore to me to have been the source and starting-point for all the dreamings of Hélène in her childhood. Thence came these visions, always

warm, luminous, highly colored, exotic, bizarre; and these brilliant apparitions, superbly dressed, in which her antipathy for her insipid and unpleasant surroundings betrays itself, her weariness of ordinary, commonplace people, her disgust for prosaic occupations, for vulgar and disagreeable things, for the narrow house, the dirty streets, the cold winters, and the gray sky.

From India to Mars, pp. 30–31.

30. "Dream Romances," p. 92.

31. Iremonger, *Ghosts of Versailles*, pp. 30 and 65.

32. Ibid., p. 73.

33. Moberly and Jourdain, *An Adventure*, p. 33.

34. In an uncomplimentary aside on Eleanor Jourdain in *The Ghosts of Versailles*, Iremonger argues that the first women to go up to Oxford and Cambridge became "unsatisfactory imitations of the men they at once envied and resented," subject to unconscious "feelings of defiance" as well as "affectations and intellectual conceit" (68–69). For a more sympathetic account of later nineteenth-century women in English universities—and of the unique social and psychological pressures they faced—see Martha Vicinus's "'One Life to Stand by Me': Emotional Conflicts of First-Generation College Women in England," as well as her *Independent Women: Work and Community for Single Women in England, 1850–1920*.

35. "Dream Romances," pp. 92–93.

36. Flournoy, *From India to Mars*, p. 27.

37. Ibid., p. 89.

38. Ibid., p. 129–31.

39. Ibid., p. 119.

40. Ibid., p. 104.

41. Cf. Evans, "An End to *An Adventure*," pp. 34–35.

42. Such a symbolic reading seems particularly appropriate given the fact that the Petit Trianon served as Marie Antoinette's private retreat and "maison de plaisir." Inside its elegant alcoves, which she had had charmingly decorated in the rococo style, she often entertained female favorites such as the comtesse de Polignac. According to Stefan Zweig, within this "inviolable kingdom"—her "island of Cythera"—not even the king himself was allowed to enter without the queen's permission. See Zweig, *Marie Antoinette: The Portrait of an Average Woman*, pp. 106–8.

43. Henrietta Keddie, *Marie Antoinette*, p. 216.

44. See, for example, Edmund Burke, *Reflections on the Revolution in France* (1790; 1969), pp. 169–70; Thomas Carlyle, *The French Revolution*, 2 vols. (1837; 1989), pp. 1:487, 2:322–25; and Charles Dickens, *A Tale of Two Cities* (1859; 1988), pp. 313 and 335. Marie Antoinette's male admirers, interestingly enough, frequently discounted the importance of her early life, including her achievements as queen, in order to concentrate instead solely on her final days and exe-

cution. As Lord Ronald Gower somewhat sententiously put it in his *Last Days of Marie Antoinette*, "The Queen's life becomes chiefly interesting as it approaches its end, and is chiefly remarkable by showing how a woman, whose early years were trifled thoughtlessly away, and who in later life, most unfortunately for her family, herself, and her adopted country, mixed herself in politics, where women are ever mischievous, was raised through suffering to an heroic level" (v–vi). This teleocentric focus was often linked with an almost prurient interest in the physical details of her so-called martyrdom and dissolution. One detects a displaced hint of this interest in *A Tale of Two Cities*, when one of Madame Defarge's accomplices contemplates condemning Lucie Darnet to the guillotine: "'She has a fine head for it,' croaked Jacques Three. 'I have seen blue eyes and golden hair there, and they looked charming when Samson held them up.' Ogre that he was, he spoke like an epicure" (444). The blue eyes and blonde hair mentioned here seem to me an unmistakable iconographic allusion to Marie Antoinette, who was noted for both. By contrast, for whatever reasons, the queen's female acolytes tended on the whole to downplay the actual horror of her demise. Their focus, almost always, was on her charmed life before the Revolution, or (as in the case of the "Dream Romances" writer) on somehow bringing her "back to life," magically, as a kind of loving and poetic apparition, in the mind's eye of the reader.

45. Zweig, *Marie Antoinette*, pp. 119–20.

46. Ibid., p. 121.

47. Zweig attributes Louis XVI's seven-year impotence to phimosis, a contraction of the orifice of the prepuce, which made it impossible for him to ejaculate; ibid., p. 21. It has often been reported—though recent biographers are more skeptical—that Louis underwent a successful operation to cure the problem in 1777 at the behest of Marie Antoinette's brother, the Emperor Joseph II of Austria. See Joan Haslip, *Marie Antoinette*, p. 100.

48. Mayer, *Marie Antoinette*, pp. 79–80.

49. Cf. Haslip, *Marie Antoinette*, pp. 64–65 and 83–84.

50. Ibid., p. 84.

51. On the publishing history of the *libelles*, see Henri d'Alméras, *Marie-Antoinette et les pamphlets*, and Hector Fleischmann, *Les Pamphlets libertins*, and *Marie-Antoinette libertine*. The pornographic pamphlets against Marie Antoinette have recently attracted considerable attention from literary critics and historians of the Old Regime. See, in particular, Chantal Thomas, *La Reine scélérate*, and the brilliant essay by Lynn Hunt (to which I am here much indebted), "The Many Bodies of Marie Antoinette."

52. Hester Thrale Piozzi, *Thraliana*, 2:740. Hearing of "Anarchy" in France and Marie Antoinette's travails at the hands of the revolutionists in December of 1790, Thrale remarked, only slightly more charitably, "God will I hope touch her noble Heart *now* with *natural* Passions, and shewing her the Vicissitudes of this Life, turn her Thoughts to Eternity" (2:788–89).

53. Zweig, *Marie Antoinette*, p. 375.

54. Haslip, *Marie Antoinette*, p. 287.

55. According to Henri d'Alméras, the *Essai historique* alone, reprinted in various forms in the 1780s, sold between twenty and thirty thousand copies; *Marie-Antoinette et les pamphlets*, 403. As Lynn Hunt notes in her essay on the *libelles*, however, he provides no evidence for this statistic.

56. See Lister, *No Priest But Love*, p. 31. Lister's diary entry—a fascinating one—supports my contention that Marie Antoinette functioned as a kind of symbolic mediator in the homosexual wooing rituals of nineteenth-century women. Lister's interlocutor here, an expatriated Englishwoman named Maria Barlow with whom she ended up sharing lodgings, made her remark shortly after the two met—as if to signal her sexual interest in Lister. Lister, taking the bait, promptly seduced Barlow. The two paid a sentimental visit to the queen's cell at the Conciergerie in March 1825.

57. Campan, *Private Life of Marie Antoinette*, p. 115.

58. Ibid., p. 115.

59. Goncourt and Goncourt, *Histoire de Marie-Antoinette*, pp. 104–5 and 116–17.

60. Goncourt and Goncourt, *Marie-Antoinette*, p. 266. Translations from the French, here and elsewhere, are my own.

61. Ibid., p. 105.

62. Ibid., p. 373.

63. Somewhat later works in the same hagiographical vein include Hilaire Belloc's *Marie Antoinette*, and Nesta H. Webster's *Louis XVI and Marie Antoinette Before the Revolution* and *Louis XVI and Marie Antoinette During the Revolution*. See also Joseph Adelman, *Famous Women*. Not content merely with romanticizing her, Marie Antoinette's early twentieth-century biographers frequently used her story as an excuse for riding various hobbyhorses of their own. Belloc's rather crabbed and neurotic account is full of gratuitous anti-Semitic asides. And in the bizarre concluding paragraphs of *Louis XVI and Marie Antoinette During the Revolution*, Webster took Marie Antoinette's fate as an occasion for warning against the international "conspiracy" of Freemasonry.

64. Catherine Hyde, *Secret Memoirs*, p. 83.

65. Campan, *Private Life of Marie Antoinette*, p. 92.

66. Keddie, *Marie Antoinette*, p. 84.

67. Ibid., p. 188.

68. Bicknell, *The Story of Marie-Antoinette*, p. 94. Admittedly, some of the revisionist biographers recognized the compromising element in the sledge party episode and tried to defuse it. In a comically bathetic passage in the fictionalized *Secret Memoirs of Princess Lamballe*, for example, the sledge parties of queen and princess are rewritten as missions of charity.

69. Montefiore, *Princesse de Lamballe*, p. 29.

70. Montefiore, *Princesse de Lamballe*, pp. 146–47.

71. Keddie, *Marie Antoinette*, p. 189.

72. Hyde, *Secret Memoirs*, p. 2.

73. Ibid., pp. 69–70.

74. Ibid., p. 72.

75. Ibid., p. 74.

76. "Catherine Hyde" here appends an ominous footnote in which, like Moberly and Jourdain later, she imagines the fateful date of August 10, 1792: "Good Heaven! What must have been the feelings of these true, sacred friends, the shadow of each other, on that fatal Tenth of August, which separated them only to meet in a better world!"; ibid., p. 86.

77. Among the errands Hyde claims to have made in boy's clothes on the queen's behalf was one to the National Assembly where she observed a debate between Mirabeau and the Abbé Maury; ibid., p. 300. On another occasion, she says, she disguised herself as a milliner and went to spy on Danton, who tried to seduce her (303–5).

78. Hyde, *Secret Memoirs*, p. 280.

79. Ibid., pp. 312–13.

80. Ibid., p. 310.

81. Ibid., p. 334.

82. Hyde, *Secret Memoirs*, pp. 344–45.

83. Ibid., p. 83.

84. According to the editors of the *Oxford Dictionary of Quotations*, 3d ed. (1979), the infamous words, "Qu'ils mangent de la brioche," were probably never uttered by Marie Antoinette. The expression antedates her: Rousseau in his *Confessions* (1740) referred to a similar remark as a well-known saying. In his *Relation d'un voyage à Bruxelles et à Coblentz en 1791* (1823) Louis XVIII attributed the phrase "Que ne mangent-ils de la croûte de pâté?" ("Why don't they eat pastry?") to Marie-Thérèse (1638–83), the wife of Louis XIV.

85. Rose Laure Allatini [A. T. Fitzroy], *Despised and Rejected* (1918; 1988), pp. 20–21.

86. Radclyffe Hall, *The Well of Loneliness*, p. 239.

87. Ibid.

88. Cf. Radclyffe Hall, *Well of Loneliness:* "The Hameau [Marie Antoinette's model village at the Trianon] no longer seemed sad to Stephen, for Mary and she brought love back to the Hameau" (329). There is evidence to suggest that the Trianon was a site of romantic pilgrimage for Radclyffe Hall and Una Troubridge as well: in the doting life of her friend she published after Radclyffe Hall's death, Troubridge mentions their sightseeing trips in the 1920s to "Versailles and the Trianon" as well as to the Conciergerie, the final prison of Marie Antoinette. See *The Life of Radclyffe Hall*, p. 88.

89. Virginia Woolf, *Orlando*, p. 45.

90. Compton Mackenzie, *Extraordinary Women*, pp. 15 and 39.

91. Djuna Barnes, *Nightwood*, p. 42.

92. Ibid., p. 44.

93. Olive Moore, *Celestial Seraglio*, in *Collected Writings*, p. 57; Antonia White, *Frost in May*, p. 121.

94. Hyde, in the *Secret Memoirs*, describes the death blow of the princesse de Lamballe thus:

> Nearest to her in the mob stood a mulatto, whom she had caused to be baptized, educated, and maintained, but whom, from ill-conduct, she had latterly excluded from her presence. This miscreant struck at her with his halbert. The blow removed her cap. Her luxuriant hair (as if to hide her angelic beauty from the sight of the murderers, pressing tigerlike around to pollute that form, the virtues of which equaled its physical perfection), her luxuriant hair fell around and veiled her a moment from view. An individual, to whom I was nearly allied, seeing the miscreants somewhat staggered, sprang forward to the rescue; but the mulatto wounded him. The Princess was lost to all feeling from the moment the monster first struck at her. But the demons would not quit their prey. She expired, gashed with wounds. (328)

In Townsend Warner's novel, the mulatto Caspar leads a Gardes Mobiles assault on the barricade where Sophia and her lover, Minna Lemuel, are loading rifles for the insurgents and then turns—equally violently—against his former mentor:

> With the certainty of a bad dream, there, when [Sophia] looked up, was Caspar's profile outlined against the smoky dusk, tilted, just as it had been on those summer evenings at Blandamer House, when he played his guitar, leaning against the balustrade. . . .
>
> "Why, it's Caspar!"
>
> It was Minna's voice, warm, inveterately hospitable. He glanced round. With a howl of rage he sprang forward, thrust with his bayonet, drove it into Minna's breast.
>
> "Drab!" he cried out. "Jewess! This is the end of you."
>
> A hand was clapped on Sophia's shoulder, a voice told her she was a prisoner.
>
> "One moment," she replied, inattentively. With her free arm she pulled out the pistol and cocked it, and fired at Caspar's mouth as though she would have struck that mouth with her hand. Having looked to aim, she looked no further. But she saw the bayonet jerk in Minna's breast, and the blood rush out.

Townsend Warner alters certain details of the original scene (as in the immediate retribution that Sophia wreaks on Caspar), but the similarities are also, I think, unmistakable. Cf. Townsend Warner, *Summer Will Show*, pp. 382–83.

95. Lennox Strong, "Royal Triangle," pp. 180–85. Among the bibliographic sources cited by Strong are two of the romanticizing biographies from the turn of the century: Bicknell's *Story of Marie-Antoinette*, and Hyde's *Secret Memoirs*.

264

96. Florence King, *Confessions of a Failed Southern Lady*, p. 70; Jeanette Winterson, *The Passion*, p. 16. King's reference, though seemingly flippant, is in fact an especially interesting one in the context of lesbian thematics. Describing several bossy grade school teachers whom she disliked intensely, King complains that "they were not happy unless everybody was engaged in an activity big enough to require what they called 'give and take,' like marching on the Tuileries with equal parts of the Princess de Lamballe's dismembered corpse on our pikes." Against such enforced jollity, the introverted King sought refuge, she says, in intimate friendships with one or two other intellectually minded and sensitive girls.

97. On Madonna's paradoxical role as lesbian (as well as heterosexual) icon, see Alice Echols, "Justifying Our Love?"

98. In her *Ladder* piece, Lennox Strong, it is true, betrays some ambivalence about Marie Antoinette's self-indulgence and lack of concern for her suffering subjects. Given the amount of money Marie Antoinette spent on "pretty fripperies" for her favorites, writes Strong, it was not surprising that the people of France ended up hating "their beautiful but expensive queen." "The rest is history," she concludes philosophically, "bloody and even evil, but not wholly unjustified"; "Royal Triangle," p. 184.

7. Haunted by Olive Chancellor

1. Cargill, *The Novels of Henry James*, p. 129.
2. Wright, *The Madness of Art*, pp. 94, 95.
3. Geismar, *Henry James and the Jacobites*, p. 65.
4. Strouse, *Alice James*, p. 250.
5. Tanner, *Henry James*, p. 53.
6. Trilling, *The Opposing Self*, p. 114.
7. Dupee, *Henry James*, p. 131.
8. McMurray, "Pragmatic Realism in *The Bostonians*," p. 341.
9. Howe, "Introduction to *The Bostonians*," pp. 165, 168.
10. Tanner, *Henry James*, pp. 54, 57.
11. Wilson, "The Ambiguity of Henry James," p. 396.
12. Foster, *Sex Variant Women in Literature*, p. 15.
13. Foster, *Sex Variant Women in Literature*, pp. 95–96. Though James's female critics have tended on the whole to treat the lesbian theme in *The Bostonians* with more equanimity than their male counterparts have, even those most sympathetic to Olive, it should be noted, have been reluctant to go very far with it. In an oddly poignant essay from the 1960s, "Henry James and the Cities of the Plain," Mildred E. Hartsock concluded that lesbianism was indeed "present in the novel" and that James himself was "recurrently interested in the theme of sexual inversion," but hedged her argument round—as if anxious not to offend—with qualifications and defensive pronouncements ("Today, confronted with this subject *ad nauseam*, we might well demur at an emphasis on it in the work of James").

Even the unusually forthright Judith Fetterley, the first critic to confront the often blatant misogyny informing some of the so-called classic readings of the novel, such as Trilling's and Philip Rahv's, steers clear—in her otherwise powerful rereading of *The Bostonians* from 1978—of the novel's sexual subtext. Though explicit about the ways in which various critics have used the lesbian "label" to defame Olive's character—and to impugn feminism itself—Fetterley is hesitant to speculate herself about the actual nature of Olive and Verena's relationship. See "Henry James's Eternal Triangle," in *The Resisting Reader*, especially pp. 109–10.

14. Edel and Powers, eds., *The Complete Notebooks of Henry James*, pp. 19–20.

15. Trilling's imposing, carefully cadenced observations are characteristic: "No American writer before James had so fully realized the contemporary, physical scene of moral action and social existence. Nor had the nature of the American social existence ever been so brilliantly suggested. Manners have changed since James wrote, but not the peculiar tenuity of the fabric of American social life" (*The Opposing Self*, p. 106).

16. Gooder, Introduction to *The Bostonians*, pp. xxiv–xxvi.

17. The most recent critic to set forth the Olive/Alice connection is Alison Lurie, in the introduction to the paperback Library of America edition of *The Bostonians*, pp. xiv–xv.

18. The phrase appears in a letter Alice James wrote to Sara Darwin in July, 1879. See Strouse, *Alice James*, pp. 194–5.

19. As Tintner notes, echoes of French "popular decadent" fiction—and of Balzac's lesbian-themed short stories in particular—can be found throughout *The Bostonians*. In her eagerness to see Balzac as the overriding influence on James's novel, however, Tintner omits entirely any reference to Zola—whose influence seems at once more direct, interesting, and pervasive. See *The Book World of Henry James*, pp. 260–71.

20. Gautier, *Mademoiselle de Maupin* (Penguin, 1981), pp. 283–84. All further references are to this edition.

21. Gautier, *Mademoiselle de Maupin*, p. 327.

22. Zola, *Nana* (Penguin, 1972), p. 335. All further references (noted parenthetically) are to this edition.

23. James uses the phrase in his working notes for *The Awkward Age* (1899). See Edel and Powers, *Notebooks of Henry James*, p. 120.

24. James, "Théophile Gautier," in *European Writers*, p. 359.

25. James, review of Swinburne, *Essays and Studies*, in *American and English Writers*, p. 1280.

26. James, *European Writers*, p. 158.

27. James, "Guy de Maupassant," in *European Writers*, pp. 536–37.

28. James, review of *Nana*, in *European Writers*, p. 865.

29. James, *European Writers*, p. 870.

30. As James himself noted in his 1880 review of the novel, *Nana* "reached, on

the day of its being offered for sale by retail, a thirty-ninth edition." See *European Writers*, p. 866.

31. The reviewer was Ulbach, in *Gil Blas*. Cited in George Holden's introduction to the Penguin edition of *Nana*, p. 15.

32. Letter to William Morton Fullerton, February 29, 1896. Cited in Edel, *Henry James: The Middle Years*, p. 104.

33. James, *The Bostonians* (Oxford and New York: Oxford University Press, 1984), p. 56. All further page references, given in parentheses, are to this edition.

34. It is Basil, of course, who applies the incriminating term "morbid" to Olive: she is, he thinks upon first meeting her, "visibly morbid; it was as plain as day that she was morbid" (8). And as James almost certainly would have known, the word is inescapable in late nineteenth- and early twentieth-century medical and psychiatric discussions of sexual deviance. (Cf. Faderman, *Surpassing the Love of Men*, pp. 241ff.) Yet it is possible that James may intend the passage more as a satire on Basil—who professes similarly crude positivistic opinions elsewhere in the novel—than as any kind of definitive statement on Olive's complex and subtle nature.

35. I am not, I realize, the first reader to sense a tragic quality in Olive; even relatively judgmental critics, such as Howe and Dupee, though antipathetic towards her sexuality, acknowledge her curious personal grandeur. What I take issue with, however, is the attitude—expressed most condescendingly by Dupee—that "we pity [Olive] all the more because James pities her so little" (*Henry James*, p. 153). The degree of James's pity for Olive is precisely the issue: in investing her with tragic power, James was (I think) expressing a certain understanding of—and compassion for—her anxious and lonely way of desiring.

36. Gooder, Introduction to the *The Bostonians*, p. xxviii.

37. See, for example, Long, *Henry James: The Early Novels*, p. 146. I take issue here, obviously, with Tintner's somewhat simplistic view that James, like Balzac, is a "nineteenth-century man" in that he believes "the 'natural' . . . must triumph over the 'unnatural.'" Tintner argues that Balzac and James both demonstrate that "presumptuous women" must fall: "the Marquise [in *La Fille aux yeux d'or*] because of her ferocity and resemblance to an animal, and Olive because of her emotional morbidity and ideological fanaticism" (*The Book World of Henry James*, p. 262). Yet to the degree that James covertly imbues Olive with something of his own sexual sensibility, he also turns away, I think, from his French models. Though Olive is brought down, she is never anathematized, it seems to me, in the way that Balzac anathematizes the Marquise de San-Réal in *La Fille aux yeux d'or*.

38. Hall, *The Well of Loneliness*, pp. 178–80.

39. Hall, *The Well of Loneliness*, p. 203.

40. Radclyffe Hall treats Stephen's heroic "martyrdom" rather more sentimentally, of course, and there is a strain of kitsch running through *The Well of*

Loneliness that is altogether absent in *The Bostonians*. Yet in Radclyffe Hall's persistent accentuation of the loneliness of her heroine—and of the strange and unhappy fatality hanging over her—one also finds more than a hint of Olive's pathos and lucklessness.

41. Barnes, *Nightwood*, p. 50.

42. The opening scene at Miss Birdseye's is a veritable orgy of watchers and watching. Just before Verena speaks, Basil sees the cagey Dr. Prance "turning over the whole assembly a glance like the flash of a watchman's bull's eye" (44); when he meets Verena's eye a moment later, he sees "she was watching him too" (45). When Doctor Tarrant performs his strange ministrations over Verena's head, while she silently prepares for her speech, Basil "watched these proceedings with much interest, for the girl amused and pleased him" (53). And later, when Olive shyly approaches Verena after her speech, the little knot of admirers around the younger woman "watched [Olive] as she arrived; their faces expressed a suspicion of her social importance, mingled with conscientious scruples as to whether it were right to recognize it" (63).

43. Bell, "The Bostonian Story," p. 111.

8. The Gaiety of Janet Flanner

1. Sischy, "White and Black," p. 145.
2. Wineapple, *Genêt*, p. 104.
3. Wineapple, *Genêt*, p. 267.
4. Wineapple, *Genêt*, p. 55.
5. Wineapple, *Genêt*, p. 74.
6. Flanner, *Paris Was Yesterday*, p. 29. In quoting from Flanner's *New Yorker* writings, I have, for convenience's sake, used Irving Drutman's edited compilations, *Paris Was Yesterday* (1972), *London Was Yesterday* (1975), and *Janet Flanner's World* (1979), along with two volumes of Flanner's essays edited by William Shawn, *Paris Journal: 1944–1965* (1965) and *Paris Journal: 1965–1971* (1971). It should be noted that Flanner and her editors made occasional small changes in the reprinted versions, usually to clarify topical references otherwise lost to time.
7. Flanner, *Paris Was Yesterday*, p. 55.
8. Wineapple, *Genêt*, p. 77.
9. Flanner, *Paris Was Yesterday*, p. 67.
10. Flanner, *Paris Was Yesterday*, pp. 70–71.
11. Ibid., p. 13.
12. Ibid., p. 73.
13. Ibid., p. 91.
14. Ibid., p. 91.
15. Flanner, "Führer," in *Janet Flanner's World*, pp. 6–7.
16. Flanner, *Darlinghissima*, p. 486.
17. Flanner, *Darlinghissima*, p. 86.

18. Wineapple, *Genêt*, p. 208.

19. Flanner, *Paris Was Yesterday*, p. 48.

20. See Flanner, *Paris Was Yesterday*, pp. 49 and 72, and *London Was Yesterday*, p. 116.

21. Flanner, *London Was Yesterday*, p. 48.

22. Flanner, *Paris Journal*, p. 218.

23. Flanner, *Paris Journal*, pp. 213–18.

24. See Spurling, *Ivy*, Glendinning, *Vita*, and Harman, *Sylvia Townsend Warner*. A number of outstanding biographies of lesbian writers and artists have been published over the last decade. See, for example, Strouse, *Alice James*, Fitzgerald, *Charlotte Mew and Her Friends*, Lempicka-Foxhall (with Charles Phillips), *Passion by Design: The Art and Times of Tamara de Lempicka*, Adam, *Eileen Gray*, Souhami, *Gluck—1895–1978*, Lee, *Willa Cather*, and Millier, *Elizabeth Bishop*.

25. Michael Baker, *Our Three Selves: The Life of Radclyffe Hall*.

9. In Praise of Brigitte Fassbaender (A Musical Emanation)

1. Brophy, *Mozart the Dramatist*, p. 40.

2. Huneker, *Bedouins*, pp. 18, 22. In *Interpreters*, invoking the "subtle fragrance" of Garden's name, Carl Van Vechten offered a similarly rhapsodic meditation: "Since Nell Gwynn no such scented cognomen, redolent of cuckoo's boots, London pride, blood-red poppies, purple fox-gloves, lemon stocks, and vermillion zinnias, has blown its delicate odour across our scene. . . . Delightful and adorable Mary Garden, the fragile Thaïs, pathetic Jean . . . unforgettable Mélisande" (92–93).

3. Brophy, *Mozart the Dramatist*, pp. 38, 43.

4. On some of the complex aesthetic, psychological, and political meanings that opera and diva-worship hold in contemporary European and American gay male culture, see Michael Bronski, *Culture Clash: The Making of Gay Male Sensibility* and Andrew Ross, *No Respect: Intellectuals and Popular Culture*. Both Bronski and Ross emphasize the culturally enfranchising power of opera: in the act of becoming fans, both argue, gay men gain access to a social world of prestige, power, and glamor. For a more diffident, and in many ways more enlightening, view, see Wayne Koestenbaum's *The Queen's Throat: Opera, Homosexuality, and the Mystery of Desire*—a brilliant fantasia on the "homoerotics" of operatic performance and its personal and public meanings.

5. See Rich, "A Queer Sensation," p. 42.

6. On the youthful Cather's use of music (especially opera) to emblematize powerful feelings for her own sex, see O'Brien, *Willa Cather: The Emerging Voice*, pp. 170–73. In emphasizing opera's enlivening and arousing effect on female spectators, I implicitly take issue with the rather more gloomy view espoused by Catherine Clément in her influential *L'Opéra, ou la défaite des femmes* (Paris: Bernard Grasset, 1979), published in English as *Opera, or the Undoing of Women* (Min-

neapolis: University of Minnesota Press, 1989). Far from seeing opera (as Clément does) simply as an institution devoted to the ritualized "undoing" and debasement of the feminine, I consider it a much more complex and subversive cultural phenomenon, precisely because of its power to evoke homoerotic *jouissance* in its female fans.

7. Esher, *The Girlhood of Queen Victoria*, 1:93.

8. Esher, *Girlhood of Victoria*, 1:94.

9. Esher, *Girlhood of Victoria*, 1:111.

10. Esher, *Girlhood of Victoria*, 1:115.

11. Holland and Rockstro, *Memoir of Jenny Lind*, 2:73.

12. Holland and Rockstro, *Memoir of Jenny Lind*, 2:153.

13. Emma Calvé, *My Life*, pp. 95–96.

14. On the notorious Gerry-flappers see Vincent Sheean, *First and Last Love*, pp. 61–62, Rupert Christiansen, *Prima Donna*, pp. 192–93, and Farrar's own autobiography, *Such Sweet Compulsion*, pp. 133 and 216. Though she complains at one point about an especially "ardent" Gerry-flapper who infected her with the measles on the eve of a performance, Farrar seems to have taken on the whole a remarkably good-humored attitude toward her female fans, and often kept in touch with them for many years. On Galli-Curci and her devotees, see Le Massena, *Galli-Curci's Life of Song*, pp. 132–33.

15. Cited in Christiansen, *Prima Donna*, p. 192.

16. See Farrar, *Such Sweet Compulsion*, p. 24, and Le Massena, *Galli-Curci's Life of Song*, p. 19.

17. Christiansen, *Prima Donna*, p. 198.

18. On Lister's veneration for Catalani and her fellow Handelian, Mrs. Salmon, see *I Know My Own Heart*, pp. 300–3. After meeting Catalani at a supper party and engaging her successfully in conversation, Lister noted with satisfaction that the singer was "certainly a very handsome, elegantly mannered & fascinating woman. I stammered on in French very tolerably" (303).

19. Sand, *Correspondance de George Sand*, 1:789–90.

20. Cate, *George Sand*, p. 177.

21. Cate, *George Sand*, p. 221.

22. Cate, *George Sand*, p. 227.

23. Smyth, *Impressions That Remained*, p. 80.

24. Smyth, *Impressions That Remained*, pp. 154–55.

25. Smyth, *Impressions That Remained*, p. 156.

26. Smyth, *Impressions That Remained*, p. 197.

27. Flanner, *Darlinghissima*, p. 302.

28. On this same occasion, the ever-provocative Garden, noticing her two fans' interest in an "enormous" photograph of Oscar Wilde on her piano, told them that "if I had only been where I am to-day, I would have gone to the prison when he came out, taken him with me, re-established him before the world." There was "nothing enveloped, nothing enveloping about Mary Garden's

charm," wrote Anderson; "It was tangible, unadorned, compelling." See *My Thirty Years' War*, p. 138.

29. Cather, *The Song of the Lark*, pp. 325–26.

30. Cather, "Three American Singers," p. 46. On the influence of Fremstad on Cather's own artistic development, see O'Brien, *Cather: The Emerging Voice*, pp. 167, 237, and 447, and Lee, *Willa Cather: Double Lives*, pp. 120–22.

31. Cushing, *The Rainbow Bridge*, pp. 13–17.

32. Cushing, *Rainbow Bridge*, p. 4.

33. Cushing, *Rainbow Bridge*, pp. 314–15.

34. Davenport's numerous works include biographies of Mozart and Toscanini, several novels, and a book of musical and personal reminiscences, *Too Strong For Fantasy*. Lena Geyer, Davenport maintained in the latter, was a composite figure based on real prototypes: "Anybody who knows the history of opera can name the prototypes" (216).

35. Davenport, *Of Lena Geyer*, p. 193.

36. Davenport, *Of Lena Geyer*, p. 205.

37. Davenport, *Of Lena Geyer*, p. 208.

38. Davenport, *Of Lena Geyer*, p. 237.

39. See Baker, *Our Three Selves*, pp. 33–38. "Ladye" (as Batten was known to her friends) studied music in Dresden and Bruges and had a "beautifully produced" mezzo voice. John Singer Sargent's 1897 portrait of her, in full vocal flight, is reproduced in Baker's biography.

40. See Margaret Anderson, *The Fiery Fountains*, especially pp. 3–14. In a letter to a friend after Monique Serrure's death at the age of ninety-one, Janet Flanner described Serrure's lifelong attachment to Leblanc, begun at the opera, as "a true stage love." See Flanner, *Darlinghissima*, p. 312.

41. An interesting counterpart to Western-style "sapphic" diva-worship can be found in contemporary Japanese society, in the often hysterical adulation bestowed on the actresses of the Takarazuka Revue—an all-female transvestite theater founded in 1914 in Tokyo—by their young female fans. The actresses who play exclusively male roles—the *otokoyaku*—are particularly popular and have huge fan followings. The revue since its founding has frequently come under attack from moralists and social reformers for promoting "abnormal sensations" in its mostly female audience. See Robertson, "Gender-Bending in Paradise," and "Theatrical Resistance, Theatres of Restraint."

42. The scene in question occurs near the end of the novel, when the heroine and the singer, Helena Buchan, stay overnight in the small Italian village of Strà on the mainland near Venice. See Brophy, *King of a Rainy Country*, pp. 256–58. In its subtle exploration of the emotional ramifications of diva-worship, Brophy's brilliant and cultivated novel remains unmatched.

43. A fascinating study might be written on the role that diva-worship has played in the evolution of contemporary lesbian identity. As it is, small pieces of this history have begun to emerge. In Van Kooten Niekerk and Wijmer's *Verkeerde*

Vriendschap, for example, there is a telling interview with "Tina B." (born 1912), who reminisces about the cult status of Kathleen Ferrier among Dutch lesbians in the 1940s and her own admiration for the singer:

> The first time I heard Kathleen Ferrier sing—now that we can tell all, literally all—*that* was erotic. This woman had something that sent me into ecstasy. It was not only that magnificent voice, that unique voice, but her whole being, her very essence, and the interpretation you took from her tone. I would sit there in tears, it was so absolutely pure that you felt yourself becoming warm inside. It was all there—eroticism, sexuality, charm, and admirability. (128–29)

(I am grateful here to Patricia Juliana Smith both for the original reference to Van Kooten Niekerk and Wijmer's book and for the translation from the Dutch.) Exactly why Ferrier became such a powerful lesbian icon is a subject yet to be taken up, it's worth noting, by any of the singer's mainstream biographers. Works such as Cardus's *Kathleen Ferrier* are hagiographical to the point of obfuscation and frustratingly silent on the subject of Ferrier's own sexuality.

44. Interview with Brigitte Fassbaender, in Matheopoulos, *Diva*, p. 273.

45. Rice, "Afterword," p. 534.

46. Gerhardt, *Recital*; cited by Alan Blyth, in liner notes to *Winterreise*, Brigitte Fassbaender, mezzo-soprano (EMI CDC-7–49846–2).

47. Jolly, "A Timeless Journey," p. 176. In other interviews, it must be said, Fassbaender sometimes reverts to the "universalist" line, as in her comment to Barbara Hammond in "A Profile of Brigitte Fassbaender": "I don't feel any difficulty [singing *Winterreise*]. There is loneliness, and lost love, and longing for death, and that emotional world is lived by women too. As long as a woman has the strength to sing it, then why not?" But even so, one often detects an ironic note. In an interview with Ingrid and Herbert Haffner in *Opernwelt*, Fassbaender says at one point: "No doubt that a woman—at least I—can identify entirely with the *Winterreise*'s walk on the edge. Of course, I am familiar with Fischer-Dieskau's incomparable recordings; yet I am fascinated by the idea that a totally new dimension is added if the cycle is sung by a woman." What this "totally new" dimension is she doesn't specify, yet it seems unlikely that she is referring to purely vocal matters.

48. She retired Octavian, for example, in 1988. "One day," she confessed in a 1990 interview, "you wake up and find that you have had enough of those pant roles, with one diet after another in order to fit into your trousers. I want to have my spaghettis now whenever I want them." See Hammond, "A Profile of Brigitte Fassbaender," p. 61.

49. Smyth, *Impressions That Remained*, p. 193.

50. Davenport, *Of Lena Geyer*, p. 55.

51. Brophy, *Mozart the Dramatist*, p. 37. The peculiar erotic charge associated with low female voices has often been noted, especially by opera buffs (like Bro-

phy) of psychoanalytic bent. In a brilliantly suggestive recent book, *The Angel's Cry*, the French Lacanian psychoanalyst Michel Poizat notes that "the voices considered most erotic, those that hold the greatest fascination for the listener, whether male or female, are voices that may be called trans-sexual—the deep voice of a woman (think of Kathleen Ferrier, or Marlene Dietrich, the 'blue angel'), the high voice in a man (the castrato, the tenor)" (105). The phenomenon can be attributed, in Poizat's view, to the complicated manner in which the voice is "inserted"—in infancy—into the network of unconscious sexual drives.

52. Susan Gould, "Brigitte Fassbaender," p. 789.

53. Gwen Hughes, Review of *Die Fledermaus*.

54. Ralph V. Lucano, Review of Schubert, *Winterreise*.

55. Part of Fassbaender's success in the role of Octavian has undoubtedly had to do with her affection for his youthful and somewhat volatile personality: she claims never to have found him "boring" (Matheopoulos, *Diva*, p. 273). By contrast, Christa Ludwig, who sang him often in the 1950s, always disliked him "because he is vapid and always uttering the stupidities of a seventeen-year-old, while all the interesting things are said by the Marschallin" (Matheopoulos, *Diva*, p. 283). Not surprisingly, Ludwig's characterization of Octavian—preserved in a famous Karajan recording from 1956—though beautifully sung, lacks almost entirely that element of enthusiastic "homovocality" so prominent in Fassbaender's.

56. Matheopoulos, *Diva*, p. 276.

57. Fassbaender has confessed to disliking the role of Geschwitz—but not, interestingly, out of any emotional discomfort with the part:

Only a couple of her phrases amount to real singing. She had a bit more to do in the three-act version, but I'm not sure the "Paris" scene is worth sitting through to get to the completed "London" scene. All those characters talking endlessly about stocks and shares—interestingly it is also the only boring scene in the original Wedekind play. I'm sure Berg would have cut it drastically. You tire your voice in the role without deriving any satisfaction from having contributed something.

See Matheopoulos, *Diva*, p. 278.

58. Matheopoulos, *Diva*, p. 273.

59. Says Te Kanawa, bluntly, on singing the Marschallin: "Once you get past these first few minutes when you are in bed with another woman, you can get on with the role." See Matheopoulos, *Diva*, p. 215.

60. Cather, "Three American Singers," p. 36.

61. Elizabeth Bowen makes a similar point in her discreetly lesbian-themed novel *The Hotel* (1928). "One has had it so ground into one," complains Bowen's young heroine, Sydney, "that admiration, any exercise of the spirit, is only valuable to its *object*, to drive her, his, somebody's mill." The fact that Sydney loves and will later be betrayed by the very person she is speaking to here, the amoral

Mrs. Kerr, adds a certain ironic resonance to her remark, but the novelist's own sympathies are clearly with her. See Bowen, *The Hotel*, p. 77.

62. Not entirely without reason, of course. Even in the relatively sedate world of opera, there has always been a lunatic fringe. During the balcony scene in a Chicago performance of Gounod's *Roméo et Juliette* in 1894, for example, a psychotic fan clambered onstage and aimed a pistol at the Roméo, Jean De Reszke, but was disarmed before he could fire. While Nellie Melba, the Juliet, hid behind the shutters on the balcony, screaming "Ring down the curtain! My voice is gone!" De Reszke, who never flinched, continued singing a moment later as though nothing had happened—to the cheers of the astonished crowd. See Nellie Melba, *Melodies and Memories*, p. 144, and Mary Garden and Louis Biancolli, *Mary Garden's Story*, pp. 20–21.

63. Brophy, *Mozart the Dramatist*, p. 37.

WORKS CITED

Ackland, Valentine. *For Sylvia: An Honest Account*. New York: Norton, 1986.

Acosta, Mercedes de. *Here Lies the Heart*. New York: Reynal, 1960.

Adam, Peter. *Eileen Gray: Architect/Designer*. New York: Abrams, 1987.

Adelman, Joseph. *Famous Women: An Outline of Feminine Achievement Through the Ages with Life Stories of Five Hundred Noted Women*. New York: Woman's World, 1926.

Alger, W. R. *The Friendships of Women*. Boston: Roberts, 1872.

Allatini, Rose Laure [A. T. Fitzroy]. *Despised and Rejected*. London: Gay Men's Press, 1988.

Alméras, Henri d'. *Marie-Antoinette et les pamphlets royalistes et révolutionnaires: les amoureux de la reine*. Paris: Librairie Mondiale, 1907.

Amours de Charlot et de Toinette. Paris, 1779.

Anderson, Margaret. *The Fiery Fountains*. New York: Hermitage House, 1951.

—— *My Thirty Years' War*. New York: Covici, Friede, 1930.

Arrowsmith, Pat. *Somewhere Like This*. London: Gay Men's Press, 1990.

Baker, Dorothy. *Cassandra at the Wedding*. Boston: Houghton Mifflin, 1962.

—— *Trio*. Cambridge, Mass.: Riverside, 1943.

Baker, Michael. *Our Three Selves: The Life of Radclyffe Hall*. New York: William Morrow, 1985.

Balzac, Honoré de. *The Girl with the Golden Eyes* (*La Fille aux yeux d'or*). Trans. Ernest Dowson. N.p.: privately printed, 1929.

Bannon, Ann. *Journey to a Woman*. New York: Arno, 1975.

—— *Odd Girl Out*. New York: Arno, 1975.

Banta, Martha. *Henry James and the Occult*. Bloomington: Indiana University Press, 1972.

Barale, Michèle Aina. "Below the Belt: (Un)Covering *The Well of Loneliness*." In Diana Fuss, ed., *Inside/Out: Lesbian Theories, Gay Theories*, pp. 235–58. New York: Routledge, 1991.

Barnes, Djuna. *Nightwood*. New York: New Directions, 1946.

Barrett, William F. *Psychical Research*. New York: Holt, 1911.

Baudelaire, Charles. *The Flowers of Evil*. Ed. Marthiel and Jackson Mathews. New York: New Directions, 1958.

—— *Oeuvres complètes*. Ed. Claude Pichois. 2 vols. Paris: Gallimard, 1975–76.

Bedford, Sybille. *A Compass Error*. New York: Knopf, 1969.

—— *A Favourite of the Gods*. New York: Simon and Schuster, 1963.

Bell, Millicent. "The Bostonian Story." *Partisan Review* (1985) 52:109–19.

Belloc, Hilaire. *Marie Antoinette*. 5th ed. London: Methuen, 1909.

Benstock, Shari. "Expatriate Sapphic Modernism: Entering Literary History." In Karla Jay and Joanne Glasgow, eds., *Lesbian Texts and Contexts: Radical Revisions*, pp. 183–203. New York: New York University Press, 1990.

Berlioz, Hector. *The Memoirs of Hector Berlioz*. Trans. David Cairns. London: Victor Gollancz, 1969.

Bicknell, Anna L. *The Story of Marie-Antoinette*. New York: Century, 1897.

Bishop, M. C. *The Prison Life of Marie Antoinette and her Children, the Dauphin and the Duchesse d'Angoulême*. London: K. Paul, Trench, Trubner, 1894.

Bogus, SDiane A. "The 'Queen B' Figure in Black Literature." In Karla Jay and Joanne Glasgow, eds., *Lesbian Texts and Contexts: Radical Revisions*, pp. 275–90. New York: New York University Press, 1990.

Bourdet, Edouard. *The Captive*. Trans. Arthur Hornblow, Jr. New York: Brentano's, 1926.

Bowen, Elizabeth. *The Hotel*. New York: Avon, 1980.

—— *The Little Girls*. Harmondsworth, Middlesex: Penguin, 1982.

Bowles, Jane. *Two Serious Ladies*. In *My Sister's Hand in Mine: The Collected Works of Jane Bowles*. New York: Ecco, 1978.

Bristow, Joseph, ed. *Sexual Sameness: Textual Differences in Lesbian and Gay Writing*. New York and London: Routledge, 1992.

Bronski, Michael. *Culture Clash: The Making of Gay Male Sensibility*. Boston: South End, 1984.

—— "She Really Did 'Want to be Alone.' " *Gay Community News*, May 6–12, 1990, p. 20.

Brontë, Charlotte. *Shirley*. Oxford: Oxford University Press, 1981.

Brophy, Brigid. *The Finishing Touch*. London: Gay Men's Press, 1987.

—— *King of a Rainy Country*. London: Virago, 1990.

—— *Mozart the Dramatist*. New York: Da Capo, 1988.

Brown, Rebecca. *The Terrible Girls*. San Francisco: City Lights, 1992.

Burke, Edmund. *Reflections on the Revolution in France*. Harmondsworth, Middlesex: Penguin, 1969.

Butler, Judith. "Imitation and Gender Insubordination." In Diana Fuss, ed., *Inside/Out: Lesbian Theories, Gay Theories*, pp. 13–31. New York and London: Routledge, 1991.

Byatt, A. S. *Possession: A Romance*. New York: Random House, 1990.

Calvé, Emma. *My Life*. Trans. Rosamond Gilder. New York: D. Appleton, 1922.

Campan, Jeanne Louise Henriette. *The Private Life of Marie Antoinette, Queen of France and Navarre, with Sketches and Anecdotes of the Court of Louis XVI*. New York: Scribner and Welford, 1887.

Caprio, Frank S. *Female Homosexuality: A Psychodynamic Study of Lesbianism*. New York: Citadel, 1954.

Cardus, Neville. *Kathleen Ferrier: A Memoir*. London: Hamish Hamilton, 1969.

Cargill, Oscar. *The Novels of Henry James*. New York: Macmillan, 1961.

Carlyle, Thomas. *The French Revolution*. Oxford: Oxford University Press, 1989.

Case, Sue-Ellen. "Tracking the Vampire." *Differences* (Summer 1991) 3:1–20.

Caserio, Robert L. "Celibate Sisters-in-Revolution: Towards Reading Sylvia Townsend Warner." In Joseph A. Boone and Michael Cadden, eds., *Engendering Men: The Question of Male Feminist Criticism*, pp. 254–74. New York and London: Routledge, 1990.

Castle, Terry. " 'Amy, who knew my Disease': A Psychosexual Pattern in Defoe's *Roxana*." *ELH: Journal of English Literary History* (1979) 46:81–96.

—— "Contagious Folly: *An Adventure* and Its Skeptics." *Critical Inquiry* (Summer 1991) 17:741–72.

—— "The Culture of Travesty." In G. S. Rousseau and Roy Porter, eds., *Sexual Underworlds of the Enlightenment*, pp. 156–80. Manchester: Manchester University Press, 1987.

—— *Masquerade and Civilization: The Carnivalesque in Eighteenth-Century English Culture and Fiction*. Stanford: Stanford University Press, 1986.

—— " 'Matters Not Fit to be Mentioned': Fielding's *The Female Husband*." *ELH: Journal of English Literary History* (1982) 49:602–22.

Cate, Curtis. *George Sand: A Biography*. Boston: Houghton Mifflin, 1975.

Cather, Willa. *The Song of the Lark*. New York: Bantam, 1991.

—— "Three American Singers: Louise Homer, Geraldine Farrar, Olive Fremstad." *McClure's Magazine* (December 1913) 42:33–48.

Charke, Charlotte. *A Narrative of the Life of Mrs. Charlotte Charke*. London, 1755; rpt. Gainesville, Fla.: Scholar's Facsimiles and Reprints, 1969.

Chauncey, George, Jr. "From Sexual Inversion to Homosexuality: Medicine and the Changing Conceptualization of Female Deviance." *Salmagundi* (Fall 1982-Winter 1983) 58–59:114–45.

Christiansen, Rupert. *Prima Donna: A History*. Harmondsworth, Middlesex: Penguin, 1984.

Chu, S., et al. "Epidemiology of Reported Cases of AIDS in Lesbians, United States, 1980–89." *American Journal of Public Health* (November 1990) 80:1380–81.

Clément, Catherine. *Opera, or the Undoing of Women*. Trans. Betsy Wing. Minneapolis: University of Minnesota Press, 1989.

Cliff, Michelle. *No Telephone to Heaven*. New York: Dutton, 1987.

Cocteau, Jean. Introduction to *Les Fantômes de Trianon* by Charlotte Anne Moberly and Eleanor Jourdain. Trans. Julliette and Pierre Barrucand. Monaco: Editions du Rocher, 1959.

Colette, Sidonie Gabrielle. *Claudine à l'école*. Paris: A. Michel, 1978.

—— *The Pure and the Impure*. Trans. Herma Briffault. New York: Farrar, Straus and Giroux, 1966.

Collis, Maurice. *Somerville and Ross*. London: Faber and Faber, 1968.

Coote, Stephen, ed. *The Penguin Book of Homosexual Verse*. Harmondsworth, Middlesex: Penguin, 1983.

Crompton, Louis. "The Myth of Lesbian Impunity: Capital Laws from 1270 to 1791." In Salvatore J. Licata and Robert P. Petersen, eds., *Historical Perspectives on Homosexuality*, pp. 11–25. New York: Haworth Press, 1981.

Crow, Christine. *Miss X, or the Wolf Woman*. London: Women's Press, 1990.

Crowley, Aleister. "The Lesbian Hell." In Stephen Coote, ed., *The Penguin Book of Homosexual Verse*. Harmondsworth, Middlesex: Penguin, 1983.

Cushing, Mary Watkins. *The Rainbow Bridge*. New York: Putnam's, 1954.

Daum, Raymond. *Walking with Garbo: Collections and Recollections*. New York: Harper Collins, 1991.

Davenport, Marcia. *Of Lena Geyer*. New York: Grosset and Dunlap, 1936.

—— *Too Strong For Fantasy*. New York: Scribner's, 1962.

Defoe, Daniel. *A True Relation of the Apparition of one Mrs. Veal*. London, 1706. Rpt. in Manuel Schonhorn, ed., *Accounts of the Apparition of Mrs Veal*. Los Angeles: Augustan Reprint Society and William Andrews Clark Memorial Library, 1965.

DeLynn, Jane. *Don Juan in the Village*. New York: Pantheon, 1990.

Dick, Kay. *The Shelf*. London: Gay Men's Press, 1984.

Dickens, Charles. *A Tale of Two Cities*. Oxford: Oxford University Press, 1988.

Diderot, Denis. *The Nun*. Trans. Leonard Tancock. Harmondsworth, Middlesex: Penguin, 1974.

—— *Diderot's Letters to Sophie Volland*. Trans. Peter France. London: Oxford University Press, 1972.

"Dream Romances." *Journal of the Society for Psychical Research* (June 1907) 13:90–96.

Dreiser, Theodore. *Sister Carrie*. New York: Doubleday, 1900.

Duffy, Maureen. *Collected Poems: 1949–1984*. London: Hamish Hamilton, 1985.

—— *The Microcosm*. London: Virago, 1989.

Dupee, F. W. *Henry James*. Westport, Conn.: Greenwood, 1973.

Echols, Alice. "Justifying Our Love? The Evolution of Lesbianism Through Feminism and Gay Male Politics." *Advocate*, March 26, 1991, pp. 48–53.

Edel, Leon. *Henry James: The Middle Years, 1882–1895*. New York: J. W. Lippincott, 1962.

Edel, Leon, and Lyall H. Powers, eds. *The Complete Notebooks of Henry James*. New York and Oxford: Oxford University Press, 1987.

Edgeworth, Maria. *Belinda*. 3 vols. London, 1801.

Edwards, Susan M. *Female Sexuality and the Law*. Oxford: Martin Robertson, 1981.

Ellmann, Richard. *Oscar Wilde*. New York: Vintage, 1988.

Erhart, Margaret. *Unusual Company*. New York: New American Library, 1987.

Eriksson, Brigitte. "A Lesbian Execution in Germany, 1721: The Trial Records." In Salvatore J. Licata and Robert P. Petersen, eds., *Historical Perspectives on Homosexuality*, pp. 27–40. New York: Haworth Press, 1981.

Esher, Viscount, ed. *The Girlhood of Queen Victoria: A Selection from Her Majesty's Diaries Between the Years 1832 and 1840*. London: John Murray, 1912.

Essai historique sur la vie de Marie Antoinette. Paris, 1781.

Evans, Joan. "An End to *An Adventure*: Solving the Mystery of the Trianon." *Encounter* (October 1976) 47:33–47.

Faderman, Lillian. *Odd Girls and Twilight Lovers: A History of Lesbian Life in Twentieth-Century America*. New York: Columbia University Pres, 1991.

—— *Surpassing the Love of Men: Romantic Friendship and Love Between Women from the Renaissance to the Present*. New York: William Morrow, 1981.

Farrar, Geraldine. *Such Sweet Compulsion*. New York: Greystone, 1938.

Farwell, Marilyn R. "Heterosexual Plots and Lesbian Subtexts: Toward a Theory of Lesbian Narrative Space." In Karla Jay and Joanne Glasgow, eds., *Lesbian Texts and Contexts: Radical Revisions*, pp. 91–103. New York: New York University Press, 1990.

Fetterley, Judith. "*My Antonia*, Jim Burden, and the Dilemma of the Lesbian Writer." In Karla Jay and Joanne Glasgow, eds., *Lesbian Texts and Contexts: Radical Revisions*, pp. 145–63. New York: New York University Press, 1990.

—— *The Resisting Reader: A Feminist Approach to American Fiction*. Bloomington: Indiana University Press, 1978.

Fielding, Henry. *The Female Husband*. London, 1746. Rpt. in Claude E. Jones, ed., *The Female Husband and Other Writings*. Liverpool: Liverpool University Press, 1960.

Fitzgerald, Penelope. *Charlotte Mew and Her Friends*. London: William Collins, 1984.

Flanner, Janet. *Darlinghissima: Letters to a Friend*. Ed. Natalia Danesi Murray. New York: Random House, 1985.

—— *Janet Flanner's World: Uncollected Writings, 1932–1975*. Ed. Irving Drutman. New York and London: Harcourt Brace Jovanovich, 1979.

—— *London Was Yesterday, 1934–1939*. Ed. Irving Drutman. New York: Viking, 1975.

—— *Paris Journal: 1944–1965*. Ed. William Shawn. New York: Harcourt Brace Jovanovich, 1965.

—— *Paris Journal: 1965–1971*. Ed. William Shawn. New York: Harcourt Brace Jovanovich, 1971.

—— *Paris Was Yesterday, 1925–1930*. Ed. Irving Drutman. Harmondsworth, Middlesex: Penguin, 1972; rpt. 1979.

Flaubert, Gustave. *The Sentimental Education*. Trans. Perdita Burlingame. New York: New American Library, 1972.

Fleischmann, Hector. *Marie-Antoinette libertine: bibliographie critique et analytique des pamphlets politiques, galants, et obscènes contre la reine*. Paris: Bibliothèque des Curieux, 1911.

—— *Les Pamphlets libertins contre Marie-Antoinette*. Paris: Les Publications Modernes, 1908.

Flournoy, Theodore. *From India to the Planet Mars: A Study of a Case of Somnambulism*. Trans. Daniel B. Vermilye. New York and London: Harper, 1900.

Forrest, Katherine V. *An Emergence of Green*. Tallahassee, Fla.: Naiad, 1987.

Foster, Jeannette. *Sex Variant Women in Literature*. 3d ed. Tallahassee, Fla.: Naiad, 1985.

Frederics, Diana [pseud.]. *Diana: A Strange Autobiography*. New York: Citadel, 1948.

Freud, Sigmund. *The Complete Psychological Works of Sigmund Freud*. Ed. James Strachey. 22 vols. London: Hogarth, 1959.

Fureures utérines de Marie Antoinette, femme de Louis XVI. Paris, 1791.

Fuss, Diana, ed. *Inside/Out: Lesbian Theories, Gay Theories*. New York and London: Routledge, 1991.

Garber, Marjorie. *Vested Interests: Cross-Dressing and Cultural Anxiety*. New York: Routledge, 1992.

Garden, Mary, and Louis Biancolli. *Mary Garden's Story*. London: Michael Joseph, 1952.

Gargano, James W., ed. *Critical Essays on Henry James: The Early Novels*. Boston: Hall, 1987.

Gautier, Théophile. *Mademoiselle de Maupin*. Trans. Joanna Richardson. Harmondsworth, Middlesex: Penguin, 1981.

Gearhart, Sally Miller. *The Wanderground*. Boston: Alyson, 1984.

Geismar, Maxwell. *Henry James and the Jacobites*. Boston: Houghton Mifflin, 1963.

Gerhardt, Elena. *Recital*. London: Methuen, 1953.

Gilbert, Sandra, and Susan Gubar. *No Man's Land: The Place of the Woman Writer in the Twentieth Century.* Vol. 2. *SexChanges.* New Haven: Yale University Press, 1989.

Gill, Brendan. *Here at the New Yorker.* New York: Random House, 1975.

Glendinning, Victoria. *Vita: A Biography of Vita Sackville-West.* New York: Knopf, 1983.

Le Godmiché royal. Paris, 1789.

Goldberg, Rita. *Sex and Enlightenment: Women in Richardson and Diderot.* Cambridge: Cambridge University Press, 1984.

Goncourt, Edmond and Jules de. *Histoire de Marie-Antoinette.* Paris: G. Charpentier, 1878.

Gooder, R. H. Introduction to *The Bostonians* by Henry James. New York and Oxford: Oxford University Press, 1984.

Gould, Lois. *A Sea-Change.* New York: Simon and Schuster, 1976.

Gould, Susan. "Brigitte Fassbaender." *Opera,* August 1981, pp. 789–95.

Gower, Lord Ronald. *The Last Days of Marie Antoinette.* London: Kegan Paul, Trench, 1885.

Grier, Barbara, ed. *The Lesbian in Literature.* 3d ed. Tallahassee, Fla.: Naiad, 1981.

Grier, Barbara and Coletta Reid, eds. *Lesbian Lives: Biographies of Women from 'The Ladder.'* Oakland, Calif.: Diana, 1976.

Grosskurth, Phyllis. *Havelock Ellis.* New York: Knopf, 1980.

Gurewitsch, Matthew. "Can a Woman Do a Man's Job in Schubert's 'Winterreise'?" *New York Times,* October 28, 1990, 2:31.

Haffner, Ingrid and Herbert. " 'Man könnte Oper viel billiger machen': Gespräch mit Brigitte Fassbaender." *Opernwelt* (June 1991) 32:14–16.

Hall, Radclyffe. *The Well of Loneliness.* New York: Anchor, 1990.

Hall, Radclyffe, and Una Troubridge. "A Veridical Apparition." *Journal of the Society for Psychical Research* (April 1921) 20:78–88.

Hammond, Barbara. "Music Makes Me Free: A Profile of Brigitte Fassbaender." *Classic CD,* November 1990, pp. 60–63.

Harman, Claire. *Sylvia Townsend Warner: A Biography.* London: Chatto and Windus, 1989.

Harris, Bertha. *Lover.* Plainfield, Vt.: Daughters, 1976.

Hartsock, Mildred E. "Henry James and the Cities of the Plain." *Modern Language Quarterly* (1968) 29:297–311.

Haslip, Joan. *Marie Antoinette.* London: Weidenfeld and Nicolson, 1987.

Hellman, Lillian. *The Children's Hour.* New York: Knopf, 1934.

Highsmith, Patricia [Claire Morgan]. *The Price of Salt.* Rev. ed. Tallahassee, Fla.: Naiad, 1984.

Hinds, Hilary. "*Oranges Are Not the Only Fruit*: Reaching Audiences Other Lesbian Texts Cannot Reach." In Sally Munt, ed., *New Lesbian Criticism: Literary and Cultural Readings*, pp. 153–72. New York: Columbia University Press, 1992.

WORKS

CITED

Hobby, Elaine and Chris White, eds. *What Lesbians Do in Books*. London: Women's Press, 1991.

Holland, Henry Scott, and W. S. Rockstro. *Memoir of Madame Jenny Lind-Goldschmidt: Her Early Art-Life and Dramatic Career, 1820–1851*. London: John Murray, 1891.

Howard, Elizabeth Jane. *Odd Girl Out*. New York: Viking, 1972.

Howe, Irving. "Introduction to *The Bostonians*." In James W. Gargano, ed., *Critical Essays on Henry James: The Early Novels*, pp. 154–69. Boston: Hall, 1987.

Hughes, Gwen. Review of *Die Fledermaus*, cond. André Previn (Philips 432 157–2). *Classic CD*, March 1992, p. 52.

Huneker, James. *Bedouins*. New York: Scribner's, 1926.

—— *Painted Veils*. New York: Boni and Liveright, 1920.

Hunt, Lynn. "The Many Bodies of Marie Antoinette." In Lynn Hunt, ed., *Eroticism and the Body Politic*, pp. 108–30. Baltimore: Johns Hopkins University Press, 1991.

Hyde, Catherine [pseud.], ed. *Secret Memoirs of Princess Lamballe: Being her Journals, Letters, and Conversations During her Confidential Relations with Marie Antoinette*. Washington, D.C., and London: M. Walter Dunne, 1901.

"Identity Crisis: Queer Politics in the Age of Possibilities." *Village Voice*, June 30, 1992, p. 27.

Iremonger, Lucille. *The Ghosts of Versailles: Miss Moberly and Miss Jourdain and Their Adventure: A Critical Study*. London: Faber and Faber, 1957.

Jackson, Shirley. *The Haunting of Hill House*. New York: Viking, 1959.

James, Henry. *The Awkward Age*. New York and Oxford: Oxford University Press, 1984.

—— *The Bostonians*. New York and Oxford: Oxford University Press, 1984.

—— *The Complete Notebooks of Henry James*. Ed. Leon Edel and Lyall H. Powers. New York and Oxford: Oxford University Press, 1987.

—— *Literary Criticism: American and English Writers*. Ed. Leon Edel. New York: Library of America, 1984.

—— *Literary Criticism: European Writers and the Prefaces*. Ed. Leon Edel. New York: Library of America, 1984.

—— *The Turn of the Screw and other Short Novels*. New York: New American Library, 1962.

Japenga, Ann. "Gay Women and the Risk of AIDS." *Los Angeles Times*, April 2, 1986.

Jay, Karla, and Joanne Glasgow, eds. *Lesbian Texts and Contexts: Radical Revisions*. New York: New York University Press, 1990.

Jeffreys, Sheila. *The Spinster and Her Enemies: Feminism and Sexuality, 1880–1930*. London: Pandora, 1985.

Johnston, David Landale. *The Trianon Case: A Review of the Evidence*. Ilfracombe, Devon: A. H. Stockwell, 1945.

Jolley, Elizabeth. *Miss Peabody's Inheritance*. Harmondsworth, Middlesex: Penguin, 1984.

—— *Palomino*. New York: Persea, 1980.

—— *The Well*. New York: Viking, 1986.

Jolly, James. "A Timeless Journey: James Jolly Talks to Brigitte Fassbaender about Recording 'Winterreise.'" *Gramophone*, July 1990, p. 176.

Juvenal. *Juvenal: The Sixteen Satires*. Trans. Peter Green. Harmondsworth, Middlesex: Penguin, 1974.

—— *The Satires of Juvenal*. Trans. Rolfe Humphries. Bloomington: Indiana University Press, 1958.

Katz, Jonathan Ned, ed. *Gay/Lesbian Almanac: A New Documentary*. New York: Harper and Row, 1983.

—— *Gay American History: Lesbians and Gay Men in the U.S.A.* New York: Crowell, 1976.

Keddie, Henrietta [Sarah Tytler]. *Marie Antoinette*. New York: Putnam's, 1883.

Kerr, Howard. *Mediums, and Spirit-Rappers, and Roaring Radicals: Spiritualism in American Literature, 1850–1900*. Urbana: University of Illinois Press, 1972.

King, Florence. *Confessions of a Failed Southern Lady*. New York: St. Martin's, 1985.

King, Katie. "Audre Lorde's Lacquered Layerings: The Lesbian Bar as a Site of Literary Production." In Sally Munt, ed., *New Lesbian Criticism: Literary and Cultural Readings*, pp. 75–94. New York: Columbia University Press, 1992.

Knopp, Sherron E. " 'If I saw you would you kiss me?': Sapphism and the Subversiveness of Virginia Woolf's *Orlando*." In Joseph Bristow, ed., *Sexual Sameness: Textual Differences in Lesbian and Gay Writing*, pp. 111–27. New York and London: Routledge, 1992.

Koestenbaum, Wayne. *The Queen's Throat: Opera, Homosexuality, and the Mystery of Desire*. New York: Poseidon, 1993.

Lauretis, Teresa de. "Queer Theory: Lesbian and Gay Sexualities—An Introduction." *Differences* (Summer 1991) 3:iii–xviii.

Lavergne, Julie. *Légendes de Trianon, Versailles, et Saint-Germain*. Paris: Palmé,1879.

Lebrecht, Norman. *The Maestro Myth: Great Conductors in Pursuit of Power*. New York: Birch Lane, 1991.

Leduc, Violette. *La Bâtarde*. Trans. Derek Coltman. New York: Farrar, Straus and Giroux, 1965.

—— *Thérèse and Isabelle*. Trans. Derek Coltman. New York: Dell, 1967.

Lee, Hermione. *Willa Cather: Double Lives*. New York: Random House, 1989.

Le Massena, C. E. *Galli-Curci's Life of Song*. New York: Paebar, 1945.

Lempicka-Foxhall, the Baroness Kizette de, and Charles Phillips. *Passion by Design: The Art and Times of Tamara de Lempicka*. Oxford: Phaidon, 1987.

Lenormant, Amélie. *Quatres Femmes au temps de la Révolution*. Paris: Didier, 1866.

Lister, Anne. *I Know My Own Heart: The Diaries of Anne Lister (1791–1840)*. Ed. Helena Whitbread. London: Virago, 1988.

——— *No Priest But Love: The Diaries of Anne Lister from 1824–1826*. Ed. Helena Whitbread. New York: New York University Press, 1992.

Long, Robert Emmet. *Henry James: The Early Novels*. Boston: Hall, 1983.

Lorde, Audre. *Zami: A New Spelling of My Name*. Trumansburg, N.Y.: Crossing, 1982.

Loulan, Joanne. *Lesbian Passion: Loving Ourselves and Each Other*. San Francisco: Spinsters/Aunt Lute, 1987.

Louÿs, Pierre. *The Songs of Bilitis*. Trans. Alvah C. Bessie. Mineola, N.Y.: Dover, 1988.

Lucano, Ralph V. Review of Schubert, *Winterreise*, sung by Brigitte Fassbaender (EMI Angel CDC 7 49846). *Fanfare* (September-October 1990) 14:378.

Lurie, Alison. Introduction to *The Bostonians* by Henry James. New York: Vintage, 1991.

Lynch, Lee. "Cruising the Libraries." In Karla Jay and Joanne Glasgow, eds., *Lesbian Texts and Contexts: Radical Revisions*, pp. 39–48. New York: New York University Press, 1990.

Mackenzie, Compton. *Extraordinary Women: Theme and Variations*. London: Hogarth, 1986.

McMurray, William. "Pragmatic Realism in *The Bostonians*." *Nineteenth-Century Fiction* (March 1962) 16:339–44.

Mahyère, Eveline. *I Will Not Serve*. Trans. Antonia White. London: Virago, 1984.

Mallet, Françoise. *The Illusionist*. Trans. Herma Briffault. New York: Farrar, Straus and Cudahy, 1952.

Manning, Rosemary. *The Chinese Garden*. New York: Farrar, Straus, 1962.

Marcus, Jane. "Sapphistory: The Woolf and the Well." In Karla Jay and Joanne Glasgow, eds., *Lesbian Texts and Contexts: Radical Revisions*, pp. 164–80. New York: New York University Press, 1990.

Martinac, Paula. *Out of Time*. Seattle: Seal, 1990.

"Mary Garden Craze Led Girl to Suicide," *New York Times*, February 18, 1913, p. 1.

Matheopoulos, Helena. *Diva: Great Sopranos and Mezzos Discuss Their Art*. London: Victor Gollancz, 1991.

Mavor, Elizabeth. *The Ladies of Llangollen: A Study in Romantic Friendship*. Harmondsworth, Middlesex: Penguin, 1973.

Maxwell, William, ed. *Selected Letters of Sylvia Townsend Warner*. London: Chatto and Windus, 1982.

Mayer, Dorothy Moulton. *Marie Antoinette: The Tragic Queen*. New York: Coward-McCann, 1968.

Mayne, Judith. "A Parallax View of Lesbian Authorship." In Diana Fuss, ed., *Inside/Out: Lesbian Theories, Gay Theories*, pp. 173–84. New York: Routledge, 1991.

Meese, Elizabeth. "Theorizing Lesbian: Writing—A Love Letter." In Karla Jay and Joanne Glasgow, eds., *Lesbian Texts and Contexts: Radical Revisions*, pp. 70–88. New York: New York University Press, 1990.

Melba, Nellie. *Melodies and Memories*. London: Thornton Butterworth, 1925.

Mendès, Catulle. *Méphistophéla*. Paris: E. Dentu, 1890.

Miller, Nancy K. *The Heroine's Text: Readings in the French and English Novel, 1722–1792*. New York: Columbia University Press, 1980.

Millier, Brett. *Elizabeth Bishop: Life and the Memory of It*. Berkeley, Ca.: University of California Press, 1992.

Miner, Valerie. "An Imaginative Collectivity of Writers and Readers." In Karla Jay and Joanne Glasgow, eds., *Lesbian Texts and Contexts: Radical Revisions*, pp. 13–27. New York: New York University Press, 1990.

Moberly, Charlotte Anne and Eleanor Jourdain [Elizabeth Morison and Frances Lamont]. *An Adventure*. 2d ed. London: Macmillan, 1913.

—— *An Adventure*. Ed. Joan Evans. 5th ed. London: Faber and Faber, 1955.

—— *Les Fantômes de Trianon*. Trans. Julliette and Pierre Barrucand. Monaco: Editions du Rocher, 1959.

Montefiore, Francis. *The Princesse de Lamballe: A Sketch*. London: Richard Bentley, 1896.

Moore, Olive. *Collected Writings: Celestial Seraglio, Spleen, Fugue, The Apple is Bitten Again*. Elmwood Park, Ill.: Dalkey Archive Press, 1992.

Mulford, Wendy. *This Narrow Place—Sylvia Townsend Warner and Valentine Ackland: Life, Letters and Politics, 1930–1951*. London: Pandora, 1988.

Munt, Sally, ed. *New Lesbian Criticism: Literary and Cultural Readings*. New York: Columbia University Press, 1992.

Mylne, Vivienne. "What Suzanne Knew: Lesbianism and *La Religieuse*." *Studies on Voltaire and the Eighteenth Century* (1982) 208:167–73.

Nestle, Joan, ed. *The Persistent Desire: A Femme-Butch Reader*. Boston: Alyson, 1992.

"News of the Weird." *Los Angeles Reader*, May 12, 1992.

Newton, Esther. "The Mythic Mannish Lesbian: Radclyffe Hall and the New Woman." *Signs* (1984) 9:557–75.

Nolhac, Pierre de. *La Reine Marie-Antoinette*. Paris: Boussod, Valadon, 1890.

O'Brien, Edna. *The High Road*. New York: New American Library, 1988.

O'Brien, Sharon. *Willa Cather: The Emerging Voice*. New York: Oxford University Press, 1987.

Parker, Pam A. "Der Rosenkavalier." In Joan Nestle, ed., *The Persistent Desire: A Femme-Butch Reader*, p. 332. Boston: Alyson, 1992.

Petrey, Sandy. "Ideology, *Écriture*, 1848: Sylvia Townsend Warner Unwrites Flaubert." *RSSI: Recherches sémiotiques, Semiotic Inquiry* (1991) 11:159–80.

Piozzi, Hester Thrale. *Thraliana: The Diary of Mrs. Hester Lynch Thrale, 1776–1809*. Ed. Katharine C. Balderston. 2 vols. Oxford: Clarendon Press, 1951.

Plant, Richard. *The Pink Triangle: The Nazi War Against Homosexuals*. New York: Henry Holt, 1986.

Poizat, Michel. *The Angel's Cry: Beyond the Pleasure Principle in Opera.* Trans. Arthur Denner. Ithaca: Cornell University Press, 1992.

Portfeuille d'un talon rouge. Paris, 1779.

Powers, Lyall H. *Henry James and the Naturalist Movement.* East Lansing: Michigan State University Press, 1971.

Ramsden, Phyllis M. "Anne Lister's Journal (1817–1840): An Unusual and Valuable Contemporary Record." *Transactions of the Halifax Antiquarian Society* (January 1970) 70:1–13.

Renault, Mary. *The Friendly Young Ladies.* New York: Pantheon, 1985.

Rex, Walter E. "Secrets from Suzanne: The Tangled Motives of *La Religieuse.*" In *The Attraction of the Contrary: Essays on the Literature of the French Enlightenment,* pp. 125–35. Cambridge: Cambridge University Press, 1987.

Rey, Léon. "Une Promenade hors du temps." *Revue de Paris,* December 1952.

Rice, Anne. *Cry to Heaven.* New York: Knopf, 1982.

Rich, Adrienne. "Compulsory Heterosexuality and Lesbian Existence." *Signs: Journal of Women in Culture and Society* (Summer 1980) 5:631–60.

Rich, B. Ruby. "A Queer Sensation." *Village Voice,* March 24, 1992, pp. 41–43.

Richardson, Joanna. Introduction to *Mademoiselle de Maupin* by Théophile Gautier. Harmondsworth, Middlesex: Penguin, 1981.

Robertson, Jennifer. "Gender-Bending in Paradise: Doing 'Female' and 'Male' in Japan." *Genders* (July 1989) 5:50–69.

—— "Theatrical Resistance, Theatres of Restraint: The Takarazuka Revue and the 'State Theatre' Movement in Japan." *Anthropological Quarterly* (October 1991) 64:165–78.

Roof, Judith. *A Lure of Knowledge: Lesbian Sexuality and Theory.* New York: Columbia University Press, 1991.

Ross, Andrew. *No Respect: Intellectuals and Popular Culture.* New York: Routledge, 1989.

Rubin, Gayle. "The Traffic in Women: Notes on the 'Political Economy' of Sex." In Rayna R. Reiter, ed., *Toward an Anthropology of Women,* pp. 157–210. New York: Monthly Review Press, 1975.

Rule, Jane. *The Desert of the Heart.* Tallahassee, Fla.: Naiad, 1985.

—— *Lesbian Images.* New York: Doubleday, 1975.

—— *Memory Board.* Tallahassee, Fla.: Naiad, 1987.

—— *This Is Not For You.* Tallahassee, Fla.: Naiad, 1982.

Russ, Joanna. *The Female Man.* New York: Bantam, 1975.

Russo, Vito. *The Celluloid Closet: Homosexuality in the Movies.* New York: Harper and Row, 1981.

Sabine, W. H. W. "Is There a Case for Retrocognition?" *Journal of the American Society for Psychical Research* (April 1950) 44:43–64.

Sadoff, Janet. *Ambivalence, Ambiguity, and Androgyny in Théophile Gautier's "Mademoiselle de Maupin".* Cambridge: Harvard University Press, 1990.

Sahli, Nancy. "Smashing: Women's Relationships Before the Fall." *Chrysalis* (Summer 1979) 8:17–27.

Said, Edward. "The Politics of Knowledge." *Raritan* (Summer 1991) 11:17–31.

Salter, W. H. " 'An Adventure': A Note on the Evidence." *Journal of the Society for Psychical Research* (January 1950) 35:178–87.

Sand, George. *Correspondance de George Sand.* Ed. Georges Lubin. 25 vols. Paris: Garnier, 1964–73.

A Sapphic Epistle from Jack Cavendish to Mrs. D****. London, 1782.

Sarton, May. *Mrs. Stevens Hears the Mermaids Singing.* New York: Norton, 1975.

—— *The Small Room.* New York: Norton, 1961.

Schanke, Robert A. *Shattered Applause: The Lives of Eva Le Gallienne.* Carbondale and Edwardsville: Southern Illinois University Press, 1992.

Schulman, Sarah. *After Delores.* New York: Dutton, 1988.

Secret Memoirs of Princess Lamballe: Being her Journals, Letters, and Conversations during her Confidential Relations with Marie Antoinette. Ed. Catherine Hyde [pseud.]. Washington, D.C., and London: M. Walter Dunne, 1901.

Sedgwick, Eve Kosofsky. "Across Gender, Across Sexuality: Willa Cather and Others." *SAQ: South Atlantic Quarterly* (1989) 88:53–72.

—— *Between Men: English Literature and Male Homosocial Desire.* New York: Columbia University Press, 1985.

—— *Epistemology of the Closet.* Berkeley: University of California Press, 1991.

—— "Privilege of Unknowing." *Genders* (Spring 1988) 1:102–24.

Sheean, Vincent. *First and Last Love.* New York: Random House, 1956.

Sischy, Ingrid. "White and Black." *New Yorker,* November 13, 1989, pp. 124–46.

Smith-Rosenberg, Carroll. "The Female World of Love and Ritual." In *Disorderly Conduct: Visions of Gender in Contemporary America.* New York: Knopf, 1985.

Smyth, Ethel. *Impressions That Remained.* New York: Knopf, 1946.

Souhami, Diana. *Gluck—1895–1978: Her Biography.* London: Pandora, 1988.

Spark, Muriel. *The Prime of Miss Jean Brodie.* New York: New American Library, 1984.

Spoto, Donald. *Blue Angel: The Life of Marlene Dietrich.* New York: Doubleday, 1992.

Spurling, Hilary. *Ivy: The Life of I. Compton-Burnett.* New York: Knopf, 1984.

Stimpson, Catharine. *Class Notes.* New York: Avon, 1979.

—— "Zero Degree Deviancy: The Lesbian Novel in English." *Critical Inquiry* (1981) 8:363–80.

Strachey, Dorothy ["Olivia"]. *Olivia.* London: Virago, 1987.

Strong, Lennox. "The Royal Triangle: Marie Antoinette and the Duchesse de Polignac." In Barbara Grier and Coletta Reid, eds., *Lesbian Lives: Biographies of Women from "The Ladder,"* pp 180–85. Oakland, Calif.: Diana, 1976.

Strouse, Jean. *Alice James: A Biography.* Boston: Houghton Mifflin, 1980.

Sturge-Whiting, J. R. *The Mystery of Versailles: A Complete Solution.* London: Rider, 1938.

Swinburne, Algernon Charles. *The Complete Works of Algernon Charles Swinburne.* Ed. Edmund Gosse and Thomas James Wise. 20 vols. London: William Heinemann, 1925.

Tanner, Tony. *Henry James: The Writer and His Work.* Amherst: University of Massachusetts Press, 1985.

Thomas, Chantal. *La Reine scélérate: Marie-Antoinette dans les pamphlets.* Paris: Editions du Seuil, 1989.

Tintner, Adeline R. *The Book World of Henry James.* Ann Arbor, Mich.: UMI Research Press, 1987.

Trefusis, Violet. *Don't Look Round.* London: Hutchinson, 1952.

—— *Violet to Vita: The Letters of Violet Trefusis to Vita Sackville-West.* Ed. Mitchell A. Leaska and John Phillips. London: Methuen, 1989.

Trilling, Lionel. *The Opposing Self.* New York: Viking, 1955.

Troubridge, Una, Lady. *The Life of Radclyffe Hall.* New York: Citadel, 1963.

Trumbach, Randolph. "London's Sapphists: From Three Sexes to Four Genders in the Making of Modern Culture." In Julia Epstein and Kristina Straub, eds., *Body Guards: The Cultural Politics of Gender Ambiguity.* New York and London: Routledge, 1991.

Tschudi, Clara. *Marie Antoinette.* Trans. E. M. Cope. London: Swan Sonnenschein, 1907.

Undank, Jack. "An Ethics of Discourse." In Jack Undank and Herbert Josephs, eds., *Diderot: Digression and Dispersion.* Lexington, Ky.: French Forum, 1984.

"Using God as a Cudgel." *New York Times,* September 1, 1992, A:16.

Vallette, Marguérite Eymery [Rachilde]. *Monsieur Vénus.* Paris: Flammarion, 1977.

Van der Meer, Theo. "Tribades on Trial: Female Same-Sex Offenders in Late Eighteenth-Century Amsterdam." *Journal of the History of Sexuality* (January 1991) 1:424–444.

Van Kooten Niekerk, Anja, and Sacha Wijmer. *Verkeerde Vriendschap: Lesbisch leven in de jaren 1920–1960.* Amsterdam: Feministische Uitgeverij Sara, 1985.

Van Vechten, Carl. *Interpreters.* New York: Knopf, 1920.

Vicinus, Martha. *Independent Women: Work and Community for Single Women in England, 1850–1920.* Chicago: University of Chicago Press, 1985.

—— " 'One Life to Stand by Me': Emotional Conflicts of First- Generation College Women in England." *Feminist Studies* (Fall 1982) 8:602–28.

—— " 'They Wonder to Which Sex I Belong': The Historical Roots of the Modern Lesbian Identity." *Feminist Studies* (Fall 1992) 18:467–97.

Vivien, Renée. *A Woman Appeared to Me.* Trans. Jeannette H. Foster. Tallahassee, Fla.: Naiad, 1976.

Wagner, Peter. "The Discourse on Sex—or Sex as Discourse: Eighteenth-Century Medical and Paramedical Erotica." In G. S. Rousseau and Roy Porter, eds., *Sexual Underworlds of the Enlightenment,* pp. 46–68. Manchester: Manchester University Press, 1987.

Walker, Alice. *The Color Purple*. New York: Pocket, 1985.

Warner, Sylvia Townsend. "An Act of Reparation." In *Stranger with a Bag*. London: Chatto and Windus, 1961.

—— *The Corner That Held Them*. London: Chatto and Windus, 1948.

—— *Kingdoms of Elfin*. London: Chatto and Windus, 1977.

—— *Lolly Willowes*. London: Chatto and Windus, 1926.

—— *Selected Letters of Sylvia Townsend Warner*. Ed. William Maxwell. London: Chatto and Windus, 1982.

—— *Summer Will Show*. London: Virago, 1987.

Webster, Nesta H. *Louis XVI and Marie Antoinette Before the Revolution*. New York: Putnam, 1937.

—— *Louis XVI and Marie Antoinette During the Revolution*. New York: Putnam, 1938.

Wedekind, Frank. *The Lulu Plays: Earth Spirit; Pandora's Box; Death and the Devil*. Trans. Carl Richard Mueller. New York: Fawcett, 1967.

Weeks, Jeffrey. *Coming Out: Homosexual Politics in Britain, from the Nineteenth Century to the Present*. London: Quartet, 1977.

Whatling, Clare. "Reading Awry: Joan Nestle and the Recontextualization of Heterosexuality." In Joseph Bristow, ed., *Sexual Sameness: Textual Differences in Lesbian and Gay Writing*, pp. 210–26. New York and London: Routledge, 1992.

White, Antonia. *Frost in May*. London: Virago, 1980.

White, Patricia. "Female Spectator, Lesbian Specter: *The Haunting*." In Diana Fuss, ed., *Inside/Out: Lesbian Theories, Gay Theories*, pp. 142–72. New York and London: Routledge, 1991.

Wilhelm, Gale. *We Too Are Drifting*. Tallahassee, Fla.: Naiad, 1984.

Wilson, Edmund. "The Ambiguity of Henry James." *Hound and Horn* (April-June 1934), vol. 8.

Wineapple, Brenda. *Genêt: A Biography of Janet Flanner*. New York: Ticknor and Fields, 1989.

Winsloe, Christa. *The Child Manuela*. Trans. Agnes Neill Scott. New York: Farrar and Rinehart, 1933.

Winterson, Jeanette. *Oranges Are Not the Only Fruit*. London: Pandora, 1985.

—— *The Passion*. Harmondsworth, Middlesex: Penguin, 1987.

—— *Sexing the Cherry*. London: Vintage, 1989.

—— *Written on the Body*. London: Jonathan Cape, 1992.

Wittig, Monique. *Les Guérillères*. Trans. David Le Vay. Boston: Beacon, 1985.

—— *The Straight Mind and Other Essays*. Ed. Louise Turcotte. Boston: Beacon, 1992.

Wolstenholme, Susan. "Possession and Personality: Spiritualism in *The Bostonians*." *American Literature* (1977–78) 49:580–91.

Woolf, Virginia. *The Letters of Virginia Woolf*. Ed. Nigel Nicolson and Joanne Trautmann. 6 vols. New York: Harcourt Brace Jovanovich, 1980.

—— *Orlando: A Biography.* New York: Harcourt Brace Jovanovich, 1956.

Wordsworth, William. *The Poetical Works of William Wordsworth.* Ed. E. De Selincourt and Helen Darbishire. 5 vols. 2d ed. Oxford: Clarendon Press, 1954.

"World View." *The Advocate*, December 15, 1992, p. 32.

Wright, Walter F. *The Madness of Art: A Study of Henry James.* Lincoln: University of Nebraska Press, 1962.

Yonge, Charles Duke. *Marie Antoinette, Queen of France.* London: Hurst and Blackett, 1876.

Zimmerman, Bonnie. " 'The Dark Eye Beaming': Female Friendship in George Eliot's Fiction." In Karla Jay and Joanne Glasgow, eds., *Lesbian Texts and Contexts: Radical Revisions*, pp. 126–44. New York: New York University Press, 1990.

—— *The Safe Sea of Women: Lesbian Fiction 1969–1988.* Boston: Beacon, 1990.

Zola, Emile. *Nana.* Trans. George Holden. Harmondsworth, Middlesex: Penguin, 1972.

Zweig, Stefan. *Marie Antoinette: The Portrait of an Average Woman.* Trans. Eden and Cedar Paul. New York: Viking, 1933.

INDEX

GENDER AND CULTURE
A Series of Columbia University Press
Edited by Carolyn G. Heilbrun and Nancy K. Miller

Designer: Teresa Bonner
Text: Janson Text #55
Compositor: The Composing Room of Michigan, Inc.
Printer: Edwards Brothers
Binder: Edwards Brothers